PENGUIN CLASSICS

THE PENGUIN BOOK OF HAIKU

ADAM L. KERN studied Japanese literature at Harvard University, where he earned a PhD in East Asian Languages and Civilizations before joining the faculty for nearly a decade. His experiences in Japan include research affiliations with the University of Kyoto, the University of Tokyo and the National Institute of Japanese Literature. Author of *Manga from the Floating World: Comicbook Culture and the Kibyōshi of Edo Japan* (Harvard University Asia Center, 2006), Kern is Professor of Japanese Literature and Visual Culture at the University of Wisconsin-Madison.

T0000271

The Penguin Book
of Haiku

Translated and Edited by
ADAM L. KERN

PENGUIN BOOKS

PENGUIN CLASSICS

UK | USA | Canada | Ireland | Australia
India | New Zealand | South Africa

Penguin Books is part of the Penguin Random House group of companies whose addresses can be found at
global.penguinrandomhouse.com.

This edition first published in Penguin Classics 2018

014

Set in Sabon Next LT Pro
Typeset by Dinah Drazin

Printed and bound in Great Britain by Clays Ltd, Elcograf S.p.A.

ISBN: 978-0-140-42476-8

www.greenpenguin.co.uk

MIX
Paper from
responsible sources
FSC® C018179

Penguin Random House is committed to a
sustainable future for our business, our readers
and our planet. This book is made from Forest
Stewardship Council® certified paper.

Contents

List of Illustrations

List of Abbreviations

Here, as throughout the present volume, the place of publication for all Japanese-language works is Tokyo unless otherwise stated. Japanese names are given in the Japanese order of family name followed by personal name, except in the case of scholars writing primarily in English (as with Makoto Ueda). In accordance with Japanese custom, well-known poets and authors are commonly referred to by their personal name (as with Issa for Kobayashi Issa). Subtitles are set off either by parentheses or a colon. Romanization follows the modified Hepburn system for Japanese and Pinyin for Chinese.

BFD	Fukumoto Ichirō, *Bashō furuike densetsu* (Taishūkan shoten, 1988)
BK	Tamaki Tsukasa (ed.), *Buson kushū: gendai goyakutsuki* (Kadokawa sofia bunko, 2011)
EB	Shunroan Shujin, *Edo bareku: ume no takarabako* (Miki shobō, 1996)
EBKI	Watanabe Shin'ichirō, *Edo bareku koi no ironaoshi* (Shūeisha, 2000)
EBYHT	Watanabe Shin'ichirō, *Edo bareku 'Yanagi no hasue' o tanoshimu* (Miki shobō, 2008)
EEBT	Shunroan Shujin, *Edo no ehon to bareku o tanoshimu* (Miki shobō, 1994)
EST	Kanda Bōjin, *Edo senryū o tanoshimu* (Shibundō, 1989)
HJAS	*Harvard Journal of Asiatic Studies*
MN	*Monumenta Nipponica*

NKBT 39   Ijichi Tetsuo (ed.), *Nihon koten bungaku taikei* 39, *Rengashū* (Iwanami shoten, 1960)

NKBT 58   Teruoka Yasutaka and Kawashima Tsuyu (eds), *Nihon koten bungaku taikei* 58, *Buson shū Issa shū* (Iwanami shoten, 1959)

NKBZ 8   Katagiri Yōichi et al. (eds), *Nihon koten bungaku zenshū* 8, *Taketori monogatari Ise monogatari Yamato monogatari Heichū monogatari* (Shōgakukan, 1972)

NKBZ 26   Minemura Fumito (ed.) *Nihon koten bungaku zenshū* 26, *Shin kokin wakashū* (Shōgakukan, 1974)

NKBZ 32   Kaneko Kinjirō, Teruoka Yasutaka and Nakamura Shunjō (eds), *Nihon koten bungaku zenshū* 32, *Renga haikaishū* (Shōgakukan, 1974)

NKBZ 41   Imoto Nōichi, Hori Nobuo and Muramatsu Tomotsugu (eds), *Nihon koten bungaku zenshū* 41, *Matsuo Bashō shū* (Shōgakukan, 1972)

NKBZ 46   Hamada Giichirō, Suzuki Katsutada and Mizuno Minoru (eds), *Nihon koten bungaku zenshū* 46, *Kibyōshi senryū kyōka* (Shōgakukan, 1971)

NKBZ 51   Ijichi Tetsuo, Omote Akira and Kuriyama Riichi (eds), *Nihon koten bungaku zenshū* 51, *Renga ronshū, Nōgaku ronshū, Haironshū* (Shōgakukan, 1973)

NMZ 26   Nihon Meicho Zenshū Kankōkai (ed.), *Nihon meicho zenshū: Edo bungei no bu* 26, *Senryū zappai shū* (Nihon meicho zenshū kankōkai, 1927)

NMZ 27   Nihon Meicho Zenshū Kankōkai (ed.), *Nihon meicho zenshū: Edo bungei no bu* 27, *Haibun haikai shū* (Nihon meicho zenshū kankōkai, 1928)

NYC 8   Nakamura Yukihiko, *Nakamura Yukihiko chojutsushū* 8, *Gesakuron* (Chūō kōronsha, 1982)

OI   Watanabe Shin'ichirō, *(Senryū Edo) Onna no isshō* (Taihei shooku, 1991)

RJS   Taira Sōsei (ed.) *Ryōran josei senryū: Meiji irai hyakunen o utai tsugu 48-nin no chisei to jōnen no sekai* (Midori shobō, 1997)

S   Azuma Masahide, *Sekushii senryū*, with illustrations by Tanaka Keiichi (Media fakutorii shinsho, 2011)

SE   Shimoyama Hiroshi, *Senryū no erotishizumu* (Shin-chōsha, 1995)

SH   Sōichi Hoshika (ed.), *Iwanami bunko* 5036–5037, *Sōgi hokkushū* (Iwanami shoten, 1953)

SMS   Yamamoto Seinosuke, *Senryū meiji sesōshi* (Makino shuppan, 1983)

SNKBT 5   Kojima Noriyuki and Arai Eizō (eds), *Shin nihon koten bungaku taikei* 5, *Kokin wakashū* (Iwanami shoten, 1989)

SNKBT 7   Komachiya Teruhiko (ed.), *Shin nihon koten bungaku taikei* 7, *Shūi wakashū* (Iwanami shoten, 1990)

SNKBT 8   Kubota Jun and Hirata Yoshinobu (eds), *Shin nihon koten bungaku taikei* 8, *Goshūi wakashū* (Iwanami shoten, 1994)

SNKBT 69   Morikawa Akira, Katō Sadahiko and Inui Hiroyuki (eds), *Shin nihon koten bungaku taikei* 69, *Shoki haikai shū* (Iwanami shoten, 1991)

SNKBT 70   Shiraishi Teizō and Ueno Yōzō (eds), *Shin nihon koten bungaku taikei* 70, *Bashō shichibushū* (Iwanami shoten, 1990)

SNKBT 72   Suzuki Katsutada, Ishikawa Hachirō and Iwata Hideyuki (eds), *Shin nihon koten bungaku taikei* 72, *Edoza tentori haikaishū* (Iwanami shoten, 1993)

SNKBZ 79   Tanahashi Masahiro, Suzuki Katsutada and Uda Toshihiko (eds), *Shinpen nihon koten bungaku zenshū* 79, *Kibyōshi senryū kyōka* (Shōgakukan, 1999)

SS   Hanasaki Kazuo, *Senryū shungashi* (Taihei shooku, 2003)

SSS   Sawada Gobyōan (ed.), *Shōhon suetsumuhana san-busaku* (*c.* 1923–6), in Taihei Shooku (ed.), *Suetsumu-hana gohen hachihen: fusai*, in *Suetsumuhana ruisho shūsei* (Taihei shooku, 2002)

SZ   Masaoka Chūsaburō et al. (eds), *Shiki zenshū*, 22 vols (Kōdansha, 1975–8)

YHZ   Okada Hajime, *Yanagi no hazue zenshaku* (Yūkō shobō, 1956)

Chronology

For more information about terms and proper names highlighted in bold, see Glossary of Terms and Glossary of Poets.

538–710 Asuka period.

538–52 Buddhism introduced into Yamato, an assemblage of semi-autonomous states (eventually becoming Japan) with diverse pantheistic folk beliefs collectively called **Shinto**.

710–94 Nara period.

*c.***711** Earliest extant Japanese text, *Kojiki* (Record of Ancient Matters), using Chinese **graph**s to represent the Japanese spoken language, lays out a Shinto world view. Contains first example of a linked exchange in Japanese poetry.

794–1185 Heian period.

late eighth century Earliest extant collection of Japanese poetry, *Man'yōshū* (Myriad Leaves Collection), containing over four thousand verses, predominantly *tanka* (short poems of thirty-one **syllabet**s) that would come to epitomize *waka* (Japanese poetry) and therefore sometimes go by that name. Also contains other poetic forms, such as *chōka* (long poems of variable length culminating in one or more 31-syllabet stanzas) and, significantly, the first 'simple linked-verse' (*tan renga*) exchange of seventeen-syllabet and fourteen-syllabet verses.

*c.***880–950** *Ise monogatari* (Tales of Ise). Collection of short prose stories of uncertain authorship, arguably built around short poems (*tanka*), adding up to a larger narrative about the romances and exile of the real-life courtier and poet Ariwara no Narihira (825–80). Many episodes contain witty poetic exchanges between Narihira and his copious lovers.

*c.*920 First imperially commissioned collection of Japanese poetry, *Kokin wakashū* (Collection of Japanese Verse Old and New), aka *Kokinshū*. Written in Japanese syllabary (**kana**) as well as graphs. One of its prefaces, by Ki no Tsurayuki (872–945), is one of the earliest sustained statements of Japanese poetics (though somewhat inspired by Chinese sources). The collection contains examples of sequences of one hundred linked verses (*hyakuin renga*) in alternating stanzas of seventeen and fourteen syllabets. It also introduced the term **haikai** to refer to approximately five dozen verses that amusingly deviated from the conventions and diction of Japanese poetry (but otherwise did not resemble witty linked verse as it would come to be normalized).

*c.*1000 *Genji monogatari* (The Tale of Genji), primarily by Murasaki Shikibu (*c.*978–1025). Widely regarded as the greatest tale (*monogatari*) of premodern Japanese literature and the world's first major 'novel' of psychological complexity. Its fifty-four chapters also feature poetic exchanges between the fictional Prince Genji (based loosely on Narihira) and others, particularly his numerous lovers.

1157 *Fukurozōshi* (Commonplace Book), by Fujiwara no Kiyosuke (1104–77). Ruled that the **hokku** (initiating stanza) in chains of linked verse (*kusari renga*) be treated as a special case, composed with greater care than the other impromptu stanzas, and stand as a complete utterance unto itself, at least momentarily, until the next stanza reinterprets it.

1175 Amidism, aka **Pure Land** (*Jōdo*) Buddhism, introduced into Japan.

1180–85 Genpei War between the Taira and Minamoto families heralding the disintegration of the aristocratic court and the rise of the warrior class. Chronicled in the epic war tale *Heike monogatari* (Tales of the Heike), compiled in or around the thirteenth century.

1190 Death of **Saigyō** (b. 1118), major *tanka* poet whose poetic travels would inspire **Bashō** five centuries later.

1185–1600 Medieval period.

1191 **Zen** introduced into Japan.

1192–1333 Kamakura period.

1192 Minamoto no Yoritomo (1147–99, r. 1192–9) becomes first shogun, or supreme military ruler of the realm, establishing the seat of the shogunate at Kamakura.

1205 *Shin kokin wakashū* (New Collection of Japanese Verse Old and New), aka *Shin kokinshū*. Commissioned by retired emperor Go-Toba (r. 1183–98) and compiled by Fujiwara Teika (1162–1241) and others. The principles of association and progression used to link together unrelated stanzas within this collection helped solidify the rules (*shikimoku*) of the emerging poetic form of 'serious minded' (*ushin*) linked verse (*renga*) – as opposed to the 'playful minded' (*mushin*) linked verse that would eventually culminate in witty linked verses (*haikai no renga*).

1338–1573 Muromachi period established after the court splits into Northern and Southern factions in 1336, eventually reuniting in 1392.

1356 Early poetry collection containing sections devoted solely to the ***hokku*** (initiating stanza) of linked-verse sequences, *Tsukubashū* (Tsukuba Collection), edited by Nijō Yoshimoto (1320–88).

1465–1600 Warring States (*Sengoku*) period of internecine warfare among warlords (*daimyō*) of the various provinces.

1486 Early collection containing only initiating stanzas, *Renga hokku*, edited by Sanjō Nishi Sanetaka (1455–1537).

1495 **Sōgi** edits the *renga* anthology *Shinsen tsukubashū* (New Linked-Verse Collection), containing sections of *hokku* treated as verses in their own right.

1499 Extant early collection of witty linked verse (*haikai no renga*), *Chikuba kyōginshū* (Hobby Horse Collection of Madcap Verse), edited anonymously. Includes 217 reply verses (***tsukeku***) and 20 *hokku*.

c.*1530** Early major collection of witty linked verse, ***Inu tsukubashū. Contains overtly humorous, scatological and even sexual verses of the sort that would come to be termed ***senryū*** and ***bareku***. The collection would prove to be widely influential, inspiring the development of **Danrin** School poetry.

1542 Portuguese land on Japan's major western island of Kyūshū. Jesuits introduce Christianity, subsequently banned.

1573–1603 Azuchi-Momoyama period. Unification of Japan initiated by warlord Oda Nobunaga (1534–82), continued by warlord Toyotomi Hideyoshi (1536–98) and concluded by Tokugawa Ieyasu (1543–1616). Hideyoshi credited with the institutionalization of the four major classes (*shinō kōshō*) of samurai, landowning farmers, artisans and merchants – though there were also untouchables (*burakumin*) and so-called non-humans (*hinin*). Hideyoshi launches failed invasions of Korea.

1600–1868 Edo or Tokugawa period.

1600 Ieyasu wins the battle of Sekigahara, unifying the country after centuries of internecine warfare.

1603 Ieyasu becomes first of the Tokugawa shoguns who for over 260 years would rule the approximately 260 semi-sovereign domains (*han*), ostensibly on behalf of the imperial line. Establishes the seat of the shogunate in a remote swamp town called **Edo** that would rapidly emerge as the major metropolis (although the imperial capital remained in Kyōto, anglicized as 'Kyoto', which had been the seat of cultural and political power for much of the preceding millennium).

1623 Commercial woodblock-printing industry established in Kamigata, resulting in a profusion of mass-published works and a dramatic rise in literacy rates.

1633 *Enokoshū*, major *haikai* repository, compiled.

1634–41 As part of a policy of self-imposed national isolationism (*sakoku*), third Tokugawa shogun Iemitsu (1604–51, r. 1623–51) in 1634 orders the construction of Dejima, a man-made islet in the bay of Nagasaki meant to contain Westerners residing in Japan. Portuguese initially inhabit the islet but are expelled after a massive uprising of Christian Japanese in the Shimabara Rebellion (1637–8). By 1641 the only Westerners allowed to remain in Japan, members of the Dutch East India Company, move in.

1651 **Teimon** (literally 'Tei[toku]'s Gate') School of *haikai* established when **Teitoku** lays out his compositional principles in *Haikai gosan* (Witty Linked-Verse Parasol).

1660s Establishment of the **Danrin** School of *haikai* of **Sōin** and followers, most notably **Saikaku**.

1663 Early appearance of the term *haiku* as an abbreviation of *haikai no renga no ku*, meaning any verse or verses (*ku*) in a witty (*haikai*) linked-verse (*renga*) sequence. Used only rarely until the late nineteenth century, when it began to acquire the present sense of a standalone verse of modern **haiku**.

1673 Early handbook of *haikai* composition, *Umoregi* (The Buried Log), by Teimon School poet **Kigin**, relates *haikai* to *waka*.

1680 Poet Tōsei, who had studied *haikai* in both the Teimon and Danrin schools, moves to a hut on the outskirts of Edo, where he adopts the new *haikai* pen name (*haigō*) **Bashō** after receiving a 'leafy plantain' (*bashō*) as a gift.

1689 Bashō meanders from Edo to Kyoto, chronicling his experiences in what would be published as a quasi-fictionalized haikuesque travel account, ***Oku no hosomichi***, hailed as his masterwork.

1690s Establishment of the Bashō School (**Shōmon**) of the *haikai* of Bashō and followers.

1690 Foundational collection of *haiku* verse capping (***maeku-zuke***), ***Futaba no matsu***, edited by **Fukaku**, helps popularize *haiku* widely, even nationally, among people not formally affiliated with any *haiku* school. Composition of the *haiku* sequence 'Akuoke no no maki' (The Washbasin Sequence) by Bashō and others (see pp. 2–7).

1691 Publication of ***Waka midori***, earliest work of *haiku* verse capping to regularly use a 'repeating challenge' verse (*jōgo*), and ***Sarumino***, a central text of the Shōmon, that includes 'Akuoke no no maki'.

1692 ***Kuzu no matsubara***, account of the composition of **Bashō**'s 'old pond' verse (see p. 172).

1694 Bashō dies. Succession dispute among disciples leads to the factionalization and eventual disintegration of the Shōmon.

1750 Publication begins of ***Mutamagawa***, containing overtly comic *haiku* in both seventeen syllabets, that would come to be called *senryū*, and fourteen syllabets.

1765 Publication begins of ***Yanagidaru***, presenting seventeen-syllabet verses selected by **Senryū** that would later be termed *senryū*. Although earlier such collections existed (e.g. *Mutamagawa*), this was probably the first major collection of *senryū* – and of any free-standing *haiku* – to reach a nationwide audience in its own day.

1766 **Bashō Revival** (*Shōfū kaiki*) launched by **Buson, Chora** and others.

1776–1801 Publication of *Suetsumuhana*, a collection of *senryū* and *bareku*.

1787–93 Series of economic and cultural edicts, collectively known as the Kansei Reforms (*Kansei kaikaku*), exhort samurai to devote themselves to the martial and literary arts (*bunbu*), especially *waka*, rather than yielding to the vices of theatres, gambling, whoring and *haiku*.

1796–7 Publication of *Yanagidaru shūi*, containing *senryū* gathered from verse-capping contests.

1800 The shogun's capital, Edo, with approximately one million inhabitants, reaches parity with Paris and London as one of the world's three largest metropolitan centres.

1835 Publication of the seminal collection *Yanagi no hazue*, consisting entirely of *bareku*.

1853 Commodore Matthew Perry (1794–1858) and his heavily armed black ships steam into Uraga Harbour near Edo, eventually forcing the limited opening of Japan to the West, effectively ending the policy of self-imposed national isolationism.

1868–1912 Meiji period.

1868 Meiji Restoration (*Meiji ishin*), customarily taken as initiating Japan's modern period. Overthrow of the Tokugawa shogunate and reinstatement of imperial rule, beginning with Emperor Meiji (1852–1912). Edo renamed Tōkyō (Eastern capital), anglicized as 'Tokyo'.

1873 Japanese adopt the Western Gregorian calendar, effective from 1 January.

1879 Bashō deified on the recommendation of the government's Ministry of Religious Instruction (*Kyōbunshō*).

1885 Tsubouchi Shōyō (1859–1935) publishes *Shōsetsu shinzui* (Essence of the Novel). He argues that, in order to modernize, Japan must abandon its disreputable literary entertainments, particularly the comic literature (*gesaku*) that was the prose counterpart to *haiku*. The Meiji government officially recognizes the *Furuike kyōkai* (Old Pond Church) as part of the Bashō sect of Shinto.

1893 D. T. Suzuki (1870–1966), who would become one of the major early popularizers of Zen Buddhism in the West, serves as interpreter at the Japanese Pavilion at the World's Columbian Exposition in Chicago.

1894 Poet and literary modernizer **Shiki**, in an essay 'Zatsu no haiku' (Miscellaneous Haiku) within the journal *Shōnippon*, uses the term 'haiku' in the modern sense of a standalone verse by an individual poet.

1894–5 Sino-Japanese War.

1904–5 Russo-Japanese War.

1912–26 Taishō period.

1912 Death of Emperor Meiji and ascension of Emperor Taishō (1879–1926).

1913 **Kyoshi** consolidates the association of the modern haiku with the *hokku* in his article 'Sate haiku (hokku) to iu mono wa donna mono deshō' (Well, What Sort of Thing is the Haiku (*Hokku*), Anyway?), published in the influential literary journal *Hototogisu*. Rabindranath Tagore (1861–1941), who translated haiku into Bengali, becomes the first non-Westerner to win the Nobel Prize in Literature.

1931 Empire of Japan invades Manchuria and by 1937 is at war with the Republic of China.

1941 Empire of Japan attacks Pearl Harbor and other American military instillations and British colonies, launching the Pacific theatre of the Second World War.

1945 United States drops a uranium bomb on Hiroshima and a plutonium bomb on Nagasaki, forcing the Empire of Japan to surrender. Women in Japan granted the right to vote.

Introduction

Haiku as global poetry – the very notion seems self-evident. After all, what began half a millennium ago as a Japanese poetic form now boasts worldwide appeal. For innumerable schoolchildren around the planet, from Aberdeen to Zhaoqing, haiku represents their first exploratory flight into the vast expanse of poetry. Haiku is composed in dozens, perhaps hundreds, of languages beyond Japanese and English: Bengali *hā'iku*, Yiddish *h'ayqw*, Arabic *al-haykw*, Greek *χαϊκού*, Russian *хайку*, Mandarin *páijù*, Esperanto *hajko*. This pervasiveness, not to mention resultant impact on literature and culture, largely owes to the fact that the haiku is – in rudimentary iteration – any unrhymed poem in three phrases of five, then seven, then five syllables. By all accounts the shortest major poetic form in the world, if not the most recognized and practised, the haiku is so simple, even a child can do it.

In more advanced articulations, challenging enough for grown-up bards, the haiku amounts to traditional Japanese micropoetry. Expressed in plain-spoken language and concrete nature imagery rooted in the seasons, particularly in their evanescence, the haiku crystallizes an intensely perceived moment into a mere seventeen syllables to paradoxically profound, even philosophical, effect. If its resonance on figurative and literal levels qualifies the haiku as almost Symbolist, its reluctance to convey emotions or cerebrations point blank is part of a quintessential restraint, suggestiveness and subtlety that have earned for the haiku, as well as for its people, a reputation of inscrutability. Hence the following T-shirt quip:

Haiku –
Sometimes it doesn't make sense.
Refrigerator!

Still, much of the appeal of the haiku derives from the irresistibly paradoxical combination of simplicity of form with the exquisite sophistication of Japanese aesthetics (see Further Reading). The notion of impersonality (*hosomi*, literally 'slenderness'), for instance, entails that the poet suspend the ego, entering into the essence of his subject matter, couching any personal feelings in the language of objective description. W. S. Merwin pinpointed the satisfying effect, esteeming 'the profound intimacy of this poetry into which the postures and qualifications and noise of an "I" obtrude relatively so little'.[1] Similarly, an empathetic sensitivity is required to fully appreciate how the forlorn existence (*sabi*) of tiny crickets under helmets of fallen warriors suggests our own radical existential aloneness in the universe. Or how the poignant beauty of ephemerality (*mono no aware*), epitomized by cherry blossoms and the like, heightens the loveliness before our eyes while signifying the fundamental Buddhist truth that, contrary to our most cherished desires, nothing lasts forever. These qualities inherently possess a mysterious profundity (*yūgen*) that can be grasped only intuitively, if at all.

In all such articulations, Japaneseness lurks somewhere in the back of the mind, when not being paraded out front and centre. Either way, the conviction that the haiku was a *purely* Japanese form, at least originally, even if watered down and adapted during its subsequent diffusion everywhere, remains ironclad. The Four Grandmasters of Haiku – Matsuo Bashō (1644–94), Yosa Buson (1716–84), Kobayashi Issa (1763–1827) and Masaoka Shiki (1867–1902) – are each, it goes without saying, Japanese. Nevertheless, this conviction bears an irreconcilable contradiction: on the one hand, it is this exclusive Japaneseness that serves as the touchstone by which the haiku derives its authenticity; on the other, it is this accessibility and universality by which the haiku derives its significance. Ultimately, the formulation of the haiku as global Japanese poetry would seem to be oxymoronic.

And so it comes as something of a revelation to most people, the least of whom are not the Japanese themselves, that the haiku was never pristinely Japanese in the first place. At least not exactly. Setting aside theories about continental influence, such as remote Chinese precursors or the Korean antecedents of certain enigmatic phrases in early Japanese poesy, if anything was ever authentically Japanese about the haiku, it was primarily its reactionary genesis during Japan's modern encounter with the West.

Prior to this, what today is called haiku historically consisted of multiple poetic practices that would come to be oversimplified, through modernization and globalization, to the point of extinction. By focusing on these little-known practices, the present volume challenges long-standing notions of the haiku as merely traditional nature poetry, for, as we will see, it was much more: erotic, funny, crude, mischievous. In contrast, the Japanese haiku as it is known today is quite a different beast – one that is 'global' less for its ubiquitous popularity (not to mention its prospect as environmental or ecological paean) than for how it was transnational from the outset.

Masaoka Shiki and the Invented Tradition of Haiku

This account of transnational origins cuts against the grain of the conventional wisdom maintaining that the haiku is a form of traditional Japanese micropoetry going back to time immemorial. Japanese poetry has indeed been around for well over a millennium (see Chronology). Yet the haiku as it is generally known – as a standalone utterance of the individual poet – was formulated relatively recently, sometime during the twilight of the nineteenth century. It has been just over a dozen decades since its inception; a century since its solidification as part of the bedrock of Japanese national culture. Accordingly, Bashō, the first of the Four Grandmasters of Haiku, the poetic genius who single-handedly elevated boneheaded wordplay to bona fide art form called haiku, the undisputed patron saint of haiku, never, strictly speaking, wrote a single haiku in his life. How could he have, when the haiku dates only to circa 1894, two centuries after the man's death in 1694?

Granted, Bashō was a master of *something*, even if that something gets routinely passed off as the inexorable prototype of the haiku. Yet, like comparing a smartphone with its rotary-dial predecessor, equating the haiku with its precursor is knotty, neither punctiliously truthful nor utterly misleading. The one is a form of modern standalone poetry of the individual; the other, to which this volume is devoted, a conspicuous part of a premodern literary word game played collaboratively. Known as 'witty linked verse' (*haikai no renga*), this word game – of which Bashō considered himself to be a practitioner – alternated seventeen-syllable stanzas with fourteen-syllable ones to various lengths (thirty-six and one hundred stanzas being most common). It did this in a wide range of manners, or what might be termed 'modes', from the inexpressibly sublime to the unutterably profane.

Naturally, only the former would do in presenting the Japanese upon the world stage, where the honour of their presence was urgently requested. Particularly after Commodore Matthew Perry steamed into Uraga Harbour near Edo (present-day Tokyo) in 1853 aboard gun-toting black ships, providing the shock and awe that forced the limited opening of Japan to the West after centuries of self-imposed isolationism, the Japanese were understandably keen to present themselves in the most favourable light. Mishima Yukio (1925–70), nominated three times for the Nobel Prize in Literature, later would characterize his fellow countrymen, with his usual macho bravado, as being 'like an anxious housewife preparing to receive guests, hiding away in closets common articles of daily use ... hoping to impress [them] with the immaculate idealized life of her household, without so much as a speck of dust in view'.[2]

With the overthrow of the authoritarian regime of Tokugawa shoguns and the establishment of a progressive government under Emperor Meiji (1852–1912), the Japanese embarked on an epochal project of modernization, Westernization, industrialization, imperialist colonization and scientific rationalization. Intellectuals reasoned that Japan could catch up with Euro-American military might and technical know-how only by reforming society drastically. In addition to a new educational system, the literary arts would play a vital role by fostering a sense of Western-style individualism. Previously popular comic literature, graphic novellas and moralistic adventure tales suddenly seemed debilitatingly backwards, and the centuries-old, collaboratively composed witty linked verse little more than sophomoric groupthink. There were calls to take up Western historical fiction, such as the novels of Benjamin Disraeli. Nowhere were such agendas more persuasively advanced than by Tsubouchi Shōyō (1859–1935) in *Shōsetsu shinzui* (Essence of the Novel, 1885). If the Japanese were to survive, let alone thrive, the logic ran, they would need to transform themselves into original thinkers, not (in the formulation of one latter-day educator) excellent sheep.[3]

Heeding this clarion call was Masaoka Shiki. Best known as the last of the Four Grandmasters, Shiki might be regarded more distinctively as Japan's foremost poetic modernizer. By boiling down the hodgepodge of collaboratively authored, premodern verse games into only the most refined morsel, straining out unsavoury impurities, Shiki can be credited with having cooked up the haiku as a form of modern standalone poetry. This he did by a rhetorical sleight of hand. He observed that the very first stanza in a linked-verse sequence, a stanza known as the *hokku*, had in the past been extracted from its collaborative milieu and presented as a kind of tasteful poem on its own. This extraction, Shiki claimed, was evidence that the Japanese had a historical precedent of individualistic standalone poetry prior to sustained contact with the West, a poetry that Shiki – in a barrage of journal articles, most emblematically one published on 9 March 1894 – retrospectively and ahistorically designated 'haiku'.[4]

Now, it is true that this initiating stanza, or *hokku*, by virtue of conferring a benediction upon the rest of the verse sequence, had been singled out for preferential treatment as far back as the twelfth century, during the early days of the serious linked verse (*renga*) that several hundred years later would give rise to witty linked verse (*haikai no renga*). The *Fukurozōshi* (Commonplace Book, 1157) mandated that because the initiating stanza set the tone for subsequent ones, it bore the burden of elegance, and so needed to be composed deliberately, even as a complete utterance unto itself.[5] In the context of collaboratively linked verse, however, this completeness was transitory, lasting only until the next stanza reinterpreted its predecessor.

It is also true that linked-verse anthologies containing sections devoted solely to the *hokku* began appearing at least by the fourteenth century. However, in works such as the *Tsukubashū* (Tsukuba Collection, 1356), these sections were apparently intended as models of how to compose stanzas initiating collaborative sequences, not as standalone poetry. In this manner over subsequent centuries, masters of serious and witty linked verse composed individual *hokku* to be extended into longer cohesive sequences. Whenever a *hokku* appeared outside its original sequence, it was almost always snapped back into another linked context, as with affiliated prose (*haibun*) and images (*haiga*). Even verse cards (*tanzaku*) featuring single verses are likely to have been understood primarily as mementos or ciphers of longer linked-verse sequences.[6]

Contrary to Shiki's claims, then, the existence of seemingly independent *hokku* does not prove that the Japanese had a tradition of free-standing, individualistic, modern poetry. For many people holding the conviction that poetry is the singular expression of an individual, the notion of collaborative verse can seem outlandish. 'Japanese classical poems, read singly and in translation, and usually without context, can give a false sense of what the poet was aiming to accomplish,' cautions J. Thomas Rimer. Their composition 'was quite often a group endeavor, an aesthetic difficult for contemporary readers to understand or find sympathy with'.[7]

Shiki himself was unsympathetic. He assailed the collaborative linked verse that he blamed as dooming the *hokku* to an oblivion he both prophesied – applying a Western mathematical theory of permutations to conclude that the days of seventeen-syllable verse were numbered (though clearly such verse had already been in decline) – and would eventually help fulfil. By insisting that the *hokku*-derived haiku was a *pure* literature on a par with Western forms, whereas linked verse was not, Shiki essentially sounded the death knell of collaborative versification. Only recently, with the benefit of hindsight, has this violence been contested. Takiguchi Susumu, scholar and past president of the World Haiku Club, has gone so far as to accuse Shiki of a kind of attempted murder, one that has been 'camouflaged under the guise of his famous *haiku kakushin* (haiku reform) for so long that no one dares to challenge the incredible authority and reputation which have decorated this great man even if it is blatantly obvious that he did something seriously wrong regarding [collaboratively linked verse]'. Later, towards the end of his brief life, Shiki would confess he had known next to nothing about such verse.[8]

It might be said that Shiki forged the modern haiku out of premodern haiku as a kind of 'invented' tradition. Traditions are constantly being constructed and revised. But what distinguishes an invented tradition in the age of modernization, according to historians, is its largely fictitious continuity with a historical past in a way that specifically authorizes the modern nation-state.[9] Such invented traditions pursue a double strategy, idealizing the past by oversimplifying disharmonious complexities, while simultaneously exploiting the authority of that idealized past in the name of Progress. Thus, Shiki streamlined a jumble of premodern verse practices into a single poetic form as national emblem when those practices had in their own day never been conceived of so monolithically, let alone in terms of a modern nation-state that had yet to be invented.

Unsurprisingly, other so-called 'traditional' symbols of Japan were similarly concocted at the same historical moment. Stephen Vlastos has observed that in 'Japan as throughout the industrialized world, the rise of the nation-state in the late nineteenth century produced an outpouring of new national symbols and rites such as flags, anthems, and holidays ... The idea of "the nation", after all, stands as the mega invented tradition of the modern era.'[10] Even the supposedly time-honoured emperor system, according to Carol Gluck, 'did not begin to emerge in earnest until around 1890'.[11]

The Grand Narrative of Haiku

Shiki's invented tradition of haiku has become so widely accepted, so automatically subscribed to, so ubiquitously naturalized, it might be described as a kind of 'grand narrative'.[12] Emerging in a hugger-mugger of writings in Japanese, English and other languages, this Grand Narrative, for a range of political, ideological, even commercial reasons, promulgates the haiku as an ancient form of traditional Japanese poetry. Yet each of these terms is disputable: the haiku is anything but ancient, let alone traditional, for its continuity with verse practices of the premodern past is mostly fabricated; these practices were not exactly poetry in the modern Western sense; nor does their existence qualify the modern haiku as purely Japanese; and since the haiku is based on merely one among what might be thought of as multiple *modes* of seventeen-syllable verseform (more about which below), to reserve the term 'haiku' exclusively for the entire verseform seems misguided.

Nevertheless, the Grand Narrative has proven amazingly robust over the past century, and flexible, providing a rich source of cultural propaganda that has promoted a positive image of Japaneseness. In the early twentieth century, the haiku was cause for Asian pride. The first Easterner to win the Nobel Prize in Literature (1913), Rabindranath Tagore (1861–1941), emulated the haiku, translating some into his native Bengali, composing haikuesque verses and making spiritual pilgrimages to Japan.[13] In extreme moments, the haiku was freighted with embracing all Taoist, Confucian, Shinto and Buddhist thought. The haiku was nothing if not 'the final channel for the deep cultural streams of the Orient, from India to Japan, distilling them all into a single bright drop'.[14] As *the* emblem of Far Eastern mysticism, the haiku was a powerful embodiment of that brand of colonial racism later termed Orientalism.

With the rise of new middle and upper classes in Japan during the early decades of the twentieth century, composing haiku became one of the standard accomplishments of the bourgeoisie, particularly among young women of marriageable age attending finishing schools. A key figure in this process of *embourgeoisement* was Takahama Kyoshi (1874–1959). Kyoshi was a favoured disciple of Shiki who, to Shiki's chagrin, declined to succeed his mentor. Years after Shiki's death, however, Kyoshi returned to champion many of his mentor's ideas in a series of influential writings collectively qualifying him as among those who most cogently solidified the Grand Narrative. He was the one who proclaimed, for instance: 'Haiku is the literature that sings of the various phenomena that arise accompanying seasonal change.'[15] Moreover, Kyoshi irrevocably equated modern haiku with pre-modern *hokku* in the title of an article in a 1913 issue of the leading literary journal *Hototogisu*: 'Well, What Sort of Thing is Haiku (*Hokku*), Anyway?'[16]

In the wake of Japan's colonial and military entanglements over the ensuing decades in Formosa, Korea, Manchuria, Hong Kong, Malaya, Okinawa, Singapore, the Philippines and Burma, not to omit Pearl Harbor or China, particularly Nanking, the haiku provided a potent counternarrative to the story of Japanese belligerence. For who but a peaceful, docile, nature-loving people would compose haiku? During the ensuing age of the so-called Economic Miracle, the haiku became an enduring symbol, like the transistor radio, of the Japanese people's innate genius for miniaturization. Indeed, the haiku has been the Japanese art form par excellence for the better part of the past century, the woodblock print notwithstanding, up until the recent juggernaut of digital games, animation and comics. It may be no coincidence that when media conglomerate Sanrio began expanding to a global market, it devised Hello Kitty, a mouthless cartoonish trademark communicating Japaneseness visually, without recourse to words, by using exactly seventeen brushstrokes – that of course being the magic number of the haiku.

The haiku has been so overburdened with the task of performing the ideological work of Japaneseness that the two terms are virtually interchangeable. So much so that to cast doubt on the validity of the Japanese haiku 'tradition' is tantamount to a certain spiritual, if not cultural, treason. Some purists have even argued that the haiku as global poetry should be written in no language other than Japanese.[17] A veritable cottage industry churns out volumes with titles such as *Haiku: The Poetic Key to Japan*.[18] Children's author Miyazawa Kenji (1896–1933) gushed about Bashō's masterpiece, *Oku no hosomichi* (Narrow Road to the Interior, 1702): 'It was as if the very soul of Japan had itself written it.'[19] Poet Ōoka Makoto (1931–2017) reckoned that Japan has more amateur poets per capita in the industrialized

world than any other nation.[20] Calling the haiku 'Japanese' or
Japan 'haikuesque' has become so redundant, so commonplace,
so clichéd, that the Japaneseness of the haiku, not unlike Japan's
post-bubble economy, has suffered a kind of deflation. Croatian
haikuist Boris Nazansky has gone so far as to christen the form a
'literary bonsai', as if to reinvest the haiku with that much more
essentialized Japaneseness.[21]

The Japaneseness of the haiku is further reinforced by its
persistent association with Zen. A sect of Buddhism maintain-
ing that spiritual enlightenment can be attained through seated
meditation (*zazen*) and the contemplation of philosophical con-
undrums (*kōan*), Zen has long been erroneously synonymous
with Japaneseness. Haiku is assuredly not Zen poetry. And con-
trary to popular belief, Bashō was no Zen master. That he shaved
his head and donned priestly garb was equivalent, during his life-
time, to wearing a beret to signify one's status as an *artiste*. This is
not to deny the existence of Zen poetry, or the Zen orientation of
a particular poet or of individual readers. But to label haiku Zen
poetry for its apparent minimalism, or emphasis on transience or
relish of the Absurd, is a bit like defining free verse as the poetry
of Libertarianism, or blank verse the poetry of Nihilism.

The triumph of the Grand Narrative has turned the haiku into
a victim of its own success. It has become so heavily formulaic,
so overly familiar, that when not being taken for granted, it is
winked away like so much kitsch, little more than the stuff of
magnetic poetry kits for the kitchen fridge, hardly taken seriously
as the poetry to which it aspires. It has become too popular. Too
ubiquitous. Too commonplace. It encapsulates film reviews.
Springs up like weeds in magazines. Appears on road safety
signs. As computer error messages. Within literary works, such
as J. D. Salinger's *Franny and Zooey*, or the Beat musings of Allen
Ginsberg, Gary Snyder and Jack Kerouac, or hip-hop albums, like
Haiku D'état. Even in the maws of zombies and werewolves and
vampires. Although it almost seems as though some contempor-
ary haiku have conjured up the repressed playfulness of their
premodern precursor, that playfulness had in the first place
probably never entirely dematerialized.

The Two Haiku

In an effort to lessen this damage, the present anthology, containing about a thousand pre-twentieth-century Japanese verses in translation, effectively describes *two* haiku. The first, and by far better known the world over, is left unitalicized throughout to indicate its entry into English (where it is pronounced *high-coo*) and languages other than Japanese.[22] Its anglicization also serves as affirmation that, while grounded in the so-called ancient form of traditional Japanese poetry, this is, to repeat, a decidedly *modern* form of global poetry. Indeed, the haiku, far from being traditional, existing long ago and continuing to the present day in the same unadulterated form, is tradition*alist*, claiming the authority of tradition, though actually brought into existence in the mid 1890s. This is hardly ancient by Western standards, let alone Japanese. Photography is older, a fact that has ramifications for the haiku as experiential snapshot.

The second, far less known *haiku* – the one this volume features and hopefully provides fresh insight into, even for haiku enthusiasts – derives from an eclectic variety of collaboratively authored witty linked-verse practices that flourished primarily during Japan's premodern Edo period (1600–1868) and into the modern Meiji (1868–1912). This *haiku* is rendered in italics from here on, in order to indicate its otherness, both as a foreign term for English speakers (*ha-i-ku* in Japanese, pronounced *hah-ee-coo*, roughly matching the cadence of 'honeydew') and as an archaic term for all readers today, including the Japanese, since this *haiku* has been largely distorted and repressed. This *haiku* is shorthand for *haikai no ku* – itself shorthand for *haikai no renga no ku* – referring to one or more stanzas (*ku*) of witty (*haikai*) linked-verse (*renga*) sequences, played as a literary word game, commencing approximately five hundred years ago, with roots going back yet further into the mists of antiquity. Even though the modern haiku is widely recognized as having been fashioned out of the initiating stanza (*hokku*) of such linked sequences, it is nevertheless still habitually taken for granted that premodern *haiku* and modern haiku are, more or less, the same thing.

It is this facile 'more or less' that creates needless confusion and perpetuates perennial misunderstandings. Although traditionalist accounts tend to gloss over the differences, modern haiku and premodern *haiku* differ in basic attitudes towards authorship, readership, individualism, culture, politics, poetry, literature and humour. The haiku, a serious written form of standalone poetry of the modern individual, may conjure up the image of the contemplative lone poet, like Bashō before a frogpond (as though Thoreau at Walden). The *haiku*, by contrast, derived from a wildly popular type of verbal repartee, often conducted orally and recorded by scribes in a convivial group setting, occasionally enlivened by nibbles and saké, played by people from all walks of life and social classes, women as well as men.

Players were expected to respond to the previous stanza, reinterpreting and morphing it into something amusingly unexpected, all on the spot with sparkling wit – that 'ability to perceive connections between ideas, and then a quickness at seeing the kind of incongruous resemblances that evoke delighted surprise'.[23] Characteristically involving a comic clash in diction between the elegant language of classical Japanese poetry and the ordinary language of the contemporary masses, clever wordplay – specifically punning – or some other humorous twist, this wit was the stuff of witty linked verse. The exception in traditionalist modern haiku, wit was the rule in premodern *haiku*.

And so two caveats. First, readers of this volume expecting the haiku, or even merely a premodern equivalent, might be in for a shock. Given the silly, satirical, scatological and sensual content of many verses, traditionalists in particular may well be scandalized, fearing that a Trojan horse has been smuggled into the Holy Citadel of Haiku. After all, for countless people, haiku is more than a cultured pastime, let alone highbrow poetry. It is a meditative technique for combating information overload. A method of getting in touch with oneself, of communing with nature, of being more observant, respectful, sensitive, mindful. A microcosmic means of imbuing life's tiny moments with titanic meaning. A way of making sense of life itself, with all its jolts, contradictions, strange abundances and mysteries. Nevertheless,

Scene of an idealized witty linked-verse session, *c.* 1886

before the twentieth century, it was this other, decidedly less highfalutin *haiku* that predominated.

The starkest specimen of which was the *bareku* (*bah-reh-coo*), an overtly comic verse with its pants down. Delighting in matters faecal as well as sexual, this 'dirty sexy' *haiku* begs comparison with naughty limericks, French *fabliaux*, college drinking songs, drunken sailor ditties and honest-to-goodness horny cowboy tunes. Ignorantly cuckolded husbands, widows succumbing to the temptation of self-pleasure if not the advances of lecherous priests, abbots kissing the asses of young rentboys devotedly, promiscuous pre-teens, insatiable chambermaids, orgasms so hyper-real as to seem faked, syphilis-ravaged body parts, farting matches between tyrannous mothers-in-law and cheeky brides – none of these were out of bounds. Like erotic woodblock prints (*shunga*), though tending to the obscene rather than the pornographic, dirty sexy *haiku* offer a refreshingly transparent, if amusingly warped, glimpse into the private lives, sick jokes and libidinous fantasies of the pre-twentieth-century Japanese. As Bennett and Rosario put it in their book on auto-eroticism, 'there is no better demonstration of naked Truth than the revelation of one's erotic imagination'.[24]

We human beings have our less-than-flattering side, deny it though we might. The verses herein do no such thing, even if their inclusion risks inadvertently reinforcing the disturbing history of eroticizing the exotic Orient. To bowdlerize the dirty sexy *haiku* (as has been standard practice for too long), given its prevalence, popping up sporadically in witty linked-verse sequences when not constituting entire dedicated collections, is to misrepresent haiku and *haiku*. Perpetuating such misrepresentations to the extent that they skew an understanding of the Japanese as flesh-and-blood human beings would be the real perversification.

The second caveat is that the sharp distinction between pre-modern and modern is admittedly an oversimplification, not without its own liberties and distortions. It is not as though one sunny morning the *haiku* had suddenly vanished and in its place stood the haiku, like some uncanny body-snatching extraterrestrial. The near-universal conflation of these two haiku by no means took hold immediately. That was a gradual process. There was a grey period, lasting into the early twentieth century, before witty linked verse had withered away, and before the modern haiku had permanently taken root. Thus, the present volume covers premodern *haiku*, with the occasional transitional modern haiku thrown in, mostly up until about 1902, the year of Shiki's death. It does not cover postwar, contemporary, avant-garde, experimental haiku, much of which has, of its own accord, broken free of traditionalist strictures, thereby becoming effectively realigned with the freewheeling spirit, diction and content of premodern *haiku*.

And yet this oversimplification may be justifiable. To the extent that it allows for a richer, more 'anatomically correct' understanding of haiku as well as *haiku* in their historical contexts and relationships to each other, without subscribing to traditionalist attitudes that have focused attention on the former to the exclusion of the latter, it certainly is less egregious than the long-standing equation of the modern haiku with the premodern *hokku*. And anyway, the paradigmatic shift from premodern to modern profoundly affected and was affected by literature in the broadest sense – particularly poetry, long central to Japanese letters and culture – for it literally provided the narrative of Japan's modernization.[25]

Season Word and Cut

The essence of the haiku has long been considered its extreme, almost excessive, brevity. One of its most appealing qualities, brevity has earned for the haiku its reputation as the shortest verseform in the world. Strictly speaking, though, there is at least one shorter: the *tanku* (pronounced *tah-n-coo*), a *haiku* in fourteen syllabets – 'syllabet', used from this point on, being the more accurate term for the Japanese (see Note on the Translation, p. LXXVII). Some modern Western poetic epigrams, albeit lacking a set form, run shorter still. Yet it is the seventeen-syllabet haiku that has set the standard for approaching a literary absolute zero, teetering on the brink of silence. Whereas most poetry cannot suffer much frou-frou or folderol, haiku cannot suffer any. It has none to suffer. Brevity *is* its meaning, not just a key feature or fortuitous side effect. Brevity makes the haiku the definition of minimalism, which, according to *The Oxford Dictionary of Literary Terms*, is a 'literary or dramatic style or principle based on the extreme restriction of a work's contents to a bare minimum of necessary elements, normally within a short form, e.g. a haiku'.

In reality, however, verses were never strictly confined to seventeen syllabets (or fourteen, in the case of the *tanku*). Syllabet count (*onsūritsu*) was always more guideline than rule, particularly when flouted to deliberate effect, even by the Grandmasters. And while it has become customary in English to compose contemporary haiku into seventeen syllables or preferably fewer – a trend impacting upon translation – historically, Japanese *haiku* took liberties by running over into extra syllabets (*jiamari*) rather than under (*jitarazu*).

According to traditionalist accounts, haiku has two major formal requirements, both of which are meant to overcome this monumental minimalism. The first though broadly undervalued requirement is the 'cutting word' (*kireji*) or 'cut' (*kire*), a device that brings about a strong dramatic pause in the meaning of a verse as well as its rhythm.[26] The cut overcomes brevity by rending the verse into two superficially unrelated portions, beckoning the reader to step in and, through a strategy of intuition or inspiration or allusional detective work, if not cold logic, search for some underlying connection. The cut, it might be said, splices as well as dices. It establishes twin cathodes that the reader must bridge by generating an imaginative spark. A technique of disjunction, according to Richard Gilbert, the cut triggers a cognitive shift.[27]

In standalone haiku, the cut is said to fall mostly after the first or second phrase, and only sometimes in the middle of a phrase as a kind of enjambment (*kumatagari*). In the linked verse that was *haiku*, however, there are also instances when the cut falls at the end of a stanza, separating one stanza from another. (Bashō's preference for such cutting corroborates the fact that he practised *haiku* rather than haiku.) Wherever the cut falls, though, it connects fragments into a larger whole, be they parts of a momentarily isolated stanza or successive stanzas within a sequence. This disjunctive logic of the cut, by creating negative space (*ma*) enjoining reader involvement, is the logic of linked verse – and of the wit in witty linked verse. To the extent that the cut substantiates this foundational logic of collaborative witty linking, it tends to be downplayed in traditionalist accounts of the modern standalone haiku.

The second requirement, the season word (*kigo*), is prioritized in such traditionalist accounts. Providing a frame of reference that calls to mind associations beyond the confines of its verse, the season word indicates the quintessence of the actual season of composition, invokes the bittersweet fleetingness of the seasons in their eternal cycles and, ideally, imparts a sense of restrained elegance grounded in the encounter between human observer and natural world. However, this hardly tells the whole story. In premodern *haiku*, stanzas also have indistinct seasons, overlapping or dual seasons (*kigasanari*) or even *no* season whatsoever. In fact, the seasonless 'miscellaneous stanza' (*zappai* or *zatsu no ku*) played a pivotal role, literally, in linked sequences, serving as a neutral transition between seasons. A sequence might have a spurt of stanzas set in autumn, for instance, then, after a seasonless stanza or two, several set in spring. 'It is as if time stopped and flowed with no regularity; in some cases, time seems to have flowed backwards,' as Makoto Ueda has put it. 'One might say that [linked verse] thrives on an atemporal sequence.'[28]

These seasons therefore progress according to artistic whimsy, rather than chronological time. Only the *hokku*, a benedictory verse serving as formal salutation by the guest of honour to the host of the verse-composing event, addresses the real-life season deliberately. When 'ordinary stanzas' (*hiraku*) within the sequence mention that season, they do so almost coincidentally, more in playful response to the previous stanza than sober reflection on the actual season. Versifiers were free to wax poetic about seasons not observed at the moment of composition. *Haiku*, in other words, was based on imagination as well as direct experience. Such licence complicates the simple biographical reading of individual stanzas, suggesting the possibility that witty linked verse was just as much imaginative role-playing as literary word game, one in which pen names (*haigō*) stood less for real people than fictitious avatars. It was even possible for a single

person to assume multiple roles when composing a 'solo se-
quence' (*dokugin*): the poet Saikaku, to take a notorious exam-
ple, once produced nearly 24,000 linked stanzas within a single
twenty-four-hour period.

Later inventors of the modern haiku took the *hokku* as their
model not merely because, as the most reliably elegant stanza in
a sequence, it had already sometimes been singled out for spe-
cial consideration, then, but because its use of the cut and season
word allowed the haiku to simultaneously sever itself from the
playful, fictional practices of collaborative witty linked verse while
selectively linking the present to an idealized, purified, imaginary,
pastoral past. This past was forever frozen in a timeless immedi-
acy in which the cherry blossoms on Mount Yoshino are always
in bloom, always scattering, always serving as inexhaustibly fresh
metaphors of the impermanence of beauty and the beauty of im-
permanence.

The season word afforded a sense of nostalgic continuity with
this imagined agrarian past in a way that provided a modicum of
stability at a time when the Japanese were genuinely apprehen-
sive not only about times to come, but also about the instability
of time itself. The Chinese zodiac, the circles of Buddhist tem-
poral cosmology, the periodic refurbishing of Shinto shrines, the
ebbs and flows of the Asian lunisolar calendar – time had, for
eons, been reassuringly cyclical. Then all of a sudden, on New
Year's day of 1873, when the solar Gregorian calendar officially
took effect in Japan, time became scientifically linear, progres-
sive, forward-looking, no longer based on the backward-glancing
search for a golden age in the distant past. Annual observances
shifted to new dates, local timepieces were synchronized nation-
ally and the national clock reset to historical global time. 'Estab-
lishing this "new time" was,' according to Stefan Tanaka, 'one of
the dominating themes of the Meiji period.'[29]

No wonder the season word itself turns out to be a modern
neologism. Earlier poetics accorded significance to seasons (*ki*)
and seasonal words (*ki no kotoba*), to be sure.[30] Yet it is not until
modernization that the 'season word' (*kigo*) and its closely allied
'seasonal topic' (*kidai*) – coined by Ōsuga Otsuji (1881–1920)
in 1908 and Shiki disciple Kawahigashi Hekigotō (1873–1937)

in 1907, respectively[31] – were formalized as part of the national haiku. If, on the surface, the season word mourned the passing of the seasons, deeper down it appealed to the authority of their predictably regular flux, as though to represent an urbanizing Japan, as well as its modern poetic emblem, as every bit as unchanging and traditional and ancient.

Shiki's Frogpond

It may be no fluke that the most celebrated of all haiku, Bashō's verse about a frog plopping into a pond, begins with the word *furu* (the grammatical stem of *furui*), suggesting something unchanged from time immemorial:

> old pond!
> a frog plunges into
> watersound

(*furuike ya / kawazu tobikomu / mizu no oto*). This verse simultaneously connects and severs itself from the past, conjuring up both continuity, in the aeonian pond, but also discontinuity, in the frog's *springing*. Given that for three-quarters of a millennium classical Japanese poetry (*waka*) had associated the poetic quintessence (*hon'i*) of frogs with *singing*, this must have seemed a radical departure in its playful subversion of poetic cliché and grandiloquent diction. In an early statement of Japanese poetics, within the first imperially commissioned anthology, *Kokin wakashū* (Collection of Japanese Poems Old and New, *c.*920), Ki no Tsurayuki had memorably proclaimed that Japanese poetry is the innate expression of human beings, just as crooning and croaking are the natural songs of warblers and frogs.

One widely circulating illustration of this verse, from *Haijin hyakkasen* (Selections from One Hundred Haiku Poets, 1855), portrays the lone poet Bashō at his writing table, inside his hut shaded by leaves of the eponymous plantain tree (*bashō*), glancing out at a leaping frog. Retrospectively portraying the originary scene of the archetypal haiku, this image is less than true-to-life

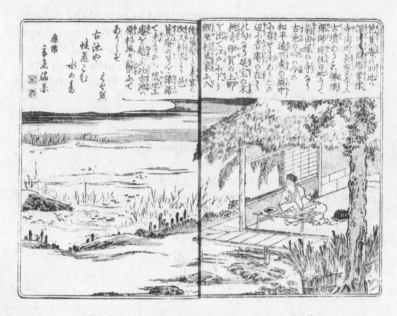

Bashō (1644–94) composing his verse on the frog
plunging into an old pond

(a distortion that might well have Bashō and his frog rolling
over in their graves); for the stanza, it turns out, was composed
at a collaborative linked-verse session (held sometime between
1681 and 1684), as per the account provided by one of Bashō's
disciples, Kagami Shikō (1665–1731).[32] Shikō did not reproduce
the entire sequence, though he recorded the response to Bashō's
stanza, a *tanku* by Takarai Kikaku (1661–1707):

> on young leaves of rush
> hangs a spider's web

(*ashi no wakaba ni / kakaru kumo no su*).[33] An illustration of the
actual moment of composition based on Shikō's account would
show Bashō, Kikaku and others collaboratively composing a
witty linked-verse sequence.[34] If the 1855 illustration seems to us

today to present Bashō as crafting a modern haiku two centuries before its invention, it is primarily because of the polemics of Masaoka Shiki. For what this illustration more likely captures is an increasing tendency, during the late eighteenth and early nineteenth centuries, towards standalone verse if not the rise of the *haiku* master as public celebrity.

Shiki himself, it should be observed, promoted imagery as central to the new haiku. Misrepresenting Bashō's verse as a Western-style standalone poem, Shiki was even more determined to align haiku with scientific objectivity and photorealism. This eventually led him to favour Buson, a professional inkwash painter and *haiku* artist whose premodern brand of verisimilitude could be conveyed in the modern phrases 'depict as is' (*ari no mama ni utsutsu*) and 'sketching from life' (*shasei*), appropriated from Tsubouchi Shōyō and Western-style painter Nakamura Fusetsu (1866–1943). That Buson also excelled at sound poetry brings into relief how traditionalist accounts of haiku frequently subordinate sound, and other sensory stimuli, to a modern regime of visuality in which images have all but displaced imagination.

Orthodox and Heterodox Schools

The blanket exaltation of Bashō's highbrow poetry and disavowal of lowbrow forms such as the dirty sexy *haiku* suggest the long-standing distinction in Japan between classics and trash. This distinction reflects the razor-sharp ideological if not societal divide, throughout the seventeenth and eighteenth centuries, between aristocratic samurai and the three major commoner classes, in descending order, of landholder-farmers, artisans and merchants. This status quo was destabilized, however, by dramatic improvements in agricultural productivity, exponential population growth and burgeoning metropolitan centres. By 1800, Edo could boast one million inhabitants, making it the largest city in the world alongside Paris and London, though arguably with a superior rate of literacy and a preferable quality of life.[35] The bottom-feeding merchants had become so filthy rich that the major socio-economic issue was the almost schizophrenic chasm between their financial hegemony and the political monopoly of the increasingly impoverished samurai.

The rising tide of commoner affluence during the seventeenth century also stimulated a buoyant – and flamboyant – urban popular culture. The 'floating world' (*ukiyo*), as it was dubbed, gleefully punning on the Buddhist 'fleeting world' of sorrow (*ukiyo*, though rendered with different Chinese characters or 'graphs'), was physically centred in the interrelated commercial entertainment spaces of kabuki and puppet theatres, street spectacles and pleasure quarters. Particularly in Edo's licensed Yoshiwara and unlicensed Nakazu districts, playboys (and the occasional well-off woman) disported themselves with haughty courtesans, talented geisha, diverting comedians, obliging bathhouse girls and alluring toyboys. A sensuous realm of fantasy and performance and role-playing, where the hierarchies of mainstream society were anything but upheld, what happened in the floating world stayed in the floating world. All were welcome – so long as they had cash. And even though the shogunate dispatched spies to deter samurai, they showed up in droves anyway, albeit incognito.

With the advent of commercial woodblock printing in Japan in the 1620s, this popular culture would come to be diffused everywhere, in the form of floating world novellas (*ukiyozōshi*), prints (*ukiyoe*), comic literature (*gesaku*) and *haiku* modes such as comic verse (*senryū*). All of these delighted in exposing the slightest whiff of hypocrisy. Authors could never lampoon the regime directly, however, for fear of corporal or even capital punishment, so they did so obliquely. The real threat, though, was symbolic. The popularity of satirical works epitomized the spectre of the irrepressible growth of an uncontrollable *mass* culture widely believed to be exacerbating fiscal and moral decay. The shogunate consequently doubled down, promoting the elite 'literary and martial arts' (*bunbu*) of classical poetry and sword fighting, while prohibiting samurai from plebeian indulgences such as gambling, theatre-going, whoring and *haiku*. The last of these, while not exactly the gangsta rap of its day, none the less struck the authorities as injurious to public morals.

It was within this context that the Bashō School – or Shōmon, in Japanese, meaning both 'Bashō's Gate' and, not coincidentally, 'Correct School' – would eventually emerge as the most respectable and orthodox. Yet there were two major rivals (and innumerable minor ones) that were more immediately long-lasting and widespread. The Teimon – or 'Teitoku School', named after Matsunaga Teitoku (1571–1653) – deserves recognition for having pioneered *haiku*. And the Danrin School, founded by Nishiyama Sōin (1605–82), attracted enormous followings, including Ihara Saikaku (1642–93), whose *haiku* sensibilities inflect the prose of his floating world novellas that qualify him as premodern Japan's pre-eminent comic author. Conversely, the Shōmon was a unified whole for a mere flash. Before Bashō's corpse grew cold, feuds among disciples fractured the school hopelessly – at least until three-quarters of a century later, when Buson laboured to revitalize its legacy in the 'Bashō Revival' (*Shōfū kaiki*). Yet traditionalist recountings of haiku tend to be limited to a single school and poet. Only within the past generation has this chokehold begun to be loosened, as when Japanese scholar Suzuki Katsutada, writing within an authoritative anthology, declared: 'The notion that the entire history of *haiku* can be adequately explained by focusing on Bashō or his school alone is no longer tenable.'[36]

To name just one of many other influential figures, Uejima Onitsura (1660–1738) was held in equally high esteem as Bashō during their day. In Buson's terse summation (in the form of a *tanku*, no less): 'In the east, Bashō; in the west, Onitsura' (*higashi no bashō / nishi no onitsura*). Although the former is customarily acclaimed for having ennobled *haiku*, the latter did something similar at roughly the same time, perhaps earlier. Onitsura infused *haiku* with the principle of poetic sincerity (*makoto*), as per his motto 'without authenticity there can be no witty linked verse' (*makoto no hokani haikai nashi*). This line of thinking is traceable to his erstwhile Teimon mentor, Matsue Shigeyori (1602–80), who extolled 'witty linked verse from the heart' (*kokoro no haikai*). Practically speaking, then, differences among schools often turn out to be arbitrary or trivial, more a matter of interpersonal politics and petty rivalries than the substance of poetics. Students not infrequently left one school for another, as did Bashō and

Onitsura themselves. Little wonder that cross-influence, adaptation, revision, parody, imitation, duplication and even what today might be called plagiarism were pervasive (as evidenced by several verses herein).

Moreover, the rise of popular culture threatened the vitality of the schools, which were based on the hereditary atelier (*iemoto*) system that for centuries had organized artistic lineages hierarchically around a poetic master (*sōshō*). This was true of linked verse. Serious linked verse (*renga*), which had begun as an urbane pastime among aristocrats at court in Kyoto during the Heian period (794–1185), became formalized among the upwardly mobile warrior class during the medieval period (1185–1600). When its intricate rules were simplified and strict diction relaxed, the resulting witty linked verse became a *popular* form. Eventually, elite schools previously closed to all but paying disciples gave way to coteries (*za*) open to just about anyone, regardless of class or gender or geography.

Haiku Verse Capping (*Maekuzuke*)

The commercial woodblock-printing revolution that was part and parcel of this popular culture posed the more immediate threat to the hereditary atelier system. Cheaply produced and thus affordable booklets permitted anyone anywhere to read, study and compose *haiku* without having to join costly schools. Printing helped relocate the primary scene of versification to vast publics, thereby popularizing *haiku* to a countrywide audience. Massive *haiku* verse-capping contests, run by workaday point-scoring judges (*tenja*) rather than poetic masters, did the trick. Naturally, as head of school Bashō frowned on such practices. Yet rivals and even some of his own disciples (notably Shikō) allegedly sold out. The Teimon and Danrin schools, and renegade Shōmon factions, conceivably flourished less in spite of *haiku* verse capping than because of it.

In its most prevalent and consequential form, *haiku* verse capping involved laying down a 'challenge verse' (*maeku*) in the form of a fourteen-syllabet *tanku*, the more confounding the better:

> however grim
> it was also funny!

(*niganigashiku mo / okashikarikeri*). To which one or more players would offer a witty seventeen-syllabet 'response verse' (*tsukeku*), as with this legendary retort by Yamazaki Sōkan (1465–1553):

> even while
> my father lay dying
> farts kept ripping!

(*waga oya no / shinuru toki ni mo / he o kokite*). *Haiku* verse capping also included sundry sorts of acrostics (*oriku*) and word games in which a player would compose two phrases of a seventeen-syllabet verse when given the first or second or third phrase as a challenge.

This challenge-plus-response pattern courses throughout pre-modern Japanese literature, going as far back as the first extant writings in Japan. The *Kojiki* (Record of Ancient Matters, *c.*711) registers a kind of verse-capping exchange in 'half verses' (*kata-uta*) of 4–7–7 and 5–7–7 syllabets.[37] Verse capping was a beloved pastime at the imperial court during the peak of classical Japanese poetry. One poet would provide a seventeen-syllabet head verse, the other a fourteen-syllabet tail, producing a 'simple linked verse' (*tan renga*) in the form of a 31-syllabet 'short verse' (*tanka*). Poetic exchange formed the backbone of classic tales combining prose and poetry, too. There is witty repartee galore between Don Juan protagonists and their copious lovers within *Ise monogatari* (Tales of Ise, *c.*880–950) and *Genji monogatari* (The Tale of Genji, *c.*1000). Masters of serious linked verse, such as Sōgi (1421–1502) and Sōchō (1448–1532), many of whose *hokku* now seem readable as modern haiku, also engaged in verse capping. Linked verse itself, after all, *is* sustained verse capping: each response becomes a challenge every time except for the last response ending a sequence. (Then again, later versifiers might allude to this last verse (*ageku*), treating it as a challenge to which they offered their own response.) In the final analysis, the challenge–response exchange of verse capping was a principal form of premodern Japanese cultural production.

Nevertheless, *haiku* verse capping has long been disparaged as poetic training wheels at best, or, at worst, a kind of gambling that was outlawed repeatedly and so, one surmises, ineffectually. It is true that during its apogee, from the end of the seventeenth century through the middle of the eighteenth, *haiku* verse capping was something of a racket. Originally a small informal game played in person (as in modern-day poetry competitions), it had become a large-scale for-profit venture, tempting people to part with their money in the hope of winning recognition and prizes despite lottery-like odds. These prizes ranged from inexpensive cotton textiles, bowls, hand towels, serving trays and the like, to the rare grand prize of valuable bolts of fine Okushima silk or even solid gold coins (worth tens of thousands of pounds today).

Typically, a referee would issue challenge verses on mass-printed flyers distributed through a network of field agents (*kai-rin*). Contestants would submit responses along with an entry fee (*tōkuryō*) or scoring charge (*tenryō*) to cover the costs of convey-ance, marking and so on.[38] The referee would then sift through the hundreds or thousands or, in some cases, tens of thousands of entries and select the wittiest ones for publication. Winning verses (*shōku*) would be announced in printed notices (*kachikuzu-ri* or *koyomizuri*) circulated back locally through the agents. Truly exceptional verses were showcased in booklets reaching a far broader audience. No matter the outcome, the referees inevitably made the biggest killing.

Originating in the Kyoto-Osaka region, *haiku* verse capping spread to Edo, where it caught on, especially among Teimon prac-titioners. The foremost popularizer among whom, Tachiba Fu-kaku (1662–1753), edited several influential publications.[39] His *Futaba no matsu* (Twin-Needled Pine, 1690), a collection gleaned from monthly gatherings (*tsukinami*), helped promote *haiku* verse capping throughout the land, from urban centres to rural peripheries.[40] One source from 1696 related: 'The whole world is having fun by playing what is known as *maekuzuke*. There is no one, not even an aged woodcutter or a young reaper, who does not amuse himself with it.'[41]

Significantly, Fukaku helped transform *haiku* verse capping from a simulated linking game into something approaching free-standing verse. The fourteen-syllabet challenge had long

Tachiba Fukaku (1662–1753)

consisted of two distinct phrases (as with 'however grim / it was also funny!'). During the closing decades of the seventeenth century, the challenge was occasionally simplified into a single seven-syllabet phrase that was repeated using a ditto mark, purportedly as a space-saving measure in printed matter. In 1691 Fukaku issued *Waka midori* (Young Greens), the earliest major work to regularly use the resultant 'repeating challenge' (*jōgo*). The standard from 1692 on, the repeating challenge swiftly eroded the role of the challenge proper – if not the fourteen-syllabet *tanku* form itself – eventually enabling the seventeen-syllabet response to stand on its own, a trend that would culminate in the full-blown *senryū*.[42]

Senryū and Other *Haiku* Modes

Although earlier collections of such free-standing verse existed, the breakthrough came in 1765, with the publication of the initial volume of *Yanagidaru* (Willow Vat).[43] Featuring the winning seventeen-syllabet responses *without* their fourteen-syllabet challenges, gleaned from *haiku* verse-capping contests hosted and judged by Karai Hachiemon (1718–90) under the pen name Senryū, *Yanagidaru* is commonly regarded as the pioneering work and main repository of what later would come to be named after the man most closely associated with this mode. Its 167 volumes were issued more or less annually until 1840, seventy-five years after its inception and half a century after the deaths of Senryū and principal editor Goryōken Arubeshi (d. 1788), both of whom masterminded the two dozen inaugural volumes. From the first of these, according to Kobayashi Masashi, *Yanagidaru* contained 'poems that could be understood on their own without their [challenge] couplet and which were still interesting and amusing as independent poems'.[44] Composed in verse-capping contests, however, these verses were not modern independent poems. Eighteenth-century *senryū*, Suzuki warns, 'remained a literature of the group and had by no means evolved into a literature of the individual'.[45]

Karai Senryū (1718–90)

Arguably, the *senryū* was the predominant mode of *haiku*, outnumbering the *hokku* and capturing the popular imagination to the point that individual verses entered proverbial wisdom (as evidenced by several verses herein). The *senryū* also embodies an early modern form of exposé (*ugachi*) of faults in common sense that was central to the comic literature and witty linked verse inspiriting the floating world with its appealing mischievousness. The *senryū* was thus the earliest poetry in Japanese history – and quite possibly world history – to be composed and consumed, with little or no time lag, by just about everybody throughout the furthest reaches of the realm. It therefore seems to have been the first *haiku* mode to be universally read on its own as a 'stand-alone verse' (*ikkudate*), without being automatically reimagined in a linked relationship (*tsukeai*) with other verses, prose or images. To the extent that the term 'haiku' designates a free-standing seventeen-syllabet poem, then, the *senryū* might be regarded as the *original* haiku. And rather than define the *senryū* as comic haiku, it would be more fitting to define haiku as less witty *senryū*.

Regrettably, the *senryū* is routinely mischaracterized twice over. First, it serves as a catch-all category for anything and everything not readily squeezed into the cookie cutter of traditionalist modern haiku. A motley assortment of modes, including *haiku* verse capping and the *bareku*, too often are muddled together as *senryū*. Second, the *senryū* is unfairly measured against haiku standards, setting it up to fall short (as a *low-coo*). If the haiku is a serious poem by a named poet about nature, deploying a season word and cut, the *senryū* is an anonymous comic verse about human nature, with no season word or cut.

Yet the presumption that a seventeen-syllabet verse is *either* a *hokku*-based haiku *or* a *senryū* is a zero-sum game. In the first place, there are far more seventeen-syllabet *hiraku* ('ordinary stanzas') with season words and cuts than there are *hokku*. Also, not all haiku have season words – and not all *senryū* lack them. Thus, the presence or absence of a season word hardly makes for a reliable litmus test to differentiate between *hokku* and *senryū*. And since the *hai* of *haiku* means 'light' or 'witty', defining *senryū* as comic haiku is redundant, like saying *comic* comic verse. Nature plays a role in many *senryū*, and many of the best haiku provide

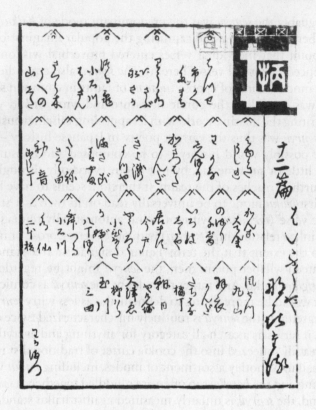

Prefatory page to *Yanagidaru* 12 (1777), presenting information
about the various authors contained in that volume

insight into human nature – not that these are mutually exclu-
sive. And contrary to the received wisdom, *senryū* often were *not*
anonymous, as evident in the prefatory page to volume 12 of
Yanigadaru.[46]

Most crucially, the seventeen-syllabet verseform by no means
is limited to two modes. Although there remains little consensus,
some scholars have informally reckoned as many as *thirty* such
modes. This figure, by counting each permutation within the
morass of overlapping *haiku* verse-capping games as a separate
mode, seems inflated. A more realistic estimate would be half a

dozen major modes: (1) *senryū* (overtly comic *haiku*); (2) *bareku* (dirty sexy *haiku*, too often dismissed as an offensive subcategory of *senryū*); (3) *maekuzuke* (*haiku* verse capping, further divisible into copious modes, as per Glossary); (4) *zappai* (seasonless miscellaneous *haiku*; when taken out of context, often mistaken for seasonless *senryū*); (5) *hokku* (initiating stanzas, the model among traditionalists for the modern haiku); and (6) *hiraku* ('ordinary stanza'; by virtue of its season word and cut habitually mistaken for the *hokku*, and therefore also sometimes an inadvertent model for the modern haiku, though falling *within* a linked sequence instead of initiating one and less beholden than the *hokku* to the imperative of gravitas). Hence, to regard the seventeen-syllabet 'verseform' as the sole preserve of the modern haiku, when that haiku was based on the *hokku* of premodern *haiku*, is problematic because seventeen-syllabet *haiku* comprised several modes other than the *hokku*, modes such as the *senryū* that eclipsed the *hokku* in terms of popularity and are more central to *haiku* in terms of overt playfulness.

Bursting onto the scene during the heyday of the *senryū* was Kobayashi Issa (1763–1827), third of the Four Grandmasters and widely considered Japan's most adored *haiku* poet. His verses come across as intensely personal, autonomous, even modern poems. They frequently seem incapable of being read any other way. Could this have been due as much to the influence of the detached *senryū* as anything else? Many of Issa's verses turn the exposé on himself, often with tremendous poignancy, in a way that lend themselves to biographical readings. This applies especially to those verses within his journals that reveal something intimate about his life, which had its fair share of heartbreak. (His mother died while he was a toddler; he later lost his wife and several young children; he suffered at the hands of a stepmother who hindered his rightful inheritance after his father passed away; his house burned down, etc.) Issa, according to Harold Henderson, 'opens his soul to us, therefore we love him'.[47] Also endearing is Issa's love for, if not identification with, small, vulnerable creatures, as though an early forerunner of the contemporary Japanese culture of the 'cute' (*kawaii*).

Women Poets

Women have often been neglected in traditionalist accounts
of haiku. In part this is because historically they are situated
lower on the social ladder in Japan than men. When women are
acknowledged, they usually serve as the exceptions who prove
the rule of male superiority. Even then, this typically is only in
connection with the men in their lives, especially if Shōmon
poets, rather than for their own poetic merits. Kawai Chigetsu
(1633–1718) gets mentioned more for her closeness to Bashō
than for how her verses were showcased in a central Shōmon text,
Sarumino (Monkey's Straw Raincape). Similarly, when Enomoto
Seifu (1732–1815) is acclaimed as one of the greatest women
haikuists – or Kaga no Chiyo (1703–75), aka Chiyoni (the nun
Chiyo), hailed as the 'female' Bashō[48] – the praise is backhand-
ed, implying these poets were more tokens of their gender than
exemplars of the art form.

Such wholesale belittling, while neither condonable nor
unique in world literary history, is relatively conspicuous in the
Japanese context. Maybe the most remarkable efflorescence of
poetry by women prior to the modern era occurred in Japan, in
the literary salons at court during the Heian period. Aristocratic
ladies have long been counted among the very finest *tanka* poets,
including Ono no Komachi (*c.*825–900) and Izumi Shikibu (b.
*c.*976). After this classical zenith, women seemed to recede into
the shadows.[49] They re-emerged noticeably in Edo-period *haiku*.
Roger Thomas has concluded: 'This renascence of the feminine
poetic voice was one of the most significant developments of the
age.'[50] Similarly, Eiko Ikegami has commented: 'the degree of
women's participation in the literary universe of the *haikai* was
unusually impressive in the standard of the eighteenth and early
nineteenth centuries in the world'.[51] More provocatively, Ikegami
suggests that the diverse membership of *haiku* clubs helped pave
the way for democratic civil society in Japan.

Women had resurfaced early on in the history of *haiku*. Verse
by 'Mitsutada's wife' is represented along with those of male
poets in the earliest major *haiku* publication, *Enokoshū* (Puppy-

Shiba Sonome (1664–1726)

dog Collection, 1633). And a few women were able to reach the
top of the *haiku* world without, as often claimed, riding on male
coat-tails. Take the case of Shiba Sonome (aka Sonojo, 1664–
1726). Legend has it that this wife of one of Bashō's disciples
was so devoted to versifying, she routinely let all the dishes pile
up, dirty, until they had to be washed in one marathon session.
Less legendarily, Sonome struck out on her own, leaving home
in Osaka for Edo after her husband's death and becoming one
of the first women to support herself solely through *haiku* point-
scoring, publishing and master instruction.

It should also be observed that, like men (even the Grandmas-
ters), women were active in lowbrow modes of *haiku* as well as
highbrow. Granted, the issue of attribution is complicated: many
verses lack pen names, and even those bearing feminine ones –
incorporating words such as 'woman' (*jo*) or 'nun' (*ni*)[52] – cannot
necessarily be relied upon to reflect an author's gender accurately.
Gender crossing has a hallowed place in Japanese arts, as with

male authors adopting feminine narrative persona within literary classics and male kabuki actors specializing in female roles.[53] Kabuki itself originated when the shrine maiden Izumo no Okuni (b. *c.* 1572) cross-dressed in male garb to perform a seductive new style of singing, dancing and acting in Kyoto (*c.* 1603).

Still, the relatively sudden mid-eighteenth-century outpouring of *senryū* and *bareku* bearing a clear female viewpoint is suggestive, leading to speculation that such verses were composed by women in part to relieve the stress of living in a male-dominated society.[54] Women are known to have composed both *senryū*, such as Goei and Goryū, and *bareku*, such as Konojo, Kisenjo and Tessen. And then there was Oei (1793–1859), third daughter of the woodblock artist Katsushika Hokusai (1760–1849), whose *Great Wave* remains iconic of Japan to this day. Oei composed *senryū* with her father, but also dirty sexy *haiku* on her own.[55]

As the subject of verses, women were not infrequently portrayed as the butts of jokes:

> the piece of ass
> slapped by mistake
> sends love letters!

(*machigai de / tataita shiri ga / fūjite ki*). Commentators overwhelmingly assume that such misogyny is indicative of male authorship. True, a good many *senryū* and *bareku* seem to adopt a male perspective. Apologists have even suggested that beneath the surface of such verses lurks *male* angst.[56] Yet this particular verse, however amusing or offensive for reducing a woman to a part of her anatomy (or amusing *because* it is offensive?), nevertheless accords that woman what must have seemed like an astounding degree of sexual agency. Such verses allow us to see the world from a woman's point of view, even if only from the limited perspective of the stereotype, irrespective of the poet's actual gender.

Well, What Sort of Thing is *Haiku*
as World Poetry, Anyway?

Women and men, young and old, poor and rich, commoners and samurai, country folk and city slickers – by the end of the eighteenth century, *haiku* had become a nationwide craze. The village headman of one small hamlet reported in his diary that *haiku* had 'reached the point where everyone in the country was playing at it – women, children, even mountain bandits'.[57]

It can be contended that *haiku* had become so popular thanks less to highbrow modes such as *hokku* (or more neutral modes such as *zappai* and *hiraku*) than to lowbrow modes such as *senryū*, *bareku* and *haiku* verse capping, modes that drew deeply from the comic literature and popular culture of the urban commoner classes. If Bashō and Onitsura were busy developing grandiose aesthetics to shore up the hereditary atelier system against the sea change of mass-printed floating-world culture, then Fukaku and Senryū rode that wave exuberantly. At any rate, the Teimon and Danrin schools initially outlived the Bashō School (until its revival by Buson), making possible the advent of charmingly idiosyncratic poets such as Issa. Shiki, taking his cue from Western poetry in his reimagining Bashō, all but annihilated collaboratively linked verse as well as lowbrow modes, reinventing the *hokku* as the modern haiku. In so doing, Shiki and his disciple Kyoshi turned this haiku into a durable national emblem. Revisionist versions of *haiku* that take into account Fukaku, Senryū and other poets, meanwhile, still tend to rely on a Great Man theory of history that, even if it could be stretched to give women their due, does not quite ring true in the context of collaborative poetry.

All things considered, then, the time seems right for a critical re-evaluation of premodern *haiku*, to reclaim those lowbrow elements that, while reappearing in much contemporary haiku in and out of Japan, have too long been denigrated or expurgated by traditionalist accounts of modern haiku. After all, the moment we inhabit has become increasingly responsive to the possibilities of group authorship in a manner that was all but unimaginable during the age of Romantic individualism. Epic social shifts, largely due to the World Wide Web, have been transforming relationships among authors and readers and publishers, changing the very concept of literature. We have witnessed not only the death of the illusion of individual authorship – though the individual author had always been a partial ventriloquist for shared humanity, anyway – but also the rebirth of more openly collective forms of authorship. These include the phenomena of internet memes, various wikis, massively multiplayer online games, even crowdsourced symphonies. Reassessing the witty linked verse that was *haiku*, while recognizing the transnational origins of modern haiku, may contribute to the discussion if not the advancement of collaborative composition in a postmodern, global twenty-first century.

NOTES

For more on the specific terms, works and proper names that appear in the Introduction, see Glossary of Terms and Glossary of Poets. See Index of Japanese Verses for verses quoted in the Introduction that are included in the Commentary.

1   W. S. Merwin, foreword to Robert Aitken, *A Zen Wave: Bashō's Haiku and Zen* (Washington, DC: Shoemaker & Hoard Publishers, 2003), p. xiv.

2   Mishima Yukio, foreword to Yato Tamotsu, *Naked Festival: A Photo-essay*, trans. Meredith Weatherby and Sachiko Teshima (New York: Walker/Weatherhill, 1969), p. 7.

3   William Deresiewicz, *Excellent Sheep: The Miseducation of the American Elite and the Way to a Meaningful Life* (New York: Free Press, 2015).

4   Shiki's article, 'Zatsu no haiku' (Miscellaneous Haiku), appeared in the journal *Shōnippon*, reprinted in *SZ* 4, pp. 64–71. Shiki actually seems to have used the term *haiku* two years earlier, in his 1892 essay 'Haijin toshite no bashō', though referring broadly to *haikai no ku*, including the initiating stanza (*hokku*), not exclusively to what would become the modern haiku.

It must be stressed that Shiki retrofitted rather than coined the term 'haiku'. The term had popped up here and there during the premodern period as a shorthand for *haikai no ku*, referring to verse sequences or any of the verses therein. Tani Sogai (1734–1823) used the term this way in the title of *(Haiku fūtei) Ehon yotsunoki* (1775), for instance. Its earliest appearance goes back to the mid seventeenth century. According to Hiroaki Sato: 'Although the term haiku seems to date from 1663, it displaced the term hokku only when Shiki dissociated hokku from [linked verse], dismissing the collaborative form as non-literature.' See Sato, *One Hundred Frogs: From Renga to Haiku to English* (New York: Weatherhill Press, 1983), p. 113.

5   See Steven D. Carter (ed. and trans.), *Haiku Before Haiku: From the Renga Masters to Bashō* (New York: Columbia University Press, 2011), pp. 1–2.

6   Although *hokku* (as well as entire linked sequences) were sometimes presented to shrines as religious offerings, these may have been intended to honour the dead by inviting them to link their own spirit verses.

7   J. Thomas Rimer, foreword to Michael F. Marra, *Seasons and Landscapes in Japanese Poetry: An Introduction to Haiku and Waka* (Lewiston, NY: Edwin Mellen Press, 2008), p. iii.

8   Shiki writes this in his preface to Takahama Kyoshi's *Haikai sankasho* (Three Excellent Books on Witty Linked Verse, 1899). See Takiguchi Susumu, 'Renku – A Baby Thrown Out with the Bath Water (A Start of Reappraising Shiki)', *Journal of Renga & Renku* 1 (2011), pp. 14–18, at p. 14.

9   Here I draw on Eric Hobsbawm and Terence Ranger (eds), *The Invention of Tradition* (Cambridge: Cambridge University Press, 1983). Focusing on English colonialism in Europe, India and Africa, Hobsbawm et al. argue that most 'traditional' national practices are surprisingly recent inventions, or at least *re*inventions, associated with the rise of modern nation-states in the late nineteenth and early twentieth centuries.

10 Stephen Vlastos (ed.), *Mirror of Modernity: Invented Traditions of Modern Japan* (Berkeley, CA: University of California Press, 1998), p. 8.

11 Carol Gluck, *Japan's Modern Myths: Ideology in the Late Meiji Period* (Princeton, NJ: Princeton University Press, 1985), p. 17.

12 Jean-François Lyotard (1924–98) coined the term 'grand narrative' in his 1979 book *La condition postmoderne: rapport sur le savoir*, published in English as *The Postmodern Condition: A Report on Knowledge*, translated by Geoff Bennington and Brian Massumi (Minneapolis: University of Minnesota Press, 1984). Lyotard used the term to refer to a kind of master narrative that he and other postmodern

thinkers would eschew. I use it to imply that haiku discourse has been dominated globally by a single viewpoint that seems to distort and repress more about actual *haiku* than it reveals.

13   None of this was lost on Inoue Kenkabō (1870–1934), who waxed nationalistic:

Tagore
hearkened the bell composed
by Bashō

(*tagōru wa / bashō no yonda / kane o kiki*). See *Inoue Kenkabō kushū* (Ichigaya shuppansha, 1966), p. 79.

14   Harold Stewart (trans.), *A Net of Fireflies: Japanese Haiku and Haiku Paintings* (Rutland, VT: Tuttle, 1960), p. 124.

15   Takahama, *Haiku to wa donna mono ka* (Kadokawa sofia bunko, 2009), p. 29.

16   'Sate haiku (hokku) to iu mono wa donna mono deshō', reprinted in ibid., p. 9. Kyoshi also seems to have been the one to introduce the term *renku* to refer to both witty and serious linked verse, so some scholars feel he can be credited with having rescued linked verse from oblivion.

17   For instance, Seegan Mabesoone writes: 'Should we not put more emphasis on the fact that the haiku spirit is often inseparable from the Japanese language? I simply believe that the international language of haiku in the 21st century should be Japanese – not English or another language.' See letter to the editor, *Japan Quarterly* 48:1 (January–March 2001), pp. 119–20, at p. 120.

18   Takahashi Mutsuo, Inoue Hakudo and Takaoka Kazuya, *Haiku: The Poetic Key to Japan*, trans. Miyashita Emiko (Tokyo: PIE Books, 2003).

19   Quoted in Howard Norman, in *National Geographic*, February 2008.

20   Ōoka Makoto, *Kotonoha gusa* (Sekai bunkasha, 1996), p. 10.

21   Quoted in Max Verhart, 'The Essence of Haiku as Perceived by Western Haijin', *Modern Haiku* 38:2 (Summer 2007), n.p.

22   Generally speaking, Japanese words introduced into English are not pluralized by the rules of English, but are left in the same form for both singular and plural, as though it were an actual Japanese word. I use the English term 'haiku' (rather than follow Jack Kerouac's term 'haikus') to refer to both the plural and the singular.

23   Jim Holt, *Stop Me If You've Heard This: A History and Philosophy of Jokes* (New York: W. W. Norton & Company, 2008), pp. 103–4.

24   Paula Bennett and Vernon A. Rosario II (eds), *Solitary Pleasures: The Historical, Literary, and Artistic Discourses of Autoeroticism* (New York: Routledge, 1995), p. 118.

25   As Thomas LaMarre has explained: 'It is not until the Meiji period . . . with the emergence of the modern nation, that we find a disciplinization of language and texts that results in a truly modern regime of reading in which the assumptions of the national imagination become the dominant logic.' See LaMarre, *Uncovering Heian Japan: An Archaeology of Sensation and Inscription* (Durham, NC: Duke University Press, 2000), p. 7.

26   In this sense, the cut is similar to the caesura in classical Western prosody (deriving from the Latin *caedere*, 'to cut'). Technically speaking, the caesura completes a metrical foot, whereas Japanese verse, being based on syllabets, lacks metre. And while conventionally rendered in English as 'cutting word', the *kireji* is more often a verbal suffix or grammatical particle than a self-sufficient word. It therefore has come to be conveyed more through emphatic punctuation (exclamation mark, dash, ellipsis, semicolon, colon) than interjection (oh, ah, alas). Although it is said that classically there were some eighteen *kireji* (*kana, mogana, shi, ji, ya, ran, kan, keri, yo, zo, tsu, se, zu, re, nu, he, ke, ikani*), in fact there were many other ways of cutting.

27   Richard Gilbert, 'The Disjunctive Dragonfly: A Study of Disjunctive Method and Definitions in Contemporary English-language Haiku', *Blithe Spirit* 18:1–3 (December 2007). Originally published in *Kumamoto Studies in English Language and Literature* 47 (Kumamoto: Kumamoto University Press, 2004), pp. 27–66; adapted in *Modern Haiku* 35:2 (2004), pp. 21–44.

28   Makoto Ueda, 'The Taxonomy of Sequence: Basic Patterns of Structure in Premodern Japanese Literature', in Earl Miner (ed.), *The Principles of Classical Japanese Literature* (Princeton, NJ: Princeton University Press, 1985), pp. 63–105, at p. 77.

29   Stefan Tanaka, *New Times in Modern Japan* (Princeton, NJ: Princeton University Press, 2004), p. 2.

30   According to Herbert Jonsson, 'The Edo-period often just talked about *ki* (season), or used an expression like *ki no kotoba* (word of the season). There seems to have been no fixed term.' See Jonsson, *Haikai Poetics: The Theory and Aesthetics of Linked Poetry in the Age of Buson* (Saarbrücken: VDM Verlag, 2008), p. 27.

31   See Richard Gilbert (ed.), 'The Heart in Season: Sampling the Gendai Haiku Non-season *Muki Saijiki*', *Simply Haiku* 4:3 (Autumn 2006), n.p.

32 Kagami Shikō, *Kuzu no matsubara* (Arrowroot Pine, 1692). For a thorough discussion, see *BFD*, pp. 77–80.

33 See *BFD*, pp. 77–92.

34 Granted, it is possible that Bashō composed this verse by himself rather than during the collaborative witty linked-verse session. It is unlikely that he did so earlier, however, since *haiku* was all about spontaneous composition, so advance drafting (*haramiku*) was frowned upon. It is known that Bashō later replaced a line about a yellow globeflower (*Kerria japonica*), associated with springtime and frogs, with the line about the old pond. Even so, this does not change the fact that the verse was a premodern *haiku*, composed first and foremost as part of a collaborative process, not a modern haiku.

35 Susan B. Hanley has argued that in terms of quantifiable and thus comparable criteria, such as diet, literacy, shelter and so on, the quality of life for the denizens of Edo circa 1800 was every bit as high, if not higher, than that of their counterparts in Paris or London. See Hanley, *Everyday Things in Premodern Japan: The Hidden Legacy of Material Culture* (Berkeley, CA: University of California Press, 1997). Studies of literacy during the Edo period show that in the major urban centres the percentage of adults with the ability to read *kana* approached 100 per cent – the highest level of literacy in the world at the time.

36 Suzuki, 'Sōron', in *SNKBT* 72, pp. 473–81, at p. 473.

37 Yamato-takeru-no-mikoto composed the *katauta*: 'Since I passed / Tsukuba and Niibari, / how many nights have I slept?' (*niibari / tsukuba o sugite / iku yo ka netsuru*). To which one Hitomoshibito of Tsukuba replied with his own *katauta*: 'Counting the days – / of nights there are nine nights, / of days there are ten days' (*kaga nabete / yo ni wa kokono yo / hi ni wa tō ka o*). See W. G. Aston, *Nihongi* (Tokyo: Charles E. Tuttle, 1972), p. 207.

38 During the late seventeenth century, a typical entry fee was twelve coppers (*mon*), about one and a half times the adult entry fee to a bathhouse. By the second half of the eighteenth century, the fee had increased to sixteen coppers, about the price of a lunch bowl of buckwheat noodles in soup. See Kobayashi Masashi, '*Senryū*: Japan's Short Comic Poetry', in Jessica Milner Davis (ed.), *Understanding Humor in Japan* (Detroit, MI: Wayne State University Press, 2006), pp. 153–77, at p. 156.

39 *NKBZ* 46, p. 205.

40 *SNKBT* 72, p. 476.

41 Kakujuken Yoshihiro (ed.), *Haikai takama no uguisu*, quoted (with

my emphasis) in Makoto Ueda (ed. and trans.), *Light Verse from the Floating World: An Anthology of Premodern Japanese Senryu* (New York: Columbia University Press, 1999), pp. 6–7.

42   *NKBZ* 46, p. 234, n. 63.

43   One earlier collection was *Mutamagawa* (1750–61) – see Glossary of Terms.

44   Kobayashi, '*Senryū*', p. 158.

45   Suzuki, 'Kaisetsu', in *NKBZ* 46, p. 212.

46   Although frequently published without a pen name, *senryū* were submitted along with a fee, so participants would have included their name and address as a matter of course to claim any prizes. The pictured page from *Yanagidaru* reads:

First tier: Hasse from Ichigae Tamachi; Ryūsui from Asabu Eizaka; Tsurugame from Koshigawa Hakusan; Sakuragi from Upper Yamashi-ta. Second tier (the second and third rows): Miyuki from Ushikomi; Wakana from Shinbori; Kakitsubata from Kanda; Kiyotaki from Yotsuya; Masago from Aoyama; Takane from Sakurada; Hatsune from Kōshichō; Kanko from Ōtenma; Nobori from Senjū; Iroha from Shitaya; Imasu from Imado; Yōrō from Kohinata; Kabuto from Hachōbori; Maizuru from Koshigawa; Suisen from Nihon'enoki. Third tier: Fūzetsu from Maruyama; Hagoromo from Kanda; Tachi-bana from Tachibanachō; Asahi from Yagenbori; Ōtsue from Yanagi-hara; and Tamagawa from Mita.

47   Harold G. Henderson (ed. and trans.), *An Introduction to Haiku: An Anthology of Poems and Poets, from Bashō to Shiki* (Garden City, NY: Doubleday Anchor Books, 1958), p. 121.

48   Patricia Donegan and Yoshie Ishibashi (ed. and trans.), *Chiyo-ni: Woman Haiku Master* (Boston and Tokyo: Charles E. Tuttle, 1998), p. 14.

49   Women had never disappeared from Japanese poetry completely. However, given the precedent of the great women *waka* poets, it was not unheard of for commoner women to study *waka* as part of their education, informal though it may have been, or to compose *waka*, even if merely in private. For more on this in English, see: Yabuta Yutaka, 'Rediscovering Women in Tokugawa Japan', *Occasional Papers in Japanese Studies*, no. 2000–2002 (May 2000); and Anne Walthall, 'The Cult of Sensibility in Rural Tokugawa Japan: Love Poetry by Matsuo Taseko', *Journal of the American Oriental Society* 117:1 (January–March 1997), pp. 70–86.

50   Roger K. Thomas, *The Way of Shikishima: Waka Theory and Practice*

in Early Modern Japan (Lanham, MD: University Press of America, 2008), pp. xix–xx.

51 Eiko Ikegami, *Bonds of Civility: Aesthetic Networks and the Political Origins of Japanese Culture* (Cambridge: Cambridge University Press, 2005), p. 187.

52 Such indications of gender being obvious in the original Japanese, the translations convey as much, though, reflecting the dearth of scholarship, a disproportionate few of these women are represented herein, unfortunately. For more on 'nun', see Glossary of Terms.

53 For an example of the former, see Ki no Tsurayuki's *Tosa nikki* (Tosa Diary, *c.*935).

54 *RJS*, pp. 12–14.

55 *RJS*, pp. 14–15.

56 Watanabe Shin'ichirō has trenchantly suggested that *bareku* were a manifestation of male sadness (*kanashimi*) and loneliness (*wabisa*). See *EB*, p. 40.

57 Quoted in Richard Rubinger, *Popular Literacy in Early Modern Japan* (Honolulu: University of Hawai'i Press, 2007), pp. 104–5.

Further Reading

For Japanese names, please see headnote to the List of Abbreviations.

Aesthetics and Poetics

Kawamoto Kōji, *Poetics of Japanese Verse: Imagery, Structure, Meter* (Tokyo: University of Tokyo Press, 2000)

Ueda, Makoto, *Literary and Art Theories in Japan* (Cleveland, OH: Press of Western Reserve University, 1967; reprinted Ann Arbor, MI: University of Michigan Press, 1991)

Edo/Tokugawa Japan

Gerstle, C. Andrew (ed.), *18th Century Japan: Culture and Society* (Sydney: Allen & Unwin, 1989)

Hall, John Whitney (ed.), *The Cambridge History of Japan*, 4: *Early Modern Japan* (Cambridge: Cambridge University Press, 1991)

Hibbett, Howard, *The Chrysanthemum and the Fish: Japanese Humor Since the Age of the Shoguns* (Tokyo, London and New York: Kodansha International, 2002)

Jones, Sumie, and Adam L. Kern (eds), *A Kamigata Anthology: Literature from Japan's Metropolitan Centers, 1600–1750* (Honolulu: University of Hawai'i Press, forthcoming)

Jones, Sumie, with Kenji Watanabe (eds), *An Edo Anthology: Literature from Japan's Mega-City, 1750–1850* (Honolulu: University of Hawai'i Press, 2013)

Nakane Chie and Shinzaburō Ōishi (eds), *Tokugawa Japan: The Social and Economic Antecedents of Modern Japan* (Tokyo: University of Tokyo Press, 1991)

Seigle, Cecilia Segawa, *Yoshiwara: The Glittering World of the Japanese Courtesan* (Honolulu: University of Hawai'i Press, 1993)

Waka

Carter, Steven D. (ed. and trans.), *Traditional Japanese Poetry: An Anthology* (Stanford, CA: Stanford University Press, 1991)

Cranston, Edwin A. (ed. and trans.), *A Waka Anthology* 1, *The Gem-Glistening Cup* (Stanford, CA: Stanford University Press, 1993)

McCullough, Helen Craig, *Brocade by Night: 'Kokin Wakashū' and the Court Style in Japanese Classical Poetry* (Stanford, CA: Stanford University Press, 1985)

Thomas, Roger K., *The Way of Shikishima: Waka Theory and Practice in Early Modern Japan* (Lanham, MD: University Press of America, 2008)

Bareku, Maekuzuke and Senryū

Blyth, R. H., *Edo Satirical Verse Anthologies* (Tokyo: Hokuseido Press, 1961)

—, *Japanese Life and Character in Senryu* (Tokyo: Hokuseido Press, 1960)

— (ed. and trans.), *Senryu: Japanese Satirical Verses* (Tokyo: Hokuseido Press, 1949)

gill, robin d., *Octopussy, Dry Kidney & Blue Spots: Dirty Themes from 18–19c Japanese Poems* (Key Biscayne, FL: Paraverse Press, 2007)

Hibbett, Howard, *The Chrysanthemum and the Fish: Japanese Humor Since the Age of the Shoguns* (Tokyo, London and New York: Kodansha International, 2002)

Kobayashi Masashi, 'Senryū: Japan's Short Comic Poetry', in Jessica Milner Davis (ed.), *Understanding Humor in Japan* (Detroit,

MI: Wayne State University Press, 2006), pp. 153–77

Screech, Timon, *Sex and the Floating World: Erotic Images in Japan 1700–1820* (London: Reaktion Books, 1999)

Solt, John (trans.), 'Willow Leaftips', in John Solt (ed.), *An Episodic Festschrift for Howard Hibbett* 24 (Hollywood, CA: Highmoonoon, 2010)

Ueda, Makoto (ed. and trans.), *Light Verse from the Floating World: An Anthology of Premodern Japanese Senryu* (New York: Columbia University Press, 1999)

Yuasa, Nobuyuki, 'Laughter in Japanese Haiku', in Stephen Henry Gill and C. Andrew Gerstle (eds), *Rediscovering Basho: A 300th Anniversary Celebration* (Folkestone: Global Oriental, 1999), pp. 63–81

Haikai and *Renga*

Hibbett, Howard S., 'The Japanese Comic Linked-Verse Tradition', *HJAS* 23 (1960–61), pp. 76–92

Horton, H. Mack, 'Renga Unbound: Performative Aspects of Japanese Linked Verse', *HJAS* 53:2 (1993), pp. 443–512

Miner, Earl, *Japanese Linked Poetry: An Account with Translations of Renga and Haikai Sequences* (Princeton, NJ: Princeton University Press, 1979)

Ramirez-Christensen, Esperanza, *Emptiness and Temporality: Buddhism and Medieval Japanese Poetics* (Stanford, CA: Stanford University Press, 2008)

Haiku and Haiku

Addiss, Stephen, *The Art of Haiku: Its History Through Poems and Paintings by Japanese Masters* (Boston, MA: Shambhala, 2012)

—, with Fumiko and Akira Yamamoto, *Haiku Humor: Wit and Folly in Japanese Poems and Prints* (Boston, MA: Weatherhill, 2007)

Bowers, Faubion (ed.), *The Classic Tradition of Haiku: An Anthology* (Mineola, NY: Dover Publications, 1996)

Carter, Steven D. (ed. and trans.), *Haiku Before Haiku: From the Renga Masters to Bashō* (New York: Columbia University Press, 2011)

Henderson, Harold G. (ed. and trans.), *An Introduction to Haiku: An Anthology of Poems and Poets, from Bashō to Shiki* (Garden City, NY: Doubleday Anchor Books, 1958)

Hoffmann, Yoel (ed.), *Japanese Death Poems: Written by Zen Monks and Haiku Poets on the Verge of Death* (Rutland, VT, and Tokyo: Charles E. Tuttle, 1986)

Marra, Michael F., *Seasons and Landscapes in Japanese Poetry: An Introduction to Haiku and Waka* (Lewiston, NY: Edwin Mellen Press, 2008)

Miyamori Asatarō (ed. and trans.), *An Anthology of Haiku, Ancient and Modern* (Tokyo: Taiseido Press, 1932), reprinted as *Haikai and Haiku* (Tokyo: Nippon Gakujutsu Shinkōkai, 1958; reprinted Westport, CT: Greenwood, 1971)

Yasuda, Kenneth, *The Japanese Haiku: Its Essential Nature, History, and Possibilities in English, with Selected Examples* (Rutland, VT, and Tokyo: Charles E. Tuttle, 1957)

Contemporary Haiku

Gurga, Lee, with Charles Trumbull, *Haiku: A Poet's Guide* (Lincoln, IL: Modern Haiku Press, 2003)

Hakutani, Yoshinobu, *Haiku and Modernist Poetics* (New York: Palgrave Macmillan, 2009)

Higginson, William J., with Penny Harter, *The Haiku Handbook: How to Write, Share, and Teach Haiku* (Tokyo and New York: Kodansha International, 1992)

Johnson, Jeffrey, *Haiku Poetics in Twentieth-Century Avant-Garde Poetry* (New York: Lexington Books, 2011)

Haiga and *Shunga*

Addiss, Stephen, *Haiga: Takebe Sōchō and the Haiku-Painting Tradition* (Honolulu: Marsh Art Gallery, University of Richmond, in association with the University of Hawai'i Press, 1995)

—, 'Interactions of Text and Image in Haiga', in Eleanor Kerkham
(ed.), *Matsuo Bashō's Poetic Spaces: Exploring Haikai Intersections*
(New York: Palgrave Macmillan, 2006), pp. 217–42

Cahill, James, 'In Edo-Period Japan', in his *The Lyric Journey:
Poetic Painting in China and Japan* (Cambridge, MA: Harvard
University Press, 1996)

Clark, Timothy, C. Andrew Gerstle, Aki Ishigami and Akiko Yano
(eds), *Shunga: Sex and Pleasure in Japanese Art* (Leiden: Hotei
Publishing, 2013)

Rosenfield, John M., *Mynah Birds and Flying Rocks: Word and Im-
age in the Art of Yosa Buson* (Lawrence, KS: Spencer Museum of
Art, University of Kansas, 2003)

Screech, Timon, *Sex and the Floating World: Erotic Images in Japan
1700–1820* (London: Reaktion Books, 1999)

Bashō

Barnhill, David Landis (ed. and trans.), *Bashō's Haiku: Selected
Poems of Matsuo Bashō* (Albany, NY: State University of New
York Press, 2004)

Gill, Stephen Henry, and C. Andrew Gerstle (eds), *Rediscovering
Basho: A 300th Anniversary Celebration* (Folkestone: Global
Oriental, 1999)

Kerkham, Eleanor (ed.), *Matsuo Bashō's Poetic Spaces: Exploring
Haikai Intersections* (New York: Palgrave Macmillan, 2006)

Miner, Earl, and Hiroko Odagiri (ed. and trans.), *The Monkey's
Straw Raincoat and Other Poetry of the Bashō School* (Princeton,
NJ: Princeton University Press, 1981)

Qiu, Peipei, *Bashō and the Dao: The Zhuangzi and the Transforma-
tion of Haikai* (Honolulu: University of Hawai'i Press, 2005)

Reichhold, Jane (ed. and trans.), *Basho: The Complete Haiku* (New
York: Kodansha International, 2008)

Shirane, Haruo, *Traces of Dreams: Landscape, Cultural Memory, and
the Poetry of Bashō* (Stanford, CA: Stanford University Press,
1998)

Ueda, Makoto (ed. and trans.), *Bashō and His Interpreters: Selected
Hokku with Commentary* (Stanford, CA: Stanford University
Press, 1992)

Buson

Crowley, Cheryl A., *Haikai Poet Yosa Buson and the Bashō Revival*,
    Brill's Japanese Studies Library, 27 (Leiden: E. J. Brill, 2007)
Jonsson, Herbert, *Haikai Poetics: The Theory and Aesthetics of Linked
    Poetry in the Age of Buson* (Saarbrücken: VDM Verlag, 2008)
Merwin, W. S., and Takako Lento (trans.), *Collected Haiku of Yosa
    Buson* (Port Townsend, WA: Copper Canyon Press, 2013)
Ueda, Makoto, *The Path of Flowering Thorn: The Life and Poetry of
    Yosa Buson* (Stanford, CA: Stanford University Press, 1998)

Issa

Bolitho, Harold, 'Issa the Poet', in his *Bereavement and Consola-
    tion: Testimonies from Tokugawa Japan* (New Haven, CT: Yale
    University Press, 2003), pp. 61–101
Hamill, Sam (trans.), illustrated by Kaji Aso, *The Spring of My Life
    and Selected Haiku by Kobayashi Issa* (Boston, MA: Shambhala
    Press, 1997)
Ueda, Makoto, *Dew on the Grass: The Life and Poetry of Kobayashi
    Issa* (Leiden: E. J. Brill, 2004)
Yuasa, Nobuyuki (trans.), *The Year of My Life: A Translation of
    Issa's Oraga Haru* (Berkeley and Los Angeles, CA: University of
    California Press, 1960)

Onitsura

Crowley, Cheryl A., 'Putting *Makoto* into Practice: Onitsura's
    Hitorigoto', *MN* 50:1 (Spring 1995), pp. 1–46

Shiki

Beichman, Janine, *Masaoka Shiki: His Life and Works* (Boston,
    MA: Twayne Publishers, 1982)

Keene, Donald, *The Winter Sun Shines In: A Life of Masaoka Shiki* (New York: Columbia University Press, 2013)

Takiguchi Susumu, 'Renku – A Baby Thrown Out with the Bath Water (A Start of Reappraising Shiki)', *Journal of Renga & Renku* 1 (2011), pp. 14–18

Watson, Burton (trans.), *Masaoka Shiki: Selected Poems* (New York: Columbia University Press, 1997)

Women Poets

Cranston, Edwin A. (ed. and trans.), *A Waka Anthology 2, Grasses of Remembrance* (Parts A and B) (Stanford, CA: Stanford University Press, 2006)

Hirshfield, Jane (trans.), with Mariko Aratani, *The Ink Dark Moon: Love Poems by Ono no Komachi and Izumi Shikibu, Women of the Ancient Court of Japan* (New York: Scribner, 1988; reprinted New York: Vintage Books, 1990)

Murasaki Shikibu, *The Tale of Genji*, trans. Royall Tyler (New York: Viking, 2001)

Sato, Hiroaki (ed. and trans.), *Japanese Women Poets: An Anthology* (Armonk, NY: East Gate, 2008)

Ueda, Makoto (ed. and trans.), *Far Beyond the Field: Haiku by Japanese Women* (New York: Columbia University Press, 2003)

Note on the Translation

Translated here are a smattering of the classics of pre-twentieth-century Japanese *haikai no ku* (witty linked verse), abbreviated as *haiku*. Most of these approximately one thousand verses – an infinitesimal fraction of the total number produced – appear in one or more Japanese anthologies. Many have been translated into English or other languages, if not retranslated, perhaps multiple times. Still, this volume also introduces less familiar modes of *haiku*. Ultimately, I have selected verses not merely of interest for some literary, cultural, human or other quality, but that also exemplify these modes in their historical range, from the lofty if lightly amusing initiating stanza (*hokku*), later taken out of context to serve as the basis of modern haiku, down to the rarely acknowledged fourteen-syllabet *tanku*, the at times forbidden verse-capping (*maekuzuke*) games, as well as over-the-top comic verse (*senryū*) and below-the-belt dirty sexy verse (*bareku*).

My translation praxis is guided by the fact that premodern *haiku* was fundamentally a collaborative literary word game in which fourteen- and seventeen-syllabet verses were linked to each other into lengthy sequences through set types of association. These included wordplay, allusion, seasonal progression, even ineffable resonances or 'whiffs' (*nioi*). So, for instance, while it has long been the vogue among translators championing minimalism to utilize little if any punctuation and to refrain from capitalizing the initial letter of a verse, let alone each line, I do as much to underscore how verses participated in a larger dialogue. Verses were required to be complete utterances unto themselves, to be sure. Yet they simultaneously occurred *in medias res*, as though preceded and/or followed by ellipses.

It may therefore be useful to regard any given verse as but one instalment – or 'stanza', as it were – in a perpetually unfolding group-authored composition. In order to link and be linked, individual stanzas had to be polyvalent, open to multiple interpretations. Since some of the best-known *haiku* represent the only portion of their sequence to survive, their full range of meanings in their original contexts has been lost. And yet including extant sequences in their entirety merely to flesh out an eminent verse or two would be to transmogrify this volume into a mass of linked-verse sequences. Most of the *haiku* herein, then, have been yanked out of their collaborative settings at the risk both of foreclosing their polyvalence and of inadvertently misrepresenting them as modern standalone haiku.

In a compensatory effort, two major strategies are deployed to showcase this practice of linking. The first is to include stanzas originally linked to each other, chiefly in the form of simple challenge (*maeku*) plus response (*tsukeku*) exchanges in verse capping, which boils down the art of linking to bare bones, but also in the form of parodies, burlesques and travesties of well-known verses. The translations furthermore begin with an excerpt from a sustained linked-verse sequence from *Sarumino* (Monkey's Straw Raincape, 1691), a central text of the Bashō School. By focusing on links, this excerpt suggests how Bashō and company themselves practised the art of collaboratively linked *haiku* rather than modern standalone haiku.

The second, more widely employed strategy is to throw originally unrelated stanzas into conversation with each other. The aim is to roughly simulate associations between stanzas, even if admittedly synthetic, transparent and ahistorical. On the one hand, this strategy departs from the way most modern anthologies organize *haiku* into some readily apparent order, especially chronologically by author, which, while helpfully suggesting historical developments, tends to misleadingly accord a primacy to the individual author too easily mistaken for modern Western individualism. On the other hand, these unauthorized rearrangements follow the lead of imperially commissioned anthologies of classical Japanese poetry (*waka*). Since their inauguration over a millennium ago, these anthologies uprooted stanzas from their organic soil, repotting them artificially, repositioning stem and blossom alike. Premodern *haiku* collections sometimes engaged in such creative flower arrangement, too. *Sarumino* itself is an example. Some of its sections and *hokku* sequences were not devised in the usual manner of people sitting together composing verse (though the sequence translated in part here, 'Akuoke no no maki', was composed in one sitting in late 1690). Rather, the compilers of *Sarumino* often plucked these stanzas out of disparate sequences and reassembled them into something resembling a single impromptu composition. (For information on the modern Japanese sources for this collection and other verses translated herein, see Sources of the Japanese Verses.)

Ideally, translations should stand on their own without props. In practice, a modicum of contextualization and commentary can enhance comprehension and appreciation of verse from another time and place, particularly when presented as isolated snippets too readily misapprehended as lacking substance. The *haiku*, as Steven Carter has observed (though for different reasons), is 'arguably the most difficult of genres to translate well, and at the same time the easiest to trivialize'.[1] In order to recoup something of the rich complexity and significance of the 'literal' meanings, from which my translations frequently depart for the sake of overall effect, the annotations in the Commentary provide detailed discussion of the wordplay, as well as romanized transliterations, of the Japanese originals. The Glossary of Terms may be consulted for more information on specific items such as literary devices and key works. In the annotations to the verses, titles of Japanese works are translated *in situ* only if the translation is relevant to the rest of the note and if the work does not appear in that glossary.

The annotations also specify authorial pen names, when known, as do the main translations. In many instances little if any information is available about the author, including the proper reading of his or her pen name, in which case an educated guess is proffered (following a Sinified rather than a Japanese reading of the Chinese graphs). Dates and further biographical information can be found in the Glossary of Poets. Within the Commentary at least, subordinating pen names to the annotations allows readers

to encounter a verse on its own before potentially being preju-
diced by knowledge of its author's identity, gender, reputation and
other such biographical factoids, as germane or fascinating as such
may well be. This move also serves as a reminder that, in collab-
orative verse, while a single stanza has a primary author, latent
meanings are drawn out by others, most immediately 'secondary'
authors of proximate stanzas, but also, less immediately, authors of
antecedent or even of future texts (to say nothing of readers them-
selves, who contribute their own textual interpretation as well).
Minor inconsistencies in punctuation and orthography within
the translations are partially meant to reinforce the range of dis-
tinctive voices among these poets.

Some readers may be startled to find end rhyme creeping into
the translations here and there, particularly in *senryū* and *bareku*,
but even in *hokku*. The consensus, after all, has long been to avoid
rhyme like the plague. This is reasonable only so far as *haiku* is as-
sumed to be unrhymed. Indeed, since Japanese word endings are
limited to half a dozen sounds – five vowels and one consonant
– end rhyme presents scant challenge. It consequently was never
prioritized let alone normalized as a formal requirement.

Even so, this does not mean that end rhyme was forbidden or
eschewed. In point of fact, both rhyme and end rhyme happen
as a matter of course, often unintentionally, but sometimes delib-
erately, especially in the hands of skilled versifiers. And anyway,
rhyme appears extensively if not ubiquitously in *haiku*, albeit in
the more footloose forms of internal rhyme, alliteration and asson-
ance. Translators ignore these at their peril. None the less, even
when not appearing in the original verse, end rhyme, used judi-
ciously, can signal the presence of a punchline, or impart a sense
of provisional completion, that otherwise might not come across
adequately in translation.

Debates on lineation and the optimal number of syllables
in translation have raged for the better part of the past cen-
tury. *Haiku* has been variously rendered into one, two, three and
even four lines. My choice of three lines for seventeen syllabets
(and two lines for the fourteen-syllabet *tanku*) is strategically
orthodox. Long the standard in English for conveying the three
rhythmic phrases of 5–7–5 syllabets of the original Japanese,

nothing shouts 'haiku!' quite like three lines. In keeping with the larger goal of reclaiming premodern *haiku* from the shadow of traditionalist modern haiku, hijacking the lineation most widely recognizable as the latter, rather than ghettoizing the former in some idiosyncratic form, seems sensible.

I have also allowed myself at times more syllabic elbow room than fashionable. This is no mere matter of favouring the scheme of short–long–short lines without punctiliously minding syllable count, a scheme that in any event has been prevalent for decades. Rather, my occasional lengthiness cuts against the grain of the trend of minimalist translation set by Reginald Blyth (1898–1964), pressed to extremes by Cid Corman and modelling the modern haiku composed in various languages. Observing that English syllables are heavier than their Japanese counterparts (*onji*), Blyth advocated a 2–3–2 accented beat scheme in translation. Granted, the English syllable does not always map directly onto Japanese, which is lighter, more fleet of poetic foot. Like the stride as a unit of measurement, the syllable is variable, ranging from shortish ('uh') to prolonged ('strengths'). Japanese syllabets tend to fall uniformly on the higher, more lightweight side of the scales. And while I follow robin d. gill in using this diminutive term 'syllabet' for the Japanese, reserving 'syllable' for the English, in my experience the briefer the translation the greater the danger of lapsing into ungrammatical fortune-cookie pithiness.[2] Why shortchange the intricacy of the original by not admitting latent meanings, let alone by not adequately conveying surface wordplay? Even at the risk of reading too much into these verses, which were subjected to multiple interpretations, 'thick' translation seems warranted.

Generally, the annotations stipulate when an original Japanese verse flouts the norm of seventeen or fourteen syllabets. For the inveterately curious who speak no Japanese but wish to try counting the syllabets of the romanized transliterations for themselves, however, a word of caution: determining the syllabet count (*onsūritsu*) can be tricky. The syllabetic-based units of sound in Japanese as rendered in syllabary writing (*kana*) cannot be transposed seamlessly into romanization, with its not-quite-equivalent syllables and lingering associations with the rules and pronunciations of other languages. That said, a full Japanese syllabet count applies in each of the following five lexical sets (listed alphabetically within each set for ease of use by English speakers):

1.   Individual vowels, when not combined with an initial consonant: *a, e, i, o* and *u* (rhyming with *ah, get, free, oh* and *you*, respectively).

2.   Indivisible combinations of one or more consonants plus a vowel: *ba, be, bi, bo, bu, bya, byo, byu, cha, chi, cho, chu, da, de, di, dja, djo, dju, do, dzu, fu, ga, ge, gi, go, gu, gya, gyo, gyu, ha, he, hi, ho, hya, hyo, hyu, ja, ji, jo, ju, ka, ke, ki, ko, ku, kya, kyo, kyu, ma, me, mi, mo, mu, mya, myo, myu, na, ne, ni, no, nu, nya, nyo, nyu, pa, pe, pi, po, pu, pya, pyo, pyu, ra, re, ri, ro, ru, rya, ryo, ryu, sa, se, sha, shi, sho, shu, so, su, ta, te, to, tsu, va, ve, vi, vo, vu, wa, wo, ya, yo, yu, za, ze, zo, zu.*

3.   Aspirated or double consonants, represented with a repeated consonant (as with *hokku* and Issa) or sometimes with a lone *t* (as with *dotchi*).

4.   Long or double vowels, indicated by a macron or a repeated vowel: *ā, ē, ī, ō* and *ū* or *aa, ee, ii, oo* and *uu* (as with Bashō or *sekushii*).

5.   The nasal *n*, when not followed by a vowel, pronounced *m* before *m-, b-* or *p-*, though still written as *n* in the modified Hepburn system of romanization used throughout. Note that the nasal *n* is differentiated from an *n* + vowel combination (*na, ne, ni, no* and *nu*) by the use of an apostrophe (as with *Man'yōshū*).

Some words appearing in the present volume can be offered as examples: *Man'yōshū* is six syllabets (*ma-n-yo-o-shu-u*); *maekuzuke* is five (*ma-e-ku-zu-ke*); *senryū* is four (*se-n-ryu-u*), as are *haikai* (*ha-i-ka-i*), *Danrin* (*da-n-ri-n*), *Teimon* (*te-i-mo-n*) and *Shōmon* (*sho-o-mo-n*); and Bashō is three (*ba-sho-o*), as are Buson (*bu-so-n*), Issa (*i-s-sa*), *bareku* (*ba-re-ku*), *hokku* (*ho-k-ku*), *kireji* (*ki-re-ji*), *onji* (*o-n-ji*), *renga* (*re-n-ga*), *tanku* (*ta-n-ku*) and, for that matter, *haiku* (*ha-i-ku*).

Location of the Translations in this Volume

Translations of the Japanese verses into English feature twice in this book. They appear first in the main section that follows, accompanied by the names of the original authors when known. This presentation may inadvertently give the impression that the premodern *haiku* was a kind of standalone poetry written by individual poets as in the West. However, as explained in the Introduction and elsewhere, premodern *haiku* were composed collaboratively and either in response to a previous verse or in anticipation of a subsequent verse, if not both. On closer inspection, therefore, one will find that the *haiku* in the main section are loosely arranged according to such collaborative flows. The second appearance of the verses in translation is in the Commentary, following the main section, where readers looking for a more in-depth encounter with these verses will find both the English translation (highlighted in bold and arranged in a single line in which the phrases or lines of verse are divided by slashes) and Japanese transliteration, accompanied by annotations. Authors of the challenge verses are all unnamed unless otherwise indicated in the Commentary. The phrase 'Author unnamed' is used throughout instead of 'Anonymous' because the name of the author was withheld rather than unknown.

NOTES

1   Steven D. Carter, review of Earl Miner and Hiroko Odagiri, *The Monkey's Straw Raincoat*, *HJAS* 42:2 (December 1982), p. 643.

2   gill claims this coinage in *Octopussy, Dry Kidney & Blue Spots: Dirty Themes from 18–19c Japanese Poems* (Key Biscayne, FL: Paraverse Press, 2007), p. 474.

THE *HAIKU*

First page of 'The Washbasin Sequence'
from *Sarumino* (1691)

The Washbasin Sequence

As an example of a witty linked-verse sequence, consider the following baker's dozen. These are only a third of the thirty-six verses in 'Akuoke no no maki' (The Washbasin Sequence), but should suffice to convey the importance of linking between verses. Although sequences could also consist of one hundred verses (*hyakuin*), one thousand verses and so on, thirty-six (*kasen*) was the game of choice among many *haiku* players. Moreover, this particular sequence appeared in *Sarumino* (Monkey's Straw Raincape, 1691). Compiled and edited by Nozawa Bonchō (*c.*1640–1714) and Mukai Kyorai (1651–1704) under the guidance of Bashō, *Sarumino* was not only a major collection of initiating stanzas (*hokku*) and witty linked verse (*haikai no renga*), it has long been a central work of the Bashō School, serving as a handbook of composition. As such, the piece has been well studied and several times translated.

Two features in the sequence are particularly worth noting. First, meaning is scarcely limited to individual verses. Rather, the link (*tsukeai*) is the thing. The art resides less in any individual verse than in how that verse links or will come to be linked to its surrounding verses. A player needed to pick up on some aspect of the previous verse, either latent or superficial, riff on it, cast it in a new light, thereby changing the perception of that verse itself. The challenge and fun of *haiku* largely resided in having the players perform this sense-shifting collaboratively and more or less on the spot. Spontaneity, the ability to think on one's feet, wit – these were the cardinal virtues. Preparing verses ahead of time (*haramiku*) was frowned upon. *Haiku* was the collaborative art of instantaneous and contingent refiguring, not unlike a jam session in improvisational jazz. It was only possible with a closely knit group of like-minded people who were able to build on shared association of ideas (*renso*).

A second feature is the fictionality of this sequence. Imagination, even memory, plays a greater role than direct observation at the moment of composition within the game. The notion that the modern haiku is a verbal snapshot of an actual experience as it unfolds is dubious in the premodern *haiku*.

initiating stanza (*hokku*):

the washbasin's
drip-dripping gives way to
crickets chirping!

Bonchō

second stanza (*wakiku*):

with oil burning low
an early-to-bed autumn

Bashō

third stanza (*daisan*):

fresh new straw mats,
having just been installed,
in the moonlight!

Yasui

fourth stanza:

delighted to have set out
five pairs of saké cups

Kyorai

fifth stanza:

here's wishing
a millennium of sundries gathered –
New Year's feast

Bashō

sixth stanza:

first song of the bush warbler
even as snow flutters down

Bonchō

seventh stanza:

reaching a gallop,
upper-arm strength no match for
the spring colt

Kyorai

eighth stanza:

atop Mount Maya
clouds hang about

Yasui

ninth stanza:

when supping
on fried lancefish
fragrant the wind

                                    Bonchō

tenth stanza:

scratching leech bites –
a feeling of relief

                                    Bashō

eleventh stanza:

putting behind
all those preoccupations –
day off from service

                                    Yasui

twelfth stanza:

return at once!
missive from her man

                                    Kyorai

thirteenth stanza:

for he who is dubbed
the feudal lord's golden boy
life must be a cinch

Bashō

[End of 'The Washbasin Sequence']

show benevolence
and they'll crap all over you!
baby sparrows

                                                                                    Issa

this life:
chowing down, shitting and then
flowery spring!

                                                                                    Jūkō

cherries abloom!
and every which way the fields
all shit and piss

                                                                                    Issa

amid the fields –
oblivious to all things
skylarks sing

                                                                                    Bashō

the cowherd
felled flat upon his ass!
skylark rising

                                                                                    Kenkabō

pheasant's rise
does a body surprise –
withered moor

Issa

wind at his back
harvesting pampas grass –
an old man

Buson

first winter drizzle –
permeating the whole world,
lightly linked verse

Issa

smug-faced
over this New Year's stanza
the light-verse master

Buson

as the year recedes
no gifts from others received –
Oh this night!

Sōkan

after receiving
the New Year's well-wisher:
who the hell was that?!

                                        Author unnamed

some people!
teeth being praised,
rue their ears!

                                        Author unnamed

no need for alarm!
inevitably precedes
need for alarm

                                        Gansui

over the clap!
right before one's nose
bloomin' wilts

                                        Author unnamed

hush-hushedly
concealing his sunstroke –
cure-all salesman

                                        Yūkō

challenge:

ain't that a shame!
ain't that a shame!

response:

though on the mend
still accepting get-well gifts,
his latest vice

Author unnamed

staving off death
on account of some gold coins
under the mattress

Gosen

nothing but faces
taking it for granted
they'll go on living

Shinpei

disregarding death
all of us nevertheless
must die

Bentenshi

truly believing
there's always a tomorrow
we all rest in peace

Author unnamed

wake for the dead –
exaggerated eulogies
and debaucheries!

Fusō

challenge:

what lechery!
what lechery!

response:

*I'd make her
as a hot-to-trot widow!*
his doctors contending

Author unnamed

terminally ill
still, tears of gratitude
for the doctor

Author unnamed

challenge:

that's life!
that's life!

response:

smug quacks,
praising the deathbed poem,
beat hasty retreats!

Author unnamed

natural causes
suspected along with
that quack doctor!

Usui

that bush doctor!
pushing dogshit onto
his patients

Bunna

challenge:

suddenly it's clear!
suddenly it's clear!

response:

fresh young widow!
her dearly departed's brother
a tad too concerned

Author unnamed

a true buddha ...
drones the funeral director
mundanely

Shōjuen

dewy with tenderness,
the high priest's condolences,
delivered slickly

Koun

slowly but surely
the widow gets sermonized
down the path serpentine

Author unnamed

Double-page spread from *Yanagidaru* 12 (1777), with the verse
'slowly but surely . . .' at far right

braided up nicely
it gets badly upbraided –
the widow's hair

Author unnamed

leaving behind
just enough to be alluring –
the widow's hair

Author unnamed

challenge:
upon closer inspection
upon closer inspection

response:
a woman
coiffuring up her hair:
setting her sights

                                                    Author unnamed

though breathtaking
women's coiffures are always
sweltery hot

                                                    Taigi

widow's conch –
no moment to spare
for tears to dry

                                                    Wakō

plying fingers
as though he were at hand –
the widow's orgasm

                                                    Ryūsha

a middle finger
trawling for some clit
her gripped clam

Mokubō

soft douching
with her own fingers
tenderly diddling

Author unnamed

should I get drunk
whatever would you do with me?
asks the widow, drinking

Author unnamed

a stabbing chill!
stepping on my dead wife's comb
in our bedroom

Buson

withered fields!
from the time of cogon grass,
women's combs

Saikaku

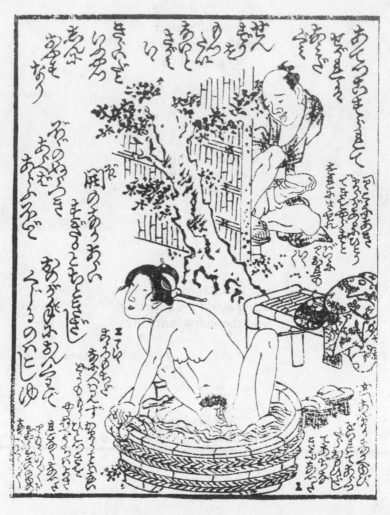

Male voyeur watching a woman in a tub, the verse 'soft douching . . .' (see p. 17) appearing on the lower left

eyes sharp
through all the blubbering:
heirloom dividing

Author unnamed

inconsolably
grabbing the choice items:
dividing the estate

Tōri

challenge:

how unfortunate!
how unfortunate!

response:

the aftermath
of dividing the estate:
relations cut off

Author unnamed

challenge:

the secret's out and yet ...
the secret's out and yet ...

response:
shares in some brothel:
the late abbot's bequeathal of
a life on the side!

                                                    Author unnamed

he who refrains
from acclaiming the first snow
amounts to somebody

                                                    Author unnamed

the grand total
of tallywacking off:
now he's the boss!

                                                    Sankō

strictly jacking off
to the daughter of his boss
did he get wed!

                                                    Futomaru

first to expose
the bridegroom's perversity:
her kid sis!

                                                    Author unnamed

challenge:

bit by bit by bit by bit
bit by bit by bit by bit

response 1:

'now I see!
it's my resemblance to *her*
he sees in me!'

Author unnamed

response 2:

studies and ladders:
skip a step and there's no
moving on up

Tōgetsu

well then, adieu!
snow viewing until
tumble, we do!

Bashō

well then, adieu!
drinking in moonlight until
tumble, we do!

Gochō

tumbling down
we have known such delight!
this snowy night

                                                    Author unnamed

chasing dragonflies ...
whither my boy this very day
never to return?

                                                    Chiyo (attrib.)

heat-shimmers –
in my eyes still lingering
his smiling face

                                                    Issa

this world of dew ...
though a world of dew it remains,
still, even so ...

                                                    Issa

this last year
not for one instant was he
out of my mind

                                                    Onitsura

Lovers taking a roll in the snow, the verse 'tumbling down . . .' appearing above the snowman

this autumn
with no child upon my lap
gazing at the moon

                                              Onitsura

until last year
scolding over muskmelons
now an offering

                                              Ōemaru

spring cleaning
turns up a baby doll
bringing tears anon

                                         Author unnamed

aboard a ferry
a woman mad with grief –
springtime waters

                                               Buson

spring dream ...
not becoming unhinged
is what's unbearable

                                               Raizan

harvest moon
appears to me alone
as darkness

Raizan

everyone gone ...
in the wake of fireworks
darkness!

Shiki

bottomless pail
thrashed along by a field-threshing
late-autumn gale

Buson

winsome in the wake
of a field-rending tempest:
red capsicum!

Buson

the market profuse
with the odour of things!
summer moon

Bonchō

foul the market
with the odour of horsepiss –
sweltering heat!

Seki Masafusa

spring disappears!
birds cry and in each fish eye
drops of tears

Bashō

feline eyes!
and beneath the icy surface
fish in a frenzy

Issa

kingfisher!
with pond water unmuddled,
the fish deeper

Shiki

dayspring –
from cormorants sprung free,
young skimming fish

Buson

knavish mosquito!
nimbly into an old well,
lying in ambush

Issa

old well ...
a fishleap for mosquitoes
echoes darkly

Buson

mosquito wrigglers ...
their puddle drying up
under a blazing sun

Taigi

tree to be felled ...
the bird unaware
builds its nest

Issa

summer cicadas
wailing so before they've finished
making love

Issa

quiescence!
voices of cicadas
piercing stone

Bashō

on the horizon
no hint of imminent death:
cicadas crying

Bashō

in the sumo ring
no hint of imminent defeat:
wrestlers parading

Author unnamed

how woeful!
the wail of a cicada
caught by a hawk

Ransetsu

springtime woods
even birds of prey
nestled asleep

Rankō

caged bird
glaring with envious eyes
at butterflies!

Issa

even in the capital,
nostalgia for the capital –
woodland cuckoo

Bashō

chopsticks dropping
not for the thunderbolts
but for the cuckoo

Muchō

mandarins!
nobles of yore taking up
bows and arrows

Buson

grass-thatched hermitage,
even it has new occupants –
festive dollhouse

Bashō

snow flurries down ...
a sign not seen yesterday
house for rent

                                              Issa

black wood-ant
flagrantly upon a bloom
of white pomegranate

                                              Buson

a jumbo ant
striding across straw mats –
what heat!

                                              Shirō

even stones and trees
incandescent to the eye –
sweltering heat!

                                              Kyorai

the joy of crossing
a river in summer,
sandals in hand!

                                              Buson

shivery cool,
feet pressed against the wall –
midday snooze!

Bashō

pampas plumes!
flimsyfrail flutterings
of the heart

Issa

a clam from its shell,
myself pried away from you –
departing autumn!

Bashō

with Genji pet names
'Perfumed Duchess' hardly stinks
for most bearded clams

Shuchin

fishmonger kiosk
pungent its dried-fish odour –
torrid heat!

Shiki

salted seabream,
chill down to its gums –
fishmonger stall!

Bashō

bluebottle flies
peck-pecking fish eyes –
such heat!

Chiryū

baby mice
squeak-squeaking for the teat –
midnight in autumn

Buson

winter drizzle:
mice skittering across
zither strings

Buson

the sound of mice
scuttling over dishes;
frigid cold!

Buson

a mouse slipped
into the crock of water –
cold the night

Taigi

nothing blacker,
no matter how regarded,
than snow

Tokugen

footsoldiers proceed
congealed into a huddle –
the frigid cold!

Shirō

lone fly
closing in around me –
winter confinement

Gyōdai

holed up for winter
it's either yellow comics
or red comics

Sōseki

paperweights
on the store's comicbooks –
spring breeze

                                                        Kitō

dubbed 'sketchy comics'
they're still inadvertently
decent portrayals

                                                        Shachō

insect tremolo
soberingly cools the heat
of farmland roads

                                                        Kogetsu

swelteringly
shines the sun's frostiness –
autumn gust

                                                        Bashō

kite breast
struck squarely by the sunlight
of nearing winter

                                                        Shirao

heartbreaking indeed!
beneath an armoured helmet,
a chirping cricket

Bashō

heartbreaking indeed!
beneath the bordello stairway,
a slipper-bearer

Shusshi

to the saké pub
a solitary warrior –
evening snowfall

Hajin

Demon Slayer –
its bouquet reeking
to high hell

Shōri

trying to walk straight
down a path of logicality
while tipsy

Meitei

tipsy reveller
used as a stepping stool
snapping blossoms!

Hōbi

mountain moon
deigns to illumine
the blossom filcher

Issa

challenge:

so this is the floating world!
so this is the floating world!

response:

sprig of blossoms
clutched by a poetic soul
passed out cold!

Author unnamed

beneath the bough
upon broth and pickled fish:
cherry petals!

Bashō

boozed-up samurai ...
the blossom-viewing party
snaps to its senses!

Author unnamed

what in the world!
someone blossom viewing
wearing a sword!

Kyorai

what in the world!
someone tooth-pulling
wearing a sword!

Hanmonsen

viewing blossoms –
how many of them I'd love
even as a wife

Haritsu

partial to autumn
or somesuch says the woman
with the slender neck

Rakusui

浪速ばよさくや乃夜ありや西春九兄

梅翁宗因

Nishiyama Sōin (1605–82), here identified by his
sobriquet Baiō (Old Man Plum)

gaze I shall!
'til the very blossoms become
a pain in the neck

Sōin

no such thing,
in the shadows of blossoms,
as blushing strangers

Issa

scatter already
and send home the gawkers!
mountain cherry

                                                              Ichū

even the shade
of the cherished cherrytree –
vanished

                                                              Issa

within a potted trap
the octopus's fleeting dream –
summer moon

                                                              Bashō

clouds of blossoms ...
those the bells at Ueno?
at Asakusa?

                                                              Bashō

petals from heaven
flurrying down it seems
oh cherry trees!

                                                              Issa

treading upon clouds
along the mountain trail –
rain of blossoms!

Kitō

come for the blossoms
how beauteous it becomes –
my very soul

Tatsujo

come for the blossoms
only to have money pinched –
country bumpkins!

Shiki

the straight and narrow
circle round other folks' pear trees
and melon patches

Tsukuda

a sneak thief
encountered by a fox –
melon field!

Taigi

challenge:
it comes to mind and yet ....
it comes to mind and yet ...

response:
trespassing forbidden
means trespassing is not
out of the question!

Author unnamed

just inside the fence
to prohibited grounds
wild violets

Yaba

here and there
upon scorched fields
wild violets

Shokyū

do not pick!
yet being picked for me:
garden plum

Taigi

upon the fence
with the 'no pissing' sign
willowstrands leak

Kindai

by false pretence
cutting through temple grounds –
the misty moon!

Taigi

passing freely
through the temple grounds –
spring butterfly

Issa

nights so chilly!
clothing so flimsy! and saké
so dreggy!

Kodō

plums in bloom!
nowhere else around
can spring be found

Ritō

spring overlooked!
on the back of a handglass,
plum blossoms

Bashō

scent of plum
in a flash of rising sun!
the mountain path

Bashō

cascade sounds
along a mountain path –
the blistering heat

Shunkō

cold the night!
to the sea cascading down,
waterfall sounds

Kyokusui

the year's first melon
clutched close to a child
fast asleep

Issa

in morning dew,
sullied for being cool –
muddy melons

Bashō

pale moonlit night . . .
in the mood to run off with
a watermelon!

Shiki

a fox sneezes
at a whiff of muskmelon –
moonlit night!

Shirao

a wild boar
warily snorts its snout –
watermelons!

Ushichi

hunting for bushpig!
swooshing through pampas grass
nocturnal voices

Issa

against a charcoal kiln
a wild boar wounded
has collapsed

Bonchō

the deer whistle
being cut short,
a gun's report!

Shiki

cumming for real
like a pig a servant girl
will squeal!

Konjin

challenge:

that was greedy!
that was greedy!

response:

squealing with delight:
'better too *big* than too *small*!'
the chambermaid

Author unnamed

inserted fully
five or six inches feel like
a perfect ten!

Kikō

the mistress –
only four or five inches
and her work is done

Author unnamed

blandishments . . .
a gold tooth gleams
repulsively

Kanehiko

his sweet nothings
the servant girl takes as
the real thing

Author unnamed

still coaxing
though the maidservant's
already cumming

Sosen

dissolving,
the maidservant's mouth and muff
all aquiver!

Shuchin

keep wheedling
perhaps the third pass
up the ass!

Ryūsha

merely diddled
the maidservant's face appears
down in the mouth

Sekishi

being possessed
of an enjoyable foible
wins approval

Goken

being skilled at
feigning infatuation
makes one popular

Shūba

heaven knows! earth knows!
the whole neighbourhood knows!
except the parents

Shishōshi

without dallying
she makes a full confession
in her third trimester

Author unnamed

*try chomping
a whole lotta chillipeppers!*
the prescription

Author unnamed

in the first place,
you were left in a basket
for clementines!

Author unnamed

the doorman:
flabbergasted! the clementine
basket: gurgling!

Author unnamed

the love child
startles at each and every
wham-bam

Gadō

oh what a world!
some pray to heaven for children,
others ditch theirs on earth

Author unnamed

smiled upon
by the babe about to be ditched,
he bursts into tears!

Shōro

piteous indeed –
more than crying the smiling
face of a waif

Rekisen

bystander to
a random crossroads slaying –
merciful buddha

Author unnamed

beneath the barrel
dangling aimlessly:
two metal balls

Shunku

dangling down
upon roses yellow:
bull testicles!

Issa

withering gust . . .
out from a treebough juts
a monkey's butt!

Kyōdai

thongless
his bum blown bare –
vernal breeze

Buson

his wife insists
he drop his pants this instant . . .
for the laundry

Author unnamed

drawing wellwater
her breasts drooping low –
such heat!

Shōhaku

pirates ashore
to draw the village water –
what a drought!

Shiki

ogre charm-print
splattered with droppings –
a passing swallow

Buson

poppy blossoms
upon which plummet
grappling sparrows!

Shirao

red plum
its fallen petals ablaze
on horse dung

Buson

a black dog
transformed into a lantern!
the way in snow

Author unnamed

glimpsed by night
eyes alone prowling along!
the jetblack cat

Author unnamed

from darkness
slinking into darkness –
cat on the prowl!

Issa

from darkness
returning unto darkness –
a sea slug?!

Gyōdai

dirty old tomcat!
nevertheless he's the one
who gets the pussy

Issa

how shocking!
the stone fence knocked down by
cats copulating

Shiki

cats mating –
in our bedroom as they finish,
misty moonlight

Bashō

crack of dawn –
even a stray for love
caterwauls

Issa

silly cat!
hamming up the yowling
with whole torso

Issa

snoozing, stirring
taking an enormous yawn –
feline passion!

Issa

no later than noon,
according to the cat's eyes ...
spring day

Onitsura

its tail
twiddling a butterfly –
the kittycat!

Issa

a butterfly
hoists the pussycat up
two, three feet

Shuchin

dandelion
sporadically snapping a butterfly
out of dreams

Chiyo

flower filcher –
a butterfly silently
in pursuit

Tomomatsu

a butterfly
chasing the spray of flowers . . .
on a casket

Meisetsu

even spring's passing
slumbered away heedlessly –
grass-perched butterfly

Suiujo

butterfly corpse . . .
ants approaching as if
on parade

Tonbo

in the spiderweb
a butterfly's empty shell –
how poignant!

Shiki

crinkly, crinkly
its body desiccated –
how now, cicada?

Saimu

on the veranda
to escape the wife and kids –
stifling heat!

Buson

autumn this morning!
realized in one footstep upon
the veranda wiped dry

Ishū

bush warbler!
crapping on ricecakes scrapped
at veranda's edge

Bashō

a fly's lot:
rubbing hands on some veranda,
whereupon the swat!

Issa

egads, swat not!
pleads the fly rubbing hands,
rubbing feet

Issa

whoooa there!
the bell-striking can wait,
for blossoms' sake!

Shigeyori

evening bell!
and still in bloom,
sweltering heat

Chiyo

quiescence!
touching not the blossoms,
temple bell's voice

Fuhaku

falling blossoms
the remaining blossoms too
falling blossoms

Ryōkan

deep down
beneath scattering blossoms
blithesome skulls!

Seifu

髑髏の上を糚ふて花見の邨

Uejima Onitsura (1660–1738),
here identified as Itami Onitsura

skeletal frames
masqueraded in finery:
blossom viewing!

Onitsura

though mortal,
skeletons every last one!
evening chill

Issa

this world of ours:
viewing blossoms on the surface
above hell

Issa

village lamplights
lambent in the raindrops
upon young leaves!

Ryōta

'yea big'
the peony sized by
a little kid

Author unnamed

a nightingale
interrupting my handiwork
at the sink

Chigetsu

cooling breeze –
the boundless sky filled with
pining voices

Onitsura

pine resin
oozing out, torrid –
broken bough

Gomei

hatchet sinking in,
amazed by the fragrance –
dead trees of winter

Buson

dog's bark
means someone passing by;
night of snow

Meimei

daybreak!
the tempest interred
in snow

Shirō

snowy morn
the *ditto ditto* marks
of wooden clogs

Sutejo

Den Sutejo (1633–98)

mountain hamlet –
beneath piled-up snows,
watersounds

Shiki

snow remaining
the mountain foot mists over –
O eventide!

Sōgi

Iio Sōgi (1421–1502)

late-thawing snow
and the village overflows ...
with little kids!

Issa

snug in my futon
on a morning so cold –
petals as snow!

Sonojo

dog barking
at a travelling salesman;
peachtrees in bloom

Buson

early-summer rains ...
blank spaces on the wall where
versecards peeled off

Bashō

ceaseless rains ...
upon the sushi pressingstone
a slug

Onitsura

dreadful the stream
without so much as a name!
early-summer rains

Buson

the blossoms
of some unheard-of creeping weed
by the riverside

Chiun

on account of spring
a no-name mountain
shrouded in mist

Bashō

no-name places
have their particular charm –
mountain cherries

Goshun

drab inkwashes
along with off-colour prints
carried home by pilgrims

Author unnamed

diddling herself
to a kabuki pin-up!
the chambermaid

Gadō

noblewoman
(under an alias)
in the cheap seats!

Gochō

among men, samurai!
so why do they come disguised
as lowly merchants?

Author unnamed

samurai rules
in the Yoshiwara
hardly pertain

Saikaku

Ihara Saikaku (1642–93)

the bachelor
feeling lonesome
plays with his flute

Shun'u

ignorant bachelor
applying *Pleasure Her* lotion
to pleasure himself

Ryūsha

'sheltered girl'
means never beholding cock
even in dreams

Bunji

the bride-to-be
at a bookshop, faintly:
'so that's how it's done!'

Author unnamed

the young lady
grasps a single volume
but gingerly!

Author unnamed

her mother away,
the young lady sneaks out
unlettered books

Karasaki

challenge:

one atop the other
one atop the other

response:

love letters
from the guy she *doesn't* fancy
she shows Mother

Author unnamed

spring rains!
fluttering in a thicket,
discarded missives

Issa

spiteful missives:
scribbles like so many
dried bonito shavings

Saikaku

the piece of ass
slapped by mistake
sends love letters!

Author unnamed

when cinched
a waistsash makes the hips
come to life!

Author unnamed

first love!
drawing close 'neath stone lantern
face to face

Taigi

under the lamplight
showing porn to turn
someone on

Author unnamed

called 'giggle pictures'
yet they almost always bring
people to tears

Wagō

the 'giggle':
an implement of sweet nothings
for self-pleasure

Author unnamed

little by little
stifling one's voice –
giggle book!

Banjin

harebrained lovers,
aping smutty woodblock prints,
dislocate their arms!

Author unnamed

bending over back
-wards to imitate porno –
strained beyond reason!

Author unnamed

judging by pictures
the netherworld's more
titillating

Ochō

just my luck!
Paradise turns out to be
a real yawner

Nanboku

at the women's bath
some guy taking a look-see
claiming 'nature calls'

Author unnamed

for woodblock artists
scrutinizing snatch is just
part of the job

Author unnamed

for woodblock artists
scrutinizing snatch is just
family business

Author unnamed

'isn't that enough
of a gander already?'
the artist's wife

Author unnamed

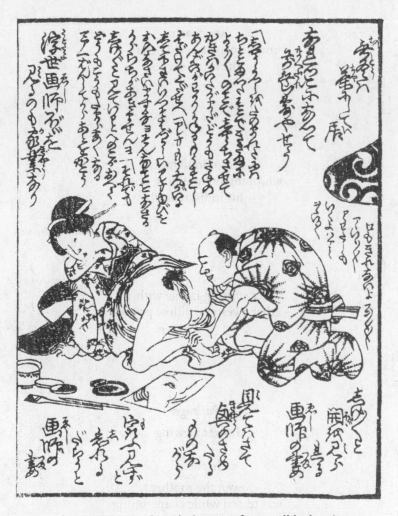

An *ukiyoe* artist at work, with the verse 'for woodblock artists ...
family business' in the upper left-hand corner

her chacha
on display in vivid detail –
the artist's wife

Author unnamed

out of loneliness
whipping out a pillow print –
his indiscretion!

Author unnamed

her spitting image within
that awesome pillow print!

Author unnamed

challenge:

flower viewing

response:

even the mother
was teased while chaperoning
their first date

Author unnamed

challenge:
butthole

response:

butts and heads alike
wholly lined up on rice girls

Author unnamed

challenge:

now that's unavoidable!
now that's unavoidable!

response:

a doctor assays
places even a husband
doesn't assay

Author unnamed

endless chatter ...
a dragonfly perches on
the speartip

Author unnamed

on a white wall
a dragonfly's passing
silhouette

Shōha

winter sun –
frozen on horseback
a silhouette

Bashō

autumn gust –
silhouette of the mountain
all aquiver

Issa

withered grass –
heat-haze shimmers upwards
inches, inches

Bashō

firefly-gazing –
with the boatman tipsy,
how tremulous

Bashō

faraway mountains
registered in its eye
dragonfly!

Issa

squid-peddler's cry
deceptively similar to that
of the cuckoo

Bashō

persimmon chewing
to the clanging of a bell –
Dharma Booming Temple

Shiki

my epitaph:
'a haiku poetaster
of persimmons'

Shiki

raggourd left to bloom –
fruitless in stopping the phlegm
that choked this buddha

Shiki

challenge:

what an inconvenience!
what an inconvenience!

response:

ceaseless praying ...
at times one gets choked up
with phlegm

                                        Author unnamed

lightningflash!
in the hollow of a bucket,
forgotten water

                                        Shiki

lightningflashes!
visible again and again,
Castle Zeze's white

                                        Sosen

a camellia plummets
the plumed rooster crows yet again
a camellia plummets

                                        Baishitsu

three trees
do not a forest make –
willow

Baishitsu

streetcorner sermon –
for all the jibberjabber,
also serene

Issa

even parrots
hailing from strange provinces
squawk Edo slang

Tsukuda

lightningflash!
penetrating the darkness,
a night heron's cry

Bashō

challenge:

how exquisite!
how exquisite!

response:

on a beauty
a wife always spots
some blemish

Author unnamed

on a beauty
not even the cunt
seems filthy

Yashū

getting stepped on
hurts only in proportion to
who does the stepping!

Nobuyuki

challenge:

the pitifulness
of he who is red-faced

response:

getting stepped on:
I didn't hurt your foot,
did I?

Daté

any girl
decent enough for their boy
they abhor

Author unnamed

any young man
cavorting with a proper lady
will never measure up!

Author unnamed

first date –
both parties engaged
in embellishment

Santarō

marriage interview –
sizing up each other's
nose or lips

Soei

challenge:

paying attention and yet ...
paying attention and yet ...

response:

when in the mood
eyes speak as much
as the lips

Romaru

when chatted up
casting a glance close by
means assent

Kōkō

challenge:

what humiliation!
what humiliation!

response:

in a nutshell
wooing is also
grovelling

Author unnamed

those hundred gold coins,
with young miss part of the deal,
yield no interest

Author unnamed

shoved into a vase
upon the wedding altar:
a pine mushroom

Kisenjo

the new bride:
picture-perfect looks
her only dowry

Author unnamed

a thing of beauty!
a new bride without a stitch
of dowry

Kōbai

still on cloud nine
the groom readily
succumbs

Author unnamed

so tender a bride
nowhere for the mother-in-law
to sink her teeth

Kiryū

no criticism,
just words of praise for the bride
next door

Author unnamed

all about the bride
the mother-in-law depicts with
mimicking gestures

Author unnamed

a bride capable
of pleasing the mother-in-law?
her nights short-lived!

Author unnamed

her only comforts:
tormenting the daughter-in-law.
attending temple.

Author unnamed

torn between
tormenting her daughter-in-law
and heeding sermons

Rishō

a wife's scolding
confirms the mother-in-law's
competence

Author unnamed

the bride's farts
like quakes, thunder and blazes
shake Mother-in-Law

Hanfu

ignobly slain
by her daughter-in-law's fart
from a squatting stance

Kanai

breaking wind
the mother-in-law also breaks
the tension

Author unnamed

the bride's fart:
exasperating; her own:
pure *jouissance*!

Kichibō

the knowing mother
pretending to be asleep
lets them go at it

Gadō

missuses
even more than mummies:
nuisances

Author unnamed

although long gone,
that hundred gold of her dowry,
her mug lingers on

Author unnamed

darkening breasts
shown to her husband setting
off on a trip

Author unnamed

challenge:

joyously overflow
the saké cups

response:

first childbirth –
the husband feeling he himself
did half the labour

Hōka

seventy-five days
of postpartum abstention
up the wazoo

Tessen

his wife
who once had caught his eye
now gets up his nose

Rakuho

challenge:

how suspicious!
how suspicious!

response:

feigned sleep –
the snoring inordinately
faithful

Author unnamed

it's the *Analects*
that his mistress snatches
out of reach

Author unnamed

challenge:

a sight to behold!
a sight to behold!

response:

that eye-popper
of a procured accessory
worn on his sleeve

Senden

challenge:

how agreeable!
how agreeable!

response:

sweet nothings
of the kept woman:
'gimme, gimme!'

Kōbai

noble ladies:
where they daintily stroke
mistresses grab hold!

Author unnamed

a lady's zither
never trumps the shamisen
of a mistress!

Shinchō

the dimples
of his mistress: the downfall
of his wife!

Shimeko

the graph for 'mistress':
a 'woman' whom one's wife
cannot 'stand'

Hakushi

whereas mistresses
might shake you down for money
maids also rock baby!

Author unnamed

challenge:

how vain! and yet ...
how vain! and yet ...

response:

novice wet nurse
glances at the man of the house
slightly askance

Author unnamed

to the napping face
the wet nurse bids farewell
then withdraws

Kashō

pushy kids!
championing their opinions,
saleswomen

Jōzen

maids' quarters –
the one who's *too* pretty
gets bullied

Author unnamed

both mistresses
every bit as dazzling
as razor-sharp blades

Author unnamed

Castle Toppler –
on account of her tears
his storehouse leaks

Kisui

spicy playboy –
salty his old man,
sweet his mother

Ribai

the mother
tops off the alibis
of her carousing son

Author unnamed

the young player
having played his mother
goes off to get played

Author unnamed

even while scolded
the boy has only one thing
on his mind

Author unnamed

even while scolded
the only thing on his mind
is girls

Author unnamed

within the heart
of every rebuking parent
resides a bride

Author unnamed

badmouthing . . .
somewhere deep down inside
he's in love!

Bishi

challenge:
. . . just try and get one!

response:
a bride
for that playboy son –

Author unnamed

he of all people
who eats us out of house and home
brushing his teeth!

Author unnamed

challenge:
what insolence!
what insolence!

response:
his mother's scolding
defied on extravagant
Chinese paper!

Author unnamed

at the bordello
the mother frets her brow into
a cliffhanger!

Utan

cutting him off
even before his father does:
the hired sidekick

Author unnamed

challenge:

now that's gentle!
now that's gentle!

response:

exclaims the father
of the silverpiped playboy:
'that *real* silver?!'

Author unnamed

silverpipe –
even this figures
in the scolding

Shiseki

getting disowned:
'take your damned silverpipe
and skedaddle!'

Author unnamed

disinherited
their lovers' suicide becomes
so much empty talk

Author unnamed

when no longer
taken with himself who else
will take him?

Author unnamed

disowned son –
taking him back along with
two extra mouths

Author unnamed

overstaying
means being voracious
for hooch

Soei

afternoon delight
stacked atop night-time delight
all on the house!

Saikaku

the poseur who claims
'my courtesan had me kidnapped!'
florid self-flattery

Author unnamed

last night's
lovers' tiff: this morning's
marital split!

Author unnamed

challenge:

unbridled fun!
unbridled fun!

response:

his return fare
the wife coughs up
with a *hmph!*

Author unnamed

challenge:

now there's an excuse!
now there's an excuse!'

response:

the bridle
to unbridledness:
one's bride!

Tōgetsu

having a wife
one's countenance
turns glum

Author unnamed

moon down,
crows caw and the wife
riled up!

Author unnamed

out all night long
upon his return the neighbours:
'there they go again!'

Gochō

challenge:

too little too late!
too little too late!

response:
only after
his philanderings does he fuss
over his wife

Author unnamed

there's no comparing
a playboy's popularity
to his wife's jealousy

Author unnamed

crazy jealous –
so the master of the house
cooks dinner

Author unnamed

squabble won
yet the master of the house simmers
the rice

Sarumatsu

even the winner
of that evening's squabble
loses sleep

Gyokutorō

being scolded
the wife refuses to bring
herself to bed

Seimu

unsmiling wife –
bootlicking her relentlessly
to get even

Author unnamed

novice courtesan!
polishing the pipe with which
she gets herself whipped

Saō

his bad posture:
even that he blames
on women

Kayū

'all women ..'
declared before glancing
over his shoulder

Author unnamed

making up,
the wife's voice returns
to normal

Author unnamed

challenge:

that's delightful!
that's delightful!

response:

making up,
he returns to the usual
watering hole

Author unnamed

piece of his mind!
and upon returning home
his wife's piece of mind

Yachō

single people
know not the perks
of marital squabbles

Sekishō

couple next door have,
judging by the heavy breathing,
kissed and made up

Senmei

darkest night!
losing track of its nest,
a plover cries out

Bashō

more chill
than the blustering wind –
midnight moon

Shōkyū

wintergrove –
a night when moonshafts
cut to the bone!

Kitō

tonight the blooms
surely fall beneath that scythe
of a crescent moon

Saigin

nothing like it,
not even its visual spoof:
crescent moon

Bashō

only thing slicker
than cormorants are cormorants
mimicked by children!

Issa

strutting along
in imitation of ploughing –
a raven

Issa

challenge:

how stirring!
how stirring!

response:

the Wolf
devours everything save
her money pouch

Author unnamed

spring drizzle ...
mallards not yet devoured
quack it up

Issa

evening squall!
scampering among the houses,
squawking ducks

Kikaku

Takarai Kikaku (1661-1707)

crack of dawn!
the citadel encircled by
quacking ducks

Kyoriku

as though flowing
with the current downstream:
swallows on the wing!

Saimaro

out of the blue
of early-morning light:
a paulownia leaf

Ryōta

paulownia leaves
scatter, crinkle, one by one
on the breeze

Ransetsu

misty spring rains ...
umbrellas high and low
aboard the ferry

Shiki

steady spring rains ...
jabbering along together,
parasol and slicker

Buson

spring drizzle ...
browsing at the picturebook stall
umbrella propped up

Shiki

fancy halfcoats
scampering away headless –
sudden downpour!

Author unnamed

sudden downpour!
no such thing as
a pensive face

Shokyū

sudden summer squall!
quick thinking of all sorts
of head coverings

Otsuyū

challenge:
staring and yet ...
staring and yet ...

response:
shelter from the rain –
the inscription on a plaque
learned by heart

Author unnamed

rain lets up
and the price of umbrellas
comes back down!

Author unnamed

storming off
the umbrella flips out
a bit too far

Author unnamed

snow-buckled,
reverting to a former life –
umbrella ribs

Shōi

giving instructions
on how to use the tattered
loaner umbrella

Kanri

paper umbrellas –
how many pass by
in snowy twilight?

Hokushi

donning a sedge hat
primping before the mirror –
tealeaf picker

Shikō

this bozo fishing
and that bozo watching him –
bozos both!

☁

only a fool
takes being made a fool of
without humour

Garyūbō

although spectacles
might do the trick for the eyes,
and dentures for the teeth ...

Mukujō

still functioning:
eyes and ears and teeth and yet
that one regret!

Kanshi

eyeglass polishing ...
even the lens on the side
with the sightless eye

Sōjō

'shall we yank 'em all?'
ejaculates the tooth doctor,
unstintingly

Author unnamed

his dead member
the wife tries frantically to
resuscitate

Ryūsha

at the hotspring
apparently not his daughter!
the scuttlebutt

Shun'u

precisely *because*
the gods are invisible
they are believed in

Shinpei

feigning ignorance
of fierce gods he cannot see –
the playboy

Maita

watermelons:
eating them with good manners
is bad manners!

Chisei

remorse
of either picking or not picking
violets

Naojo

swellfish broth:
folly to take a sip
and folly not to!

Shōchō

challenge:

ever-changingly!
ever-changingly!

response:

taken for a ride –
an accomplice from last night's
swellfish dinner

Author unnamed

nothing drastic?
yesterday came and went?
swellfish broth

Bashō

hardly charred newts ...
but gold coins are still potent
aphrodisiacs

Author unnamed

challenge:

how gratifying!
how gratifying!

response:

it's a wonder
Narihira didn't contract
a rash of cockiness!

Author unnamed

orchids by night –
within their fragrance looms
their blossoms' white!

Buson

first snowfall . . .
scarcely enough to cover
the dogshit

Issa

throughout fields, mountains,
not one thing stirring:
snowy morn

Chiyo

Kaga no Chiyo (1703–75)

neither hills nor plains
obliterated in snow
and nothing else

Jōsō

lofty wooden clog
drifts away beneath the ice
and disappears

Banan

Kawai Chigetsu (1633–1718)

awaiting spring –
sprinkled into the ice
ashes and dust

Chigetsu

deep underground
male and female quintessences
hibernating

Nakajō Kakujirō

traversed without
coming across any wolves –
winter's mountain

Shiki

challenge:

how vexing!
how vexing!

response:

one stray ant
scares a girl in full bloom
right out of her clothes!

Author unnamed

challenge word:

come to a standstill –

response:

the easygoing ants
change directions

Author unnamed

colliding head-on,
'whatnots' whispered a mite,
ants part ways

Suikyō

challenge:
look at that!

response:
footprints of the cat,
strewn plum petals

Author unnamed

they both meet
scowling at the other:
catty love

Shiki

whiskers
on the both of 'em –
cats in heat

Raizan

'til blooming,
nobody pines after them –
rhododendrons

Haritsu

throughout the shop
the only one *not* in the know:
her boss

Author unnamed

throughout town,
her husband alone
in the dark

Author unnamed

'thanks for carrying on
while I was away from my wife!'
said unknowingly

Author unnamed

'thanks for keeping
my wife unmolested!'
said unknowingly

Yamaki

challenge:
proposed half-jokingly
for having a little fun

response:

fastest of friends –
so let me take advantage of
your nubile wife!

Chikusui

her so-called 'cousin'
always seems to be visiting
when hubby's away

Author unnamed

challenge:

from gaps in the duckboards
a draught wafting upwards ...

response:

for goosebumps,
a twin pillow for lovebirds?!
her sultry coo!

Hakukei

challenge:

how admirable!
how admirable!

response:
bachelors
withdraw to their rooms
and groan

Author unnamed

belly-cutting scene
suspended to watch a brawl
in the *audience*!

Kyūsei

challenge:
cheered up, yet still ...
cheered up, yet still ...

response:
the mother back home
struts along cradling
the birth announcement

Author unnamed

when at last
one longs to be filial
both parents are gone

Author unnamed

nostalgic
even for the scoldings!
parents' grave

Fūshō

challenge:

however grim
it was also funny!

response:

even while
my father lay dying
farts kept ripping!

Sōkan

having children
one learns appreciation
all too late

Shakujin

having children
one gets filial piety
all too late!

Gyokushu

Yamazaki Sōkan (1465–1553)

not until nabbing
the flea that bit her baby
will she sleep easy

Hōrō

even while sleeping
the hand fan sweeps to and fro –
a parent's devotion

Author unnamed

that gentle breeze
from the slumbering fan –
a mother's love

Author unnamed

even asleep
one's hand fan keeps swaying –
blazing heat

Fukoku

the drowsy fan
bit by bit becomes
a faint breath

Author unnamed

the morning after
their sleeping child caught cold,
the parents bicker

Author unnamed

a child cries
throughout the night about to break –
affliction

Shirao

monsoon rains
gathered into the torrential
Mogami River!

Bashō

scorching day
washed away into the sea –
River Mogami!

Bashō

whoosh whoosh
washing summer away:
Mogami River

Shiki

a crimson sun
slumps into the sea –
the heat!

Natsume Sōseki

challenge:
unsteady the heart!
unsteady the heart!

response:
our little princess
in the hands of a nursemaid
with tattooed arms!

Author unnamed

down to her tattoos
a courtesan's business:
turning a profit

Ukō

where to keep
her severed finger
has him stumped!

San'en

the high priest
shows devotion by licking
his rentboy's bunghole

Mokubō

the rentboy
as though heaving a sigh
lets go a fart

Yokose

short the distance
between great monks and baboons
as the crow flies

Author unnamed

nowhere to dump
all the dirty bathwater –
insect voices!

Onitsura

even splash baths
become less frequent –
insect voices!

Raizan

bright the moon!
for dumping an ashtray,
no dark corner

Fugyoku

bright the moon!
from locations pitch-dark,
insect voices

Bunson

the other breast!
the first stirrings of desire
does grabbing it beget!

Jinsei

'so, Nanny,'
poking with his footsie,
'this your *furry goblin*?'

Jakuchō

nanny's cunny:
catching sight of it, sonny
bursts into tears!

Shumoku

challenge:

'off to play hide 'n' seek!'
so Mother let down her guard

response 1:

playing house –
into her tiny shellclam
his hot chillipepper!

Shōki

response 2:

'he's put his willy
into the little one's mouth!'
Big Sis exclaims

Mokubō

shell-gathering
within a clear line of sight ...
still, a mother worries

Kinchō

the first grandchild
comes along and suddenly
everything's dangerous

Toshiko

challenge:

can't hardly wait!
can't hardly wait!

response:

jumping out
in order to be found –
lil' hide-and-seeker!

Author unnamed

all those sighs
exhaled into some corner –
hide-and-seek!

Author unnamed

sparklers in hand,
come on, be dark already!
be dark already!

Gochō

in the midst
of children thronging ...
an overwhelmed sparrow

Issa

scold as one might,
little kids prefer their shoes
too big to fill

Author unnamed

playing house:
the one who gets to be wifey
the most sassy

Shiseki

challenge:

what a nuisance!
what a nuisance!

response:

playing house:
the homewrecker shows up
as the spoiled child

Author unnamed

playing the parent
in a game of hide-and-seek –
the kittycat

Issa

kittycats
playing hide-and-seek:
bushclover blooms!

Issa

pleasure women
sleeping beneath this very roof!
bushclover and moon

Bashō

challenge:
completely compatible!
completely compatible!

response:
shophand and maidservant
abstain from fraternizing
in broad daylight

Author unnamed

the young master –
jacking off by night
telling off by day

Author unnamed

the maidservant:
obliging whims by night
disregards them by day

Baishi

having obliged demands
the maidservant no longer
obliges commands

Author unnamed

fleas, lice
and a horse taking a whizz
beside my pillow

Bashō

evening rainburst!
brought back from the dead,
a collapsed steed

Kitō

challenge:

crowded out!
crowded out!

response:

clutching porno
he gets kicked out from
their heating table

Author unnamed

challenge:

now, that's harsh!
now, that's harsh!

response:

smutty pictures,
when voiced out loud,
get one told off

Author unnamed

pillow pictures –
to a new spot every day
hidden away

Author unnamed

it's the real stud
who on the morning after
gets dicked

Author unnamed

for his peccadillos
to the bordello he goes,
the fool gung-ho!

Ryūsen

on a roofed boat
doing it with fingers praying
to the tiny goddess!

Sanchō

even when ill
bachelors never feel
like groaning

Kinbō

about to shout,
'hey look, a firefly!'
though all alone

Taigi

on windless days
scattering that much more ...
cherry blossoms

Chora

falling too soon
after so long awaited:
the blossom's essence!

Sōgi

up and out early
spotting malicious graffiti –
the hilarity!

Kitō

spotting graffiti
by acquaintances of mine –
autumn dusk

Issa

the name
of you whom I adore
there in graffiti!

Bashō

viewing blossoms
only to return to a home
engulfed in flames!

Kenkabō

storehouse burnt down
nothing to impinge upon
the incandescent moon

Masahide

others gone home
now there's nothing between
the moon and me

Seifu

guests gone home
yet loath to drape the bed netting
this moonlit night

Ryōta

all are aboard boats,
upon bridges, atop drying racks
moon viewing!

Shiki

from time to time
clouds provide a respite from
moon viewing

Bashō

upon sleepy homes
as though glancing askance:
harvest moon!

Otsuyū

up from amongst
tempest-buffeted grasses:
harvest moon!

Chora

out from the shadows
of every thing in this world:
harvest moon!

Nangai

rainy season gloom –
then one night through pines, slyly,
the pined-for moon!

Ryōta

luminous moon!
upon strawmats your pined-for
shadow of pines!

Kikaku

bright the moon!
emerging shapes of pine trees
unseen by day

Kakō

lazing in shadows,
conceding the drawing room
to moonrays

Seibi

one by one
the stars come into view –
frigid cold!

Taigi

one by one
the stars, shimmeringly
the crickets, profusely

Tatsuko

darkening seas ...
the call of a mallard,
faintly white

Bashō

evening squall!
the squawk of geese, white
the pond, dark

Rohan

scolded
the cat shuts its eyes;
spring draws nigh

Mantarō

the upshot
of jotting and scrubbing out:
a scrubland of poppies

Hokushi

my night ending
I shall resound in the blooms!
Pure Land Gate

Saimu

challenge:

the way of the world:
oxen with oxen!

response:

only an illiterate
can make out the scribblings
of other illiterates!

Kōchiku

pharmacy shopsign –
illiterates make out only
its 🍶

Yamaimo

no shopsign
for white facepowder
is lily white

Wabun

the peddler's cry
smoothes over the crumples
in his dried radishes

Yūkō

floating-world moon –
let pass disregarded
these last two years

Sodō

in the twinkling
a saké shot slides down the throat ...
up rises the moon!

Sōin

springtime hovel:
its nothingness precisely
its everythingness

Sodō

obligingly,
a tea seller set up shop:
summer grove

Buson

my, oh my, oh my!
all to be said of the blossoms
on Mount Yoshino

Teishitsu

my, oh my, oh my!
all to be said of the headlice
through a microscope

Author unnamed

a plover
taken for a great egret –
the telescope!

Author unnamed

steady spring rains ...
both dream and reality
Mount Yoshino!

Ryōta

was it for real,
this dream of being cut to shreds?
bitemarks of a flea!

Kikaku

dreading its own
reflection in the water –
a firefly

Sutejo

fervent for the grass
at the bottom of the pond –
fireflies

Buson

tread not yonder
where last night dwelt fireflies
upon the banks

Issa

never dreaming
that within my garden grasses
fireflies!

Takuchi

when chased
taking cover in moonrays:
fireflies!

Ryōta

jumbo firefly,
undulating, pendulating,
flits on by

Issa

to know the plum:
along with the heart alone
the nose alone

Onitsura

pining away,
the heart's passions in spring –
blossoms at their pique

Sōgi

half-asleep eyes
open to a dreamlike world
of blossoms

Seibi

plum, cherry –
hopping from bed to bed
of flowers

Sōzei

plum blossoms scatter
and it's peach; peach scatters
and it's cherry

Kyōma

even Hollanders
have come for the blossoms!
quick, saddle up!

Bashō

bright moon
in the sky even for *them* –
shaggy barbarians!

Issa

within the nose
of Buddha Colossus
chirping baby sparrows!

Issa

stray cat
using the Buddha's lap
as pillow!

Issa

within the heat-haze
shimmeringly a cat
snores away!

Issa

bursting open
disgorging its rainbow:
peony dynamo!

Buson

peony petals
scattering gently, nestle
in twos and threes

Buson

cockscombs:
up to fourteen . . . fifteen
stalks, even

Shiki

people so horrid!
to haggle over the price
of orchids

Shiki

within the narcissus
not the least shadow exists
of man's murkiness!

Roten

once fallen
its after-image arises:
peony!

Buson

the nightingale:
some days it shows up twice,
others not at all

Kitō

nightingale!
then suddenly at the gate
a tofu peddler

Yaba

nightingale!
even before his lordship
that same voice

Issa

mighty warlord
forced down from his mount!
cherry blossoms

Issa

thud-thudding
upon cherry petals –
horse dung!

Issa

the entire world
moved beneath the trees –
cherry blossoms!

Atsujin

blooming for the sake
of this light-verse racket:
cherry blossoms!

Author unnamed

cherry blossoms
at the untouchables' temple
bloom defiantly

Issa

in the garden
blossoming whitely:
camellia

Onitsura

'though in winter,
summer ain't so bad,'
or so it's said

Onitsura

'come! come!'
yet still the fireflies go
flitting away

Onitsura

over and over,
sprinkled over by blossoms,
drowsily, drowsily

Onitsura

accustomed to,
even poverty still has
the moon and blooms

Jisshi

moon, blossoms –
a world that will now know
the third verse

Ryūho

an excess of love
the pussycat just as frisky
as a courtesan!

Saimaro

cat bell
amidst the peonies
...here!...there!

Issa

now here, now there,
emerging from the snowfall:
evening smoke

Rankō

day after day after day
at the wood-burning brazier
watching for bamboo

Issa

Konishi Raizan (1654-1716)

with continued thawing
everything is turning green –
spring snow

Kikusha

lush green, lush green,
spring shoots so lushly green –
snowy field

Raizan

whitish clouds
brushed away by summer trees
with fresh green leaves!

Saimaro

autumn breeze
taking shape in a mess
of pampas grass

Kigin

in the riverbreeze
a cluster of willowtrees:
spring revealed

Sōchō

拾穂軒季吟

友寂と
うき
泊を
なみだ
の邪

Kitamura Kigin (1624–1705)

within loneliness
there is also happiness –
autumn dusk

Buson

out of loneliness
my walking stick left behind –
autumn dusk

Buson

persimmons so tart
not even crows
give 'em a glance!

Bokusui

persimmons sold out
not even crows visit
the mountain hamlet

Shūda

even in hamlets
where unseen the blossom and bream –
harvest moon!

Naniwa Saikaku

spring days –
people taking it easy
in a small town

Shiki

wisteria spray
left withered in a vase –
wayside inn

Taigi

blossoming
in forgotten flowerpots:
a spring day

Shiki

green seaweed:
in the recesses of a reef,
forgotten tide

Kitō

rather dried up
a mere tuft of grass
between stones

Shōha

washing the mountain
a colourless rain of autumn,
waters unseen

Muchō

upon withered bough
a crow has come to its rest ...
autumnal twilight

Bashō

Painting of a lone crow by Morikawa Kyoriku (1656–1715),
with calligraphy by Bashō (1644–94) of his verse
'upon withered bough . . .'

snowmelt!
through mountain vapours,
crow-cawing

Gyōdai

nest feathering!
even the much-despised crow,
a parent's heart

Shirao

fresh green leaves:
cats and crows
squabbling!

Issa

at a roadside shrine
glowing before the stone buddha ...
fireflies!

Buson

perched asleep
on the massive temple bell:
a butterfly!

Buson

at daybreak
hailstones pitter-pattering
upon camellia

Buson

evening breeze –
water lapping the shins
of a blue heron

Buson

steady spring rains . . .
doubtlessly growing dark,
this day lingers on

Buson

against the stormclouds
seemingly plum-blossom stars
despite the daylight

Onitsura

challenge:
no help whatsoever!
no help whatsoever!

response:

hungover yawn –
eyeing offertory saké
upon the altar!

Author unnamed

butterflies!
fluttering a girl's way,
ahead, behind

Chiyo

a fallen petal
back to its bough, reviewed:
a butterfly!

Moritake

water whirligigs?
or butterflies whirling round?
wavelets of petals!

Baisei

but for the call
all but indistinguishable –
white heron and snowball

Tayojo

Arakida Moritake (1472–1549)

beak and legs alone –
inkwash of a white heron
in the snow

Kingyo

a line of geese!
and upon the mountain crest
the moon as impress

Buson

Dutch scribbling:
wild geese in the sky
flying sideways!

Ishŭ

skewers of dumplings
more than sprigs of blossoms:
geese flying home

Teitoku

the fragrance
resides more in the nose
than the nosegay

Moritake

blowing her nose
with a nosegay of moonflowers –
the young lady

Issa

drops of dew?
or rays of moon
upon the grass!

Zenma

vernal seas ...
all day long swelling, falling
swelling, falling!

Buson

rising sun
and nothing else –
misty sea!

Shirō

rowing clear
through the hazy dimness –
the vast sea

Shiki

cloud and mist alike
rendered unnoticeable –
bright moon tonight!

Kensai

bright enough
to lose sight of it –
tonight's moon

Seika

mountain fog –
performing shrine safekeeping,
conchshell-sounds

Taigi

glancing behind,
the person met in passing
shrouded in mist

Shiki

even behind
even ahead ...
distant mist!

Ryōta

heaven and earth
still not rent asunder –
morning mist

Genkaibō

bit by bit
the mountainside changes hue –
moonlit night!

Fuhaku

autumn begins!
the summer rainburst blends into
a crisp night drizzle

Taigi

after sunset
suffuses its vermilion –
autumn dusk

Kitō

falling clear through
the bottom of loneliness –
freezing rain!

Jōsō

cricket
upon hearth's pothook climbs –
frigid night

Buson

the lamplight
holding steady freezes –
frosty night!

Seira

'the wind is freezing!
freezing, freezing!'
says the night lamp

                                                                Issa

first spring breeze
in the lamplight flickering
within the outhouse

                                                              Ōemaru

examined in the palm
the year's first hailstones
revert to water

                                                               Sakijo

within my grasp
sadly vanishing!
a firefly

                                                               Kyorai

morning glories –
just try to capture their image
and they droop

                                                              Haritsu

morning glories –
just try to sketch their portrait
and they droop

                                                            Shiki

challenge:

a sight to behold!
a sight to behold!

response:

the classy ones
even when catching z's
grasp books

                                                   Author unnamed

naptime book –
page by page the breeze
ravishes

                                                   Author unnamed

concealing the face
of the snoozing sneak thief,
Vatful of Light Verse

                                                            Higan

the burglar
on his way home commends
the bountiful moon

Yasharō

the burglar
left it behind –
moon in the window

Ryōkan

bumping into
a woman pickpocket –
hazy moon

Taigi

through countless rimes
gently this Plantain serves
as my New Year's pine

Bashō

plantain-shredding windstorm –
rain upon a washbasin heard
all night long!

Bashō

Bashō's plantain
Senryū's riverwillow
equally palmy!

Keisuke

tree-withering gust!
later bursting forth in buds,
the riverwillow

Senryū

come for a loan
he momentarily appears
trustworthy

Author unnamed

more woeful
even than the death poem:
he who lent money!

Tamagawa

snail
bit by bit ascend!
Mount Fuji

Issa

to the very brink
of smouldering Mount Asama
cultivated fields

Issa

Mount Asama
amidst its fumes and ash
fresh young leaves!

Buson

bindweed blooms
opening toward the hiss-hissing
sizzling stones

Issa

worthless weeds!
the taller you grow
the longer the days

Issa

bush warbler!
only a drab-coloured bird
with a song thrown in

Onitsura

a bush warbler
with too many syllabets
draws out its song

Buson

barely springtime
but lo that bush warbler!
in a voice of yore

Buson

bush warbler!
alighting upon plum trees
since aeons ago

Onitsura

the years pass ...
greying hairs have I concealed
from my parents

Etsujin

over there
appears nice and cool –
pines on the ridge

Shikō

支考肖像真蹟

杉子の三の指
猫を三の腰てん
猫のわくんうれ

蓮莊坊

支考美濃人天資高邁才識
過人少入禪室早游其會柢弦頁
質頌異常論法與其徒許故疾忌
互生終捨鉢還(似以通)因經其間自取
給時介炎人凉寇擇蓑箱於伊勢旅寓一語
摧其氣鋭倒才歸降爲人博學多通不甘從
人步趨號自閑一徑以導衆徳咪著書數十篇皆以呂
傳始號見龍後白狂蓮三華表人桃花仙東花西花野盤
子神子諸號随手繼阪之此世俗知秀別號可謂達聞者哉

活齋

Kagami Shikō (1665–1731)

emerging from
the edge of coolness –
ocean moon

Shiki

how enviable!
falling while still resplendent,
the maple leaf

Shikō

looking as though
spring would nevermore return:
scattered leaves!

Ryōta

inner side revealed
outer side being revealed –
tumbling maple leaf

Ryōkan (attrib.)

city folk
adorned with red maple leaves
on the train home

Meisetsu

heat-shimmers:
even mosquito breeding grounds
brimming with beauty

                                                                    Issa

sure enough!
mushrooms that will kill you,
also gorgeous

                                                                    Issa

resplendent,
the kite soaring high above
the shanty town

                                                                    Issa

however sublime,
even the blossoms cannot compare:
tonight's bright moon

                                                                    Sōin

plum blossoms
one by one toward
spring's warmth!

                                                                    Ransetsu

a barren woman
coddling festival dolls –
how poignant

Ransetsu

doll's face ...
mine unavoidably
wizened with age

Seifu

door ajar
though nobody home ...
peach blossoms

Chiyo

lull in the rain ...
drifting into the bedroom
a butterfly!

Seifu

spring rains ...
every thing transformed
exquisitely

Chiyo

blossoms falling,
it has become still:
the human heart

Matsumoto Koyū

the wife
buried in their burrow of snow,
while he hawks coal

Author unnamed

challenge:

ain't that the truth!
ain't that the truth!

response:

horse farts perturb
four or five passengers
aboard the ferry

Wakamatsu

roused by horse farts
to catch a glimpse of
flitting fireflies

Issa

challenge:

beyond a doubt!
beyond a doubt!

response:

loan shark
lying in wait outside
the pawnshop

Author unnamed

valley stream:
stones too do songs croon
'neath mountain blooms!

Onitsura

willow, bare
clear stream, dry stones
here and there

Buson

hands pressed down
offering up a song –
the frog!

Sōkan

old pond!
a frog plunges into
watersound

Bashō

philandering ways –
laying off them deflates
his manliness!

Author unnamed

nobody ever
glances behind himself
in wintry rain

Author unnamed

for a beauty
forty is from head to toe
hideous

Author unnamed

from forty
when looking in the mirror
one is galled!

Author unnamed

in my handglass
begrudging the departing spring
all alone

                                                            Seibi

with great ardour
the freed bird flies smack into
the great arbour!

                                                    Author unnamed

white heron
manoeuvring legs as though
the paddy were unclean

                                                    Author unnamed

hew hew!
howls the wind through the sky –
winter peonies

                                                            Onitsura

one by one
praising and withdrawing inside –
winter moon

                                                            Senjō

winter orb:
admired then shut out
with a slam

Author unnamed

luminescent
yet completely shut out –
winter moon

Ryūichi

winter moon!
pebbles felt beneath the sole
of one's shoe

Buson

wintry river ...
from the trudging ferrymen,
nary a melody

Goyō

cool breeze
breathing deeply into my mouth
a bush mosquito!

Issa

smoked out
by the next-door neighbour –
bush mosquitoes!

Issa

challenge:

beyond one's control!
beyond one's control!

response:

the widow first off
feels lonesome at the emptiness
of the bed netting

Ōkubo

struggling to rise,
to sleep, in searching . . . our bed netting's
desolateness!

Ukihashi

diddle weary
Chiyo concocted that bug verse
by a stroke of luck!

Chikuga

sleeping alone
beneath mosquito netting
the wife fuming

Useki

challenge:

obsessed with the old in-and-out!
obsessed with the old in-and-out!

response:

the mosquito speaketh:
'can't even sneak a peep,
damn paper netting!'

Author unnamed

bed netting up,
even mosquitoes are delightful,
flitting in moonlight

Baishitsu

the net that screws not
the mosquitoes screwing her –
swatting all to hell!

Rekisen

swarm of mosquitoes –
fed full with the blood of
fed-up meditators!

Taigi

mosquito swatting –
the covers of a war epic,
stained with blood!

Shiki

poised to retreat,
driving off a yellowjacket
with a book of verse

Amenbō

riled up
by the shears' bare blades:
hornets!

Shirao

bumblebee,
having chased off some person,
returns to its blooms

Taigi

the maidservant
slept right past their rendezvous
deeply in her cups

Author unnamed

challenge:

given the cold shoulder,
bored alone in bed

response:

feigning sleep,
then losing sleep before
falling asleep for real!

Shōsui

from snowy slumber
bamboo trees shaken awake:
morning sun

Nyoshun

challenge:

how devious!
how devious!

response:

to awaken
a late-morning riser
just say it's midday!

Author unnamed

challenge:

looking frightened
out of one's wits!

response:

a tall tale –
the remedy to cut short
the hiccoughs!

Shōjin

challenge:

wanting both to slash
and not to slash

response 1:

that branch
of blossoms concealing
the dazzling moon!

Author unnamed

response 2:
that housebreaker
caught and unmasked:
my own kid!

Sōkan

the sneak thief
apprehended, his mother
stops shrieking

Kinchō

'lock up tightly
before sleeping!' repeated,
leaving to thieve

Author unnamed

to his wife:
'lock up tightly before sleeping!'
leaving for a job

Author unnamed

'lock up tightly
before sleeping ... with me!'
the widow's depravity

Author unnamed

challenge:

jumping right out!
jumping right out!

response:

more beguiling
than that stunning face:
her put-ons!

Author unnamed

challenge:

finally settled down!
finally settled down!

response:

from this day on
she makes herself up
for one man only

Author unnamed

challenge:

how despicable!
how despicable!

response:

the Dear Jane letter,
upon closer inspection,
in a *woman*'s hand!

Ryūmon

challenge:

a pleasant surprise!
a pleasant surprise!

response:

had it been a dream
her comb would have no business
being here for real

                                                           Author unnamed

challenge:

the prank of poking a hole
in the paper sliding-door

response:

'once crawling, stand!
and once standing, run!'
parental love

                                                                      Chōryū

challenge:

a secret that must be kept!
a secret that must be kept!

response:

'bumper crop!'
lyrics not to leave the mouth
in peasant songs

                                                                      Suisen

rice-planting chant –
not one single aggrievement
goes unaddressed!

Issa

challenge:

an extreme grudge
followed by disgrace!

response:

the letter snatched
out of his wife's hands
... from her mother!

Suiha

challenge:

looking forward to it!
looking forward to it!

response:

unblackened teeth
and a blank slate of hair –
delightful Miss Carte Blanche!

Fūso

sooner or later
down and dirty in white makeup –
the widow's face!

Tōjin

for all people
the seed of daytime napping:
summer moon!

Teitoku

Matsunaga Teitoku (1571–1653)

sold filially
into slavery though redeemed
unfilially

                                        Author unnamed

the lucre
for selling his daughter
gone in a flash!

                                        Author unnamed

the follow-up *ah
choo!* for which one is braced
goofy-faced

                                        Rekisen

challenge:

now that's unavoidable!
now that's unavoidable!

response:

exasperation
occasionally makes the face
a work of art

                                        Author unnamed

some blokes
imbibing their winter coats
bundle up with drink!

Author unnamed

crying out
in the driving rain
as though slain

Kibun

the rain lets up
yet still just as expected
the same heat!

Keira

what rumbling!
rat-grey thunderclouds rouse
summer from slumber

Ichū

rumbling thunder
heard off in the distance
of the night heat

Ganshitsu

without a moon
to cool down the day –
the night heat!

Rōsen

irregular shape
clothiers' secret jargon
for a rare beauty

Sakakidori

'monthly visitor'
the pillow word a woman
can rest her head on

Kinsai

snagging his clog
with that seeing eye of a stick,
the blindman triumphs

Teika

his seeing eyes ...
yet still he itches to whip
his dog with his stick!

Sesshū

harvest moon ...
a blindman running smack into me
bursts out laughing!

Buson

arrived at the blossoms!
seems like people are laughing
upon springtime hill

Mōichi

'they've bloomed!'
relishing plums with his nose,
a blind bloke

Author unnamed

rent asunder
by the sound of footsteps:
their silhouette

Kakō

the wind blows,
twining and untwining
willowstrands

Gessonsai Sōseki

tree-withering gust
reaching its ultimate end:
sound of the ocean

Gonsui

tree-withering gust
reaching its ultimate end:
firewood for a hut!

Shūba

tumultuous seas!
stretched out to Sado Isle,
the River of Heaven

Bashō

how sublime!
through holes in the paper door
the River of Heaven

Issa

cold the wind ...
through tattered paper doors,
a godless moon

Sōkan

stars on the pond ...
again the pitter-pattering
freezing drizzle

Hokushi

some starlight
spared from being scooped up –
four-handed net

Kinsha

in morning haze
a breeze yearned for and yet ...
boat upon the moon!

Baisei

spring rain –
the belly of a frog
not yet wet

Buson

sunlight on snow ...
the price of oil for desk lamps
falls in Cathay!

Muchō

the ninth shogun –
with his demise dog poison
spiked in price

Author unnamed

short-sighted,
a centipede chatting up
a real louse

Author unnamed

as though his own,
the cashier makes change
grudgingly

Bunshō

uttered drunk,
true feelings the morning after
turn into lies

Sennosuke

those boozers
with the most perverse quirks
compose verse!

Author unnamed

within *Who's Who*
nowhere is it written
'dances when sloshed!'

                                                                    Saika

completely different:
one's expression when playing
or paying

                                                                    Shigetsune

at a pawnshop
falling in love sight unseen –
summer clothes airing

                                                                    Ryūge

on a lone pole
white belly-cutting attire!
midsummer airing

                                                                    Kyoriku

challenge:

everything in moderation!
everything in moderation!

response:
he who hangs himself
over spiteful remarks:
a real numbskull!

Author unnamed

facing Yoshiwara,
a working stiff from Ueno
hanging by the neck

Author unnamed

'wonder if
I talked in my sleep?'
says Rosei

Author unnamed

mortified
Urashima Tarō
chomped his gums

Wari

Urashima –
his buttocks riddled
with hexagons!

Tsukuda

Urashima's cock
must've shrivelled up
on the spot!

Kinsui

Urashima's wife
upon his homecoming:
'and you would be . . . ?'

Muho

my hometown:
however misted over,
still grotesque

Issa

hitting rock bottom
everyone helps each other –
that's humanity

Nokōrō

giving up his seat
only when disembarking –
whatta guy!

Ryūsei

ticket window
our kid suddenly grows one year
younger

Author unnamed

childless
contemplating a seascape
the aged couple

Deirei

sleeping together
their copious dream was for
their child's prosperity

Tessen

the bureaucrat's tot
learns about grabby-grabby
an awful lot!

Author unnamed

one's shadow
reaching the ceiling of rank
breaks bad!

Gosei

rustic samurai!
muckin' around now more in paddies
than with poetry

Author unnamed

even walls have *mouths*!
prospering imperial reign
of the telephone

Author unnamed

telegraph pole
toppled down by
the tempest

Shiki

photographers eat
by capturing and roasting
their clientele!

Fukui Junko

summer grass!
in the wake of dreams
of legion warriors

Bashō

Nakazu today!
in the wake of dreams
of legion partiers

Chikushi

in such snow!
the footprints remain
of legion drivellers

Tagyo

the Milky Way ...
the sieging camp far below
comes into view!

Shiki

the rose mallow
gracing the side of the road –
devoured by my horse!

Bashō

challenge:

now that's crowded!
now that's crowded!

response:

a tie post
facing the cheap-eats joint –
devoured by my horse!

Author unnamed

unwell on the road
dreams running rampant
o'er withered moors!

Bashō

unwell in the head
running rampant in dreams
o'er red-light whores!

Richō

challenge:

a real laugh, *but ...*
a real laugh, *but ...*

response:

head over heels
from behind and yet head-on
dead in one's tracks!

Author unnamed

challenge:

giggling and yet ...
giggling and yet ...

response:

the house burglar
overhearing sweet nothings
sticks out his tongue

Author unnamed

'never hang out
with that pecker!' say the fathers
of both peckers

Author unnamed

challenge:

called out to play ...
called out to play ...

response:

their friendship
does not at all please
their fathers

Author unnamed

Vixen Isle spunk:
dildos fashioned out of fans
from the Shady Shop

Ryūsha

Vixen Isle –
so much as sneeze and *wham bam*
the midwife's summoned

Author unnamed

challenge:

suddenly it's clear!
suddenly it's clear!

response:

the doctor
takes Kiyomori's pulse
buck naked

Author unnamed

New Year's greetings
exchanged in a bathhouse
butt naked

Author unnamed

New Year's day
even next-door neighbours
stand on ceremony

Yamaki

in want of laughs
a New Year's comic duo
gets one laughing!

Kijaku

laughing loudly
that the loneliness
might be forgotten

Chigusa

as peonies bloom
Christian icons get trampled
at Pure Land temples

Shiki

crowned by both
setting moon and rising sun –
the peony!

Ōemaru

yellow mustardblooms!
moon to the east
sun to the west

Buson

yellow mustardblooms!
not even whales in the offing
of a sea gone dark

Buson

upon a world
of yellow mustardblooms,
the setting sun!

Tantan

even the kerchief
worn during a migraine –
woebegone!

Author unnamed

second night of the year –
a new flurry of nightmares
the dream beast devours

Kinga

for dream beasts
the second night of the year
is New Year's Eve!

Izutsu

'better not turn into a butterfly!'
says the dream beast
about to chow down

Kizui

when there appear
phoenixes and unicorns,
dream beasts get thin

Banjin

dreams of Mount Fuji
get divvied up evenly
among dream beasts

Author unnamed

embroidered ballads
set women's idle grumblings
to sweet music

Author unnamed

shrine gate
run aground on the riverbank
or so it seems

Monryū

challenge:

how singular!
how singular!

response:

King of Hell
calls in Sniffing Nose
to buy mackerel

Author unnamed

challenge:

although it came off well ...
although it came off well ...

response:

getting loose in bed
nothing's so interminable
as a sash!

Author unnamed

upon the golden screen
whose negligee could this be?!
– autumn breeze

Buson

the young master
smutty prints his handbook
practising strokes!

Author unnamed

Sukeroku
hidden beneath her skirts
diddles away

Bunchi

Full-page spread from *Willow Vat's Exposé of 'The Treasury of Loyal Retainers'* (c.1830–44). In this famous scene, Yuranosuke reads a letter scroll – also read by Kudayū, crawling beneath the veranda – while Okaru raises her hand to shield herself from the sword of her brother, Heiemon

Willow Vat's Exposé of
'The Treasury of Loyal Retainers'

Originally appearing in *Yanagidaru* 50 (1811). The following eight verses were later gathered together in *(Naniwa miyage) Chūshingura anasagashi yanagidaru* or Willow Vat's Exposé of 'The Treasury of Loyal Retainers': Souvenirs from Naniwa (*c.* 1830–44). This woodblock-printed comicbook was a sophisticated adaptation, told through *senryū* originally appearing in *Yanagidaru* (Willow Vat) and elsewhere, of the perennial favourite kabuki and puppet play about the forty-seven masterless samurai (*rōnin*), entitled *Kanadehon chūshingura* (The Treasury of Loyal Retainers; first performed in 1748 as a puppet play).

The play, using fictional names to sidestep government censorship, dramatized a sensational real-life event that shocked the nation. Known as the Akō Incident (*akō jiken*) of 1701, the honourable lord of Akō domain, Asano, unsheathed his sword in the shogun's castle in Edo in indignant response to being forced to bribe an official, one Kira Yoshinaka. Although Kira was never seriously reprimanded, Lord Asano was ordered to commit mutually assisted suicide (*seppuku*) for his breach of conduct. Nearly four dozen of his loyal samurai retainers, led by the intrepid Ōishi Kuranosuke, allowed their lord's death to go unavenged for nearly two years, as though they had decided to let bygones be bygones. Suddenly one night, most of the retainers stormed the fortress of their nemesis Kira, cut him down, placed his severed head as an offering before the memorial to their dead lord and then, having at long last satisfied their blood vendetta, turned themselves in, eventually taking their own lives honourably.

The image shown here, featuring verses from *Yanagidaru* 50 (1811), depicts the play's celebrated letter-reading scene in which the hero Ōboshi Yuranosuke (the fictional name of Ōishi Kuranosuke) reads a letter scroll about the secret vendetta. Unbeknown to him, others are reading the letter too. Okaru, a young married woman who has allowed herself to be sold into a brothel so that her husband can raise the money to join the vendetta, reads the letter backwards in her mirror from a second-floor balcony (not pictured here). Simultaneously, the

treacherous Ono Kudayū, who has literally sold out his comrades,
manages to read the scroll by crawling beneath the veranda,
where Yuranosuke is standing. When Okaru drops her hairpin,
Yuranosuke realizes she has read the letter and therefore must die.
Before he can cut her down, Okaru's brother and loyal retainer
Heiemon (pictured here) offers to kill her himself, whereupon
Yuranosuke decides to spare Okaru. Realizing someone else has
also read the letter, however, Yuranosuke drives his sword through
the veranda, killing Kudayū.

dead drunk
on the outside though deep within
cold sober!

Author unnamed

playing drunk –
the very mirror of this age
of decadence!

Sokō

strike the enemy
just like striking a gong –
that's the plan!

Kokusui

her hairpin
smack-dab between loyalty
and betrayal

Shukō

Heiemon
makes a terrible demand
of his sister

Ryōju

Kudayū,
hopeful there's silver in it,
gets his hands dirty!

Hantō

Kudayū
treading with his palms
on cat shit!

Tōjin

samurai dog
fated to fall underneath
the veranda!

Shidō

[End of *Willow Vat's Exposé of
'The Treasury of Loyal Retainers'*]

pinch her booty
and a maid will brandish
rice-bran hands

Author unnamed

salted rice-bran broth:
with just one gulp losing weight
in the wallet

Rakuho

'first cicada!'
no sooner thus proclaimed than
it takes a leak

Issa

those who piss and run:
kept women,
cicadas

Rekisen

thunder letting up,
sunset shining on one tree
where cry cicadas

Shiki

woodpecker
upon its one little speck
the sun sets

Issa

brocade weaving ...
only a single dragon
and the day darkens

Author unnamed

challenge:

her raiment of mist
moistened at the hems

response:

Princess Sao
springing up and spreading wide
makes peepee!

Sōkan

Princess Sao
swaying, softly, pissing down
the spring rains!

Teitoku

divinely appearing
upon Luxuriant Reed Plain
His thang dang-a-lang!

Shuchin

high priest
in withered fields piously
taking a crap

Buson

even monks
cannot help but ogle
lady flowers

Shigeyori

stunning nun –
several souls get turned on
to religion

Author unnamed

with fingertips
searching for scenic spots –
wide bush pilgrimage

Yashū

as a rule
nothing tastes quite like
poontang

Sekishi

for the master,
it's a boy, for his wife,
a girl!

Tōgan

challenge:

ah, how sweet – and yet ...
ah, how sweet – and yet ...

response:

stretching out
as far as Two Hole street blocks –
the widow's pride

Author unnamed

first husband dead
so all the way to Dandytown
for a dandy time

Author unnamed

women, men –
everybody serviced just dandy
in Dandytown

Author unnamed

when craving cock
a widow will head off
to Dandytown

Mokubō

just like a clit
bareback riding a dick –
Kindaka's sensation!

☁

a maidservant
would have him do *her*
all ninety-nine nights

Kinshi

outta one hole
but thanks to another hole
into one more hole!

Author unnamed

outta one hole
all the way into another hole
thanks to another hole!

Author unnamed

born of a hole
fooling around with a hole
buried in a hole!

Aryū

how amusing!
the word 'hole' rubbed raw
with red ink

Konojo

cherries pink
folks moving in and out –
mound's opening

Ginkō

on the threshold
of the cherry-red home
a thick bush

Kisenjo

at her barred gate
the roaming monk tried his hand
every which way

Oei

floating world –
newspapers unearth its loopholes
with the pen!

Author unnamed

newspapers
serve as karmic mirrors
of the world

Author unnamed

shining the light
on social enlightenment –
electric lamps!

Author unnamed

civilized skies
stretching out into writing
gone sideways

Author unnamed

even love letters
by civilized young ladies
in block style!

Author unnamed

beefsteak
as well as Western languages –
just a *soupçon*!

Author unnamed

when all else fails,
the interpreter resorts
to hand gestures

Busui

socialism:
nothing up and running
except taverns!

Sakai Kuraki

insufferable
even for politicians –
women's suffrage!

Author unnamed

misconstruing
libertarianism ...
the widow's looseness!

Author unnamed

Buddha Colossus
batting not an eye
under hailstones!

Shiki

no telling
its head from its ass –
the sea slug

Kyorai

heaven and earth:
neither exists apart from
snow fluttering down

Hashin

sky cleared up,
they share a single hue:
moon and snow

Matsumoto Koyū

winter moon!
above a gateless temple,
heaven's vastness

Buson

autumn wind –
for me there are no gods,
no buddhas

Shiki

from first
to final cleansing tub:
all gobbledygook!

Author unnamed

from first
to final cleansing tub –
all a dream!

Author unnamed

from first
to final cleansing tub –
a mere fifty years!

Zeraku

from first
to final cleansing tub –
one long dream!

Sajisuke

in all eternity
there's less pain and suffering
than just this one life

Senkyō

even the pine
I planted has grown ancient –
autumnal twilight

Issa

this very autumn
how could I have grown so old?
a bird unto clouds

Bashō

Commentary

This section contains notes on the English translations of the verses (highlighted in bold and arranged in a single line in which the phrases are divided by slashes), with a transliteration of the original Japanese verse in italics beneath. The transliterations are listed alphabetically, according to the first word, in the Index of Japanese Verses. For information on the modern editions of the original verses, see Sources of the Japanese Verses. Any bibliographical details that do not appear in the Sources are otherwise provided in the individual notes. Abbreviations to reference works in Japanese are explicated in the List of Abbreviations. For more on the specific terms, works and proper names that appear in the Introduction and elsewhere, including the dates of the poets when known, see Glossary of Terms and Glossary of Poets.

The Washbasin Sequence

Previous translations of *Sarumino* include: Cana Maeda (trans.), *Monkey's Raincoat* (New York: Mushinsha/Grossman, 1973); Earl Miner and Hiroko Odagiri (eds and trans.), *The Monkey's Straw Raincoat and Other Poetry of the Bashō School* (Princeton, NJ: Princeton University Press, 1981); and Lenore Mayhew (trans.), *Monkey's Raincoat (Sarumino): Linked Poetry of the Bashō School with Haiku Selections* (Rutland, VT, and Tokyo: Charles E. Tuttle, 1985).

initiating stanza (hokku):
the washbasin's / drip-dripping gives way to / crickets chirping!
akuoke no / shizuku yamikeri / kirigirisu
> Bonchō. The autumn scene is set outside, where a washbasin (*akuoke*) has been dripping (*shizuku*), after having been used or because a rain shower has let up. With the gradual cessation of the dripping, one

realizes that chirr-chirring crickets (*kirigirisu*) – and the autumn they symbolize – are suddenly present, or perhaps have been present all along.

second stanza (*wakiku*):
with oil burning low / an early-to-bed autumn
abura kasurite / yoine suru aki
 Bashō. Listening to the crickets and thinking plaintively about autumn, the speaker is now indoors, where the lantern is a mere flicker, continuing the idea of cessation of the dripping in the previous verse. This is also the second verse in a row to end with a noun. Even though the second verse of a sequence (*wakiku*) is not typically considered a modern haiku, since being a fourteen-syllabet *tanku* it lacks the requisite seventeen syllabets, it is nevertheless a *haiku*. The echo of *aki* (autumn) in the *waki* of *wakiku* may be a kind of self-reflexive gag.

third stanza (*daisan*):
fresh new straw mats, / having just been installed, / in the moonlight!
aradatami / shiki narashitaru / tsukikage ni
 Yasui. With the dimming of the lantern in the preceding stanza, our eyes can now adjust to the beautiful glimmer of moonlight upon fresh new straw mats (*aradatami*), slightly green in hue and, synaesthetically, green in scent. The moonlight in this rural abode, perhaps newly constructed, where a person of refined if eccentric taste has come to dwell, is most elegant. Just as the speaker in the previous verse is early to bed, so too is the moon early to rise in this, the third verse (*daisan*) – two stanzas ahead of its usual position in the fifth verse – in what amounts to another self-reflexive gag.

fourth stanza:
delighted to have set out / five pairs of saké cups
narabete ureshi / tō no sakazuki
 Kyorai. The link with the previous stanza is tenuous, but may involve the feeling of anticipation befitting something new. The season being obscure, this fourteen-syllabet 'ordinary verse' (*hiraku*) is also a miscellaneous verse (*zatsu no ku*), allowing the sequence to pivot into a new season. The occupant of this house is pleased to host a small gathering of some kind, even though not a large banquet – perhaps not unlike a *haikai*-composing party? – and this amounts to a kind of overt challenge for the composer of the next stanza.

fifth stanza:

here's wishing / a millennium of sundries gathered – / New Year's feast

chiyo fubeki / mono o samazama / nenobi shite

Bashō. *Chiyo fubeki mono* refers to those things that one wishes would last a thousand years. Here, this serves not just to refer to young pine trees, but as a toast among guests at a New Year's party, thereby responding to the challenge of the previous stanza. *Nenobi* (also *nenohi*), a season word (*kigo*) associated with the New Year and the coming spring, is the annual ritual of collecting herbs and pulling out young pine trees by the roots. The feeling of delight in the previous stanza is continued here in the well-wishing. Normally in linked verse, the moon is supposed to appear in the fifth stanza, but since the moon arose early, in the third stanza, Bashō must refrain from mentioning it again here.

sixth stanza:

first song of the bush warbler / even as snow flutters down

uguisu no ne ni / tabira yuki furu

Bonchō. The song of the *uguisu* – the Japanese nightingale or bush warbler (*Horornis diphone*) – is heard in early spring. *Tabira* refers to the soft fluttering of a thin light snow. By coupling this bird with the New Year's food gathering of the previous verse, Bonchō alludes to a well-known verse by Saigyō: 'while collecting herbs and pines / through the mist / trailing on the moors / one hears the cry / of the first bush warbler!' (*nenohi shi ni / kasumi tanabiku / nobe ni dete / hatsu uguisu no / koe o kiku kana*; quoted in *NKBZ* 32, p. 478; the verse appears in Saigyō's anthology *Sankashū* (Mountain Home Anthology, *c*. late Heian period)).

seventh stanza:

reaching a gallop, / upper-arm strength no match for / the spring colt

noridashite / kaina ni amaru / haru no koma

Kyorai. The young 'spring colt' (*haru no koma*) galloping through spring fields, presumably with great vigour, befits the seventh stanza where momentum needs to pick up. This vigorousness makes for a lovely contrast with the gently fluttering snow and first song of the warbler of the previous stanza. This verse implies that although the rider is about to bring the colt to full speed, he is no match for the animal's power. Were this verse plucked out of this context, one might suppose that Kyorai himself were galloping along, though in reality he would have been inside relaxing, perhaps sipping saké.

eighth stanza:
atop Mount Maya / clouds hang about
maya-ga-takane ni / kumo no kakareru

Yasui. Another miscellaneous verse, one alluding obliquely to robust warriors and the colts they ride. The mountain peak, near present-day Kobe, is associated with the famous military attack of the Genji against the Heike at a stronghold there during the battle of Ichi-no-tani in the twelfth century, where the seasoned warrior Kumagae killed the young general Atsumori. Also, an annual event held in early spring at a temple there involves colts. The clouds atop the mountain peak resemble, in a visual pun (*mitate*), a rider astride his horse. If so, then this verse may well humorously recast the rider of the previous stanza (if not its poet?) as white-haired with old age, thereby explaining why his arm strength is no match for the young colt – and why we suddenly have slowed down to the pace of clouds hovering about a mountain. In this interpretation, the *ni*, 'atop', may also function as 'like' (*no yō ni*).

ninth stanza:
when supping / on fried lancefish / fragrant the wind
yūmeshi ni / kamasugo kueba / kaze kaoru

Bonchō. From the clouds hanging over Mount Maya in the previous verse, perhaps now threatening a summer squall, we move down to a humble scene by the shore. As a sweet-smelling summer breeze wafts across the strand, the speaker enjoys a dish of fried, previously dried, lancefish (*kamasugo*), a kind of cheap food associated with the Osaka area near Kobe.

tenth stanza:
scratching leech bites – / a feeling of relief
hiru no kuchido o / kakite kimi yoki

Bashō. Water leeches (*hiru*), no doubt picked up unwittingly while catching the lancefish of the previous stanza, are associated with summer, evening squalls and rice planting. *Kuchido*, literally 'mouthed spot', was contemporary slang for the part of the body bitten by an insect.

eleventh stanza:
putting behind / all those preoccupations – / day off from service
monoomoi / kyō wa wasurete / yasumu hi ni

Yasui. A miscellaneous verse. Whereas relief in the previous stanza was obtained by scratching leech bites, here it is had by taking time off work, with all its preoccupations (*monoomoi*). This is a striking re-figuring of the term *monoomi*, which classically had denoted lovelorn yearning.

twelfth stanza:
return at once! / missive from her man
mukae sewashiki / tono yori no fumi

Kyorai. Another miscellaneous verse, though this 'missive' (*fumi*) be-ing understood as a love letter, Kyorai deliberately reinterprets the preoccupation of the previous verse as the 'love' that it avoided. The 'return!' (*mukae*) orders the subject of the verse not only to go back to her man, but also to reciprocate his love.

thirteenth stanza:
for he who is dubbed / the feudal lord's golden boy / life must be a cinch
kintsuba to / hito ni yobaruru / mi no yasusa

Bashō. The 'man' of the previous verse is reinterpreted here as a feudal lord. A 'golden flange' (*kintsuba*) is a sword guard of gold rather than mere steel, more to dazzle than to protect, thereby suggesting some-thing more showy than functional. This affectation began during the early 1600s, but was outlawed in the sumptuary regulations of the Kanbun era (1660s–70s). The term also suggested a samurai who was his lord's favourite, or else a chief retainer who accompanies a young prince.

[End of 'The Washbasin Sequence']

show benevolence / and they'll crap all over you! / baby sparrows
jihi sureba / hako o suru nari / suzume no ko

Issa. Apart from the comic disparity between highfalutin and vulgar, there is the ironic message that no good deed goes unpunished. The reference to 'benevolence' or 'mercy' (*jihi*) here suggests that what is covered in bird droppings (*hako*) is a stone buddha or, more precisely, Kannon, the so-called goddess of mercy.

this life: / chowing down, shitting and then / flowery spring!
yo no naka wa / kūte hakoshite / hana no haru

Jūkō. Alludes to a celebrated verse widely attributed to Ikkyū Sōjun (1394–1481): 'this life – / eating, shitting, / sleeping, rising / and after that / death' (*yo no naka wa / kūte hakoshite / nete okite / sate sono ato wa / shinuru narikeri*).

cherries abloom! / and every which way the fields / all shit and piss
hana saku ya / sokora wa noguso / noshōben
Issa. The combination of crowds of people and saké at cherry-blossom parties often gives rise to uninhibited behaviour and the need for 'outdoor relief' (*noshōben*). Although blossoms and faeces seem polar opposites, night soil ultimately helps make the ground fertile for future trees.

amid the fields – / oblivious to all things / skylarks sing
haranaka ya / mono nimo tsukazu / naku hibari
Bashō.

the cowherd / felled flat upon his ass! / skylark rising
ushikai o / ketsumazukaseru / agehibari
Kenkabō. The herdsman, who has complete control over his cows, is knocked flat onto his backside by the sudden flight of a small skylark (*Alauda arvensis*).

pheasant's rise / does a body surprise – / withered moor
kiji tatte / hito odorokasu / kareno kana
Issa.

wind at his back / harvesting pampas grass – / an old man
oikaze ni / susuki karitoru / okina kana
Buson. *Susuki*, Japanese pampas grass (*Miscanthus sinensis*), which is native to China and other parts of East Asia as well as Japan, grows near rivers and mountain plains.

first winter drizzle – / permeating the whole world, / lightly linked verse
hatsushigure / haikai rufu no / yo narikeri
Issa.

smug-faced / over this New Year's stanza / the light-verse master
saitan o / shitarigao naru / haikaishi
Buson. *Saitan*, literally 'New Year's day', was shorthand for *saitanbira-ki*, a gathering in which a linked-verse master composes the first verse of the New Year with his or her students – or the collection emanating from such a session. *Saitan o* was the title of the collection by Buson

and his students in which this very verse appeared. The word *shitari* in *shitarigao* is a pivot (*kakekotoba*) between the two phrases *saitan o shitari*, 'doing a New Year's poetry session' and *shitarigao*, 'smug-faced'.

as the year recedes / no gifts from others received – / Oh this night!
toshi kurete / hito mono kurenu / koyoi kana

Sōkan. This verse has gained notoriety as typifying the fatuous word-play above which Sōkan and other early pioneers of *haiku* were allegedly incapable of rising. Yet there is more to their versifying than such verbal pyrotechnics as punning *kurete* (closes) and *kurenu* (receives not). Wit being the hallmark of *haiku*, this verse engages in the tongue-in-cheek, drama-queen-like self-mockery of a supposedly lonesome linked-verse master who, not receiving the customary New Year's gifts from his students, must content himself with such strained puns. On the contrary, not only would his students have showered him with presents, but the teasing pose of loneliness was belied by their presence in the linked-verse session in which this very verse was composed.

after receiving / the New Year's well-wisher: / *who the hell was that?!*
nenrei o / ukete ima no wa / dare datta

Author unnamed.

some people! / teeth being praised, / rue their ears!
ha ga ii to / homereba mimi o / munengari

Author unnamed.

no need for alarm! / inevitably precedes / need for alarm
ki ni wa kake- / rare na to kakeru / koto o ii

Gansui. In *Yanagidaru* 24 (1791). Some verses in the *senryū* mode are so aphoristic they virtually ensure their own entrance into proverbial wisdom. An example of verse straddling (*kumatagari*).

over the clap! / right before one's nose / bloomin' wilts
supparito / naorimashita to / hana ga ochi

Author unnamed. In *Yanagidaru* 16 (1781). A burlesque of the poetic cliché 'fallen blossom' (*hana ga ochi*) to refer to the 'collapsed nose' of late-stage syphilis (and not gonorrhea per se), a disease that left untreated seems to clear up temporarily (when the bacteria become dormant) before progressively worsening, causing the cartilage in the bridge of the nose to disintegrate. Although the related term 'saddle nose' (*hanakuta*) typically referred to afflicted prostitutes, male clients were by no means immune from the condition.

hush-hushedly / concealing his sunstroke – / cure-all salesman
gokunai de / kakuran o suru / jōsaiuri
Yūkō. In *Yanagidaru* 52 (1811). The pun on *kakuran*, 'conceal' and 'sunstroke', is aptly applied here to cure-all salesmen, known for summertime peddling of their wares, which they advertised by loud rattle-shaking.

challenge:
ain't that a shame! / ain't that a shame!
aware narikeri / aware narikeri

response:
though on the mend / still accepting get-well gifts, / his latest vice
yamiagari / itadaku koto ga / kuse ni nari
Author unnamed. In *Yanagidaru* 1 (1765). Appeared earlier in *Mutamagawa* 6 (1754) (in *NYC* 8, p. 115). No doubt it was some other kind of bad habit (*kuse*) that led to his broken health in the first place.

staving off death / on account of some gold coins / under the mattress
shi ni kaneru / futon no shita ni / nisan ryō
Gosen. In *Yanagidaru* 23 (1789).

nothing but faces / taking it for granted / they'll go on living
itsumademo / ikiteiru ki no / kao bakari
Shinpei.

disregarding death / all of us nevertheless / must die
shinu koto o / wasureteitemo / minna shini
Bentenshi.

truly believing / there's always a tomorrow / we all rest in peace
asu ari to / shinjite minna / shin ni tsuki
Author unnamed. *Shin ni tsuki*, 'entering sleep', contains *shinni*, 'verily', which in turn suggests *shi ni*, 'into death'. *Minna* is a less formal way of saying *Mina* (everyone).

wake for the dead – / exaggerated eulogies / and debaucheries!
tsuya no seki / yatara kojin o / homete kui
Fusō. The term *kui* covers a lot of ground, from 'eating' and 'living', to 'making fun of', to 'receiving something unfavourable (literally "to eat the cost")', to the vulgar 'screwing a woman (often for the first time)'.

challenge:
what lechery! / what lechery!
yokubari ni keri / yokubari ni keri

response:
I'd make her / as a hot-to-trot widow! / his doctors contending
yoi goke ga / dekiru to hanasu / isha nakama
Author unnamed. In *Yanagidaru* 5 (1770). Wordplay spices up this wry comment on the universal comic themes of sex, death and cynicism towards doctors. *Dekiru*, 'can be', also means 'do (someone sexually)'. *Hanasu*, 'quip' just as much as 'discuss', has two related homonyms, functioning less syntactically than suggestively: 'release', referring to how the death of the husband – not directly mentioned – would free the wife from the bond of matrimony, making her sexually available; and 'divide', gesturing to the coming disintegration of the apparent unity of this medical team in the free-for-all competition over the affections of this sexy young widow-to-be.

terminally ill / still, tears of gratitude / for the doctor
korosarete / katajikenai mo / isha no rei
Author unnamed. In *Senryūhyō mankuawase* (1757–89).

challenge:
that's life! / that's life!
inochi narikeri / inochi narikeri

response:
smug quacks, / praising the deathbed poem, / beat hasty retreats!
ishashū wa / jisei o homete / tataretari
Author unnamed. In *Yanagidaru* 2 (1767). *Jisei* can mean 'self-restraint' as well as 'death verse' (a verse written in one's final moments, typically on the theme of death), and *tataretari* can mean 'honourably rise to leave' or 'screw things up'. *Yanagidaru shūi* 3 (c.1796–7) has a similar version.

natural causes / suspected along with / that quack doctor!
jumyō to wa / omoedo yabuisha / to mo omoi
Usui. The extra syllabet of the second line emphasizes that the doctor is a charlatan (*yabuisha*).

that bush doctor! / pushing dogshit onto / his patients
takenoko ga / sashiageteiru / inu no kuso
Bunna. In *Yanagidaru* 164 (1838). Although literally 'the bamboo shoot pushes up a dog turd', this verse has an even less pleasant meaning.

challenge:
suddenly it's clear! / suddenly it's clear!
hatsumeina koto / hatsumeina koto

response:
fresh young widow! / her dearly departed's brother / a tad too concerned
wakagoke wa / hotoke no ani o / urusagari
> Author unnamed. In *Yanagidaru* 7 (1772). Although the husband of this 'young widow' (*wakagoke*) is now a *hotoke*, 'dearly departed' but literally a 'buddha' (thus jibing with *hatsumei*, 'enlightenment', of the challenge), his brother takes the opportunity to behave in a less saintly way.

a true buddha ... / drones the funeral director / mundanely
hotokesama / nado to sōguya / nareta mono
> Shōjuen.

dewy with tenderness, / the high priest's condolences, / delivered slickly
shippori to / oshō no kuyami / nareta mono
> Koun. In *Yanagidaru* 25 (1794). An *oshō* is not only a high priest in various Buddhist sects, but also any master of a trade or an art – here, apparently, including the art of seduction.

slowly but surely / the widow gets sermonized / down the path serpentine
sorosoro to / goke o jahō e / susumekomi
> Author unnamed. In *Yanagidaru* 12 (1777). Stereotype of the susceptible if lusty widow meets the stereotype of the lascivious preacher, who is so devious as not to appear in the verse himself, except, perhaps, in the barely noticeable if phallic guise of the 'serpent' (*ja*) lurking just beneath the shimmering veneer of 'evil' (*ja*). Then again, serpents are also vaginal symbols because of their ability to swallow things whole.

braided up nicely / it gets badly upbraided – / the widow's hair
yoku yū to / waruku yuwareru / goke no kami
> Author unnamed. The *yū*, 'do up (hair)', has a homonym in 'say'. In premodern Japan, a widow was expected to remain faithful to her deceased husband by becoming a celibate 'secular nun' (*goke*, short for *gokeni*, 'house nun') with shaved head. Those who were determined not to follow suit, however, would shave only the back of the head,

putting up the rest of their hair in a special ponytail (not braids or
plaits per se), suggesting their availability for remarriage. The first
two lines, when spoken, can also mean 'speaking seductively / she gets
badly spoken of'.

leaving behind / just enough to be alluring – / the widow's hair
horerareru / hodo wa nokoshite / goke no kami
Author unnamed. In *Yanagidaru* 30 (1804). Appeared earlier in *Sue-
tsumuhana* 3 (1791). Although normally it is the deceased who leaves
a bequeathal, here it is the widow who leaves just enough of her
hair unshaved in the hope of finding new love without also drawing
criticism.

challenge:
upon closer inspection / upon closer inspection
chikazuki ni keri / chikazuki ni keri

response:
a woman / coiffuring up her hair: / setting her sights
kami o yū / toki ni onna wa / me ga suwari
Author unnamed. In *Yanagidaru* 2 (1767). The more closely one ex-
amines a woman at her toilette, the more it seems she is looking at
something more than her own reflection.

though breathtaking / women's coiffures are always / sweltery hot
medetaki mo / onna wa kami no / atsusa kana
Taigi.

widow's conch – / no moment to spare / for tears to dry
goke no bobo / namida no kawaku / hima wa nashi
Wakō. In *Yanagi no hazue* (1835). Wetness is manifest here in the appo-
site opposites of sadness and arousal. The graph can be read as either
bobo or *kai* (as Watanabe glosses it), referring to 'slit' or 'shell' (like a
cowrie) – slang terms for 'vulva' (*EBYHT*, p. 27). The verse burlesques
a *waka* by Lady Sanuki, appearing in the celebrated *Hyakunin isshu*
(One Hundred Poems by One Hundred Poets; initially compiled by
Fujiwara Teika, 1162–1241), that uses the figure of an unseen rock
submerged in water as a metaphor for a sleeve that 'never has even the
time to dry' (*kawaku ma mo nashi*), suggesting limitless sorrow.

plying fingers / as though he were at hand – / the widow's orgasm
waga yubi de / imasu ga gotoku / goke yogari
Ryūsha. In *Yanagi no hazue* (1835). Allowing a grieving widow the

space for sexual self-satisfaction, this verse burlesques a line from the *Analects* of Confucius about 'sacrificing to the spirits as if they were present' (*matsuru koto masu ga gotoku*; *EBKI*, pp. 58–9; see also *EEBT*, pp. 21–2). The full passage (from 3:12) runs: 'Sacrifice implies presence. One should sacrifice to the gods as if they were present. The Master said: "If I do not sacrifice with my whole heart, I might as well not sacrifice"' (in Simon Leys (trans.), *The Analects of Confucius* (New York: W. W. Norton & Company, 1997), p. 12).

a middle finger / trawling for some clit / her gripped clam
nakayubi de / sane o tsutteru / nigiri bobo

Mokubō. In *Yanagi no hazue* (1835). 'Trawling' (*tsutteru*), a slang term for 'diddling' or 'stimulating', is not unrelated to 'gripping' (*nigiri*), which also refers to moulding rice for sushi.

soft douching / with her own fingers / tenderly diddling
onoga te ni / onka de kujiru / no wa koshiyu

Author unnamed. In *Yuki no hana* (*c.*1848–54). As visible in the accompanying image (see p. 18), this female bather does more than merely douche herself, much to the apparent enjoyment of a masturbating voyeur.

should I get drunk / whatever would you do with me? / asks the widow, drinking
yōta nara / dō shinasaru to / goke wa nomi

Author unnamed.

a stabbing chill! / stepping on my dead wife's comb / in our bedroom
mi ni shimu ya / naki tsuma no kushi o / neya ni fumu

Buson. At the heart of this well-known verse lies the phrase 'pierce' (*shimu*) one's soul as much as one's 'body' (*mi*). Just as the comb of the speaker's dead wife – or the autumn chill – violently, perhaps even phallically, penetrates his flesh, with an extra syllabet in the second line no less, so too does her memory abruptly pierce him to the core. Other wordplay includes *kushi*, 'comb', which written differently means 'skewer'; *neya*, referring to the bedroom of a married couple, or an inner sanctum, can also be the colloquial 'ain't'; and *fumu*, 'to tread on', can also mean 'to experience'. As tempting as it might be to conflate the speaker with Buson the poet himself, in real life his wife was quite robust and would go on to outlive him.

withered fields! / from the time of cogon grass, / women's combs
kareno kana / tsubana no toki no / onnagushi
  Saikaku. *Tsubana*, 'cogon grass' (*Imperata cylindrica*), is associated with mid spring. The flower of these reeds appears white and in the shape of a woman's hair comb (*onnagushi*).

eyes sharp / through all the blubbering: / heirloom dividing
nakinagara / manako o kubaru / katamiwake
  Author unnamed. In *Yanagidaru* 13 (1778). One of many verses about the distribution of mementos (*katamiwake*) of the deceased among the surviving family members and relatives.

inconsolably / grabbing the choice items: / dividing the estate
nakinaki mo / ii hō o toru / katamiwake
  Tōri. In *Yanagidaru* 17 (1782).

challenge:
how unfortunate! / how unfortunate!
kinodokuna koto / kinodokuna koto

response:
the aftermath / of dividing the estate: / relations cut off
katamiwake / igo wa inshin / futsū nari
  Author unnamed. In *Yanagidaru* 6 (1771). *Inshin*, 'communications', can also mean 'sexual passion' – in both cases here, presumably between relatives.

challenge:
the secret's out and yet … / the secret's out and yet …
hikari koso sure / hikari koso sure

response:
shares in some brothel: / the late abbot's bequeathal of / a life on the side!
chaya kabu ga / sen sōjō no / katami nari
  Author unnamed. In *Yanagidaru* 7 (1772). In a radical twist on the subject of estate dividing (*katami*), this verse exposes a late abbot as a kind of 'two-faced' (*katami*) performer. This was the 'doubly disguised mendicant actor show' (*katami kawari no monomorai shibai*), a one-man performance popular at the time in which an actor played two roles simultaneously by dressing the left and right sides of his body as different characters. In the context of the pleasure quarters, a *chaya*

is a 'teahouse' of assignation – a place where a male client could enjoy refreshments and entertainment while waiting for a lower-ranked courtesan to be summoned.

he who refrains / from acclaiming the first snow / amounts to somebody
hatsuyuki o / homenu musuko ga / mono ni nari

Author unnamed. And he who, resisting cliché, composes when his heart is genuinely moved, becomes a poet.

the grand total / of tallywacking off: / now he's the boss!
senzuri o / kaki-ōseta ga / shihainin

Sankō. In *Yanagi no hazue* (1835). The irony is that masturbation (*senzuri*, literally 'thousand rubs'), typically regarded as a matter of a *lack* of self-control, in this case turns out to be the opposite, allowing a shop assistant or bookkeeper to get ahead by virtue of not wasting his time with romantic entanglements.

strictly jacking off / to the daughter of his boss / did he get wed!
ategaki mo / chigawazu shū no / muko ni nari

Futomaru. In *Yanagi no hazue* (1835). It was precisely *because* he masturbated to (*ategaki*) his boss's daughter unerringly (*chigawazu*), rather than playing around with multiple partners, that he ended up marrying her – and into the family business.

first to expose / the bridegroom's perversity: / her kid sis!
muko no kuse / imoto ga saki e / mitsuke dashi

Author unnamed. In *Yanagidaru 2* (1767). On the surface, the humour of this verse is that the bride's younger sister divulges the groom's perversity (*kuse*) – perhaps his inability to keep his hands off young girls? Or boys? Or himself? Still, it is possible that what is really being exposed is the *bride's* quirk of not acknowledging to herself her groom's proclivities. Kanda, however, citing the cool detachment of the younger sister, suggests the verse is a character study of an unmarried girl's interest in the opposite sex (*EST*, p. 298).

challenge:
bit by bit by bit by bit / bit by bit by bit by bit
shidai shidai ni / shidai shidai ni

response 1:
'now I see! / it's my resemblance to *her* / he sees in me!'
ore ni nita / shiru hito no aru / hito sōna

Author unnamed. In Kojui Taiō (ed.), *Urawakaba* (1732). Although the informal first-person pronoun *ore* is masculine in modern Japanese, women used it in premodern Japanese as well.

response 2:
studies and ladders: / skip a step and there's no / moving on up
gakumon to / hashigo wa tonde / noborarezu
   Tōgetsu. In *Yanagidaru shūi* 10 (*c.*1796-7).

well then, adieu! / snow viewing until / tumble, we do!
iza saraba / yukimi ni korobu / tokoro made
   Bashō. A playful verse celebrated for how its breathless exuberance conveys a refined feeling for nature (*fūryū*).

well then, adieu! / drinking in moonlight until / tumble, we do!
iza saraba / tsukimi ni nomeru / tokoro made
   Gochō. In *Yanagidaru* 54 (1811). A parody of Bashō's verse above.

tumbling down / we have known such delight! / this snowy night
korondemo / ureshi ya shirenu / yo no yuki
   Author unnamed. In *Yuki no hana* (*c.*1848-54). Pivoting on *shirenu*, 'has known', in both intellectual and carnal senses, this verse is a loose send-up of Bashō's *iza saraba / yukimi ni korobu / tokoro made*. The associated image (see p. 23) depicts a samurai (with two swords) and a courtesan having a roll in the snow, as a snowman seems to watch on (see *SE*, p. 201). In Japan, snowmen (*yuki daruma*) are modelled on the doll of Bodhidharma (*c.* fifth or sixth century; Daruma in Japanese), an Indian monk in China who founded Chan Buddhism, known in Japan as Zen. Legend has it that Bodhidharma spent nine years in wall-gazing meditation, during which time he not only lost his limbs to atrophy, but also amputated his own eyelids to prevent himself from dozing off. Daruma dolls are made with two blank eyes that are meant to be inked in, the first when making a wish, the second when the wish comes true. Here, both eyes of the snowman are filled in, suggesting a happy ending.

chasing dragonflies . . . / whither my boy this very day / never to return?
tonbotsuri / kyō wa dokomade / itta yara
   Attributed to the nun Chiyo. Supposedly written after the death of her only child, a boy some nine or ten years old.

heat-shimmers – / in my eyes still lingering / his smiling face
kagerō ya / me ni tsukimatō / waraigao

    Issa. Written after the death of his son Ishitarō, only a toddler. Heat-shimmers (*kagerō*), associated with spring and thus young life, here take on a spectral quality. *Tsukimatō* has a double sense of 'lingering' in the eyes as a kind of after-image and of 'tagging along', as dogs or young children are wont to do.

this world of dew … / though a world of dew it remains, / still, even so …
tsuyu no yo wa / tsuyu no yo nagara / sari nagara

    Issa. In *Oraga haru* (Spring of My Life, 1819). A renowned verse on the death of his young daughter. The pointed repetition of *nagara*, 'despite', effectively unravels the meaning of this verse, suggesting the poet's own unravelling. And the haunting repetition of *tsuyu no yo*, 'world of dew', suggesting that the poet cannot quite grasp the reality that has brought him to this point, begs pondering. *Tsuyu*, 'dew', has two not-unrelated sets of associations: first, an image of freshness, beauty and moisture associated with autumn – though, ironically, his daughter was in the springtime of her life and died on the day of the summer solstice; and second, a venerable symbol of Buddhist impermanence, as with a well-known line from the *Diamond Sutra* (*Vajracchedikā Prajñāpāramitā Sūtra* in Sanskrit; *Kongōkyō* in Japanese): 'all conditioned things are like a dream, a phantom, a drop of dew, a lightning flash'. The *sari*, 'thus', in the verse's final phrase *sari nagara*, 'be that as it may', has homonyms in 'leaving' (from *saru*) and in the desiccated 'remains' (also rendered *shari*) of a cremated corpse. Unpacked, the verse seems to be saying: 'Intellectually, I understand the truth that this world is as impermanent as dew, but somehow that insight offers no consolation as I grieve over the charred remains of my beautiful-as-dew young daughter, whose death has shaken me to the core.'

this last year / not for one instant was he / out of my mind
kyonen yori / mono hitotoki mo / wasurarenu

    Onitsura. Nearly mad with grief, Onitsura composed this verse on the first anniversary of the death of his eldest son, Eitarō, in 1700 at the age of six.

this autumn / with no child upon my lap / gazing at the moon
kono aki wa / hiza ni ko no nai / tsukimi kana

    Onitsura.

until last year / scolding over muskmelons / now an offering
kyonen made / shikatta uri o / tamukekeri

Ōemaru. Composed on the first anniversary of the death of his child. It has long been customary in Japan to place before a gravemarker or upon a household altar an offering (*tamuke*) in the form of an object that provided comfort to the departed when he or she was alive.

spring cleaning / turns up a baby doll / bringing tears anon
susuhaki ni / ningyō ga dete / mata nakase

Author unnamed. In *Mutamagawa* 6 (1754).

aboard a ferry / a woman mad with grief – / springtime waters
hirubune ni / kyōjo nosetari / haru no mizu

Buson. The 'madwoman' (*kyōjo*) inconsolable over the death of a child was a stock figure in literature and drama. Here, the torrential 'waters of spring' (*haru no mizu*) suggest her unsettled state of mind, a profusion of tears and the youthfulness of her lost child, if not the actual cause of that loss in the first place.

spring dream ... / not becoming unhinged / is what's unbearable
haru no yume / kigachigawanu ga / urameshii

Raizan. Composed after the death of his only son.

harvest moon / appears to me alone / as darkness
kyō no tsuki / tada kuragari ga / mirarekeri

Raizan. *Kyō no tsuki*, literally 'moon of this day', refers to the harvest moon, known for its luminescence. Grief stricken, Raizan reputedly drank himself blind.

everyone gone ... / in the wake of fireworks / darkness!
hito kaeru / hanabi no ato no / kurasa kana

Shiki.

bottomless pail / thrashed along by a field-threshing / late-autumn gale
soko no nai / oke kokearuku / nowaki kana

Buson. The 'field-sundering' (*nowaki*) windstorm that buffets (*koke*) a discarded bucket so that it appears to stagger along (*aruku*) helter-skelter – acoustically mimicked by *oke koke* – also threshes (*koke*) from the chaff what grain remains in a field (the *no* of *nowaki*) at autumn's end. Although widely reputed as a visual poet, Buson also excelled at sound poetry.

winsome in the wake / of a field-rending tempest: / red capsicum!
utsukushi ya / nowaki no ato no / tōgarashi

Buson. (1776). Standing out vibrantly against the desiccated lifeless-ness, drab colours and stark textures of fields rent asunder by autumnal windstorms are red peppers (*Capsicum annuum*), perhaps with beads of moisture glistening in the sunshine, though with a firm crispness in the ever-so-slight hint of chill in the air. Buson aurally links *utsukushi* (beautiful), *nowaki* ('field-rending' tempest) and *tōgarashi* (capsicum) by their final vowels. Two of these words end in the syllabet *shi*, a hom-onym of 'death', which in turn reverberates with 'wake', the secondary meaning of *ato*, usually implying a more neutral 'afterwards'.

the market profuse / with the odour of things! / summer moon
ichinaka wa / mono no nioi ya / natsu no tsuki

Bonchō. This was followed by a 7-7-syllabet verse taking note of the heat.

foul the market / with the odour of horsepiss – / sweltering heat!
ichi uma no / shito no ka kusaki / atsusa kana

Seki Masafusa. In *Omoigo* (1669).

spring disappears! / birds cry and in each fish eye / drops of tears
yuku haru ya / tori naki uo no / me wa namida

Bashō. In *Oku no hosomichi* (1702). Supposedly written for his dis-ciple Sanpū, who had connections to the fishing industry.

feline eyes! / and beneath the icy surface / fish in a frenzy
neko no me ya / kōri no shita ni / kurū uo

Issa. Singling out those 'ice-cold capricious' (*neko no me*) 'eyes of a cat' (*neko no me*) suggests the lens-like magnification, from the point of view of the fish gone berserk (*kurū*), through the surface of ice.

kingfisher! / with pond water unmuddled, / the fish deeper
kawasemi ya / mizu sunde ike no / uo fukashi

Shiki. *Kawasemi*, literally 'river cicada', is the common kingfisher (*Al-cedo atthis*). *Mizu*, 'water', can also mean 'unseen'. The extra syllabet of the second line reinforces the sense of sudden clarity.

dayspring – / from cormorants sprung free, / young skimming fish
shinonome ya / u o nogaretaru / uo asashi

Buson. Even as the 'fish' (*uo*) break free 'from' (*o*) the 'cormorant' (*u*), they are united by the *u o* and *uo* sounds, the way that *asashi* (shallow) sounds like the *asahi* (morning sun) that is associated with daybreak.

knavish mosquito! / nimbly into an old well, / lying in ambush
abare ka no / tsuito furu i ni / shinobikeri
  Issa. The phrase *abare ka*, 'knavish mosquito', calls to mind *abarekko*, 'naughty child'. *Tsuito*, 'finally', may also suggest *tsuitō*, 'hunting down to kill'. This crafty insect lies in wait at a well in the hope of ambushing some unsuspecting soul too distracted by quenching his or her thirst to swat.

old well ... / a fishleap for mosquitoes / echoes darkly
furuido ya / ka ni tobu sakana / oto kurashi
  Buson. The way that *kurashi* pulls double duty as 'livelihood' as well as 'dark' suggests a paradoxical statement about the mosquito's impending death (even as this verse plays off Bashō's verse about the old pond – *furuike ya / kawazu tobikomu / mizu no oto*).

mosquito wrigglers ... / their puddle drying up / under a blazing sun
bōfuri ya / teru hi ni kawaku / nenashi mizu
  Taigi. *Bōfuri*, also *bōfura*, are mosquito larvae. *Nenashi mizu* (literally 'rootless water') is a body of water that has stopped flowing or otherwise is stagnant.

tree to be felled ... / the bird unaware / builds its nest
kiru ki to wa / shirade ya tori no / su o tsukuru
  Issa.

summer cicadas / wailing so before they've finished / making love
natsu no semi / koi suru hima mo / naki ni keri
  Issa. Embedded within this verse is the phrase *hima mo naki*, 'without free time', referring to the brief lifespan of cicadas.

quiescence! / voices of cicadas / piercing stone
shizukasa ya / iwa ni shimiiru / semi no koe
  Bashō. The cicada (*semi*) emerges only briefly from its thirteen to seventeen years underground, yielding the most enduring symbol of impermanence in Japan other than the cherry blossom. The shrill wail raised by groups of males when courting is deafening, often reaching over one hundred decibels.

on the horizon / no hint of imminent death: / cicadas crying
yagate shinu / keshiki wa mienu / semi no koe
  Bashō. *Keshiki* can mean 'sign' as well as 'landscape'.

in the sumo ring / no hint of imminent defeat: / wrestlers parading
dohyōiri / makeru keshiki wa / mienu nari
> Author unnamed. In *Yanagidaru* 15 (1780). Originally composed in
> 1777. A loose parody of Bashō's verse above. In the *dohyōiri* (ring-
> entering ceremony) wrestlers parade with tremendous bravura. A
> more literal rendering: 'no sign within / the ring-entering ceremony
> / resembling defeat!'

how woeful! / the wail of a cicada / caught by a hawk
ana kanashi / tobi ni toraruru / semi no koe
> Ransetsu. The summer cicada is seized by a *tobi*, a black kite (*Milvus
> migrans*) and not a 'hawk' per se (a winter bird of prey), though the lat-
> ter helps to more closely approximate the sound effects of the original.

springtime woods / even birds of prey / nestled asleep
haru no mori / tori toru tori mo / neburi keri
> Rankō.

caged bird / glaring with envious eyes / at butterflies!
kago no tori / chō o urayamu / metsuki kana
> Issa.

even in the capital, / nostalgia for the capital – / woodland cuckoo
kyō nite mo / kyō natsukashi ya / hototogisu
> Bashō. Although the *hototogisu*, the lesser cuckoo (*Cuculus polioceph-
> alus*), appears in classical poetry (particularly in the travel sections of
> the great *waka* anthologies) as a sign of longing for home, here the
> speaker already *is* home – at least physically. Emotionally, he yearns
> either for a capital (*kyō*) that, having receded into the past, no longer
> exists, or else for an ideal capital that, having never existed, never-
> theless conflicts with the mundane one before him. Those travelling
> far from home hearing the plaintive song of the *hototogisu* coming
> from deep within the forest supposedly become seized with nostal-
> gic (*natsukashi*) feelings, perhaps because the bird, beginning to sing
> day and night in early summer but stopping suddenly with the onset
> of autumn, is associated with the passing of a pleasant season for a
> harsher one.

chopsticks dropping / not for the thunderbolts / but for the cuckoo
kaminari ni / otosanu hashi o / hototogisu
> Muchō (better known as Ueda Akinari).

mandarins! / nobles of yore taking up / bows and arrows
tachibana ya / mukashi yakata no / yumiya tori

Buson. In *Shin hanatsumi* 46 (1777). Clementines (*tachibana*), perhaps attracting 'birds' (*tori*), emit a fragrance that, especially when their flowers are 'plucked' (*tori*), evokes nostalgia for the good 'old days' (*mukashi*), when the warrior 'nobility' (*yakata*) – like the Tachibana lineage of nobles during the Nara and Heian periods (roughly 710–1185) or the unrelated Tachibana lineage of samurai during the medieval and Edo periods – 'took up' (*tori*) arms. The verse also refers subtly to two contemporary kinds of Shinto: Tachibana (established by Tachibana no Mitsuyoshi (1635–1703) as a sect of Suika Shinto) and Yumiya (established by Mitsuyoshi's disciple, Mukasa Tamba, presumably after the practice of shooting bows and arrows, *yumiya*, as part of its festivals).

grass-thatched hermitage, / even it has new occupants – / festive dollhouse
kusa no to mo / sumikawaru yo zo / hina no ie

Bashō. There is a contrast between the implied reclusiveness of the previous owner of the hut – Bashō's persona – and the freer mood of the new residents, who apparently have a young girl who celebrates the doll festival (*hinamatsuri*), held on the third day of the third lunisolar month.

snow flurries down … / a sign not seen yesterday / *house for rent*
yuki chiru ya / kinō wa mienu / shakuya fuda

Issa. People living in snow country, as Issa did, well know what it means when light snow starts falling in autumn, signalling the early onset of winter.

black wood-ant / flagrantly upon a bloom / of white pomegranate
yamaari no / akarasama nari / hakubotan

Buson. *Hakubotan*, literally 'white peony', is a kind of pomegranate (*Punica granatum*). Its fruit being tart, the presence of one or more ants is surprising, then, not only for the black-and-white contrast with the blossoms that resemble large white carnations.

a jumbo ant / striding across straw mats – / what heat!
ōari no / tatami o aruku / atsusa kana

Shirō.

even stones and trees / incandescent to the eye – / sweltering heat!
ishi mo ki mo / manako ni hikaru / atsusa kana
    Kyorai.

the joy of crossing / a river in summer, / sandals in hand!
natsugawa o / kosu ureshisa ya / te ni zōri
    Buson.

shivery cool, / feet pressed against the wall – / midday snooze!
hiyahiya to / kabe o fumaete / hirune kana
    Bashō.

pampas plumes! / flimsyfrail flutterings / of the heart
hosusuki ya / hosoki kokoro no / sawagashiki
    Issa. *Hosoki*, 'flimsyfrail', not only echoes *hosusuki*, 'fronds of pampas grass' (*Miscanthus sinensis*), whose feathery plumes flutter about in the wind in early autumn, it also serves as a pivot between those fronds and the heart (*kokoro*) all aflutter (*sawagashiki*).

a clam from its shell, / myself pried away from you – / departing autumn!
hamaguri no / futami ni wakare / yuku aki zo
    Bashō. An erotically charged verse. *Futami* can mean 'divided self' as well as 'clam shell' – slang for 'vulva'.

with Genji pet names / 'Perfumed Duchess' hardly stinks / for most bearded clams
genjina mo / kai wa ōkata / nioumiya
    Shuchin. In *Yanagi no hazue* (1835). This dirty sexy verse is a tour de force of wordplay alluding to various aspects of *Genji monogatari* (The Tale of Genji, *c.*1000): *kai* – the graph for which, literally meaning 'shell', conjures up the 'shell-matching' (*kaiawase*) episode – is slang for 'vulva'; *nioumiya* refers both to the 'Fragrant Prince', a male character, but also to 'fragrant palace', a euphemism for 'vulva' – though *nio* alternatively could be read *niau*, meaning 'befit', another allusion to matching contests using shells inscribed with old Japanese and Chinese poems; and, finally, *genjina* refers both to the professional names of ladies of the night and to the practice of assigning nicknames to characters derived from chapter titles – real life and art/fiction brought together by the *haiku* poet Kikaku in *Yoshiwara Genji gojūshikun* (Yoshiwara's Fifty-four Genji Ladies, n.d.), a book providing critiques of Yoshiwara courtesans in terms

of female characters from the fifty-four chapters of *The Tale of Genji* (in Kokusho Kankōkai (ed.), *Zoku enseki jusshu* 2 (Kokusho kankōkai, 1927), pp. 70–95; also in Shuzui Kenji (ed.), *Mikan bungei shiryō* 3 (Koten bunko, 1953)).

fishmonger kiosk / pungent its dried-fish odour – / torrid heat!
amagaya ni / hizakana no niou / atsusa kana
  Shiki. The second line contains an extra syllabet.

salted seabream, / chill down to its gums – / fishmonger stall!
shiodai no / haguki mo samushi / uo no tana
  Bashō. The grotesquely grinning 'gums' (*haguki*) of dead fish in winter is not something likely to be found in classical poetry. This verse exemplifies the aesthetic concept of 'slenderness' (*hosomi*) associated with Bashō and his school whereby the poet suspends his ego, impersonally entering into the essence of a subject.

bluebottle flies / peck-pecking fish eyes – / such heat!
aobae no / uo no me seseru / atsusa kana
  Chiryū. *Aobae*, literally 'blue fly', or bluebottle (*Calliphora vomitoria*), is a type of blowfly whose larvae feed on animal carcasses.

baby mice / squeak-squeaking for the teat – / midnight in autumn
konezumi no / chichi yo to naku ya / yowa no aki
  Buson. *Chichi* has a range of possible meanings, including 'squeak' and 'breast' (and also 'milk' and even 'daddy'). *Yowa*, 'weak', referring to the manner of squeaking as well as meaning 'dead of night' (reinforced by secondary meanings of *yo* and *ya* as 'night'), can also be read *yahan* – a self-allusion to Buson's *haikai* circle, the Yahantei.

winter drizzle: / mice skittering across / zither strings
shigururu ya / nezumi no wataru / koto no ue
  Buson. Perhaps the same cold winter drizzle that drove the mice indoors in the previous verse also drove the occupant to take out the zither to relieve the boredom of being cooped up? *Wataru koto* can mean both 'crossing over' and 'zither that (someone or something) crosses'.

the sound of mice / scuttling over dishes; / frigid cold!
sara o fumu / nezumi no oto no / samusa kana
  Buson.

a mouse slipped / into the crock of water – / cold the night
mizugame e / nezumi no ochishi / yosamu kana
> Taigi. *Mizugame*, an earthenware pot of water for drinking or washing, was especially associated with Buddhist temples. A homonym of *mizu*, 'water', is 'unseen'.

nothing blacker, / no matter how regarded, / than snow
nanto mitemo / yuki hodo kuroki / mono wa nashi
> Tokugen. Literally meaning 'black', *kuroki* implies 'evil'. The first line contains an extra syllabet.

footsoldiers proceed / congealed into a huddle – / the frigid cold!
ashigaru no / katamatte yuku / samusa kana
> Shirō.

lone fly / closing in around me – / winter confinement
hae hitotsu / ware o meguru ya / fuyugomori
> Gyōdai. A feeling of cabin fever comes across loud and clear.

holed up for winter / it's either yellow comics / or red comics
fuyugomori / kibyōshi aruwa / akabyōshi
> Sōseki. In 1895, when this verse was composed, the slight choice between the yellow-covered comicbooks (*kibyōshi*) of a bygone age and red-covered ones (*akabyōshi*) suggests the feeling of winter confinement (*fuyugomori*). In real life, the famous novelist drew inspiration from both.

paperweights / on the store's comicbooks – / spring breeze
ezōshi ni / shizu oku mise ya / haru no kaze
> Kitō. Woodblock-printed comicbooks have a venerable history in Japan, emerging as a mass industry during the mid eighteenth century.

dubbed 'sketchy comics' / they're still inadvertently / decent portrayals
manga to wa / iedo midaride / nai tehon
> Shachō. In *Yanagidaru* 96 (1827). A jokey lament that the series of sketchbooks by the famous artist Hokusai (1760–1849) titled *Hokusai manga*, published in woodblock-printed form from 1814 onwards, did not purvey any pornography.

insect tremolo / soberingly cools the heat / of farmland roads
mushi no koe / noji no atsusa no / same ni keri
> Kogetsu. The cry of insects makes both the lingering summer heat feel more 'cool' (*same*) and, by hinting at the approach of autumn with its associations of death, the traverser more 'sober' (*same*). An example of a verse with blended or double seasons (*kigasanari*).

swelteringly / shines the sun's frostiness – / autumn gust
akaaka to / hi wa tsurenakumo / aki no kaze
> Bashō.

kite breast / struck squarely by the sunlight / of nearing winter
fuyu chikaki / hi no atarikeri / tobi no hara
> Shirao.

heartbreaking indeed! / beneath an armoured helmet, / a chirping cricket
muzan ya na / kabuto no shita no / kirigirisu
> Bashō. The opening phrase is famously associated with the death of the warrior Saitō (Bettō) Sanemori (1111–83) in *Heike monogatari* (c. thirteenth century) and the noh play *Sanemori* by Zeami Motokiyo (c.1363–1443). A *kirigirisu* is a kind of cricket, associated with autumn, named onomatopoetically for its chirr-chirring.

heartbreaking indeed! / beneath the bordello stairway, / a slipper-bearer
muzan ya na / hashigo no shita no / zōritori
> Shusshi. In *Yanagidaru* 85 (1825). The same verse appeared earlier in *Yanagidaru shūi* 4 (c.1796–7) and *Mutamagawa* 8 (1755). A burlesque of Bashō's verse above, replacing the warrior's helmet (*kabuto*) and cricket with a stairway (*hashigo*) – presumably to the second floor of a bordello – and a slipper valet (*zōritori*), pathetically waiting for his master to finish.

to the saké pub / a solitary warrior – / evening snowfall
sakaya made / tsuwamono hitori / yoru no yuki
> Hajin.

Demon Slayer – / its bouquet reeking / to high hell
onigoroshi / jigoku de nioi wa / kitsui koto
> Shōri. In *Yanagidaru* 69 (1817). *Onigoroshi*, 'demon slayer', refers to a particularly pungent brand of saké. The second line has an extra syllabet.

trying to walk straight / down a path of logicality / while tipsy
sujimichi o / tate yō to suru / yopparai
    Meitei.

tipsy reveller / used as a stepping stool / snapping blossoms!
namayoi o / fumidai ni shite / hana o ori
    Hōbi. In *Yanagidaru* 10 (1775). No doubt the blossom filcher is only
    slightly less soused (*namayoi*), since using a boozed-up flower viewer
    as a booster step (*fumidai*) is not the best idea. Depending on how high
    up the blossoms are, it might well be one's neck that gets snapped.
    Still, there is something charming about people carried away by their
    enthusiasm, even to the extent of believing that theft will somehow
    prolong the beauty of a flower whose splendour is short-lived.

mountain moon / deigns to illumine / the blossom filcher
yama no tsuki / hana nusubito o / terashi tamau
    Issa. Although typically the enemy of the professional thief, here
    the bright moon draws attention (with an extra syllabet in the third
    line) to an amateur who, no doubt at a saké-fuelled cherry blossom-
    viewing party, is moved to spontaneously filch a sprig.

challenge:
so this is the floating world! / so this is the floating world!
ukiyo narikeri / ukiyo narikeri

response:
sprig of blossoms / clutched by a poetic soul / passed out cold!
hana no eda / motte fūgana / taoremono
    Author unnamed. In *Yanagidaru* 8 (1773). A bit of fun at the expense
    of those who fancy themselves poetical enough to be moved to drink
    by the beauty of cherry blossoms.

beneath the bough / upon broth and pickled fish: / cherry petals!
ko no moto ni / shiru mo namasu mo / sakura kana
    Bashō. The wordplay on *namasu*, a pickled fish salad, and *namazu*,
    piebald skin, triggers a playful visual comparison.

**boozed-up samurai ... / the blossom-viewing party / snaps to its
senses!**
samurai ga / yotte hanami no / kyō ga same
    Author unnamed. In *Senryūhyō mankuawase* (1757-89). Typically,
    it is the cherry blossoms that awaken people to the impermanence
    of life, not drunk swordsmen. But what is to be expected when saké

enlivens blossom-viewing parties? Particularly during the last decades of the Edo period, when their class was sinking into debt and poverty, many samurai felt they had good reason to drink.

what in the world! / someone blossom viewing / wearing a sword!
nanigoto zo / hana miru hito no / nagagatana

Kyorai. Although samurai, the only class to have the privilege of wearing a long sword (*nagagatana*), enjoyed blossom viewing, which is all about appreciating the fleeting beauty of life, for one to do so while actually armed would have been outrageous.

what in the world! / someone tooth-pulling / wearing a sword!
nanigoto zo / ha o nuku hito no / nagagatana

Hanmonsen. A close parody of the preceding verse by Kyorai, perhaps suggesting that while in premodern Japan it was a samurai's prerogative, however uncouth, to go blossom viewing girded with a long sword, in the modern age of economic decline, former samurai have resorted to taking up undignified professions such as dentistry. Throughout the Edo and Meiji periods, itinerant peddlers offering tooth-extraction services typically advertised their skills by performing 'sword unsheathing' (*iainuki*).

viewing blossoms – / how many of them I'd love / even as a wife
tsuma nimo to / ikutari omou / hanami kana

Haritsu. This verse plays on the truism that, while some go out to gaze upon the blossoms, others are blossoms who go out to be gazed upon.

partial to autumn / or somesuch says the woman / with the slender neck
aki ga suki / nado to onna no / hosoi kubi

Rakusui. In *Waka midori* (1691). This verse pokes fun at the superficiality of those men who pay more attention to women's looks than their thoughts (the neck having been considered a major erogenous zone). Then again, this particular woman seems aware that she is being eyed up while eyeing the autumn foliage, judging by her coquettish use of the word *suki*, 'partial to'.

gaze I shall! / 'til the very blossoms become / a pain in the neck
nagamu tote / hana ni mo itashi / kubi no hone

Sōin. A renowned spoof of another renowned verse, by Saigyō, changing the original 'very' (*itaku*) to 'painful' (*itashi*): 'wishing to gaze / upon the cherry blossoms / close drew I / only to part with such / deep sorrow!' (*nagamu tote / hana ni mo itaku / narenureba / chiri wakere koso / kanashi karikere*; poem number 126 in *NKBZ* 26, p. 72).

no such thing, / in the shadows of blossoms, / as blushing strangers
hana no kage / aka no tanin wa / nakarikeri
    Issa. The shade beneath the tree of the cherry blossom, with its ephemeral beauty, provides a kind of intimacy – or eroticism, as suggested by the colours. The red of 'blushing strangers' also calls to mind flushed cheeks under the influence of saké, typically drunk beneath the blossoms, and the pink of blossoms perhaps evokes female genitalia, a notion reinforced by the fact that the graph for 'shadows' (*kage*) is also read *in*, denoting the gentle, passive, female force or recessive space – the *yin* of *yin-yang*. Since 'blossom' (*hana*) was a common metaphor for a beautiful woman, a more overt rendering might be: 'no such thing, / thanks to Blossom's recesses, / as blushing strangers!' Thus, although cherry blossoms symbolize the bittersweet beauty of love as well as life, public lovemaking itself is not only inspired by the blossoms but facilitated by their recesses.

scatter already / and send home the gawkers! / mountain cherry
toku chirite / miru hito kaese / yamazakura
    Ichū. A wry comment on the misbehaviour of blossom viewers, presumably city folk who have come to a rustic locale to party. *Yamazakura* is a wild cherry (*Cerasus jamasakura*) often found in the mountains.

even the shade / of the cherished cherrytree – / vanished
ki ni itta / sakura no kage mo / nakarikeri
    Issa.

within a potted trap / the octopus's fleeting dream – / summer moon
takotsubo ya / hakanaki yume o / natsu no tsuki
    Bashō.

clouds of blossoms ... / those the bells at Ueno? / at Asakusa?
hana no kumo / kane wa ueno ka / asakusa ka
    Bashō. One of his acclaimed verses (perhaps inspiring Rabindranath Tagore, according to Kenkabō).

petals from heaven / flurrying down it seems / oh cherry trees!
ten kara demo / futtaru yōni / sakura kana
    Issa. The first line contains an extra syllabet.

treading upon clouds / along the mountain trail – / rain of blossoms!
kumo o fumu / yamaji ni ame no / sakura kana
  Kitō.

come for the blossoms / how beauteous it becomes – / my very soul
hana ni kite / utsukushiku naru / kokoro kana
  The woman poet Tatsujo. From one of the works (*c.* 1689) comprising *Haikai shichibushū* (the seven major works of the Bashō School). *Ni kite* can mean either 'coming for' or 'thanks to'.

come for the blossoms / only to have money pinched – / country bumpkins!
hana ni kite / zeni surarekeri / inakabito
  Shiki.

the straight and narrow / circle round other folks' pear trees / and melon patches
shōjikina / hito wa tōranu / rika kaden
  Tsukuda. In *Yanagidaru* 113 (1831). A Chinese proverb advises that, while acting uprightly is good, acting to avoid the slightest outward impression of impropriety is better, even if that entails taking the long way around other people's 'pear trees and melon patches' (*rika kaden*). Riffing on that proverb, this verse suggests that the straightest distance morally might not be the shortest distance geometrically.

a sneak thief / encountered by a fox – / melon field!
nusubito ni / deau kitsune ya / uribatake
  Taigi. The graph for 'fox' contains the graph for 'melon'.

challenge:
it comes to mind and yet … / it comes to mind and yet …
omoi koso sure / omoi koso sure

response:
trespassing forbidden / means trespassing is not / out of the question!
tōrinuke / muyō de tōri- / nuke ga shire
  Author unnamed. In *Yanagidaru* 8 (1773) and *Yanagidaru shūi* 10 (*c.*1796–7). This kind of sophistry, reinterpreting words to validate their opposite meaning, is a mainstay of comic literature (*gesaku*) as well as of comic poetry. Another instance of verse straddling (*kumatagari*).

just inside the fence / to prohibited grounds / wild violets
hottoba no / kaki yori uchi wa / sumire kana
    Yaba. Within the word for the natural wild violets (*sumire*) lurks the act of 'entering' (*ire*) that violates the human prohibition.

here and there / upon scorched fields / wild violets
yakeshino no / tokorodokoro ya / sumiregusa
    The nun Shōkyū. Although stated in terms of the annual prescribed burning of fields (*yakeshino*) in spring, according to a headnote Shōkyū returned home at the end of the third lunisolar month to find her hut destroyed by fire.

***do not pick!* / yet being picked for me: / garden plum**
na oriso to / orite kurekeri / sono no ume
    Taigi. Although customarily rendered as 'plum', the *ume* (also *mume*) is strictly speaking a kind of apricot tree (*Prunus mume*). Its pink, white and red fragrant blossoms, highly regarded in China (*meihua* in Chinese) as well as Japan, are an early harbinger of spring.

upon the fence / with the 'no pissing' sign / willowstrands leak
shōben wa / muyō no hei ni / yanagi tare
    Kindai. In *Yanagidaru* 71 (1819). Just as overgrown willow branches transgress the rules of human society, so do comic verses – like this one – named after Senryū, literally 'River Willow'.

by false pretence / cutting through temple grounds – / the misty moon!
azamuite / yukinuke dera ya / oborozuki
    Taigi. *Yukinuke*, 'keep on going', may pivot into *dera*, 'temple', to yield *nukedera*, which suggests either 'if stealing away' or 'not steal away'.

passing freely / through the temple grounds – / spring butterfly
tōrinuke / yurusu tera nari / haru no chō
    Issa. Temple patrons were expected to make a donation.

nights so chilly! / clothing so flimsy! and saké / so dreggy!
yo ya samushi / koromo ya usushi / nigorizake
    Kodō. In *Yanagidaru* 28 (1799).

plums in bloom! / nowhere else around / can spring be found
ume saite / atari ni haru wa / nakarikeri
    Ritō. Sometimes blooming with snow still on the ground, the plum is an early harbinger of spring.

spring overlooked! / on the back of a handglass, / plum blossoms
hito mo minu / haru ya kagami no / ura no ume
  Bashō. Which is truer to life: a painted image of spring; a reflection of spring in a mirror in which one's own image predominates; or a verse about this conundrum? Since the plum blossom in Japanese poetry has long evoked scent (particularly that of a woman in a sensual way), the suggestion here might be that spring is best sensed through smell. Aida Gozan (*c.*1717–87), in his discussion in *Akemurasaki* (Red and Purple, 1784) of some fifty of Bashō's verses, commented: 'I think the poet was moved to write this hokku when he smelled the fragrance of plum blossoms that had begun to bloom by his rustic hut. He thought those blossoms blooming in the small yard were as unnoticed as a design on the back of a mirror' (quoted in Makoto Ueda (ed. and trans.), *Bashō and His Interpreters: Selected Hokku with Commentary* (Stanford, CA: Stanford University Press, 1992), p. 335).

scent of plum / in a flash of rising sun! / the mountain path
ume ga ka ni / notto hi no deru / yamaji kana
  Bashō. On a frosty, perhaps still snowy, but undoubtedly lonely mountain road, the speaker encounters the first whiff of spring. Somehow, a sunrise seems to carry greater significance at such moments.

cascade sounds / along a mountain path – / the blistering heat
taki no oto wa / arite yamaji no / atsusa kana
  Shunkō. The first line has an extra syllabet.

cold the night! / to the sea cascading down, / waterfall sounds
samuki yo ya / umi ni ochikomu / taki no oto
  Kyokusui.

the year's first melon / clutched close to a child / fast asleep
hatsuuri o / hittoramaete / neta ko kana
  Issa.

in morning dew, / sullied for being cool – / muddy melons
asatsuyu ni / yogorete suzushi / uri no doro
  Bashō. This verse, set in late summer, accords with an interest in things 'reeking of mud' (*dorokusai*).

pale moonlit night ... / in the mood to run off with / a watermelon!
usuzuki yo / suika o nusumu / kokoro ari
  Shiki. A homonym of *ari*, 'has', is 'ant'.

a fox sneezes / at a whiff of muskmelon – / moonlit night!
uri no ka ni / kitsune no hanahiru / tsukiyo kana
  Shirao. The second line has an extra syllabet.

a wild boar / warily snorts its snout – / watermelons!
inoshishi no / hana gusutsukasu / suika kana
  Ushichi.

**hunting for bushpig! / swooshing through pampas grass /
nocturnal voices**
shishi ou ya / susuki o hashiru / yoru no koe
  Issa. The *shishi* (wild boar rather than bushpig per se) and *susu* (pampas grass) intimate the sound of rushing through tall grass.

against a charcoal kiln / a wild boar wounded / has collapsed
sumigama ni / teoi no shishi no / taorekeri
  Bonchō.

the deer whistle / being cut short, / a gun's report!
shikabue no / yamikeri yagate / tsutsu no oto
  Shiki. The word *tsutsu* for 'gun' is onomatopoeic.

cumming for real / like a pig a servant girl / will squeal!
gejo masa ni / yogaru toki sono / koe buta
  Konjin. In *Yanagi no hazue* (1835). A loose burlesquing of a line from the Confucian *Analects* (8:4) in which Master Zeng, having fallen ill, says: 'When a bird is about to die, his song is sad; when a man is about to die, his words are true' (in Leys (trans.), *The Analects of Confucius*, p. 35). *Yogaru*, literally 'be elated', was slang for reaching orgasm (see *EBKI*, p. 18).

challenge:
that was greedy! / that was greedy!
yokubari ni keri / yokubari ni keri

response:
**squealing with delight: / 'better too *big* than too *small*!' / the
chambermaid**
dai wa shō / kaneru to warau / nagatsubone
  Author unnamed. In *Yanagidaru* 1 (1765). The verse would also appear, by Kiryū, in *Yanagidaru* 134 (1834). Playing on the stereotype of the sex-starved chambermaid (*nagatsubone*), this *bareku* has its subject take matters into her own hands, just as much as with a sex toy as with an actual penis. This stereotype may be a kind of projection of male

sexual fantasies onto women. Yet it may also reflect the assertion of
sexual feelings of women as members of a gender too often objecti-
fied as passive.

inserted fully / five or six inches feel like / a perfect ten!
goroku sun / irete jūbun / kimaru nari
 Kikō. In *Yanagidaru* 33 (1806). Aside from the pun on *jūbun* ('ten
 parts' and 'sufficient'), *kimaru* means both 'to be settled' and for a rela-
 tionship between lovers – or a client and courtesan – 'to go well'. The
 length mentioned here is on the long side for a penis (though not ne-
 cessarily for a dildo), at least judging by a slightly later source (*Keichū
 kibun makura bunko*, 1822) that categorizes the male member into
 three ascending tiers: short, 3 *sun* 8 *bun* (4½ inches/11.4cm); average,
 4 *sun* (4¾ inches/12cm); and long, 4 *sun* 8 *bun* (5¾ inches/14.4cm).
 (See *EB*, pp. 171–2.) Precisely speaking, a *sun* being about 1⅕ inches
 (3cm), 5 *sun* would be about 6 inches (15cm) and 6 *sun* about 7
 inches (18cm).

the mistress – / only four or five inches / and her work is done
omekake wa / tatta shi go sun / shigoto nari
 Author unnamed. In *Suetsumuhana* 2 (1783).

blandishments . . . / a gold tooth gleams / repulsively
gotsuishō / iyana kinba ga / hikaru nari
 Kanehiko. Embedded within *gotsuishō*, 'honourable blandishments',
 is the word *gotsui*, 'unrefined' or 'harsh'.

his sweet nothings / the servant girl takes as / the real thing
aisō ni / itta o gejo wa / hon ni suru
 Author unnamed. In *Yanagidaru* 11 (1773). Or as *his* real thing, since
 hon, 'real', can also be a counter word for long cylindrical objects.

still coaxing / though the maidservant's / already cumming
mada kudoi- / teru noni gejo wa / mō yogari
 Sosen. In *Yanagi no hazue* (1835). Another instance of verse straddling
 (*kumatagari*) since *kudoiteru*, 'coaxing', is not usually split across two
 phrases.

dissolving, / the maidservant's mouth and muff / all aquiver!
gejo kietsu / atama mo bobo mo / ōwarawa
 Shuchin. In *Yanagi no hazue* (1835). The last two phrases present a
 veritable palindromic orgasm of vowels: *ah-ah-ah oh oh-oh oh / oh-oh
 ah-ah-ah.*

keep wheedling / perhaps the third pass / up the ass!
danjitara / ketsu mo sase sona / sankaime
> Ryūsha. In *Yanagi no hazue* (1835). *Sankaime* can mean 'third hole' as well as 'third time'.

merely diddled / the maidservant's face appears / down in the mouth
kujirareta / bakari monouki / gejo ga tsura
> Sekishi. In *Yanagi no hazue* (1835). *Tsura* (face) is also a colloquial contraction of *tsurai* (pained).

being possessed / of an enjoyable foible / wins approval
omoshiroi / ketten ga ari / mitomerare
> Goken.

being skilled at / feigning infatuation / makes one popular
horeta mane / jōzuni suru de / hayaru nari
> Shūba. In *Yanagidaru* 46 (1808).

heaven knows! earth knows! / the whole neighbourhood knows! / except the parents
ten shiru chi / shiru kinjo shiru / oya shirazu
> Shishōshi.

without dallying / she makes a full confession / in her third trimester
massugu ni / hakujō o suru / itsutsukime
> Author unnamed. In *Yanagidaru* 9 (1774). Of course, there never would have been any unintended consequences to dilly-dally about confessing had there been no dalliance in the first place. *Itsutsukime*, literally meaning 'fifth month' of the lunisolar calendar, contains the interrogative word *itsu*, 'when?'.

try chomping / a whole lotta chillipeppers! / the prescription
shikotama ni / karashi o kutte / mina to iu
> Author unnamed. Although many cultures regard spicy foods as aphrodisiacs, in Japan hot chillies (*karashi*) were believed to be an abortifacient. *Kutte* covers a range of meanings, from 'chomp', to 'make a living', to 'screw (a woman, especially for the first time)'. If *karashi* is taken as a slang term for 'penis', an alternative meaning of the verse would be: 'It's okay to put my entire penis inside you, since you won't get pregnant!'

in the first place, / *you* were left in a basket / for clementines!
dete ushō / nanji genrai / mikan kago

Author unnamed. *Yanagidaru* 1 (1765). One of many verses on the theme of the abandoned child. Nakamura Yukihiko singles this verse out as an example of the exposé (*ugachi*): 'This *senryū* is in the voice of a father who finds an abandoned baby in a clementine basket and raises him, enduring many a struggle with the child as he grows up. The entire saga of their relationship could easily be expanded into a full-length novel' (*NYC* 8, p. 125).

the doorman: / flabbergasted! the clementine / basket: gurgling!
monban wa / tamage mikanba- / ko wa warai

Author unnamed. *Tamage*, 'flabbergasted', is echoic of *tamagu shiryō*, an offering to the Shinto gods. Although this verse might be read more naturally in 5-8-4- or even 5-6-6-syllabet phrases, in 5-7-5 form the word *mikanbako*, 'clementine box', is split to 'straddle' two phrases (*kumatagari*), thereby emphasizing *-ko*, 'child'.

the love child / startles at each and every / *wham-bam*
chon no ma de / dekita ko bikuri / bikuri oji

Gadō. In *Yanagi no hazue* (1835). Popular belief held that children born out of wedlock startled easily. The *chon no ma de*, 'in a flash', works both with *dekita ko*, 'child conceived during a quickie', and with *bikuri bikuri oji*, 'scared out of one's wits lickety-split'.

oh what a world! / some pray to heaven for children, / others ditch theirs on earth
yo no naka yo / ten ni inoriko / chi ni sutego

Author unnamed. In Chōgetsu (ed.), *(Haikai) Azuma karage* (1755), a collection of verse published two years prior to the first publication of *Senryūhyō mankuawase* (1757).

smiled upon / by the babe about to be ditched, / he bursts into tears!
sute ni yuku / ko ni warawarete / naki idashi

Shōro. In *Yanagidaru* 99 (1828). A paradoxical reversal – the adult crying, the baby smiling – in unusual, extreme, brutal circumstances.

piteous indeed – / more than crying the smiling / face of a waif
naku yori mo / aware sutego no / waraigao

Rekisen. In *Yanagidaru* 44 (1808). The same verse, by one Kaneshige, appears in *Yanagidaru* 65 (1814).

bystander to / a random crossroads slaying – / merciful buddha

tsujigiri o / mite owashimasu / jizōson

Author unnamed. In *Yanagidaru* 1 (1765). Outlawed throughout the eighteenth century, *tsujigiri* was the practice of testing a new sword, or of honing one's swordsmanship, on a random passerby. The verse seems to blame the impassivity of the statue of the deity as much as the one doing the slaying (not directly mentioned), since Jizō (Kṣitigarbha-bodhisattva) is the protector of travellers (among others, including expectant mothers and miscarried or aborted foetuses). However, since Jizō was also responsible for easing the suffering of those in hell, the victim here may not be so innocent as the verse might otherwise let on.

beneath the barrel / dangling aimlessly: / two metal balls

teppō no / shita ni furari to / futatsu tama

Shunku. In *Yanagidaru* 51 (1811). *Teppō*, 'gun', was also a slang term for 'penis'.

dangling down / upon roses yellow: / bull testicles!

yamabuki ni / burari to ushi no / fuguri kana

Issa. Although *yamabuki* is a Japanese yellow rose (*Kerria japonica*), it was also a term for gold coins – in turn slang for testicles (*fuguri*).

withering gust . . . / out from a treebough juts / a monkey's butt!

kogarashi ya / ki kara ochitaru / saru no shiri

Kyōdai.

thongless / his bum blown bare – / vernal breeze

fudoshi senu / shiri fukare yuku ya / haru no kaze

Buson. Aside from the comic disjunction in tone between the two parts of this verse, the humour derives less from the exposed buttocks, which by standards of the time was not shockingly naked, than from the fact that the loincloth is mentioned for its absence, whereas the man's buttocks (sticking out conspicuously like the extra syllabet in the second line) are exposed by the wind blowing a robe not present. Mentioned as far back as the *Kojiki* (*c.*711), the *fudoshi*, or *fundoshi*, was the major form of male undergarment – in the form of a G-string, veiling the genitals but not the buttocks – up until the postwar period. It is still visible today on sumo wrestlers and on men participating in festivals.

his wife insists / he drop his pants this instant ... / for the laundry
fundoshi o / nyōbo saisoku / shite arai
> Author unnamed. In *Yanagidaru* 22 (1788). For *fundoshi*, see note to previous verse.

drawing wellwater / her breasts drooping low – / such heat!
chichi tarete / mizu kumu shizu no / atsusa kana
> Shōhaku.

pirates ashore / to draw the village water – / what a drought!
kaizoku no / mura ni mizu kumu / hideri kana
> Shiki.

ogre charm-print / splattered with droppings – / a passing swallow
ōtsue ni / fun otoshi yuku / tsubame kana
> Buson. Typically depicting an ogre holding a gong, mallet and list of temple donors, the *ōtsue* was a folksy genre of inkwash picture that served as a popular souvenir for travellers to the town of Ōtsu near Kyoto. Thus, on the surface, this verse seems to be a wry if blandly scatological reminder that human beings are not the only ones passing through. Still, double entendres on *ō-tsue*, 'large rod', slang for an enormous penis, and *tsubame*, 'martin', slang for a younger male partner of an older man, suggest the possibility, however remote, of a sexualized reading: 'on his huge rod / shit plunges with the movement / of the young toyboy!'

poppy blossoms / upon which plummet / grappling sparrows!
hanageshi ni / kunde ochitaru / suzume kana
> Shirao.

red plum / its fallen petals ablaze / on horse dung
kōbai no / rakka moyuran / uma no fun
> Buson. If the red tinge of the Japanese apricot (*kōbai*) resembles an ember, then the steam rising off manure (*fun*) in late winter or early spring resembles smoke.

a black dog / transformed into a lantern! / the way in snow
kuroinu o / chōchin ni suru / yuki no michi
> Author unnamed. In *Yanagidaru* 1 (1765). The riddle of the first two phrases, in the form of a visual pun (*mitate*), is resolved in the last.

glimpsed by night / eyes alone prowling along! / the jetblack cat
yoru mireba / me bakari aruku / karasuneko
    Author unnamed. In *Yanagidaru* 23 (1789).

from darkness / slinking into darkness – / cat on the prowl!
kuraki yori / kuraki ni iru ya / neko no koi
    Issa. A burlesque of a celebrated *waka* (in *Shūishū* 20, poem number
    1342) by Izumi Shikibu (b. *c.*976) that refers to the parable of the
    'magic city' within the *Lotus Sutra*. In order to boost the morale of
    travel-weary pilgrims, their guide conjures up the image of a phantom
    city: 'Now from out the dark / Into yet a darker path / I must enter: /
    Shine upon me from afar, / Moon on the mountain crest' (*kuraki yori
    / kuraki michi ni zo / irinubeki / haruka ni terase / yama no ha no tsuki*;
    in Edwin A. Cranston (ed. and trans.), *A Waka Anthology* 2, *Grasses of
    Remembrance* (Stanford, CA: Stanford University Press, 2006), p. 432).

from darkness / returning unto darkness – / a sea slug?!
kuraki yori / kuraki ni kaeru / namako kana
    Gyōdai. Issa may have been aware of this burlesque of Izumi Shiki-
    bu's verse in the commentary above when he wrote his own.

dirty old tomcat! / nevertheless he's the one / who gets the pussy
yogore neko / soredemo tsuma wa / mochi ni keri
    Issa.

how shocking! / the stone fence knocked down by / cats copulating
osoroshi ya / ishigaki kuzusu / neko no koi
    Shiki. The vowels alone paint a randy picture: *o o o i a / i i a i u u u /
    e o o o i.*

cats mating – / in our bedroom as they finish, / misty moonlight
neko no koi / yamu toki neya no / oborozuki
    Bashō. Cats in heat wake the speaker, who realizes that the springtime
    moon has misted over – mist being a euphemism for sexual climax.

crack of dawn – / even a stray for love / caterwauls
ariake ya / ienashi neko mo / koi o naku
    Issa. At the reluctant parting after a passionate night, seeming oppo-
    sites voice their yearning, be they human being or cat, or he who 'has'
    (the *ari* embedded in *ariake*, literally 'has light') and he who 'has not'
    (the *nashi* in *ienashi*, 'homeless', reinforced by the homonym 'with-
    out' of *naku*, 'to cry out').

silly cat! / hamming up the yowling / with whole torso
baka neko ya / shintai-giri no / ukaregoe
Issa. *Kiri*, 'cutting' (rendered *giri* here), has special uses meaning 'just' (i.e. cut off from), but also 'finale' (since it implies cutting something off dramatically). *Ukare*, to be 'buoyant' or 'festive', also implies being cut off from something.

snoozing, stirring / taking an enormous yawn – / feline passion!
nete okite / ōakubi shite / neko no koi
Issa. Within *ōakubi*, 'great yawn', may lurk *ōaku*, 'huge sin'.

no later than noon, / according to the cat's eyes … / spring day
neko no me no / mada hiru suginu / haruhi kana
Onitsura.

its tail / twiddling a butterfly – / the kittycat!
chōchō o / shippo de naburu / koneko kana
Issa.

a butterfly / hoists the pussycat up / two, three feet
nisanjaku / chōchō neko o / tsuriageru
Shuchin. In *Yanagidaru* 58 (1811). A reworking of an earlier verse by an unnamed author: 'a pussycat / hoisted up by a butterfly / two, three feet' (*chōchō ni / neko no tsurarete / nisanjaku*) in *Haikai kei* 10 (1789).

dandelion / sporadically snapping a butterfly / out of dreams
tanpopo ya / oriori samasu / chō no yume
The nun Chiyo. *Samasu* can mean to awaken from sleep or illusion. The butterfly, especially when coupled with reference to sleep or waking, invokes perhaps the most well-known dream in East Asia: the one in which the Taoist philosopher Zhuangzi (aka Chuang Tzu) dreams of himself as a butterfly, only to wake up and wonder if he is not a butterfly dreaming of himself as Zhuangzi.

flower filcher – / a butterfly silently / in pursuit
hanadorobo / chō wa mugon de / okkakeru
Tomomatsu. In *Yanagidaru* 63 (1813). *Hanadorobo* is the clipped form of *hanadorobō* (flower thief).

a butterfly / chasing the spray of flowers … / on a casket
chōchō no / shitau hanawa ya / kan no ue
Meisetsu. *Shitau* means both 'follow' and 'yearn for'.

even spring's passing / slumbered away heedlessly – / grass-perched butterfly

haru yuku mo / shirade ya nemuru / kusa no chō

    The woman poet Suiujo.

butterfly corpse … / ants approaching as if / on parade

chōchō no / mukuro e ari no / matsuri meki

    Tonbo.

in the spiderweb / a butterfly's empty shell – / how poignant!

kumo no su ni / kōcho no kara no / aware nari

    Shiki.

crinkly, crinkly / its body desiccated – / how now, cicada?

karakara ni / mi wa narihatete / nanto semi

    Saimu.

on the veranda / to escape the wife and kids – / stifling heat!

hashii shite / saishi o sakuru / atsusa kana

    Buson.

autumn this morning! / realized in one footstep upon / the veranda wiped dry

aki ya kesa / hitoashi ni shiru / nuguien

    Ishū (aka Shigeyori). Dew signifies the onset of autumn.

bush warbler! / crapping on ricecakes scrapped / at veranda's edge

uguisu ya / mochi ni fun suru / en no saki

    Bashō. Instead of singing, as is its wont, this bush warbler (*uguisu*) has other business to tend to. Since bush warblers come out in early spring, the offertory ricecakes here must be discarded leftovers from the New Year's festivities.

a fly's lot: / rubbing hands on some veranda, / whereupon the swat!

en no hae / te o suru tokoro o / utarekeri

    Issa. At first blush the fly is about to rub his 'hands' together seemingly in gratitude, perhaps for finding a sunny resting spot (whose line is marked by an extra syllabet), or for the prospect of leftover food from inside the house. However, once the fly is swatted, the hand rubbing retrospectively seems an act of prayer. *En*, 'veranda', also refers to a kind of 'interconnected fate' (the Buddhist *pratyaya*).

egads, swat not! / **pleads the fly rubbing hands,** / **rubbing feet**
yare utsuna / hae ga te o suri / ashi o suru
    Issa.

whoooa there! / **the bell-striking can wait,** / **for blossoms' sake!**
yaa shibaraku / hana ni taishite / kane tsuku koto
    Shigeyori. His motto being that witty linked poetry (*haikai*) should
emanate 'from the heart' (*kokoro no haikai*), Shigeyori no doubt in-
fluenced his disciple Onitsura's even more famous dictum that witty
linked poetry needs to be based on authenticity (*makoto*). In this rare
example of double hypermetre (*jiamari*), the extra syllabet in both the
first and last lines suggests spontaneity.

evening bell! / **and still in bloom,** / **sweltering heat**
banshō ni / chirinokoritaru / atsusa kana
    The nun Chiyo.

quiescence! / **touching not the blossoms,** / **temple bell's voice**
shizukasa ya / hana ni sawaranu / kane no koe
    Fuhaku.

falling blossoms / **the remaining blossoms too** / **falling blossoms**
chiru sakura / nokoru sakura mo / chiru sakura
    Ryōkan. Take a long view and everything, even a cherry in blossom,
is in decline.

deep down / **beneath scattering blossoms** / **blithesome skulls!**
chiru hana no / moto ni medetaki / dokuro kana
    The nun Seifu. A profound statement about the nature of existence
just as much as a literal description of the gruesome aftermath of the
great famines of the 1770s and 1780s, which claimed tens if not hun-
dreds of thousands of souls, for the phrase *moto ni*, 'at root', can mean
'fundamentally' as well as 'beneath'. This poignant verse itself is built
upon the remains of the past, alluding to a celebrated twelfth-century
waka by the priest and great poet Saigyō: 'I pray to die / under cherry
blossoms / in spring / when the moon is full / in the lunar second
month' (*negawakuba / hana no moto ni te / haru shinamu / sono kisaragi
no / mochizuki no koro*; in Makoto Ueda (ed. and trans.), *Far Beyond
the Field: Haiku by Japanese Women* (New York: Columbia University
Press, 2003), p. 57, n. 1).

skeletal frames / masqueraded in finery: / blossom viewing!
gaikotsu no / ue o yosōte / hanami kana
    Onitsura. Extending the lesson of impermanence of the previous
    verses from the cherry blossom to its gazers, one realizes that we our-
    selves appear as human beings only momentarily. And even then we
    are merely in disguise, the way that blossoms distract from the skel-
    etal boughs.

though mortal, / skeletons every last one! / evening chill
kō iru mo / mina gaikotsu zo / yūsuzumi
    Issa.

this world of ours: / viewing blossoms on the surface / above hell
yo no naka wa / jigoku no ue no / hanami kana
    Issa. A sober twist on clichés about how cherry blossoms make the
    world appear heavenly.

village lamplights / lambent in the raindrops / upon young leaves!
sato no hi o / fukumite ame no / wakaba kana
    Ryōta.

'yea big' / the peony sized by / a little kid
kore hodo to / botan no shikata / suru ko kana
    Author unnamed.

a nightingale / interrupting my handiwork / at the sink
uguisu ni / temoto yasumen / nagashimoto
    The woman poet Chigetsu. A melodious tribute to the arresting song
    of the Japanese nightingale or bush warbler (*Horornis diphone*), heard
    in early spring. Apart from the pun on *temoto* as 'close at hand' and
    'handiwork', there is the nice repetition of *moto* in *temoto* and *na-
    gashimoto* (sink).

cooling breeze – / the boundless sky filled with / pining voices
suzukaze ya / kokū ni michite / matsu no koe
    Onitsura.

pine resin / oozing out, torrid – / broken bough
matsuyani no / nadarete atsushi / eda no ore
    Gomei.

hatchet sinking in,/ amazed by the fragrance – / dead trees of winter
ono irete / ka ni odoroku ya / fuyukodachi
> Buson. The vibrant scents typically associated with trees derive from their flowers and leaves in spring or summer, not from their apparently lifeless wood when put under the axe in winter. Trees survive the cold by going into a kind of suspended animation involving the molecular conversion of starches into sweet-smelling sugars. *Kodachi*, 'grove of trees', has a homonym in 'small blade' that resonates with *ono*, 'hatchet'.

dog's bark / means someone passing by; / night of snow
inu no koe / hito ya sugiken / yoru no yuki
> Meimei.

daybreak! / the tempest interred / in snow
akebono ya / arashi wa yuki ni / uzumorete
> Shirō.

snowy morn / the *ditto ditto* marks / of wooden clogs
yuki no asa / ninoji ninoji no / geta no ato
> The woman poet Sutejo.

mountain hamlet – / beneath piled-up snows,/ watersounds
yamazato ya / yuki tsumu shita no / mizu no oto
> Shiki.

snow remaining / the mountain foot mists over – / O eventide!
yuki nagara / yamamoto kasumu / yūbe kana
> Sōgi. Seasonal transitions are not always smooth, as with this overlap (*kigasanari*) of the remnants of winter and the misty harbinger of spring, known for its evenings (*haru no yūbe*).

late-thawing snow / and the village overflows ... / with little kids!
yuki tokete / mura ippai no / kodomo kana
> Issa. Snow melting as late as mid spring typically results in flooding, especially in small villages at the foot of a mountain. The twist here is that as soon as weather permits, it is children, cooped up for a longer-than-usual winter, that come flooding out into the streets. Nearly half a millennium earlier, Reizei Tamesuke (1263–1328) composed in a similar vein: 'Frost melts – / drenching fallen leaves / in sunlight' (*shimo kiete / hikage ni nururu / ochiba kana*; in Steven D. Carter (ed.

and trans.), *Haiku Before Haiku: From the Renga Masters to Bashō* (New York: Columbia University Press, 2011), pp. 22–3).

snug in my futon / on a morning so cold – / petals as snow!
futon maku / asa no samusa ya / hana no yuki
> Sonojo. More chilling than snow falling in winter is the scattering of cherry blossoms in spring.

dog barking / at a travelling salesman; / peachtrees in bloom
akyūdo o / hoeru inu ari / momo no hana
> Buson. In late spring (signified by the peaches), signs of life return outside after a long winter.

early-summer rains … / blank spaces on the wall where / versecards peeled off
samidare ya / shikishi hegitaru / kabe no ato
> Bashō. One of the poet's many verses that refer to verses, or to the act of representation, or to the poet himself.

ceaseless rains … / upon the sushi pressingstone / a slug
samidare ya / sushi no omoshi no / namekujiri
> Onitsura. This arresting if unappetizing verse captures how the interminable early-summer rains transmogrify the human world into a damp morass, even to the extent that slugs (*namekujiri*, a variation on *namekuji*) end up on sushi pressingstones (*omoshi*). Yet it also suggests the gloominess of the season by invoking the slothfulness of the slug and the weightiness of the stone.

dreadful the stream / without so much as a name! / early-summer rains
samidare ya / na mo naki kawa no / osoroshiki
> Buson. Although known for gloominess, the rains of early summer, in Buson's hands, take on a menacing quality.

the blossoms / of some unheard-of creeping weed / by the riverside
na mo shiranu / ogusa hana saku / kawabe kana
> Chiun. In *Nanihito hyakuin* (1447). *Ogusa* is a kind of creeping bugleweed (*Ajuga decumbens*).

on account of spring / a no-name mountain / shrouded in mist
haru nare ya / na mo naki yama no / usugasumi
> Bashō. Shinten'ō Nobutane, author of *Oi no soko* (1795), commented that 'This poem is haikai because it mentions a nameless hill. Singing

of famous mountains is left to waka poets' (quoted in Ueda (ed. and trans.), *Bashō and His Interpreters*, p. 126).

no-name places / have their particular charm – / mountain cherries
na no tsukanu / tokoro kawayushi / yamazakura
Goshun.

drab inkwashes / along with off-colour prints / carried home by pilgrims
nishikie to / sumie to gyōja / motte kuru
Author unnamed. In *Yanagidaru* 30 (1804). Similar versions appeared earlier in *Senryūhyō mankuawase* (1757–89) and in *Yanagidaru* 23 (1789). The religious pilgrimage was a common pretext for a pleasure jaunt. It was also a euphemism for a visit to the floating world (*ukiyo*) of kabuki or puppet theatre, street spectacles and pleasure quarters. For such 'pilgrims' (*gyōja*), 'brocade prints' (*nishikie*) of this titillating world served as polychromatic mementos, some of them no doubt risqué, whereas the 'inkwash pictures' (*sumie*) available at temples served as black-and-white alibis.

diddling herself / to a kabuki pin-up! / the chambermaid
nigaoe de / ateire o suru / nagatsubone
Gadō. In *Yanagi no hazue* (1835). Watanabe explains that the chambermaid uses a dildo while ogling a portrait of a kabuki actor (*EBYHT*, pp. 57–8). Literally 'likeness prints', *nigaoe* were stylized, almost cartoonish images, with some realistic touches, of actors in character. One wonders if the actor in question here was playing a male or female role. The *nagatsubone*, or chambermaid, was often depicted as oversexed.

noblewoman / (under an alias) / in the cheap seats!
okugata ni / imyō o tsukeru / kiriotoshi
Gochō. In *Yanagidaru* 26 (1796). Although the upper classes publicly looked down their noses at plebeian forms of art and culture, in private many were huge fans. This meant that they would typically disguise themselves when visiting the pleasure quarters or theatre district. In this verse, a noble lady (*okugata*) is watching kabuki from the unpartitioned standing-room-only 'crush' (*kiriotoshi*) of the theatre, up against the very front of the stage where visibility was limited. No doubt she can afford a better seat but is leery of government spies on the lookout there for people like her. Or else she is such an avid fan, she can only attend regularly if she buys the cheapest tickets so as not to drain the family coffers, which would raise the suspicions of her nobleman husband.

among men, samurai! / so why do they come disguised / as lowly merchants?

hito wa bushi / naze chōnin ni / natte kuru
>   Author unnamed. In *Yanagidaru* 5 (1770). According to the idiom, samurai are kings among men, yet here they are, in a cowardly disguise, presumably in some floating-world establishment such as the popular theatre or pleasure quarter – or are they crashing a *haiku* party, perhaps even the one in which this very verse was composed?

samurai rules / in the Yoshiwara / hardly pertain

yoshiwara de / budō shōri o / ezaru koto
>   Saikaku. The usual social hierarchy, dominated by the samurai, did not apply in the liminal world of the infamous licensed pleasure quarters in Edo. It might be said that, even for samurai, what happens in Yoshiwara, stays in Yoshiwara.

the bachelor / feeling lonesome / plays with his flute

hitorimono / samishiku naru to / fue o fuki
>   Shun'u.

ignorant bachelor / applying *Pleasure Her* lotion / to pleasure himself

bakana doku- / shin yotsumeya o / tsukete kaki
>   Ryūsha. In *Yanagi no hazue* (1835). Adult shops, such as the Yotsumeya in Edo, sold aphrodisiacs, elixirs and sensual lotions, including concoctions to stimulate women. Here, the verse straddling (*kumatagari*) isolates the *doku* of *dokushin* (bachelor) to suggest 'poison'.

'sheltered girl' / means never beholding cock / even in dreams

yume ni damo / henoko o minu ga / ohimesama
>   Bunji. In *Yanagi no hazue* (1835). A loose burlesquing of a passage from the Confucian *Analects* (7:5) replacing 'Duke (of Zhou)' (*Shūkō*) with 'dick' (*henoko*): 'It has been a long time since I last saw in a dream the Duke of Zhou' (in Leys (trans.), *The Analects of Confucius*, p. 29).

the bride-to-be / at a bookshop, faintly: / 'so that's how it's done!'

yomeiri wa / kō da to hon'ya / sotto mise
>   Author unnamed. In *Senryūhyō mankuawase* (1766). Supposedly, a virgin about to be married would receive a crash course in sex education from some kind of pornography, though who knows if she had not already seen such materials – or really was a virgin in the first place (see

COMMENTARY FOR PAGES 66–8

S, p. 52)? Although *mise* means 'to let see' (in which case the bookseller would be showing the porn to her), it can also be an honorific meaning 'regard'. The term *sotto*, 'quietly', 'furtively' or 'bashfully', calls to mind the near-homonym *sottō*, 'swooning'.

the young lady / grasps a single volume / but gingerly!
taisetsu ni / musume issatsu / motteiru
Author unnamed.

her mother away, / the young lady sneaks out / unlettered books
haha no rusu / musume muhitsu no / hon o dashi
Karasaki. In *Senryūhyō mankuawase* (1778). Since the young lady is probably *not* illiterate, the hidden book is undoubtedly porn.

challenge:
one atop the other / one atop the other
kasanari ni keri / kasanari ni keri

response:
love letters / from the guy she *doesn't* fancy / she shows Mother
waga sukanu / otoko no fumi wa / haha ni mise
Author unnamed. In *Yanagidaru* 4 (1769). It is not only the love letters from her secret lover (no doubt containing intimate details) that lie on top of each other.

spring rains! / fluttering in a thicket, / discarded missives
harusame ya / yabu ni fukaruru / sutetegami
Issa. The repeated *u* and *a* sounds, as in *fukaruru*, 'is blown', are quite striking.

spiteful missives: / scribbles like so many / dried bonito shavings
uramibumi / katsuo kaku hodo / kakichirashi
Saikaku.

the piece of ass / slapped by mistake / sends love letters!
machigai de / tataita shiri ga / fūjite ki
Author unnamed. The unanticipated results of presumably unwanted sexual advances in which male fantasies are projected onto women – but which also, perhaps, allow women the opportunity to exert some sexual agency of their own. *Fūjite*, referring to one or more sealed love letters, but also meaning a 'sealed move' in Japanese chess or 'forbidden hands' in sumo wrestling, is vaguely echoic of *fūjikomu*, 'ensnare'. See also Introduction, p. lvi.

when cinched / a waistsash makes the hips / come to life!
koshiobi o / shimeru to koshi wa / ikite kuru

Author unnamed. In *Yanagidaru* 1 (1765). Similar versions of the verse appear in *Mutamagawa* 6 (1754) and *Senryūhyō mankuawase* (1757–89).

first love! / drawing close 'neath stone lantern / face to face
hatsukoi ya / tōro ni yosuru / kao to kao

Taigi. In *Taigi kusen kōhen* (1777). One of the great love *haiku*, capturing an intimate moment of first-time passions ignited. Two fledgling lovers rendezvous by the light of a garden lantern that illuminates their faces against the shadows of a secluded area beyond parental surveillance. Such lanterns, typically made of stone, often with flimsy paper lampshades to shield the flame from the wind, suggest something at once immobile, rock-hard and erect, yet also fragile, uncertain and perhaps frail against the oncoming autumn, associated with the loss of innocence. The *i* in *koi*, 'love', was routinely written with *hi*, a homonym of 'fire'. Also implied here may be the associative word *tobosu*, 'turn on (a lantern)', a slang term for arousal.

under the lamplight / showing porn to turn / someone on
chōchin ni / waraie misete / tobosaseru

Author unnamed. In *Kyōku umeyanagi* 15 (c. Tenpō era, 1830–44). The phrase 'get turned on' (*tobosaseru*) is slang for sexual arousal as well as referring to a lantern (*chōchin*) – itself a phallic symbol (see previous verse). *Waraie*, 'laughing pictures', are those that bring a smile to one's face.

called 'giggle pictures' / yet they almost always bring / people to tears
waraie to / iedo taigai / naiteiru

Wagō. In *Yanagidaru* 138 (1835). No doubt both the people depicted within the pornographic prints as well as the people looking at the prints are weeping tears of joy. Many pornographic images during the period routinely included pictorial devices to engender viewer identification with the acts represented therein. (For more on this, see Timon Screech, 'Symbols in *Shunga*', in *Sex and the Floating World: Erotic Images in Japan 1700–1820* (London: Reaktion Books, 1999), pp. 133–97.)

the 'giggle': / an implement of sweet nothings / for self-pleasure
warai to wa / soragoto yogaru / dōgu nari

Author unnamed. In *Suetsumuhana* 4 (1801).

little by little / stifling one's voice – / giggle book!
dandanni / koe o hisomeru / waraibon
   Banjin. In *Yanagidaru* 34 (1806).

harebrained lovers, / aping smutty woodblock prints, / dislocate their arms!
baka fūfu / shunga no manete / te o kujiki
   Author unnamed. In *Kotodama yanagi* 1 (1861). *Kujiku*, 'sprain', also means 'dampen (enthusiasm)'. It is interesting to note how some verses pooh-pooh the erotic prints (*shunga*) of the day as unrealistic.

bending over back / -wards to imitate porno – / strained beyond reason!
murini shun- / ga no mane o shite / sujichigai
   Author unnamed. In *Kyōku umeyanagi* 15 (c. Tenpō era, 1830–44). Although it may be less awkward to parse this into 6–6–5-syllabet lines, having *shunga* straddle two lines humorously suggests unreasonably contorted bodies. The resonance between *sujichigai*, 'straining' reason or a muscle, and *murini*, 'impossible', mirrors the act of imitation itself.

judging by pictures / the netherworld's more / titillating
e de mite wa / jigoku no hō ga / omoshiroshi
   Ochō. In *Yanagidaru* 71 (1819). *Jigoku*, the Buddhist 'purgatory', also refers to the demi-monde. *Omoshiroshi* (or *omoshiroi* in modern Japanese – see note to Baishitsu's *kaya tsureba / ka mo omoshiroshi / tsuki ni tobu*) implies both the literally 'white-faced' courtesans in their grease paint and their variously 'coquettish' performances.

just my luck! / Paradise turns out to be / a real yawner
gokuraku wa / taikutsurashii / akubi nari
   Nanboku. *Gokuraku*, Amitabha's Pure Land (*Sukhāvatī* in Sanskrit), calls to mind an alternative meaning of *akubi*, 'yawn', as 'unlucky day'.

at the women's bath / some guy taking a look-see / claiming 'nature calls'
onnayu e / otoko no nozoku / kyūna yō
   Author unnamed. *Kyūna yō*, 'urgent business', was a euphemism for going to the toilet.

for woodblock artists / scrutinizing snatch is just / part of the job
ukiyoeshi / bobo o miru no mo / tosei nari
> Author unnamed. In *Yanagi no hazue* (1835). It might be said that for an artist of pornographic woodblock prints (*shunga*), rendering a lady's business *is* his business.

for woodblock artists / scrutinizing snatch is just / family business
ukiyoeshi / bobo o miru no mo / kagyō nari
> Author unnamed. In *Beni no hana* (c. 1848–54). In this dirty sexy *haiku*, which reimagines the artist's model of the previous verse as his wife, the family trade involves making her private parts public. The present verse appears in the upper left-hand corner of the image (see p. 71), and the following two at the bottom.

'isn't that enough / of a gander already?' / the artist's wife
mō mizu to / shireru darō to / eshi no tsuma
> Author unnamed. In *Beni no hana* (c. 1848–54).

her chacha / on display in vivid detail – / the artist's wife
shigeshigeto / bobo o mirareru / eshi no tsuma
> Author unnamed. In *Beni no hana* (c. 1848–54).

out of loneliness / whipping out a pillow print – / his indiscretion!
sabishisa ni / makurae no deru / mufunbetsu
> Author unnamed. In *Miyage* 26 (1708). Perhaps the indiscretion that provides temporary relief from loneliness is the same one that brought about the loneliness in the first place. For *makurae*, see note to the following verse.

her spitting image within / that awesome pillow print!
yoku nita kao no / nikuki makurae
> Author unnamed. In *Oriku taizen* 48 (1683). This *tanku* appears within a collection of acrostic verse (*oriku*). *Ma-kurae*, literally 'pillow pictures', were woodblock-printed pornographic images that could be stored beneath the pillow for handy use in bed alone or with someone else. *Nikuki*, 'despicable', here is a clipped slang for *kokoronikuki*, 'awesome'. Hanasaki suggests that the speaker is delighted to recognize within a pornographic image the familiar face of a courtesan whom he frequents (*SS*, p. 50).

challenge:
flower viewing
hanami

response:
even the mother / was teased while chaperoning / their first date
hahaoya mo / naburarete deru / miai no hi
> Author unnamed. A seventeen-syllabet acrostic verse (*oriku*) in which the first syllabet of each phrase, *ha na mi*, together spell out the challenge word *hanami* (flower viewing).

challenge:
butthole
ana

response:
butts and heads alike / wholly lined up on rice girls
atama mo shiri mo / narabu saotome
> Author unnamed (see *EBKI*, p. 79). An acrostic verse (*oriku*) in fourteen syllabets in which the first syllabet of each phrase, *a na*, together spell out the challenge word *ana* (butthole).

challenge:
now that's unavoidable! / now that's unavoidable!
zehi mo nai koto / zehi mo nai koto

response:
a doctor assays / places even a husband / doesn't assay
otto sae / shiranu tokoro o / isha ga shiri
> Author unnamed. In *Yanagidaru* 30 (1804). *Shiri*, 'knowing', can also mean 'ass'.

endless chatter ... / a dragonfly perches on / the speartip
nagabanashi / tonbo no tomaru / yari no saki
> Author unnamed. In *Yanagidaru* 1 (1765). Kanda suggests that a warrior has stopped along a road to have a good long chat with an acquaintance, who, growing increasingly bored, notices a dragonfly – a harbinger of autumn, often associated with clear blue skies – alighting on the warrior's spearhead (*EST*, p. 265).

on a white wall / a dragonfly's passing / silhouette
shirakabe ni / tonbō suguru / hikage kana
> Shōha. In *Shundei kushū* (1777). *Suguru* can mean 'expire' as well as 'go by'.

winter sun – / frozen on horseback / a silhouette
fuyu no hi ya / bajō ni kōru / kagebōshi
> Bashō. *Bajō*, 'horseback', when written in the historical orthography, can also be read 'Bashō', in which case an alternative interpretation of this verse would be: 'winter sun – / freezing into Bashō, / a silhouette'.

autumn gust – / silhouette of the mountain / all aquiver
akikaze ya / hyorohyoro yama no / kagebōshi
> Issa.

withered grass – / heat-haze shimmers upwards / inches, inches
kareshiba ya / yaya kagerō no / ichini sun
> Bashō.

firefly-gazing – / with the boatman tipsy, / how tremulous
hotarumi ya / sendō yōte / obotsukana
> Bashō. The image of fireflies near a summer party boat, where even the boatman is drinking, is not to be found earlier in the poetic canon.

faraway mountains / registered in its eye / dragonfly!
tōyama ga / medama ni utsuru / tonbo kana
> Issa. Dragonflies have compound eyes, not eyeballs (*medama*) per se. *Utsuru*, 'be reflected' or 'be projected', can also mean 'elapse (in time)' and even 'be permeated by'. The act of visual reflection is echoed in the acoustic repetition of *a* sounds in *medama* and *tōyama* (distant mountains) if not *kana*.

squid-peddler's cry / deceptively similar to that / of the cuckoo
ikauri no / koe magirawashi / hototogisu
> Bashō.

persimmon chewing / to the clanging of a bell – / Dharma Booming Temple
kaki kueba / kane ga narunari / hōryūji
> Shiki. Hōryūji, in Nara, is one of the oldest temples in Japan (and a UNESCO World Heritage Site).

my epitaph: / 'a haiku poetaster / of persimmons'
kaki kui no / haiku konomishi to / tsutaubeshi
> Shiki. This verse poignantly refers not only to the poet's fondness for persimmon (*kaki*) eating (*kui*), but also, by way of homophones, to his obsession for scratching out (*kaki*) verses (*ku i*, literally 'verse

meanings'), like this very one, in a mode he himself was mostly responsible for reinventing. The phrase *kaki kui no haiku konomishi* is grammatically ambiguous, meaning either 'partial to haiku about eating persimmons' or 'persimmon eater partial to haiku'. Other versions of this verse substitute *hokku* for *haiku* and *konomi* for *konomishi* (to avoid an extra syllabet in the second line).

raggourd left to bloom – / fruitless in stopping the phlegm / that choked this buddha
hechima saite / tan no tsumarishi / hotoke kana

Shiki. (1902). One of the poet's several death verses (*jisei*) about the raggourd or sponge gourd (*hechima*, or *Luffa acutangula*) in his garden, a plant with medicinal uses as an expectorant for relieving the symptoms of tuberculosis. So closely is it associated with Shiki's death on 19 September, that the day has come to be commemorated as Raggourd Day (*hechima ki*). This one seems to bloom with an extra syllabet in the first line. 'Buddha' (*hotoke* or *butsu*) is a conventional way of referring to the dearly departed.

challenge:
what an inconvenience! / what an inconvenience!
meiwakuna koto / meiwakuna koto

response:
ceaseless praying . . . / at times one gets choked up / with phlegm
jōnenbutsu / orifushi tan ga / hikkakari

Author unnamed. In *Yanagidaru* 4 (1769). The *nenbutsu*, a prayer to Amida Buddha, literally means 'mindful of the Buddha'. Here, the idea is that the phlegm that occasionally gets caught in the throat while praying around the clock (emphasized by the extra syllabet in the first line) to Buddha makes one think one is going to die.

lightningflash! / in the hollow of a bucket, / forgotten water
inazuma ya / tarai no soko no / wasuremizu

Shiki. *Mizu* means 'unseen' as well as 'water'.

lightningflashes! / visible again and again, / Castle Zeze's white
inazuma ya / shibashiba miyuru / zeze no shiro

Sosen. A homonym of *shiro*, 'castle', is 'white'. Zeze is on Lake Biwa near Kyoto (see Miyamori Asatarō (ed. and trans.), *Haikai and Haiku* (Westport, CT: Greenwood, 1971), p. 608).

a camellia plummets / the plumed rooster crows yet again / a camellia plummets

tsubaki ochi / tori naki tsubaki / mata ochiru

Baishitsu. The unity of this moment is suggested both aurally, the vowels and consonants being stunningly interwoven, and visually, for one can imagine the scene: in the dim light of dawn, just as a cockerel crows with ascending head, its red comb and wattles bearing an uncanny resemblance to the pink or red camellia blooms, those blooms themselves abruptly drop, as is their wont in late winter or early spring. The *tsubaki* (*Camellia japonica*) is actually a rather drab evergreen shrub whose contrastingly showy blooms all too suddenly fall from the branch in their entirety.

three trees / do not a forest make – / willow

miki aredo / mori ni wa naranu / yanagi kana

Baishitsu. The wordplay here derives from the fact that the graph for 'forest' consists of three 'trees' rather than three 'willows'. Shiki was not the first to deride such 'superficial' wordplay.

streetcorner sermon – / for all the jibberjabber, / also serene

tsujidangi / chinpunkan mo / nodoka kana

Issa.

even parrots / hailing from strange provinces / squawk Edo slang

ikoku kara / kitemo ōmu wa / edo kotoba

Tsukuda. In *Yanagidaru* 71 (1819). A study in the centrifugal force of the shogun's capital, Edo.

lightningflash! / penetrating the darkness, / a night heron's cry

inazuma ya / yami no kata yuku / goi no koe

Bashō. The *goi*, a black-crowned night heron (*Nycticorax nycticorax*), not unlike a penguin in appearance, has a black cap and other bits set against a white belly. Although such a stark contrast should be made visible by the flash, which normally precedes a thunderclap, Bashō instead supplies only the sound of the heron – which, in turn, emphasizes the muteness of the lightning. This surprise mimics the abruptness of the lightning but also of the heron itself, which typically perches invisibly by night on the water's edge waiting to ambush prey.

challenge:
how exquisite! / how exquisite!
rippa narikeri / rippa narikeri

response:
on a beauty / a wife always spots / some blemish
yoi onna / doko zo ka nyōbo / kizu o tsuke
 Author unnamed. In *Yanagidaru shūi* 2 (*c.*1796–7). Although seem-
 ingly a misogynistic swipe at the jealous wife, the implication is also
 that men hypocritically overlook flaws in the case of beautiful wom-
 en – perhaps even their own wives when originally courting. The
 phrase *kizu o tsuke*, 'harming', also means 'stalking for flaws'.

on a beauty / not even the cunt / seems filthy
ii onna / bobo mo kitanaku / omowarezu
 Yashū. In *Yanagi no hazue* (1835). A not-so-subtle criticism of how
 some people – presumably most men – are blinded by beauty.

**getting stepped on / hurts only in proportion to / who does the
 stepping!**
fumaretemo / aite ni yoreba / itaku nashi
 Nobuyuki. In *Senryūhyō mankuawase* (1757–89). *Aite* means 'the
 other party', though it ranges in tone from 'partner' to 'opponent'.

challenge:
the pitifulness / of he who is red-faced
sekimen shitaru / hito shōshi nari

response:
getting stepped on: / *I didn't hurt your foot, / did I?*
ore funde / sonata no ashi wa / itamanu ka
 Daté from the town of Koori in Ōshū Province. In Fukaku (ed.),
 Herazuguchi (1694).

any girl / decent enough for their boy / they abhor
tame ni naru / onna wa musuko / kirai nari
 Author unnamed. In *Yanagidaru* 16 (1781).

**any young man / cavorting with a proper lady / will never
 measure up!**
jionna ni / biretsuku musuko / taka ga shire
 Author unnamed. In *Yanagidaru* 17 (1782).

first date – / both parties engaged / in embellishment
shotaimen / dotchi mo uso o / tsuiteiru
  Santarō.

marriage interview – / sizing up each other's / nose or lips
miai taga- / i ni ki o tsukeru / hana to kuchi
  Soei. In *Yanagidaru* 138 (1835). An *omiai* (also *miai*) is the first formal
  interview between a man and a woman as part of an arranged mar-
  riage that has, of course, yet to be consummated. Another instance of
  verse straddling (*kumatagari*).

challenge:
paying attention and yet … / paying attention and yet …
todoki koso sure / todoki koso sure

response:
when in the mood / eyes speak as much / as the lips
ki ga areba / me mo kuchi hodo ni / mono o ii
  Romaru. In *Yanagidaru shūi* 2 (*c.*1796–7). The last two phrases have
  become proverbial.

when chatted up / casting a glance close by / means assent
kudokarete / atari o miru wa / shōchi nari
  Kōkō. In *Yanagidaru shūi* 2 (*c.*1796–7). Although a fixed glance
  off into the distance would convey indifference, perhaps counter-
  intuitively so too would a direct glance back, since that would reveal
  that one has no feelings to be kept hidden. In fact, such was even
  sometimes taken as a sign of scorn (as with *uba ni dete / sukoshi otto
  o / hizundemi*). *Atari*, 'vicinity', can also mean a 'hit' on a target – or a
  'bite' on a fishing line.

challenge:
what humiliation! / what humiliation!
hazukashii koto / hazukashii koto

response:
in a nutshell / wooing is also / grovelling
temijikani / ieba kudoki mo / mushin nari
  Author unnamed. In *Yanagidaru shūi* 6 (*c.*1796–7). The succession of
  graphs here for 'hands' or 'arms' (*te* of *temijikani*), 'mouth' (*ku* of *ku-
  doki*), then 'heart' (*shin* of *mushin*) suggests the general progression of
  courtship.

those hundred gold coins, / with young miss part of the deal, / yield no interest

musume ga tsuku / de moraite nashi / hyakuryō

> Author unnamed. In *Yanagidaru* 24 (1791). As it would be odd for the word *tsuku* to be straddled, this verse most naturally falls into a 7–6–4- or even a 6–7–4-syllabet pattern.

shoved into a vase / upon the wedding altar: / a pine mushroom

konrei no / seki de kabin e / matsu o oshi

> The woman poet Kisenjo. In *Ryūfū kyōku kaisei jinmeiroku* (1899). *Matsu* here is a truncated form of *matsutake*, 'pine mushroom', a well-worn phallic symbol in Japan.

the new bride: / picture-perfect looks / her only dowry

e no yō na / nyōbo nannimo / motte kozu

> Author unnamed (see *S*, p. 51). In the popular imagination, men would only marry women without a dowry if they were beautiful.

a thing of beauty! / a new bride without a stitch / of dowry

rippa naru / mono hanayome no / maruhadaka

> Kōbai. In *Yanagidaru* 10 (1775). When it comes to brides, 'naked' (*hadaka*) refers to lacking a dowry as well as being undressed.

still on cloud nine / the groom readily / succumbs

hyōhyō no / uchi wa teishū ni / nedari yoi

> Author unnamed. The second line contains an extra syllabet.

so tender a bride / nowhere for the mother-in-law / to sink her teeth

yawarakana / yome wa shūto no / ha ga tatazu

> Kiryū. In *Yanagidaru* 45 (1808). *Ha ga tatazu* can mean 'can't put a dent in' or 'hard to chew'.

no criticism, / just words of praise for the bride / next door

shikarazu ni / tonari no yome o / homete oki

> Author unnamed (see *EST*, p. 234).

all about the bride / the mother-in-law depicts with / mimicking gestures

yome no koto / shūto miburi o / shite hanashi

> Author unnamed. In *Yanagidaru* 8 (1773). *Hanashi* means 'separation' as well as 'talk'. So animated in her disdain is this mother-in-law that

she 'gesticulates' (*miburi o shite*) like an 'overzealous fan' (*miburizuki*) of some domestic melodrama on the kabuki stage.

a bride capable / of pleasing the mother-in-law? / her nights short-lived!

shūtome no / ki ni iru yome wa / yo ga hayashi
Author unnamed. In *Yanagidaru* 4 (1769). A new bride who works hard enough to satisfy the proverbially impossible-to-please mother-in-law 'ain't long for this world' (*yo ga hayashi*), since (as suggested by a homonym) her 'nights are short', without ample time to rest, let alone to perform other marital duties.

her only comforts: / tormenting the daughter-in-law. / attending temple.

tanoshimi wa / yome o ibiru to / teramairi
Author unnamed. In *Yanagidaru* 17 (1782).

torn between / tormenting her daughter-in-law / and heeding sermons

odangi mo / kikitaku yome mo / ijiritashi
Rishō. In *Yanagidaru* 39 (1807). One suspects that sermons merely fortify the mother-in-law's resolve to continue behaving badly.

a wife's scolding / confirms the mother-in-law's / competence

nyōbō ni / shikarareteiru / ii shūto
Author unnamed.

the bride's farts / like quakes, thunder and blazes / shake Mother-in-Law

yome no he o / jiraika hodo ni / shūto fure
Hanfu. In *Yanagidaru* 156 (1838-40?). A virtually identical verse, with slightly different orthography, appears later in the same volume.

ignobly slain / by her daughter-in-law's fart / from a squatting stance

yome no he wa / kakato no ue de / notarejini
Kanai. In *Yanagidaru* 161 (1838-40?). Kanai's verse reappears later in the same volume (though with slightly different orthography). In-law relations are likened here to a combat sport, for in Japanese fencing, sumo wrestling and so on, *kakato no ue* is a squatting position from which one springs to attack.

breaking wind / the mother-in-law also breaks / the tension
shūtome no / he o hitta node / ki ga hodoke
> Author unnamed. In *Yanagidaru* 1 (1765). There is a pun on *hodoke*, 'working out (a disagreement)' and 'relieving'. The *e* sound in fart (*he*) is echoed sporadically.

the bride's fart: / exasperating; her own: / pure *jouissance*!
yome no he wa / okori jibun no / he wa warai
> Kichibō. There is more to this verse than the overt hypocrisy of the mother-in-law perceiving her own farts as less offensive than those of her daughter-in-law. The word for 'laughter' or 'smiling' (*warai*) was loosely associated with sexual release, as evidenced by the way 'giggle picture' (*waraie*) was a euphemism for pornography. Thus, there is a veiled contrast here between the vaguely sexual if vicarious pleasure that the mother-in-law derives from comparing farts on the one hand and the no-doubt full-fledged sexuality of the newly-weds on the other. After all, given the cramped quarters of most housing during the period, if the mother-in-law was close enough to detect her daughter-in-law's farts, she would also have been close enough to hear her moans.

the knowing mother / pretending to be asleep / lets them go at it
suina haha / soraneiri shite / hajimesase
> Gadō. In *Yanagi no hazue* (1835). The couple might not have been so fortunate had this verse been about a mother-in-law (*shūto*) instead of a mother (*haha*).

missuses / even more than mummies: / nuisances
nyōbō wa / ofukuro yori mo / jamana mono
> Author unnamed. In *Yanagidaru* 6 (1771). Although early on in the marriage it is the husband's 'mummy' (*ofukuro*) who interferes with his happiness, eventually it is his 'wife' (*nyōbō*).

although long gone, / that hundred gold of her dowry, / her mug lingers on
hyakuryō wa / nakunari kao wa / nokotteru
> Author unnamed. In *Yanagidaru* 23 (1789). Although *kao* means 'face' in both senses of the word, honour as well as visage, here it is probably the latter that more disturbs the husband.

darkening breasts / shown to her husband setting / off on a trip
chi no kuromi / otto ni misete / tabidatase
> Author unnamed. In *Yanagidaru* 1 (1765). According to Taira, this
> woman shows the dark spots on her nipples and areolae to her hus-
> band, before he leaves on a trip, in order to suggest that, because preg-
> nant, she will not have an adulterous affair in his absence – and to
> urge him to be faithful to her (*RJS*, p. 12).

challenge:
joyously overflow / the saké cups
amari ureshiku / furuu sakazuki

response:
**first childbirth – / the husband feeling he himself / did half the
labour**
uizan wa / otto hanbun / umu kokoro
> Hōka. In Fukaku (ed.), *Herazuguchi* (1694). Taking the *furuu*, 'over-
> flow', of the challenge and reinterpreting it as 'mustering up courage',
> this response pokes fun at how men tend to take more than their fair
> share of the credit even when it comes to something like giving birth
> (not to mention conceiving).

seventy-five days / of postpartum abstention / up the wazoo
umareru to / nanajūgo nichi / mujōkan
> The woman poet Tessen. In *Yanagidaru* 71 (1819). Seventy-five days
> refers to both the proverbial length of time that gossip lasts and the
> usual period of abstention from sexual intercourse for a woman after
> giving birth. (Another verse promises that on the seventy-sixth day a
> woman cannot say no; see *OI*, p. 228.) *Mujōkan*, 'period of uncertain-
> ty', plays on *fujōkan*, literally 'chamber of impurity', a room dedicated
> to childbirth or menstruation – but also a euphemism for vagina.
> Taira speculates that the interest of this verse largely resides in seeing
> how sex after childbirth is described from a woman's point of view
> (*RJS*, p. 14).

his wife / who once had caught his eye / now gets up his nose
me ni tsuita / nyōbo konogoro / hana ni tsuki
> Rakuho. In *Yanagidaru* 62 (1812).

challenge:
how suspicious! / how suspicious!
okashikarikeri / okashikarikeri

response:
feigned sleep – / the snoring inordinately / faithful
sorane iri / amari ibiki ga / richigi sugi

Author unnamed. In *Yanagidaru* 4 (1769) and *Yanagidaru shūi* 8 (*c.*1796–7). The repetition of the vowel *i* (in ten of seventeen syllabets) mimics the word for snoring (*ibiki*) as well as the act of snoring. There is a double sense to *richigi*, not only meaning an artifice that is *too* (*sugi*) faithful to life, but also implying that the reason for this artifice has to do with infidelity in the relationship.

it's the *Analects* / that his mistress snatches / out of reach
rongo o ba / mekake soba kara / hittakuri

Author unnamed. In *Yanagidaru* 21 (1786). As though an extramarital affair alone did not violate Confucian precepts of morality. A relevant passage in the *Analects* (9:18) runs: 'The Master said: "I have never seen anyone who loved virtue as much as sex"' (in Leys (trans.), *The Analects of Confucius*, p. 41).

challenge:
a sight to behold! / a sight to behold!
kore wa migoto ya / kore wa migoto ya

response:
that eye-popper / of a procured accessory / worn on his sleeve
katta toki / deta me no tama o / koshi ni sage

Senden from Udagawachō. In *Kinkōhyō mankuawase* (1737). Most likely the stunning (literally 'eyeball popping') fashion accessory is a netsuke, or carved figurine. Often made of ivory (or some other durable material such as fossilized wood, coral, deer antlers or even copper), sometimes with inlaid jewels (*tama*), netsuke were used as toggles to adjust cords securing a tobacco pouch or coin purse to a belt at the waist – not unlike the little plastic figurines accessorizing modern-day mobile phones. However, *tama* was also slang for 'courtesan'. The phrase 'affixed to the waist' (*koshi ni sage*) suggests something worn conspicuously (*hissageru*), perhaps as a conversation piece.

challenge:
how agreeable! / how agreeable!
kokoroyoi koto / kokoroyoi koto

response:
sweet nothings / of the kept woman: / 'gimme, gimme!'
omekake no / mutsugoto kurero / kurero nari

> Kōbai. In *Yanagidaru* 21 (1786). *Kurero* is a double entendre, referring to the mistress's desire for additional recompense for letting her sugar daddy have his way with her.

noble ladies: / where they daintily stroke / mistresses grab hold!
okugata wa / hameru mekake wa / nigiru nari

> Author unnamed. Apart from the obvious sexualized reading, bolstered by double entendres on *hameru* ('fuck' as well as 'stroke') and *nigiru* ('grasp (balls)' as well as 'clutch'), this verse applies stereotypes of class preference for musical instruments to the dynamics of romantic relationships. Supposedly, upper-class ladies prefer the refined zither (*koto*), which one plucks or strums with a plectrum lightly clasped (*hameru*), whereas lower-class women prefer the twangy shamisen, which one grips firmly (*nigiru*) by the neck. The implication is that both kinds of women keep their men in line, respectively, either by applying pressure gently or by seizing the upper hand through threats or blackmail or the like.

a lady's zither / never trumps the shamisen / of a mistress!
okugata no / koto o shamisen / mekakegata

> Shinchō. In *Yanagidaru* 37 (1807).

the dimples / of his mistress: the downfall / of his wife!
omekake no / ekubo wa oku no / metsubo nari

> Shimeko. In *Yanagidaru* 65 (1814). The heart of this verse resides in how *metsubo* (downfall) reverberates with *ekubo* (dimples).

the graph for 'mistress': / a 'woman' whom one's wife / cannot 'stand'
shō no ji wa / nyōbo no hara no / tatsu onna

> Hakushi. In *Yanagidaru* 146 (1838–40?). In a bit of orthographic play not at all rare in *haiku* – though the challenges of translation make it seem rare – the graph for 'mistress' is here observed to combine component graphs for 'woman' and 'stand'.

whereas mistresses / might shake you down for money / maids also rock baby!
mekake no wa / nedari gejo no wa / yusuru nari
Author unnamed. In *Senryūhyō mankuawase* (1757–89). A slightly different version appears in *Yanagidaru* 21 (1786). Either the maid has discovered the husband's secret affair with a kept woman, who is blackmailing him, or else it is the maid herself with whom the husband is having an affair. Either way, at the end of the day it is the maid who holds the trump card.

challenge:
how vain! and yet ... / how vain! and yet ...
ogori koso sure / ogori koso sure

response:
novice wet nurse / glances at the man of the house / slightly askance
uba ni dete / sukoshi otto o / hizundemi
Author unnamed. In *Yanagidaru* 1 (1765). The new wet nurse apparently did not realize that discharging her duties might draw the wandering eye of her male employer.

to the napping face / the wet nurse bids farewell / then withdraws
sagaru uba / hirune no kao e / itomagoi
Kashō. In *Yanagidaru* 77 (1823). Probably not the *kibyōshi* author Iba Kashō (*c.* 1747–83). There is a pun on *itomagoi*, 'withdraw', but also 'pay a farewell visit'.

pushy kids! / championing their opinions, / saleswomen
nedaru ko no / mikata ni natte / joten'in
Jōzen. More than a swipe at overeager salespeople, this verse plays on the stereotype of maids, nannies, shopgirls and other kinds of service women as being childishly aggressive themselves.

maids' quarters – / the one who's *too* pretty / gets bullied
jochūbeya / utsukushi sugiru / no o ijime
Author unnamed.

both mistresses / every bit as dazzling / as razor-sharp blades
mekake futari / hamono no yō ni / utsukushiki
Author unnamed. The suggestion of something masculine within female aggression, in the phallic image of edged blades, somehow emasculates the man, who is syntactically absent. Yet the homophonous

'teeth' (*ha*) of these 'cutting tools' (*hamono*) suggests a biting violence. The mistresses are staring daggers and smiling menacingly at each other, but also at the missing male member of the love triangle.

Castle Toppler – / on account of her tears / his storehouse leaks
keisei no / namida de ie no / kura ga mori

Kisui. In *Yanagidaru* 27 (1798). A similar version in *Yanagidaru* 82 (1825) by Shōken runs: 'Castle Toppler – / on account of her tears / his storehouse roof leaks' (*keisei no / namida de kura no / yane ga mori*). In both versions the tears of the gorgeous home-wrecker bring about the literal leaking of the man's family storehouse by the figurative depletion of his funds. Simply put, the man is lavishing money on his dalliance instead of his domestic obligations. 'Castle Toppler' (*keisei*) referred to any beautiful woman, though particularly a courtesan, who brings about a man's downfall. The term derives from a Chinese story of the Tang dynasty (618–907), immortalized in the classic 'Song of Everlasting Sorrow' ('Chang hen ge', 806) by the poet Bai Juyi (772–846), about how the obsession of Emperor Xuanzong (685–762) with his consort, the beauty Yang Guifei (Yōkihi in Japanese; 719–56), led to national as well as personal ruination.

spicy playboy – / salty his old man, / sweet his mother
sui musuko / karai oyaji ni / amai haha

Ribai. In *Yanagidaru* 55 (1811). The verse appears twice in the same volume. Beneath the surface wordplay of flavouring the son sour (*sui*), the father salty (*karai*) and the mother sweet (*amai*), this verse describes the prototypical story of the sophisticated (*sui*) young playboy who, living large in the pleasure quarters at the expense of the family fortune, is chastised, perhaps even disowned, by the harsh (*karai*) father, but defended, perhaps even financially supported in secret, by the indulgent (*amai*) mother.

the mother / tops off the alibis / of her carousing son
hahaoya wa / musuko no uso o / tashite yari

Author unnamed. In *Yanagidaru* 16 (1780). In an act of wilful deceit, the mother defends the son against the father's scathing criticism – perhaps even to the point of threatening disinheritance – for squandering the family fortune in the pleasure quarters. This reason is suggested only indirectly, both by the secondary meaning of *tashite*, 'reinforcing (a lie)', as 'replenishing (a drink)' and by the special use of 'son' (*musuko*) to refer to an aspiring playboy.

the young player / having played his mother / goes off to get played
haha o dama- / shite damasare ni / musuko yuki
   Author unnamed. Another instance of verse straddling (*kumatagari*).

even while scolded / the boy has only one thing / on his mind
iken kiku / musuko no mune ni / ichimotsu ari
   Author unnamed. The phrase *mune ni ichimotsu*, referring to a secret
plan, here contains a double entendre on *ichimotsu*, literally 'one
thing', but also a slang term for penis, which may explain the bulge
in the syllabet count (*onsūritsu*) of the third line.

even while scolded / the only thing on his mind / is girls
iken kiku / musuko no mune ni / onna ari
   Author unnamed. In *Yanagidaru* 11 (1776).

within the heart / of every rebuking parent / resides a bride
iken suru / oyaji no mune ni / yome ga ari
   Author unnamed. In *Yanagidaru* 22 (1788).

badmouthing ... / somewhere deep down inside / he's in love!
warukuchi no / otoko dokoka de / horesasu ki
   Bishi.

challenge:
... just try and get one!
tottemiru

response:
a bride / for that playboy son –
dōraku na / musuko ni yome o
   Author unnamed. An example of a 'footgear-linking' (*kutsuzuke*)
verse. The resultant verse reads: 'a bride / for that playboy son – / just
try and get one!'

**he of all people / who eats us out of house and home / brushing his
teeth!**
kuitsubusu / yatsu ni kagitte / ha o migaki
   Author unnamed. In *Yanagidaru* 1 (1765). A light-hearted exposé of
the cavalier attitude of the omnivorous prodigal son. A similar verse
by Utan runs: 'eating us out of home / his quirk is brushing his teeth
/ scrupulously!' (*kuitsubushi / sono kuse ha o ba / yoku migaki*). In *Ya-
nagidaru* 63 (1813).

challenge:
what insolence! / what insolence!
wagamamana koto / wagamamana koto

response:
his mother's scolding / defied on extravagant / Chinese paper!
karakami e / haha no iken o / tatetsukeru
 Author unnamed. In *Yanagidaru* 1 (1765). To his mother's warning
against squandering the family fortune, the prodigal playboy cava-
lierly replies in a note jotted on expensive paper that in and of itself
is defiant.

at the bordello / the mother frets her brow into / a cliffhanger!
chaya e kuru / haha wa hitai e / hachimonji
 Utan. In *Yanagidaru* 65 (1814). The punchline, *hachimonji*, pivots
between the phrase *hitai e hachinoji o yoseru*, 'furrow one's brows'
(likening furrowed brows to the graph for 'eight'), and *Hachimonji-ya*,
'Figure of Eight Shop', a Kyoto publisher specializing in popular epi-
sodic novellas. A mother braving the demi-monde in order to track
down her child – presumably a playboy son squandering the family
fortune or else a daughter sold into sexual slavery – was itself the stuff
of melodrama.

cutting him off / even before his father does: / the hired sidekick
oyaji yori / mazu mikagiru wa / taiko nari
 Author unnamed. In *Yanagidaru* 24 (1791). A young playboy typi-
cally hired a 'drum-bearer' (*taikomochi* or *taiko*), a paid escort to the
pleasure quarters, to keep him company while smoothing over any
awkward or dull moments with light banter. The sharp contrast be-
tween such jokey demeanour and this harsh rejection is reinforced
by the comic incongruity of a stranger knowing a young man better
than his own father does. Then again, it is only natural that a plea-
sure-quarter establishment worth its salt would catch on to the cash-
flow problems of a playboy earlier than his parents realize the full
extent of his embezzlement.

challenge:
now that's gentle! / now that's gentle!
sunao narikeri / sunao narikeri

response:
exclaims the father / of the silverpiped playboy: / 'that *real* silver?!'
gingiseru / gin no yō da to / oyaji ii

Author unnamed. In *Yanagidaru* 7 (1772). Strictly speaking, 'silver-pipe' (*gingiseru*) is something of a misnomer, for while fitted with a sterling silver mouthpiece and bowl, the elegantly long stem was fashioned of wood. In the Edo vernacular, the term came to be applied to the sophisticated playboy who wielded this flashy emblem of extravagance.

silverpipe – / even this figures / in the scolding
gingiseru / kore mo iken no / kazu ni iri
Shiseki. In *Yanagidaru* 40 (1807). For *gingiseru*, see note to previous verse.

getting disowned: / 'take your damned silverpipe / and skedaddle!'
kandō ni / motte ushō to / gingiseru
Author unnamed. For *gingiseru*, see note to *gingiseru / gin no yō da to / oyaji ii*.

disinherited / their lovers' suicide becomes / so much empty talk
kandō o / sarete shinju ga / uso ni nari
Author unnamed. Neither of the two lovers – presumably a playboy and his courtesan – who have been planning a double suicide wishes to admit to now having cold feet. Reading between the lines, both of them had secretly counted on eloping at the last minute on his parents' money. The graph for 'falsehood' (*uso*) consists of component graphs for 'mouth' (suggesting 'talk') and 'empty'.

when no longer / taken with himself who else / will take him?
unubore o / yamereba hokani / horete nashi
Author unnamed. In *Yanagidaru* 24 (1791) and *Suetsumuhana* 4 (1801). It appears later by one Maita in *Yanagidaru* 38 (1807).

disowned son – / taking him back along with / two extra mouths
kandō o / yurushite kuchi ga / futatsu fue
Author unnamed. In *Yanagidaru* 3 (1768). The prodigal son, once disowned for ignoring parental rebukes against carousing in the pleasure quarters, now accompanied by both the cause and result of his romantic escapades, returns home chastened.

overstaying / means being voracious / for hooch
itsuzuke wa / kai no atohiki / jōgo nari
Soei. In *Yanagi no hazue* (1835). Paying up front for three nights with a courtesan was cheaper than booking only two nights and 'overstaying'

(*itsuzuke*) one, since an overage fee was charged on top of the extra time. Still, the latter, being spontaneous, was considered more debonair.

afternoon delight / stacked atop night-time delight / all on the house!

hiru no chigiri / yoru no chigiri o / kasanekeri

Saikaku. *Chigiri*, 'pledge', was a euphemism for making love, the spontaneity of which is underlined here with an extra syllabet in the first line. *Kasanekeri* has a range of meanings, from 'piled up (on top of each other)' and 'repeated (many times)' (both derived from *kasane*) to 'without having rented' (the negative form of *kasu*), which in the context of the pleasure quarters refers to being 'on the house'.

the poseur who claims / 'my courtesan had me kidnapped!' / florid self-flattery

tsukamikomi- / mashita to teishu / hana no miso

Author unnamed. In *Yanagidaru* 6 (1771). When a courtesan discovered that one of her regular clients was frequenting another bordello, she might have him physically forced back to her. The straddling (*kumatagari*) of the word *tsukamikomimashita*, 'had kidnapped', across two phrases humorously intimates the putative two-timing. *Hana*, 'flower', also implies a beautiful woman.

last night's / lovers' tiff: this morning's / marital split!

yūbe no wa / kuzetsu kesa no wa / kenka nari

Author unnamed. In *Yanagidaru* 8 (1773) and *Yanagidaru shūi* 7 (c.1796-7). The same verse would later be claimed by one Ryūshi in *Yanagidaru* 33 (1806). To placate his courtesan lover after a quarrel, a playboy ends up spending the night in the pleasure quarters, only to return home to even more trouble.

challenge:
unbridled fun! / unbridled fun!
zonbunna koto / zonbunna koto

response:
his return fare / the wife coughs up / with a *hmph*!
kagochin o / yatte nyōbo wa / tsun to suru

Author unnamed. In *Yanagidaru* 1 (1765). The word *kagochin* (palanquin fare) is vaguely reminiscent of *chinko* (willy), which intimates what he might have been up to the previous night.

challenge:
now there's an excuse! / now there's an excuse!'
wake no aru koto / wake no aru koto

response:
the bridle / to unbridledness: / one's bride!
chōhōna / mono no jamana wa / nyōbo nari
    Tōgetsu. In *Yanagidaru shūi* 6 (c.1796–7). Also in *Mutamagawa* 9
    (1759). The double entendre on *chōhōna mono* exposes the hypocrisy
    of those men who regard having a wife as a 'matter of convenience'
    only so far as she does not hinder their flings with 'women of con-
    venience' in the pleasure quarters.

having a wife / one's countenance / turns glum
nyōbō o / motte ninsō- / zura ni nari
    Author unnamed. In *Yanagidaru* 17 (1782). Another instance of verse
    straddling (*kumatagari*).

moon down, / crows caw and the wife / riled up!
tsuki ochi / karasu naite nyōbo / hara o tate
    Author unnamed. In *Kawazoi yanagi* 1 (1780), a five-volume collec-
    tion of miscellaneous verse (*zappai*), often in non-standard forms,
    selected by Karai Senryū. This 4–9–5-syllabet verse, about a husband
    returning home late after a night on the town to a wife who is less
    than thrilled, spoofs a well-known Tang dynasty poem, Zhang Ji's
    'Night Mooring at Maple Bridge' ('Fūkyō yahaku' in Japanese), that
    begins: 'the moon sets, a crow caws, frosty vapours fill the heavens'
    (*tsuki ochi karasu naite shimo ten ni mitsu*).

**out all night long / upon his return the neighbours: / 'there they go
again!'**
asagaeri / sorya hajimaru to / ryōdonari
    Gochō. In *Yanagidaru* 38 (1807). An earlier version by an unnamed
    author appeared in *Yanagidaru* 7 (1772) with the challenge verse:
    'now that's harsh! / now that's harsh!' (*kitsui koto kana / kitsui koto
    kana*). This must not be the first time the marital fracas is overheard.

challenge:
too little too late! / too little too late!
osoi koto kana / osoi koto kana

response:
only after / his philanderings does he fuss / over his wife
ireagete / kara nyōbō o / kawayugari

Author unnamed. In Kojui Taiō (ed.), *Urawakaba* (1732). This response was republished later as a free-standing verse in *Senryūhyō mankuawase* (1770). *Ireagete*, 'overindulge', implies sexual as well as financial immoderation in the pleasure quarters.

there's no comparing / a playboy's popularity / to his wife's jealousy

nyōbō no / yaku hodo teishu / mote mo sezu

Author unnamed. Another *senryū* that has become proverbial wisdom. There is a slight pun in the phrase *yaku hodo*, 'to the extent of burning (with jealousy)', for *hodo* can be a smith's forge for 'firing' metal. This verse thus might also be rendered: 'no *match* / for her *fuming* jealousy – / his e*steem*!'

crazy jealous – / so the master of the house / cooks dinner

yoppodo no / rinki teishu ga / meshi o taki

Author unnamed. The phrase *meshi o taki*, literally 'simmering rice', means to cook a meal, particularly dinner. However misogynistic the implication that the jealousy belongs to the wife, the husband comes across not only as having behaved badly to cause such jealousy, but also as being too weak to stand up to his wife directly – which he might feel caused his bad behaviour in the first place.

squabble won / yet the master of the house simmers / the rice

kenka ni wa / katta ga teishu / meshi o taki

Sarumatsu. In *Yanagidaru* 48 (1809). *Taki*, 'cook', can also mean 'seethe'. See also note to previous verse.

even the winner / of that evening's squabble / loses sleep

iikatta / kata mo sono yo o / nesobireru

Gyokutorō.

being scolded / the wife refuses to bring / herself to bed

shikarareta / nyōbo wa neyō / to mo shinai

Seimu. A pun yields two meanings: 'the wife wouldn't *even say* (*to mo*) "let's to bed"!' and 'the wife wouldn't be *together* (*tomo*) with him in bed'.

unsmiling wife – / bootlicking her relentlessly / to get even

warawanai / nyōbo e oseji / shikiri nari

Author unnamed. This wife's frigidity must be something that incurs – if not is incurred by – the husband's passive-aggressive toadyism. After all, one is expected to reply with a smile to kindness, particularly in public, even kindness meant to kill.

novice courtesan! / polishing the pipe with which / she gets herself whipped
tatakareru / kiseru kamuro wa / migaiteru
 Saō. In *Yanagidaru* 27 (1798). This courtesan-in-training not only is ridiculously complicit in her own corporal punishment, but also has unwittingly brought it upon herself in the first place: for judging by the sexually charged imagery, a fully fledged courtesan must be cruelly penalizing this young teenage trainee of hers with the symbolically fitting chore out of jealousy over a male client who was beginning to show signs of interest in the younger woman – perhaps even *on account* of her comparative *naiveté*?

his bad posture: / even that he blames / on women
izumai no / warui mo onna / tsumi ni nari
 Kayū. In *Yanagidaru* 27 (1798).

'all women ..?/ declared before glancing / over his shoulder
subete onna / to iu mono to / sokora o mi
 Author unnamed. In *Yanagidaru* 9 (1774). This can be rendered as a 6–6–5-syllabet verse, as here, or else the word *onna*, 'women', needs to be cut in half to straddle the first two lines.

making up, / the wife's voice returns / to normal
nakanaori / moto no nyōbo no / koe ni nari
 Author unnamed. In *Yanagidaru* 15 (1780).

challenge:
that's delightful! / that's delightful!
omoshiroi koto / omoshiroi koto

response:
making up, / he returns to the usual / watering hole
nakanaori / moto no sakaya e / tachikaeri
 Author unnamed. In *Yanagidaru* 4 (1769).

piece of his mind! / and upon returning home / his wife's piece of mind
iken shite / kaereba tsuma ni / iken sare
 Yachō. No doubt the husband has been complaining to a friend about his wife – whose castigation of him for staying out is just the kind of thing he has been complaining about in the first place.

single people / know not the perks / of marital squabbles

hitorimono / fūfu kenka no / ri o shirazu

 Sekishō. In *Yanagidaru* 65 (1814).

couple next door have, / judging by the heavy breathing, / kissed and made up

hanaiki de / shireru tonari no / nakanaori

 Senmei. In *Yanagidaru* 32 (1805). Just as much a comment on snoopy neighbours as on the notorious lack of privacy in Edo's tenement row housing, even for a couple enjoying make-up sex in their own room (as opposed to any number of other spots just out of public scrutiny).

darkest night! / losing track of its nest, / a plover cries out

yami no yo ya / su o madowashite / naku chidori

 Bashō. The desolation of a seemingly interminable winter is captured here by a winter bird in the dead of night being unable to find its nest and, by implication, the springtime that nests symbolize.

more chill / than the blustering wind – / midnight moon

fuku kaze no / oto yori samushi / yowa no tsuki

 Shōkyū.

wintergrove – / a night when moonshafts / cut to the bone!

fuyukodachi / tsuki kotsuzui ni / iru yo kana

 Kitō. The eponymous opening verse to Buson's linked sequence *Fuyu-kodachi* (Wintergrove, 1780). Rays of the moon (*tsuki*) shine through the ghostly barren trees, penetrating (*tsuki*) like daggers (*kodachi*, a homonym of 'grove of trees').

tonight the blooms / surely fall beneath that scythe / of a crescent moon

shingetsu no / ono ni chiruran / hana no kyō

 Saigin.

nothing like it, / not even its visual spoof: / crescent moon

nanigoto no / mitate nimo nizu / mika no tsuki

 Bashō. If any verse can come close to capturing the essence of the moon, it is a verse that openly admits to its inability to do so.

only thing slicker / than cormorants are cormorants / mimicked by children!

u no mane o / u yori kōshana / kodomo kana

Issa. Sometimes art is even better than life, or at least an imitation can seem more artful than its original.

strutting along / in imitation of ploughing – / a raven

hatauchi no / mane o shite aruku / karasu kana

Issa. The second line contains an extra syllabet.

challenge:
how stirring! / how stirring!

setsusetsuna koto / setsusetsuna koto

response:
the Wolf / devours everything save / her money pouch

ōkami wa / saifu bakari o / kuinokoshi

Author unnamed. In *Yanagidaru* 7 (1772). As with the English 'wolf', an *ōkami* is a predatory carnivorous beast interested only in getting one thing from a woman. This response plays on both meanings of the challenge, 'how moving!' and 'how impassioned!'.

spring drizzle ... / mallards not yet devoured / quack it up

harusame ya / kuwarenokori no / kamo ga naku

Issa. Although *naku* here means 'quack', its homonym, 'be no more', portends that while these wild ducks (*kamo*) have survived the winter, maybe (*ka mo*) they are not quite yet out of the woods.

evening squall! / scampering among the houses, / squawking ducks

yūdachi ya / ie o megurite / naku ahiru

Kikaku. A vignette of a sudden evening thunderstorm causing domestic ducks (*ahiru*) to run around one or more houses frantically quacking.

crack of dawn! / the citadel encircled by / quacking ducks

akegata ya / shiro o torimaku / kamo no koe

Kyoriku. The moat around a castle is brought into relief by the sound of the ducks upon it.

as though flowing / with the current downstream: / swallows on the wing!

mizu ni tsurete / nagaruru yōna / tsubame kana

Saimaro. The river or stream is brought into relief by the sight of swallows, who usually hunt in groups, following its flow. The first line contains an extra syllabet.

out of the blue / of early-morning light: / a paulownia leaf

akebono no / aoki naka yori / kiri hitoha

Ryōta. This single leaf from a paulownia tree (*kiri*, or *Paulownia tomentosa*) is a sudden harbinger of early autumn.

paulownia leaves / scatter, crinkle, one by one / on the breeze

hitoha chiru / totsu hitoha chiru / kaze no ue

Ransetsu. A fitting death verse (*jisei*) for a poet, since the leaf of the paulownia tree (*kiri* – see previous verse), with its three prongs of buds in clusters of 5–7–5, symbolizes the seventeen-syllabet verse-form itself. Just as *hana* (blossom) normally indicates the cherry blossom in particular, since it is the cherry that epitomizes all blossoms, so too does *hitoha* (single leaf) normally indicate the paulownia.

misty spring rains ... / umbrellas high and low / aboard the ferry

harusame ya / kasa takahiku ni / watashibune

Shiki. *Harusame* refers to the light, almost misty, steady rains of spring that prototypically give rise to feelings of wistfulness or dreaminess.

steady spring rains ... / jabbering along together, / parasol and slicker

harusame ya / monogatari yuku / mino to kasa

Buson. (1782). After an undoubtedly long winter, people come out of doors 'to take a stroll' (*yuku*) and have 'a chat' (*monogatari*) with one another in spite of the soft, continuous, spring rains (*harusame*). Wetting everything and everybody, these rains imbue the scene with a certain intimacy, if not eroticism, bringing together even polar opposites, such as the owners of a straw raincape (*mino*) and a lacquered paper umbrella (*kasa*). Whoever this odd couple might be – man and woman, provincial and urbanite, merchant and samurai, rich and poor, some combination thereof? – the spectacle of their ostensibly headless bodies playfully conjures up the old 'tales' (*monogatari*) of romance as well as ghosts. Moreover, *monogatari* and *mino to kasa* (straw raincape and parasol) are tethered together aurally by the *o-o-a-a* vowel pattern. This famed verse reputedly inspired the superpository technique of Ezra Pound (1885–1972) and of John Gould Fletcher (1886–1950) before him.

spring drizzle ... / browsing at the picturebook stall / umbrella propped up
harusame ya / kasa sashite miru / ezōshiya
Shiki.

fancy halfcoats / scampering away headless – / sudden downpour!
kubi no nai / haori ga hashiru / niwakaame
Author unnamed. However amusing the image of one or more headless fine jackets heedlessly beating a hasty retreat may or may not be, this verse lightly pokes fun at being caught off guard without rain gear even in a season when rain is known to come from out of the blue.

sudden downpour! / no such thing as / a pensive face
yūdachi ni / monoomou kao wa / nakarikeri
The nun Shokyū. A sudden evening shower has caught everyone off guard, so people are scrambling to get out of the rain with looks varying from intense concentration and panic to sheer relief from the summer heat. The second line contains an extra syllabet.

sudden summer squall! / quick thinking of all sorts / of head coverings
yūdachi ya / chie samazama no / kaburimono
Otsuyū. There may be a slight pivot on *sama*, yielding the phrases *chie-sama*, 'Mr and Mrs Wits', and *samazama no kaburimono*, 'various head coverings'.

challenge:
staring and yet ... / staring and yet ...
nagame koso sure / nagame koso sure

response:
shelter from the rain – / the inscription on a plaque / learned by heart
amayadori / gaku no monji o / yoku oboe
Author unnamed. In *Yanagidaru* 1 (1765). An alternative version in *Senryūhyō mankuawase* (1757–89) replaces *amayadori* (rain shelter) with *niwaka ame*, 'rain shower'. Caught without an umbrella under the eaves of a building, one has nothing else to do but read the plaque there, over and over.

rain lets up / and the price of umbrellas / comes back down!
ame no yamu / uchi karakasa o / nekitte i
> Author unnamed. In *Yanagidaru shūi* 9 (*c.*1796–7).

storming off / the umbrella flips out / a bit too far
hara tatte / deru kasa wa / hirakisugi
> Author unnamed. In *Yanagidaru shūi* 10 (*c.*1796–7). This is an alternative version of a verse that originally appeared in *Mutamagawa* 16 (1771).

snow-buckled, / reverting to a former life – / umbrella ribs
yukiore ya / mukashi ni kaeru / kasa no hone
> Shōi.

giving instructions / on how to use the tattered / loaner umbrella
sashiyō o / shinan shite kasu / yaburegasa
> Kanri. In *Yanagidaru* 51 (1811).

paper umbrellas – / how many pass by / in snowy twilight?
karakasa no / ikutsu sugiyuku / yuki no kure
> Hokushi.

donning a sedge hat / primping before the mirror – / tealeaf picker
sugegasa o / kite kagami miru / chatsumi kana
> Shikō. Perhaps not uncoincidentally, *kagami* (mirror) reflects the surname of the poet.

this bozo fishing / and that bozo watching him – / bozos both!
tsuru yatsu mo / tsuru yatsu miteiru / yatsu mo yatsu
> ☙ (Hanasanjin). In *Yanagidaru* 151 (1838–40?). Fools who feel superior when scrutinizing (*miteiru*, emphasized by an extra syllabet) other fools may not be limited to the fools within this verse that we ourselves are reading.

only a fool / takes being made a fool of / without humour
baka dakara / baka ni sareta o / ikidōri
> Garyūbō. The corollary presumably being that someone who is no fool takes being made a fool of in good part.

although spectacles / might do the trick for the eyes, / and dentures for the teeth ...
me wa megane / ha wa ireba nite / ma ni aedo
Mukujō. In *Yanagidaru* 38 (1807). Also appears later in the same volume. The infirmities of age in men progress, according to popular belief, by afflicting first dental health, then eyesight and finally sexual virility (see *EBKI*, p. 138). In this context, *ma ni aedo*, 'can suffice and yet ...', may be a double entendre that also means 'can encounter a crack and yet ...'.

still functioning: / eyes and ears and teeth and yet / that one regret!
me mo mimi mo / ha mo yokeredomo / zannensa
Kanshi. In *Yanagidaru* 88 (1825).

eyeglass polishing ... / even the lens on the side / with the sightless eye
mienu me no / hō no megane no / tama mo fuku
Sōjō.

'shall we yank 'em all?' / ejaculates the tooth doctor, / unstintingly
mina nuite / shimae to haisha / oshigenashi
Author unnamed. *Nuite*, 'extracting', is also vulgar slang for 'ejaculation'.

his dead member / the wife tries frantically to / resuscitate
shini mara o / nyōbo tōtō / katsu o ire
Ryūsha. In *Yanagi no hazue* (1835). *Tōtō* has a range of meanings: an onomatopoeic word for a pounding or clanging noise, as in the sound of swords clashing; an adverb referring to the torrential gushing of water or any kind of rapid but smooth action; or an adverb meaning 'as a last resort'.

at the hotspring / *apparently not his daughter!* / the scuttlebutt
tōjiba no / uwasa musume ja / nai rashii
Shun'u. *Musume*, 'daughter', also refers to a respectable young lady, though either way the related phrase *uwasa no musume* suggests a 'girl in the rumour'.

precisely *because* / the gods are invisible / they are believed in
me ni mienu / kami nareba koso / shinjirare
Shinpei. Often, not seeing is believing.

feigning ignorance / of fierce gods he cannot see – / the playboy
me ni mienu / onigami o musuko / shirageru

    Maita. In *Yanagidaru* 52 (1811). If not a 5-8-4-syllabet verse, as here, *musuko* can be straddled across the second and third lines. One wonders who the young playboy is trying to fool here: his rebuking parents who have invoked vengeful gods? Himself? A little bit of both?

watermelons: / eating them with good manners / is bad manners!
teineini / suika o kū to / gebiru nari

    Chisei. In *Yanagidaru* 26 (1796). Although commenting on how consuming some foods properly entails making a mess, this verse also seems to suggest that manners of the East and West are diametrically opposed. The word for watermelon (*suika*) consists of the two graphs 'Western' and 'melon', since Westerners introduced the fruit into Japan (apparently the Portuguese during the sixteenth century).

remorse / of either picking or not picking / violets
tsumu mo oshi / tsumanu mo oshiki / sumire kana

    The woman poet Naojo. *Sumire* are wild violets (*Viola mandshurica*).

swellfish broth: / folly to take a sip / and folly not to!
fugujiru o / kuwanu tawake ni / kū tawake

    Shōchō. In *Yanagidaru* 87 (1825). Also in *Senryūhyō mankuawase* (1763) and *Yanagidaru shūi* 1 (*c.*1796-7). The swellfish or pufferfish (*fugu*) has long been a cherished if notoriously risky gourmet dish in Japan. Its liver contains a poison, tetrodotoxin (the byproduct of the symbiotic bacteria *Pseudoalteromonas tetraodonis*), toxic to human beings. When prepared precisely, however, in the right non-lethal dose, the liver can produce a pleasurable tingling sensation, making it a sought-after aphrodisiac (on the level of Spanish fly, oysters, spicy peppers, ginseng and horny goat weed). There is a related proverb: 'He who consumes swellfish broth is a fool, he who consumes it not is a fool' (*fugujiru kū baka kuwanu baka*). Indeed, among the foolhardy (*tawakemono*, clipped to *tawake*), there is one Milquetoast for every bon vivant.

challenge:
ever-changingly! / ever-changingly!
kawari kawari ni / kawari kawari ni

response:
taken for a ride – / an accomplice from last night's / swellfish dinner
katabō o / katsugu yūbe no / fugu nakama

Author unnamed. In *Yanagidaru* 1 (1765). *Katsugu* means 'to take for a ride' in both the figurative sense of a deception and the literal sense of bearing someone on one's shoulders – even to the grave. For the potential risks entailed in eating *fugu* (swellfish or pufferfish), see note to verse above the challenge.

nothing drastic? / yesterday came and went? / swellfish broth
ara nan tomo na ya / kinō wa sugite / fugutojiru

Bashō. The opening phrase, which contains an extra three syllabets, was an idiomatic expression. For more on the infamous *fugu* (swellfish or pufferfish) and the broth made from it, see note on previous page.

hardly charred newts . . . / but gold coins are still potent / aphrodisiacs
kuroyaki ni / sezu to koban wa / horegusuri

Author unnamed. In the traditional Japanese medicine of charred remedies (*kuroyaki*), a blackened and broiled concoction of fire belly newt (*imori no kuroyaki*) – which like *fugu* (see previous verse) contains the poison tetrodotoxin – was used as a love potion (*horegusuri*). This use supposedly goes back at least to the time of the legendary ladies' man and poet Narihira (see note to verses below) according to Saikaku in *Saikaku jichū dokugin hyakuin* (Saikaku's Hundred Linked Verses, Annotated by Himself, 1691; in Ebara Taizo, Teruoka Yasutaka and Noma Kōshin (eds), *Teihon saikaku zenshū* 12 (Chūō kōronsha, 1972), pp. 269–313).

challenge:
how gratifying! / how gratifying!
honbōna koto / honbōna koto

response:
it's a wonder / Narihira didn't contract / a rash of cockiness!
narihira no / kasa o kakanu mo / fushigi nari

Author unnamed. In *Yanagidaru* 4 (1769). This verse pokes holes in *Ise monogatari* (c. 880–950), the classic literary work that romanticizes the amorous exploits of Ariwara no Narihira (825–80), a high-ranking courtier, poet and fabled lover (who served as the primary model of the eponymous womanizing anti-hero of *Genji monogatari, c.*1000). The phrase *kasa o kakanu*, 'not cavalier', also means 'not contract a rash'. During the eighteenth century sexually transmitted diseases such as syphilis ran rampant in Edo's pleasure quarters and beyond.

orchids by night – / within their fragrance looms / their blossoms' white!
yoru no ran / ka ni kakurete ya / hana shiroshi
  Buson. Apart from its synaesthetic mix of scent and colour, this verse may intimate that, in spite of the orchid's prototypical association with mid autumn, there lurks in the dark of late-autumn nights a whiff of the coming white stuff.

first snowfall … / scarcely enough to cover / the dogshit
hatsuyuki ya / furi nimo kakurenu / inu no kuso
  Issa. The world is hardly ever as pure as it looks. The second line has an extra syllabet.

throughout fields, mountains, / not one thing stirring: / snowy morn
no ni yama ni / ugoku mono nashi / yuki no asa
  The nun Chiyo.

neither hills nor plains / obliterated in snow / and nothing else
no mo yama mo / yuki ni torareta / nanimo nashi
  Jōsō. In Morikawa Kyoriku and Kōno Riyū (eds), *Hentsuki* (*c.*1699). Only the absence of the hills and plains register their buried presence.

lofty wooden clog / drifts away beneath the ice / and disappears
takaashida / kōri no shita o / nagare saru
  Banan. The previous verse in the original sequence describes a year-end scene involving a debt collector. High clogs were worn by top-ranking courtesans or religious ascetics.

awaiting spring – / sprinkled into the ice / ashes and dust
matsu haru ya / kōri ni majiru / chiriakuta
  The woman poet Chigetsu.

deep underground / male and female quintessences / hibernating
tsuchi fukaku / shiyū no sei mo / tōminsu
  Nakajō Kakujirō.

traversed without / coming across any wolves – / winter's mountain
ōkami ni / awade koekeri / fuyu no yama
  Shiki.

challenge:
how vexing! / how vexing!
tsurai koto kana / tsurai koto kana

response:
one stray ant / scares a girl in full bloom / right out of her clothes!
ari hitotsu / musumezakari o / hadaka ni shi

    Author unnamed. In *Yanagidaru* 2 (1767) and *Yanagidaru shūi* 3 (*c.*1796–7). Apart from the charming contrast between the modest young lady and her immodest behaviour, there is the semantic and aural wordplay between 'ant' (*ari*) and 'in full bloom' (*~zakari*). Related verses include: 'one stray ant / and a virtuous lady / strips off her sash!' (*ari hitotsu / teijo ni obi o / tokasekeri*) from *Mutamagawa* 17 (*c.*1771–5); and 'one stray flea / and the most chaste of women / strips off her sash!' (*nomi hitotsu / teijo ni obi o / tokasekeri*), from the *kibyōshi* (comicbook) of 1791 by Takizawa Bakin, *Katakiuchi nomitori manako* (for an English translation, see Leon M. Zolbrod, 'The Vendetta of Mr. Fleacatcher Managorō, The Fifth (Kataki-uchi Nomi-tori Manako)', *MN* 20:1–2 (1965), pp. 121–34).

challenge word:
come to a standstill –
tachidomari

response:
the easygoing ants / change directions
yasashi ya ari no / yuki chigai

    Author unnamed. In *Aka eboshi* (Red-lacquered Cap, 1702), a collection of 'crown-linking verses' (*kanmurizuke*) in which one tries to cap a five-syllabet challenge with a twelve-syllabet response. As is sometimes the case with verses composed in verse-capping (*maekuzuke*) games, the resultant linked verse is relabelled a *senryū*: 'come to a standstill – / the easygoing ants / change directions' (*tachidomari / yasashi ya ari no / yuki chigai*).

colliding head-on, / 'whatnots' whispered a mite, / ants part ways
tsukiatari / nani ka sasayaki / ari wakare

    Suikyō. *Yanagidaru* 101 (1828). No doubt a retort to the previous verse in *Aka eboshi*. The *ka sasayaki* of Suikyō's verse calls to mind the phrase 'whisper in hushed tones like a mosquito' (*ka no sasayaku yō na koe*).

challenge:
look at that!
are o miyo

response:
footprints of the cat, / strewn plum petals
neko no ashiato / kobore ume
> Author unnamed. In *Aka eboshi* (1702). The resultant crown linking (*kanmurizuke*): 'look at that – / footprints of the cat, / strewn plum petals!'

they both meet / scowling at the other: / catty love
ryōhō de / niramiaikeri / neko no koi
> Shiki.

whiskers / on the both of 'em – / cats in heat
ryōhō ni / hige no haeteru / neko no koi
> Raizan.

'til blooming, / nobody pines after them – / rhododendrons
saku made wa / matsu hito motanu / tsutsuji kana
> Haritsu. The rather drab rhododendron or azalea bush (*tsutsuji*) blooms spectacularly in late spring, producing vibrantly coloured blossoms in reds, pinks and purples.

throughout the shop / the only one *not* in the know: / her boss
tanajū de / shiranu wa teishu / hitori nari
> Author unnamed. In *Yanagidaru* 7 (1772).

throughout town, / her husband alone / in the dark
chōnai de / shiranu wa teishu / bakari nari
> Author unnamed. In *Suetsumuhana* 4 (1801). Nakamura Yukihiko suggests that this exposé portrays the husband with some sympathy (*NYC* 8, p. 123). Although a slightly different version was published a quarter of a century earlier, this verse has become proverbial of an ignorant cuckold. Aside from the double entendre on *shiru*, 'to know' (present in the word *shiranu*, 'does not know', in the second phrase), which as in English means both to be aware of and also to know someone *carnally* (as in the expression *aishiru*, 'to love mutually'), *teishu* is used ironically, meaning 'master' as well as 'husband'.

'thanks for carrying on / while I was away from my wife!' / said unknowingly
to wa shirazu / sate rusuchū wa / osewasama
> Author unnamed. This verse appears in a comic skit from the time (*c.*1774). The phrase *to wa shirazu*, literally 'not knowing about it', was a euphemism for a secret affair. *Shirazu*, 'not *knowing*', implies that someone other than the husband 'knows' in both senses of the word.

'thanks for keeping / my wife unmolested!' / said unknowingly
to wa shirazu / kanai anzen / nado to share
> Yamaki. In *Yanagidaru* 47 (1809).

challenge:
proposed half-jokingly / for having a little fun
muri iikakete / nagusami ni sen

response:
fastest of friends – / so let me take advantage of / your nubile wife!
sochi to ware / nengoro gai ni / nyōbo kase
> Chikusui. In Fukaku (ed.), *Niiki* (1693). The absurd logic here depends on the almost seamless slippage from one set of punning meanings to another: *sochi*, from 'you' to 'yours'; and *nengoro*, from 'many years', through 'hospitable' and 'intimate', to 'marriageable age'.

her so-called 'cousin' / always seems to be visiting / when hubby's away
itoko nimo / shiro yō kuru to / tabi no rusu
> Author unnamed. In *Yanagidaru* 12 (1777). Although *shiro* here with *nimo* means 'even if', *shiro* also carries the associations of 'innocent person' and, even more tellingly, 'substitute'.

challenge:
from gaps in the duckboards / a draught wafting upwards ...
sunoko no ai o / fukiaguru kaze

response:
for goosebumps, / a twin pillow for lovebirds?! / her sultry coo!
torihada wa / hiyoku no makura / kotoba nari
> Hakukei. In Fukaku (ed.), *Chiyomigusa* (1692). The response is a tour de force of wordplay. Both *torihada* (goosebumps) and *hiyoku no makura* (an extra-long 'pillow for lovebirds') are associated with *kaze* ('breeze' – or, in the case of an upwards one, 'draught') and *sunoko* (the

wood-slatted 'duckboard' base in a closet for storing a futon and its bedding). Although the *ai* of the challenge means 'gap', the response plays not only on this word's alternative meanings of 'love' and 'rendezvous', but also on its orthographic rendering as *ahi* (though still pronounced *ai*), the *hi* of which can mean 'fire', by virtue of a homonym of *hiyoku* (lovebird) as *hi* (sun) and *yoku* (thoroughly). Moreover, *makura* (pillow) pivots between the phrases *hiyoku no makura* (pillow for lovebirds) and *makura kotoba* (a set epithet in poetry, though literally 'pillow words').

challenge:
how admirable! / how admirable!
yukashikarikeri / yukashikarikeri

response:
bachelors / withdraw to their rooms / and groan
hitorimono / uchi e kaeru to / unari dashi
Author unnamed. In *Yanagidaru* 1 (1765).

belly-cutting scene / suspended to watch a brawl / in the *audience*!
hara o kiri / kakete kenka o / kenbutsu shi
Kyūsei. In *Yanagidaru* 52 (1811). One or more kabuki actors on stage momentarily stop a samurai disembowelment scene to watch a real-life drama among the theatregoers. Similarly that same year, the comic author Shikitei Sanba (1776–1822) published his popular *Kyakusha hyōbanki* (Critique of Theatregoers, 1811), which cleverly turned the tables on the genre of actor reviewbooks (*yakusha hyōbanki*) by treating the audience members as the real celebrities. (For more on this in English, see Jacob Raz, 'The Audience Evaluated: Shikitei Sanba's *Kyakusha Hyōbanki*', *MN* 35:2 (Summer 1980), pp. 199–221.)

challenge:
cheered up, yet still ... / cheered up, yet still ...
isami koso sure / isami koso sure

response:
the mother back home / struts along cradling / the birth announcement
kuni no haha / umareta fumi o / dakiaruki
Author unnamed. In *Yanagidaru* 1 (1765). Although the birth announcement is a surprising proxy for a newborn, the more subtle comic twist has to do with how the 'mother' simultaneously is *not* the mother of the newborn yet *is* the mother of the newborn's mother.

This provincial grandmother's momentary conflation of herself as *the* mother evokes the larger pathos of urbanization, already underway at the time, whereby the infant's real mother, not mentioned directly, has relocated to a no doubt far-off metropolitan centre such as Edo.

when at last / one longs to be filial / both parents are gone
kōkō no / shitai jibun ni / oya wa nashi

Author unnamed. In *Yanagidaru* 22 (1788). A deservedly proverbial verse. Try as one might to live up to the Confucian ideal of respecting one's parents, one can never fully appreciate something until having experienced it oneself. This poignant message is reinforced through subtle wordplay (sometimes with different graphs): at 'the time of life' (*jibun*) when one 'oneself' (*jibun*) becomes a parent and realizes how challenging it is to raise children, one has a newfound appreciation for one's own parents, making one 'desire' (*shitai*) being 'filial' (*kōkō*), though it remains an 'incurable condition' (*kōkō*) that by then those parents may 'not be around' (*nashi*) much longer, and sometimes even are already lifeless 'corpses' (*shitai*).

nostalgic / even for the scoldings! / parents' grave
shikarareta / koto mo natsukashi / fubo no haka

Fūshō. *Yanagidaru* 117 (1832). The verse appears twice in the same volume.

challenge:
however grim / it was also funny!
niganigashiku mo / okashikarikeri

response:
even while / my father lay dying / farts kept ripping!
waga oya no / shinuru toki ni mo / he o kokite

This infamous response was penned by Sōkan. In *Inu tsukubashū* (*c.*1530). Teitoku, titular head of the rival Teimon School, railed against Sōkan's disrespectfulness as inappropriate, not funny. But this criticism misses the point that very often something is funny precisely because it is grossly inappropriate. Such earthiness informs the lowbrow branch of *haiku* even in the hands of its most famous practitioners.

having children / one learns appreciation / all too late
ko o motte / shiru to wa osoi / omoitsuki

Shakujin. In *Yanagidaru* 26 (1796).

having children / one gets filial piety / all too late!
ko o motte / shiru to wa osoi / oya no on
   Gyokushu. In *Yanagidaru* 156 (1838-40?).

not until nabbing / the flea that bit her baby / will she sleep easy
ko o kutta / nomi o toru made / nyōbo nezu
   Hōrō (probably not *the* Hōrō, one of the three masters of the Tenpō
   era, 1830-44).

**even while sleeping / the hand fan sweeps to and fro - / a parent's
devotion**
neteite mo / uchiwa no ugoku / oyagokoro
   Author unnamed. In *Yanagidaru* 1 (1765). *Uchiwa*, a non-folding fan,
   often varnished with persimmon juice, has as a homonym 'family
   circle'.

that gentle breeze / from the slumbering fan - / a mother's love
utatane no / uchiwa no kaze ga / haha no on
   Author unnamed. In *Yanagidaru shūi* 9 (c.1796-7).

even asleep / one's hand fan keeps swaying - / blazing heat
nemuredomo / ōgi wa ugoku / atsusa kana
   Fukoku.

the drowsy fan / bit by bit becomes / a faint breath
utatane no / uchiwa shidaini / mushi no iki
   Author unnamed. The phrase *mushi no iki*, literally 'insect's breath',
   can also mean 'dying whisper'.

**the morning after / their sleeping child caught cold, / the parents
bicker**
ko no nebie / yokujitsu fūfu- / genka nari
   Author unnamed. In *Yanagidaru* 11 (1776). The same verse, by one
   Mabu Ichiku, appears in *Yanagidaru* 21 (1786).

a child cries / throughout the night about to break - / affliction
akeyasuki / yo o naku chigo no / yamai kana
   Shirao.

monsoon rains / gathered into the torrential / Mogami River!
samidare o / atsumete hayashi / mogamigawa
   Bashō. One of the three fastest rivers in Japan, the Mogamigawa

originates in Yamagata Prefecture (or Dewa Province, in Bashō's day, due north of Edo) and empties into the Sea of Japan.

scorching day / washed away into the sea – / River Mogami!
atsuki hi o / umi ni iretari / mogamigawa
Bashō. Revised from an earlier verse in which the river (see note to previous verse) merely empties into the sea.

whoosh whoosh **/ washing summer away: / Mogami River**
zunzun to / natsu o nagasu ya / mogamigawa
Shiki. The mere sight of the Mogamigawa (see note on previous page) cools the soul on even the hottest of summer days.

a crimson sun / slumps into the sea – / the heat!
akaki hi no / umi ni ochikomu / atsusa kana
Natsume Sōseki.

challenge:
unsteady the heart! / unsteady the heart!
kokoromotonashi / kokoromotonashi

response:
our little princess / in the hands of a nursemaid / with tattooed arms!
hime o moru / uba sae ude no / irebokuro
Author unnamed. In Matsumoto Seiemon (ed.), *Shussemaru* (1720), a collection of verse-capping (*maekuzuke*), crown-linking (*kanmuri-zuke*) and other miscellaneous verse (*zappai*). The response cleverly re-interprets the surface meaning of the 'uneasy heart' (*kokoromotonashi*) of the parents as the 'fickle heart' of a loose woman.

Tattoos have long been associated in Japan with criminals, prostitutes and other elements of society with whom the bourgeoisie was loath to mix openly. Although *irezumi* is the modern Japanese for 'tattoo', during the Edo period that term was reserved specifically for the permanent markings forced on convicts as a form of painful punishment and public humiliation, whereas the term used here, *ire-bokuro*, 'inserted mole' (like *horimono*, 'carving'), denoted body art (see Sugiura Hinako, *Edo e yōkoso* (Chikuma bunko, 1989), p. 23).

down to her tattoos / a courtesan's business: / turning a profit
horimono mo / yūjo no saku wa / kane ni nari
Ukō. In *Yanagidaru* 65 (1814). A tattoo (*horimono*) of the name of a lover was by no means indelible proof of a courtesan's love for a

client, for there were ways of removing tattoos, such as burning them off with moxibustion (*mogusa*), in which cones of dried mugwort are ignited on one's skin.

where to keep / her severed finger / has him stumped!

yubi o morate– / te okidokoro ni / komaru nari

San'en. In *Yanagidaru* 53 (1811). Lampooning the courtesan practice of demonstrating love for a special client by presenting him with her severed finger (*yubikiri*), usually the last section of the pinkie, this verse raises the practical matter of what to do with the thing. The awkwardness of the situation – if not the cutting of the finger itself – is conspicuously reinforced by the verse straddling: *moratte*, 'receiving', is dramatically split across two lines. Also exposed here is the selfishness of those men who care more about being imposed upon slightly than about the greater welfare of their lovers. Still, in the duplicitous floating world of the pleasure quarters, where male clients boasted of romantic entanglements with multiple courtesans – who themselves juggled numerous clients – such 'demonstrations of sincerity' (*shinjū*) could well be faked. Indeed, there was something of a cottage industry of robbing bodies in open graves to supply the pleasure quarters with substitute fingers.

Other forms of *shinjū* ranged from cutting a lock of hair (*kamigiri*), composing a love letter (*seishi*), getting inked with a tattoo (*irebokuro* or *horimono*), excising a fingernail (*tsumegiri*), to the extreme of mutually assisted double suicide (*shinjūshi*), committed in the belief that the lovers would be reborn together on the same lotus blossom in the Western Paradise. These practices are described in Fujimoto Kizan's (1628–1704) *Shikidō ōkagami* (Grand Mirror of the Way of Love, 1678). (In English, see Lawrence Rogers, 'She Loves Me, She Loves Me Not: *Shinjū* and *Shikidō ōkagami*', *MN* 49:1 (1994), pp. 31–60.)

the high priest / shows devotion by licking / his rentboy's bunghole

shinjū ni / oshō kagema no / ketsu o name

Mokubō. *Yanagi no hazue* (1835). Wordplay here pokes fun at how monastic Buddhist priests, who were supposed to 'experience' (*name*) hardships such as 'scarcity' (*ketsu*), were nevertheless reputed for their same-sex affairs, hence 'licking' (*name*) a younger partner's 'ass' (*ketsu*). Kizan, in the *Grand Mirror of the Way of Love* (see note to verse above), makes no mention of rim jobs.

the rentboy / as though heaving a sigh / lets go a fart
tameiki no / yō ni kagema wa / he o tareru
Yokose. In *Yanagidaru* 33 (1806).

short the distance / between great monks and baboons / as the crow flies
meisō no / baka wa saru koto / tōkarazu
Author unnamed. Animating this verse are several oblique puns on animals – *baka*, 'fool', is typically written with the graphs for 'horse' and 'deer'; *saru*, 'depart', has the homonym 'monkey'; and *tōkarazu*, 'not far', can also be read (in the historical orthography) as 'distant crow' (*tō karasu*). The upshot is to suggest either the asinine nature of even a great Buddhist bonze or perhaps the secret beastly breach of the Buddhist restriction against consuming animal flesh.

nowhere to dump / all the dirty bathwater – / insect voices!
gyōzui no / sutedokoro naki / mushi no koe
Onitsura. Although a champion of poetic authenticity (*makoto*), here Onitsura no doubt is having some tongue-in-cheek fun. In as much as Buddhism places tremendous value on the sanctity of all life – including insects – the speaker finds himself in a catch-22: where can one discard used cleansing water without further incurring defilement by inadvertently killing insects? The way this single act of disposal has a double meaning is enacted verbally by the pivot on *naki*, meaning both 'lacking (a place)' and 'crying (insects)', and by the two meanings of *gyōzui* as 'bathwater' and 'ritual purification water'.

even splash baths / become less frequent – / insect voices!
gyōzui mo / himaze ni narinu / mushi no koe
Raizan. With the coming autumn cool associated with loudly chirping insects, the decrease in outdoor bathing day by day might result less from an altruistic concern for respecting all life than the more selfish worry about not catching cold.

bright the moon! / for dumping an ashtray, / no dark corner
meigetsu ya / haifuki sutsuru / kage mo nashi
Fugyoku. Although the full moon may well be the stuff of classical art and poetry – where it sometimes was associated with groves of bamboo (here humorously invoked by the *haifuki*, a simple ashtray fashioned from a stalk of bamboo) – it presents a more pragmatic challenge for those not wishing to be seen.

bright the moon! / from locations pitch-dark, / insect voices
meigetsu ya / kuraki tokoro wa / mushi no koe
  Bunson.

the other breast! / the first stirrings of desire / does grabbing it beget!
katachibusa / nigiru ga yoku no / deki hajime
  Jinsei. In *Yanagidaru* 26 (1796). Nearly identical versions would be published later by two other named poets, Rekisen in *Yanagidaru* 58 (1811) and Gan'en in *Yanagidaru* 59 (1812). Sexual yearnings have their origin in early childhood as a matter of course. *Deki* is a double entendre, meaning 'emerge' and 'be intimate with'.

'so, Nanny,' / poking with his footsie, / 'this your *furry goblin*?'
uba koko wa / momonjii ka to / ashi o yari
  Jakuchō. In *Yanagidaru* 50 (1811). Perhaps not so innocently, the young male charge of a nursemaid probes her euphemism (drawn from storybooks they have presumably read together) as they share a bath, or sit at a quilt-covered heating table, or lie about with robes aloose in the summer heat. The comparison of female external genitalia to a hirsute goblin (*momonjii*) works visually, for this kind of goblin (loosely based on the Japanese flying squirrel) is typically depicted with hair covering all but its oversized maw. Yet the comparison also works aurally, for *momo* echoes the unstated slang, *bobo*, for 'vulva' as well as its stated proxy, *koko*, 'here'. *Yari* means 'spear', a weapon associated with goblins, and 'poking' in the vulgar sexual as well as neutral non-sexual sense.

nanny's cunny: / catching sight of it, sonny / bursts into tears!
uba no bobo / mite obōsan / watto naki
  Shumoku. In *Yanagi no hazue* (1835). The young male charge of a nursemaid, beholding a vulva perhaps for the first time after only having heard about it euphemistically, mistakes it for an actual 'furry goblin' (see previous verse). *Obōsan*, 'monk', was used to refer to an innocent young man from a good family (not unlike the modern Japanese term *botchan*).

challenge:
'off to play hide 'n' seek!' / so Mother let down her guard
kakurenbō to / yūdan shita haha

response 1:
playing house – / into her tiny shellclam / his hot chillipepper!
mamagoto wa / shijimikkai ni / tōgarashi
> Shōki. In *Yanagidaru* 71 (1819). A rare instance of a hypermetric challenge verse, above, with an extra syllabet in the second phrase. In Shōki's response, *shijimikkai*, literally a freshwater clam, also refers to a young girl – or her genitals.

response 2:
'he's put his willy / into the little one's mouth!' / Big Sis exclaims
chinboko o / ano ko no kuchi to / ane no koe
> Mokubō. In *Yanagi no hazue* (1835). *Tōgarashi*, a kind of Chinese pepper, is also slang for 'penis'. Okada observes of this response that babies will suck on just about anything (*YHZ*, p. 37).

shell-gathering / within a clear line of sight … / still, a mother worries
mitōshi ni / iru noni shiohi / haha anji
> Kinchō. In *Yanagidaru* 26 (1796). A nearly identical version by Shise-ki appears in *Yanagidaru* 45 (1808). There is something similar about gathering shells and tending young children. Perhaps not uncoincidentally, the pen name puns on 'anxiety'.

the first grandchild / comes along and suddenly / *everything*'s dangerous
hatsumago ga / dekite abunai / koto bakari
> Toshiko.

challenge:
can't hardly wait! / can't hardly wait!
machikane ni keri / machikane ni keri

response:
jumping out / *in order* to be found – / lil' hide-and-seeker!
tazunuru o / kotchi kara deru / kakurenbo
> Author unnamed. In *Kuchiyosegusa* (1736).

all those sighs / exhaled into some corner – / hide-and-seek!
tameiki o / sumikko e suru / kakurenbo
> Author unnamed (see *OI*, p. 30).

sparklers in hand, / come on, be dark already! / be dark already!
hanabi o mo- / rai hi ga kurero / hi ga kurero
> Gochō. In *Yanagidaru* 17 (1782). The same verse, by one Ryūjin, appears in *Yanagidaru* 38 (1807). Another instance of verse straddling (*kumatagari*), here emphasizing breathless impatience.

in the midst / of children thronging ... / an overwhelmed sparrow
ōzei no / ko ni tsukaretaru / suzume kana
> Issa.

scold as one might, / little kids prefer their shoes / too big to fill
shikattemo / ōkina geta o / kodomo suki
> Author unnamed.

playing house: / the one who gets to be wifey / the most sassy
mamagoto no / kakasan ni naru / ochappii
> Shiseki. In *Yanagidaru* 50 (1811). Although the colloquial term *kakasan* can mean 'mama', it also means 'wifey', suggesting that the children hear their father referring to their mother in this way.

challenge:
what a nuisance! / what a nuisance!
meiwakuna koto / meiwakuna koto

response:
playing house: / the homewrecker shows up / as the spoiled child
mamagoto no / setai-kuzushi ga / amaete ki
> Author unnamed. In *Yanagidaru* 1 (1765). Here, the children's game of playing house is used to convey the adult drama of a brattish mistress showing up on the doorstep of her lover and his wife.

playing the parent / in a game of hide-and-seek – / the kittycat
oya to shite / kakurenbo suru ko / neko kana
> Issa. In many Japanese children's games, the one who is 'it' is called *oni*, 'ogre', or *oya*, 'parent'.

kittycats / playing hide-and-seek: / bushclover blooms!
neko no ko no / kakurenbo suru / hagi no hana
> Issa. Less an actual scene of one or more kittens in play than the resemblance of billowing white-flowered stems of the upright Japanese bushclover, *hagi* (*Lespedeza japonica*), when buffeted about fitfully by the breeze, to the tails of kittens in play.

pleasure women / sleeping beneath this very roof! / bushclover and moon

hitotsuya ni / yūjo mo netari / hagi to tsuki

Bashō. In *Oku no hosomichi* (1702). This verse is usually read in terms of the shocking incongruence between lodgers at the same inn: the courtesans as lovely but ground-hugging bushclovers (*hagi*) versus Bashō (with his monkish travelling companion Sora – a homonym of 'sky') as austere lofty moon (*tsuki*). Secondary wordplay on *hagi* as 'conjoining' and on *tsuki* as 'thrusting', however, casts a ray of moonlight (suggesting an amorous rendezvous) on the possibility of a mischievous sexual subtext.

challenge:
completely compatible! / completely compatible!
mutsumashii koto / mutsumashii koto

response:
shophand and maidservant / abstain from fraternizing / in broad daylight

sono tedai / sono gejo hiru wa / mono iwazu

Author unnamed. In *Yanagidaru* 1 (1765). *Mono iwazu* is the negative of *mono ifu*, 'say something', which can also refer to being physically intimate. Workplace romances were not merely frowned upon as a threat to solidarity within merchant houses, but strictly prohibited as a danger to public morals. Shimoyama praises this verse for its understated pathos (*SE*, p. 72).

the young master – / jacking off by night / telling off by day

wakadanna / yoru wa ogande / hiru shikari

Author unnamed. From *Senryūhyō mankuawase* (1766). *Ogande*, literally 'worshipping', either by bringing one's hands together or by fingering a Buddhist rosary (*jūzū*), was Edo slang for masturbation.

the maidservant: / obliging whims by night / disregards them by day

iu koto o / yoru kiku gejo wa / hiru kikazu

Baishi. In *Yanagidaru* 51 (1811). The contrast of 'heeds' and 'heeds not' (*kiku* and *kikazu*) matches the reversal of the usual social situation, i.e. a female employee who need not obey her male employer's orders by day because, we can surmise, she is sleeping with him at night.

having obliged demands / the maidservant no longer / obliges commands

iu koto o / kiite iu koto / gejo kikazu

Author unnamed. In *Yanagidaru* 34 (1806).

fleas, lice / and a horse taking a whizz / beside my pillow
nomi shirami / uma no nyō suru / makuramoto
  Bashō. In a passage from *Oku no hosomichi* (1702), the Bashō character
finds himself bunking down in a barn. Although *nyō* is a relatively
tame term for urine, *uma*, 'horse', was also slang for an oversized
member.

evening rainburst! / brought back from the dead, / a collapsed steed
yūdachi ya / yomigaeritaru / taore uma
  Kitō.

challenge:
crowded out! / crowded out!
oshiai ni keri / oshiai ni keri

response:
clutching porno / he gets kicked out from / their heating table
makurae o / motte kotatsu o / oidasare
  Author unnamed. In *Yanagidaru* 1 (1765). Shimoyama suggests that
the man of the house is leering at pornography while at the
family's quilt-covered heating table (*kotatsu*) (*SE*, p. 57).

challenge:
now, that's harsh! / now, that's harsh!
kibishikarikeri / kibishikarikeri

response:
smutty pictures, / when voiced out loud, / get one told off
makurae o / takaraka ni yomi / shikarareru
  Author unnamed. In *Yanagidaru* 10 (1775) and *Suetsumuhana* 4
(1801) (in *SE*, p. 58). Usually one is scolded for squandering family
funds in the pleasure quarters. Even though this young man is saving
money by staying at home, he still gets scolded.

pillow pictures – / to a new spot every day / hidden away
makurae wa / mainichi kawaru / okidokoro
  Author unnamed. In *Senryūhyō mankuawase* (1762). Although called
'pillow pictures' (*makurae*), since pornography was supposedly kept
beneath the pillow for use in bed, the joke here is that, once discov-
ered, they are hidden anywhere else around the house except under
the pillow.

it's the real stud / who on the morning after / gets dicked

gokugoku no / mote kinuginu ni / mara o sare

Author unnamed (see *S*, pp. 24–6). Although men frequently fancy themselves as being in charge, the woman here (as elsewhere) wears the trousers. The term *gokugoku*, 'exceedingly', can also mean 'gulp down repeatedly'.

for his peccadillos / to the bordello he goes, / the fool gung-ho!

machigae de / imo no ha e noru / baka mōja

Ryūsen. *Yanagidaru* 106 (1829). The surface meaning of this complex verse is deceptively simple: 'by mistake / boarding the leaf of a potato, / foolish lost soul!'. The rather ho-hum implication is that a deceased person who blunders onto the wrong kind of leaf is unlikely to be reborn into Buddhist paradise. Yet the popularity of this verse, appearing an unprecedented three times within the same volume, no doubt owes much to deeper wordplay featuring a missing punchline (*kangaeochi*) that readers had to supply for themselves. The key to the puzzle is that the only kind of potato (*imo*) whose leaf visually resembles the pad of the lotus – associated in Buddhism with rebirth and purity – is the taro root plant (*satoimo*). The word omitted from the verse being *sato* (village), slang for 'pleasure quarters', secondary meanings of *machigae*, 'blunder', as 'sexual indiscretion' (contrasting ironically with purity), and *mōja*, 'the deceased', as 'aficionado', come to the fore. Additionally, as noted previously (see the verse *meisō no / baka wa saru koto / tōkarazu*), the graphs for *baka* (fool), 'horse' and 'deer', connote dumb beasts – the state of existence into which great sinners were said to be reborn. More than an inability to differentiate between lotus and taro, then, it is his asinine attachment to sensual pleasures that prevents this player from ever reaching paradise.

on a roofed boat / doing it with fingers praying / to the tiny goddess!

yanebune de / shinagara ogamu / kanzeon

Sanchō. In *Yanagi no hazue* (1835). According to Watanabe, a man and woman have hired a party boat on the Sumida River in Edo (*EBYHT*, p. 26). Just as a boatman is busy punting past the famous statue of the goddess of mercy in Asakusa near the Yoshiwara pleasure quarter, a couple unobserved below engaging in foreplay. *Ogamu*, 'to pray', was slang for 'self-stimulate'. Solt has also suggested that *kanzeon*, 'goddess of mercy' (aka Kannon), was slang for 'clitoris' (see John Solt (trans.) 'Willow Leaftips', in John Solt (ed.), *An Episodic Festschrift for Howard Hibbett* 24 (Hollywood, CA: Highmoonoon, 2010), p. 49).

even when ill / bachelors never feel / like groaning
hitorimono / byōki mo unaru / ki ni narezu
    Kinbō.

about to shout, / 'hey look, a firefly!' / though all alone
tobu hotaru / are to iwan mo / hitori kana
    Taigi.

on windless days / scattering that much more . . . / cherry blossoms
nakanaka ni / kaze no naki hi o / chiru sakura
    Chora. Cherry blossoms being expected to scatter on windy days, the
    relatively few that fall on windless days are lamented disproportion-
    ately.

falling too soon / after so long awaited: / the blossom's essence!
toku chiru mo / matareshi hana no / kokoro kana
    Sōgi. In *Jinensai hokkushū* (1506).

up and out early / spotting malicious graffiti – / the hilarity!
oki idete / rakushu yomikudasu / okashisa yo
    Kitō. In *Nanohana ya* (1774). *Rakushu*, literally 'dropped verses', were
    typically anonymously written, politically satirical verses (*kyōka*) that
    were either posted or distributed in public as a kind of pasquinade.
    Here, the second line contains an extra syllabet.

spotting graffiti / by acquaintances of mine – / autumn dusk
chikazuki no / rakugaki miete / aki no kure
    Issa. Apparently, when visiting Zenkō Temple, Issa spotted graffiti
    signed by old friends of his.

the name / of you whom I adore / there in graffiti!
rakugaki ni / koishiki kimi ga / na mo arite
    Bashō. In *Yamanaka sangin* (c.1689). A playful miscellaneous verse,
    this is not typically categorized as one of Bashō's *hokku*.

viewing blossoms / only to return to a home / engulfed in flames!
hanami kara / kaereba ie wa / yaketeiru
    Kenkabō. Although cherry-blossom viewing can be an occasion for
    contemplating ephemerality, thereby stimulating an appreciation
    of such teachings as the 'burning house' parable (*upaya*) of the *Lotus
    Sutra*, one hardly expects to return home to find it literally ablaze.

storehouse burnt down / nothing to impinge upon / the incandescent moon
kura yakete / sawaru mono nashi / kyō no tsuki
  Masahide. Although long read as a stoic exaltation of the spiritual over the material, the complex of wordplay in this poet's best-known verse suggests a necessary interrelatedness. *Kura*, 'storehouse', calls to mind 'dark' (*kurai*). *Yakete*, 'burned', also refers to the reddish afterglow of a sunset. *Tsuki*, 'moon', a symbol of Buddhist enlightenment, can also mean both 'protrusion' (associated with *sawaru*, 'to obscure') and 'set on fire' (conjuring up the 'burning house' parable of the *Lotus Sutra*).
  Expanded upon in the extreme, just as one can fully appreciate the harvest moon (*kyō no tsuki*) when day grows dark (*kurai*), past the afterglow of the sunset (*yakete*), when the moon (*tsuki*) itself seems ablaze (*yakete*), so too can one gain enlightenment if unencumbered (*mono nashi*), or at least not benighted (*kurai*), by burning away darkness itself (*kura yakete*), obliterating all protrusions (*tsuki*) or obstacles (*sawaru mono*), as though these were but a storehouse (*kura*) to be burned down (*yakete*).

others gone home / now there's nothing between / the moon and me
hito inete / naka ni mono nashi / tsuki to ware
  The nun Seifu.

guests gone home / yet loath to drape the bed netting / this moonlit night
kyaku tatte / kaya tsuri oshimu / tsukiyo kana
  Ryōta. If not to die for, the moon is beautiful enough to warrant the exposure to mosquitoes.

all are aboard boats, / upon bridges, atop drying racks / moon viewing!
fune ni hashi ni / monohoshi ni mina / tsukimi kana
  Shiki. The eight *i* sounds establish a dynamic rhythm and, since *ii* can mean 'good' as well as 'says', may suggest the *oohs* and *ahs* of the spectators, whose enthusiasm spills over into an extra syllabet in the first line.

from time to time / clouds provide a respite from / moon viewing
kumo oriori / hito ni yasumuru / tsukimi kana
  Bashō. The first line contains an extra syllabet.

upon sleepy homes / as though glancing askance: / harvest moon!
neta ie o / niramu yō nari / kyō no tsuki
    Otsuyū.

up from amongst / tempest-buffeted grasses: / harvest moon!
arashi fuku / kusa no naka yori / kyō no tsuki
    Chora. *Tsuki* can mean 'moon' or 'thrusting' up.

out from the shadows / of every thing in this world: / harvest moon!
yo no naka no / mono no kage yori / kyō no tsuki
    Nangai.

rainy season gloom – / then one night through pines, slyly, / the pined-for moon!
samidare ya / aru yo hisokani / matsu no tsuki
    Ryōta. *Matsu* is a pivot (*kakekotoba*) working with other words to yield two overlapping meanings: 'secretly *pining* (for someone)' and 'the moon faintly through the *pines*'. *Tsuki*, 'moon', is a homophone of 'poking', which only adds to the romantic if not erotic subtext.

luminous moon! / upon strawmats your pined-for / shadow of pines!
meigetsu ya / tatami no ue ni / matsu no kage
    Kikaku. The standard pun on *matsu* as 'pine tree' and 'pining for' here yields a novel paradox between 'shadow of my pining (for someone *not* present)' and 'pined-for silhouette (of someone *now* present)'. Hope for the speaker may reside in the fact that the fine-grained texture of pine needles lost in their shadowy form cast upon the tatami mats is regained within the woven strands.

bright the moon! / emerging shapes of pine trees / unseen by day
meigetsu ya / hiru minu nari no / matsu ga deru
    Kakō (see Miyamori (ed. and trans.), *Haikai and Haiku*, p. 399). (The Kakō here is not to be confused with the author of *ashioto de / futatsu ni wareru / kagebōshi*.)

lazing in shadows, / conceding the drawing room / to moonrays
kage ni ite / tsuki ni zashiki o / yuzurikeri
    Seibi. There may be a sexual undertone here, for *kage*, 'shadows', also connotes feminine recesses, and *tsuki*, 'moon', is a homophone of 'poking'.

one by one / the stars come into view – / frigid cold!
sorezore no / hoshi arawaruru / samusa kana
   Taigi.

one by one / the stars, shimmeringly / the crickets, profusely
dandanni / hoshi akaraka ni / mushi shigeshi
   Tatsuko. Strictly speaking, *shigeshi* (profuse) is an adjective.

darkening seas … / the call of a mallard, / faintly white
umi kurete / kamo no koe / honokani shiroshi
   Bashō. This renowned verse, featuring a synaesthetic mix of sound
   with colour, is typically taken as an example of a rare 5–5–7-syllabet
   pattern (though, strictly speaking, *honokani* could be forced to
   straddle the second and third lines) used to emphasize the boundary-
   defying cry of the duck. *Kurete*, 'darken', can also mean 'lost in
   despair'.

evening squall! / the squawk of geese, white / the pond, dark
yūdachi ya / ga no koe shiroku / ike kurashi
   Rohan.

scolded / the cat shuts its eyes; / spring draws nigh
shikararete / me o tsuburu neko / haru tonari
   Mantarō. The expression *haru tonari*, 'spring next door', is an anti-
   quated expression, going back to classical *waka* of the Heian period,
   if not earlier.

the upshot / of jotting and scrubbing out: / a scrubland of poppies
kaite mitari / keshitari hate wa / keshi no hana
   Hokushi. The image of a poppy (*keshi*), a summer flower whose petals
   fall all too easily, is well suited to a death verse (*jisei*). Punning on *keshi*
   is *keshitari*, 'erasing'. The first line contains an extra syllabet.

my night ending / I shall resound in the blooms! / Pure Land Gate
yo no akete / hana ni hibiku ya / jōdomon
   Saimu. The surface meaning of this death verse (*jisei*), referencing the
   Pure Land Buddhist gate that represents the passage from this world
   (*yo*) of sorrows into the next, is 'dawn breaking, / [the bell] reverber-
   ates in the flowers – / Pure Land Gate', though through homonyms
   it can also be read 'my life ending, / I will remain with you in the
   blooms/return into blooms, / at Pure Land Gate'.

challenge:
the way of the world: / oxen with oxen!
yo no majiwari yo / ushi wa ushizure

response:
only an illiterate / can make out the scribblings / of other illiterates!
muhitsu yoku / muhitsu no hito no / fumi yomite
   Kōchiku. In Fukaku (ed.), *Niiki* (1693).

pharmacy shopsign – / illiterates make out only / its ⚱
aramonoya / ⚱ bakari / muhitsu yomi
   Yamaimo. In *Yanagidaru* 139 (1835). Example of a rebus (*hanjie*) verse, deploying a picture-puzzle that must be read as a word. It could be glossed as 'pestle and mortar', the joke being that for every uncouth reader reminded of copulation there is a couth reader who gets caught up between a reading of 'pestle' (*surikogi*) and 'mortar' (*suribachi*) when both objects are depicted. Alternatively (though also signifying sexual arousal), Okada Hajime reads the image as 'candle' (*rōsoku*) (see Okada (ed.), *(Haifū) Yanagidaru zenshū* 13 (Sanseidō, 1999), p. 38). In either case, such rebus play was beginning to become popular in eighteenth-century Japan. Entire books were written this way, as with *Heart Sutra for Illiterates* (*Mekura shinkyō* in Japanese), reproduced within *Tōzai yūki* (Travelogue of East and West, 1795) by Tachibana Nankei (1753–1805). Some commentators have even speculated that the rebus would give rise to the modern emoji.

no shopsign / for white facepowder / is lily white
oshiroi no / kanban shiroku / dekinu nari
   Wabun. In *Yanagidaru* 57 (1811). Even if a shopsign could be painted pure white (*shiroku*), cosmetics – particularly the white facepowder (*oshiroi*) popular at the time (and still worn by geisha and kabuki actors today) – are by definition, like advertising itself, always a kind of deception.

the peddler's cry / smoothes over the crumples / in his dried radishes
urigoe wa / shiwa no nobiteru / hoshidaiko
   Yūkō. In *Yanagidaru* 60 and 61 (1812). Although *daiko*, a clipped form of *daikon*, 'radish', is a phallic image, it also calls to mind the phrase *daikon yakusha*, 'ham actor'. The silky voice of the radish peddler belies his wilted wares.

floating-world moon – / let pass disregarded / these last two years
ukiyo no tsuki / misugoshi ni keri / sue ninen
   Sodō. The first line contains an extra syllabet.

in the twinkling / a saké shot slides down the throat . . . / up rises the moon!
sake hitotsu / nodo tōru ma ni / tsuki idete
> Sōin. Not only can saké put one in the mood for love, but the very thought of something slipping down the throat can be erotic. *Tsuki idete*, 'moon emerging', plays on *tsukidasu*, 'to get erect'.

springtime hovel: / its nothingness precisely / its everythingness
yado no haru / nani mo naki koso / nani mo are
> Sodō. In praise of the eremitic ideal.

obligingly, / a tea seller set up shop: / summer grove
kashikokumo / chamise dashikeri / natsu kodachi
> Buson.

my, oh my, oh my! / all to be said of the blossoms / on Mount Yoshino
kore wa kore wa / to bakari hana no / yoshinoyama
> Teishitsu. In this renowned ode to the stunning cherry blossoms of Mount Yoshino (in modern-day Nara Prefecture), the artfulness resides both in the paradoxically put-on air of artlessness in the plain-spoken first line – its astonishment overbrimming into an extra syllabet – and in the palindromic vowel pattern of *hana no . . . no yama* at the end, mimicking the kind of inversion perhaps experienced when beauty turns one's world upside down.

my, oh my, oh my! / all to be said of the headlice / through a microscope
kore wa kore wa / to bakari shirami o / kenbikyō
> Author unnamed. In Honekawa Dōjin (ed.), *Kokon senryū ichimanshū*, in *Tōyō bungei zensho* 17 (1892). A parody of Teishitsu's verse above. The optical microscope, apparently invented in the Netherlands, was introduced into Japan by the Dutch East India Company during the eighteenth century (see *SMS*, p. 96).

a plover / taken for a great egret – / the telescope!
chidori o ba / sagi ni shiteoku / tōmegane
> Author unnamed. In *Mutamagawa* 1 (1750). The telescope was introduced into Japan during the early seventeenth century.

steady spring rains . . . / both dream and reality / Mount Yoshino!
harusame ya / yume mo utsutsu mo / yoshinoyama
> Ryōta. For more on Mount Yoshino, see note to Teishitsu's *kore wa kore wa / to bakari hana no / yoshinoyama*.

was it for real, / this dream of being cut to shreds? / bitemarks of a flea!

kiraretaru / yume wa makoto ka / nomi no ato
Kikaku.

dreading its own / reflection in the water – / a firefly

minasoko no / kage o kowagaru / hotaru kana
The woman poet Sutejo.

fervent for the grass / at the bottom of the pond – / fireflies

minasoko no / kusa ni kogaruru / hotaru kana
Buson. There is a lovely resonance between *kogaruru*, 'be burning for', and *hotaru*, 'firefly'.

tread not yonder / where last night dwelt fireflies / upon the banks

soko fumuna / yūbe hotaru o / ita atari
Issa.

never dreaming / that within my garden grasses / fireflies!

niwakusa ni / hotaru ari to wa / shirazarishi
Takuchi.

when chased / taking cover in moonrays: / fireflies!

owarete wa / tsuki ni kakururu / hotaru kana
Ryōta. Typically in poetry the moon gets concealed (by clouds or some other obstacle) rather than does the concealing.

jumbo firefly, / undulating, pendulating, / flits on by

ōhotaru / yurari yurari to / tōrikeri
Issa. *Ōhotaru*, 'gigantic firefly' (*Luciola cruciata*), was also referred to as *genjibotaru* (Genji firefly).

to know the plum: / along with the heart alone / the nose alone

ume o shiru / kokoro mo onore / hana mo onore
Onitsura. Grasping the essence of the plum blossom is a matter of both the heart and the nose, but both experiences are so all-consuming that they seem somehow not just discrete but mutually exclusive – a paradox that somehow has greater implications. The last line contains an extra syllabet.

pining away, / the heart's passions in spring – / blossoms at their pique
matsu hodo wa / kokoro ya sakari / haru no hana
Sōgi. When spring blossoms are at their 'peak' (*sakari*), so too are the heart's passions 'piqued' (*sakari*).

half-asleep eyes / open to a dreamlike world / of blossoms
nebuki me o / hirakeba hana no / ukiyo kana
Seibi. *Ukiyo*, the floating world of pleasure, specifically referred to the pleasure quarters with its various beautiful women (*hana*, literally 'blossoms') as well as to popular theatre and street spectacles.

plum, cherry – / hopping from bed to bed / of flowers
ume sakura / hana yori hana ni / utsuru kana
Sōzei.

plum blossoms scatter / and it's peach; peach scatters / and it's cherry
ume chireba / momo momo chireba / sakura kana
Kyōma.

even Hollanders / have come for the blossoms! / quick, saddle up!
oranda mo / hana ni kinikeri / uma ni kura
Bashō. Every spring, about the time the cherry blossoms are in bloom, members of the Dutch East India Company would make their annual visit to Edo to pay tribute to the shogunate.

bright moon / in the sky even for *them* – / shaggy barbarians!
meigetsu mo / sonata no sora zo / ketōjin
Issa. The derogatory term *ketōjin*, originally referring to Tang Chinese, was retrofitted for Western foreigners.

within the nose / of Buddha Colossus / chirping baby sparrows!
daibutsu no / hana de naku nari / suzume no ko
Issa. Among the most famous of Japan's many *daibutsu*, or colossal statues of the Buddha, are the ones at Kōtokuin in Kamakura and Tōdaiji in Nara (today a national treasure as well as UNESCO World Heritage Site).

stray cat / using the Buddha's lap / as pillow!
noraneko ga / hotoke no hiza o / makura kana
Issa. An act of insolence, obliviousness or enlightenment? In Buddhism, at least, there is a long-standing debate over the indifference of

cats in general. One line of thought holds that their refusal to mourn the death of the historical Buddha is tantamount to cold irreverence. Another line maintains that their cool detachment is a matter of wise realization that the Buddha's death signified an end to rebirth and thus was actually not to be mourned in the first place.

within the heat-haze / shimmeringly a cat / snores away!
kagerō ni / guigui neko no / ibiki kana

Issa. *Guigui* can refer to the shimmering of the heat-haze (*kagerō*) or to the sound of snoring (*ibiki*) – a word reinforced here by the *i* sound in six out of seventeen syllabets.

bursting open / disgorging its rainbow: / peony dynamo!
niji o haite / hirakan to suru / botan kana

Buson. The phrase *niji o haite*, literally 'rainbow disgorging', is an idiomatic expression for a human dynamo. Although it can be read *niji o haki*, avoiding hypermetre (*jiamari*), the extra syllabet in *haite* suggests ample energy.

peony petals / scattering gently, nestle / in twos and threes
botan chirite / uchikasanarinu / nisan pen

Buson. The first line contains an extra syllabet.

cockscombs: / up to fourteen ... fifteen / stalks, even
keitō no / jūshigohon mo / arinubeshi

Shiki. One of the poet's best-known if most controversial verses, written, according to its headnote, while gazing upon his garden. A *keitō* is a plumed cockscomb (*Celosia argentea*), whose vibrant red flowers, resembling the crest of an actual cock, are associated with autumn (when in point of fact they bloom from late summer through late autumn). Although some critics have condemned this verse as little more than straightforward description deploying conspicuously unconventional numbers (fourteen and fifteen) in a strained effort to appear uncontrived, others have hailed it as a masterpiece for the pathos beneath its unemotional objective surface. Since cockscomb stalks grow in clusters, adding to the impression of their robustness, they are hard to count precisely, especially from a distance. Even if Shiki guessed well, however, that would be no consolation for the fact that the cockscomb is highly resilient to disease – unlike the frail poet, whose tuberculosis that would kill him within a few years was already advanced enough to prevent Shiki from simply walking out into his garden and counting the stalks for himself.

people so horrid! / to haggle over the price / of orchids
hito iyashiku / ran no atai o / ronjikeri
  Shiki. The first phrase has an extra syllabet, no doubt to underline
  Shiki's disgust over those people who miss the forest for the trees by
  valuing money over beauty.

within the narcissus / not the least shadow exists / of man's murkiness!
suisen ni / hito no nigori no / kuma mo nashi
  Roten.

once fallen / its after-image arises: / peony!
chirite nochi / omokage ni tatsu / botan kana
  Buson.

the nightingale: / some days it shows up twice, / others not at all
uguisu no / nido kuru hi ari / konu hi ari
  Kitō. For the Japanese nightingale or bush warbler (*uguisu*), see note
  to Bonchō's *uguisu no ne ni / tabira yuki furu*.

nightingale! / then suddenly at the gate / a tofu peddler
uguisu ya / kado wa tamatama / tōfu uri
  Yaba.

nightingale! / even before his lordship / that same voice
uguisu ya / gozen e detemo / onaji koe
  Issa. Unlike the Japanese nightingale, no doubt some people change
  their tune based on who is listening.

mighty warlord / forced down from his mount! / cherry blossoms
daimyō o / uma kara orosu / sakura kana
  Issa. Normally, people had to grovel before the procession of a war-
  lord (*daimyō*), but before the beauty of cherry blossoms, even a war-
  lord must bow his head. At Ueno in Edo, well known for its cherry
  blossoms, there was a placard before one of the shrines to the first
  Tokugawa shogun, Ieyasu (r. 1603-5), ordering everyone to dismount
  from their horses, presumably so they would not bump into the
  branches and make the blossoms scatter prematurely (see Maruyama
  Kazuhiko, *Issa haiku shū* (Iwanami shoten, 1993), p. 344).

thud-thudding / upon cherry petals – / horse dung!
dokadoka to / hana no ue naru / bafun kana

Issa. A crowded blossom-viewing scene is captured acoustically with *dokadoka*, 'thud thud', onomatopoeia for hoofbeats as well as the sound of footsteps, crowds, something thudding down – everything, in other words, except for the gentle fluttering of cherry petals.

the entire world / moved beneath the trees – / cherry blossoms!
yo no naka o / ki no shita ni suru / sakura kana

Atsujin.

blooming for the sake / of this light-verse racket: / cherry blossoms!
haikai no / kuchisugi ni saku / sakura kana

Author unnamed. A bit of self-reflexive fun, ribbing *haiku* poets for whom cherry blossoms are nothing more than their 'stock-in-trade' (*kuchisugi*).

cherry blossoms / at the untouchables' temple / bloom defiantly
etadera no / sakura majimaji / saki ni keri

Issa. Issa deliberately uses the shocking term *eta*, 'great filth' – a shamefully hateful epithet not unlike the N-word in English – for the untouchable class in Japan (more neutrally referred to as *burakumin* and analogous to India's Harijan). Aside from playing on the fertilizing power of excrement, Issa's point is that such terms, like the social conventions they signify, are arbitrary, for nature bows not to human law.

in the garden / blossoming whitely: / camellia
teizen ni / shiroku saitaru / tsubaki kana

Onitsura. A well-known verse whose simplicity belies its profundity and influence on subsequent poetics. Although the Japanese camellia (*Camellia japonica*) can be red, white or pink, the poetic tradition recognized only the first of these, even in cases when the actual flower was another colour. When the Zen monk Kūdō asked Onitsura about the secret of composing *haiku*, Onitsura responded with this verse as if to say that one must write from a position of experiential truthfulness (*makoto*) rather than through the filter of poetic convention. This kind of insistence on a relative verisimilitude over artifice would retroactively be credited primarily to Bashō and his school.

'though in winter, / summer ain't so bad,' / or so it's said
fuyu wa mata / natsu ga mashi ja to / iwarekeri
  Onitsura. Even though two seasons are mentioned, point blank, the actual season of composition is not clear. The colloquial copula *ja*, 'ain't', is also used here to dramatic effect.

'come! come!' / yet still the fireflies go / flitting away
koi koi to / iedo hotaru ga / tonde yuku
  Onitsura. Supposedly his inaugural verse, written at an extremely young age. In its original orthography, the *i* of *koi* (come) could have been written as *hi*, a homonym of 'fire', in which case a light flickers on and off in the early part of the verse, until the fireflies flee.

over and over, / sprinkled over by blossoms, / drowsily, drowsily
mata mo mata / hana ni chirarete / utsura utsura
  Onitsura. Repetition and a hypermetric last line brilliantly reinforce the sense of stupor.

accustomed to, / even poverty still has / the moon and blooms
binbō mo / narereba tsuki mo / hana mo ari
  Jisshi.

moon, blossoms – / a world that will now know / the third verse
tsuki hana no / sankume o ima / shiru yo kana
  Ryūho. A suitable deathbed poem (*jisei*) for a *haiku* poet, since the moon and the blossoms are the two great themes, the third yet to be discovered in the next world. *Yo*, meaning 'night' as well as 'world', suggests the darkness of death, while the *sanku* of *sankume*, 'third verse', can mean 'terrible pain'.

an excess of love / the pussycat just as frisky / as a courtesan!
ai amaru / neko wa keifū no / kobi o karu
  Saimaro. The second line contains an extra syllabet.

cat bell / amidst the peonies / ... here! ... there!
neko no rin / botan no atchi / kotchi kana
  Issa.

now here, now there, / emerging from the snowfall: / evening smoke
tokorodokoro / yuki no naka yori / yūkemuri
  Rankō. The first phrase has an extra syllabet.

day after day after day / at the wood-burning brazier / watching for bamboo

kyō mo kyō mo / kyō mo take miru / hioke kana

Issa. Not only is bamboo a harbinger of spring, but the speaker may be running out of firewood. The extra syllabet in the first line, not to mention the three appearances of *kyō* (today), emphasizes the tedium – if not desperation – of late-winter confinement.

with continued thawing / everything is turning green – / spring snow

tokete yuku / mono mina aoshi / haru no yuki

The nun Kikusha. Note the play of *yuku* (going) and *yuki* (snow).

lush green, lush green, / spring shoots so lushly green – / snowy field

aoshi aoshi / wakana wa aoshi / yuki no hara

Raizan. Another verse capturing the transition of the seasons (*kigasanari*), in this case from late winter to early spring, with an extra syllabet in the first phrase.

whitish clouds / brushed away by summer trees / with fresh green leaves!

shirakumo o / fukinagashitaru / shinju kana

Saimaro. At first blush this verse seems affected for feigning ignorance that it is of course the wind that blows (*fukinagashitaru*) both white clouds (*shirakumo*) and newly green trees (*shinju*). Yet all three elements are united acoustically by the swish-swishing sound *shi*. Moreover, the contrast of green and white, associated with young shoots against late snow in early spring, is playfully twisted here, in a master stroke of seasonal overlap (*kigasanari*), into an image of early summer.

autumn breeze / taking shape in a mess / of pampas grass

akikaze no / sugata narikeri / murasusuki

Kigin. The same trope of pampas grass (*Miscanthus sinensis*) making visible the invisible appeared in his history of homoerotic love in Japanese literature, *Iwatsutsuji* (1676): 'It was this poem [from the *Kokinshū*] that first *revealed, like plumes of pampas grass waving boldly in the wind*, the existence of this way of love, and even serious people came to know and practice it' (my emphasis; quoted in Paul Gordon Schalow, 'The Invention of a Literary Tradition of Male Love: Kitamura Kigin's *Iwatsutsuji*', *MN* 48:1 (Spring 1993), pp. 1-31, at p. 5. The poem in question, number 495 in the *Kokinshū* (*c.* 920), is translated by Schalow: 'Memories of love revive, / like wild azaleas bursting into

bloom / on mountains of evergreen; / my stony silence only shows /
how much I love you' (*omoi izuru* / *tokiwa no yama no* / *iwatsutsuji* /
iwaneba koso are / *koishiki mono o*)).

in the riverbreeze / a cluster of willowtrees: / spring revealed
kawakaze ni / *hitomura yanagi* / *haru miete*
Sōchō. In *Minase sangin hyakuin* (1488).

within loneliness / there is also happiness – / autumn dusk
sabishisa no / *ureshiku mo ari* / *aki no kure*
Buson. This verse runs against the grain of most gloom-and-doom
autumn verses.

out of loneliness / my walking stick left behind – / autumn dusk
sabishimi ni / *tsue wasuretari* / *aki no kure*
Buson. The walking stick generally implies old age.

persimmons so tart / not even crows / give 'em a glance!
kono kaki wa / *shibui ka karasu* / *mite nomi zo*
Bokusui. One can perhaps hear the exasperation of hungry crows in
late autumn within the five *k* sounds, three of which are truncated
caws (*ka*) suggesting distance.

persimmons sold out / not even crows visit / the mountain hamlet
kaki urete / *karasu mo towanu* / *yamaga kana*
Shūda.

**even in hamlets / where unseen the blossom and bream – / harvest
moon!**
tai wa hana wa / *minu sato mo ari* / *kyō no tsuki*
Naniwa Saikaku. A verse within a *haiga* in *Kōmyōshū* (1682). In vil-
lages so remote that neither sea bream (*tai*) nor cherry blossom (*hana*)
– the emblems of bountiful good luck and delicate impermanence,
respectively – are beheld, at least the moon can still be enjoyed during
the moon-viewing festival (*tsukimi*) on the fifteenth day of the eighth
lunisolar month. The first phrase is hypermetric.

spring days – / people taking it easy / in a small town
haru no hi ya / *hito nanimo senu* / *komura kana*
Shiki.

wisteria spray / left withered in a vase – / wayside inn
fuji ikete / shioreshi mama ya / tabi no yodo
> Taigi. The feeling of loneliness is discovered within this sign of neg-
> lect at an inn where the speaker has stopped to stay while travelling
> off the beaten trail.

blossoming / in forgotten flowerpots: / a spring day
wasure orishi / hachi ni hana saku / harubi kana
> Shiki. The first phrase has an extra syllabet.

green seaweed: / in the recesses of a reef, / forgotten tide
aonori ya / ishi no kubomi no / wasurejio
> Kitō. *Aonori* is an edible green seaweed (*Enteromorpha*) sometimes
> called sea lettuce. *Jio* can mean 'opportunity' as well as 'tide'.

rather dried up / a mere tuft of grass / between stones
isasakana / kusa mo karekeri / ishi no ai
> Shōha. In *Shundei kushū* (1777).

**washing the mountain / a colourless rain of autumn, / waters
unseen**
yama arau / ame no iro nashi / aki no mizu
> Muchō. A homonym of *mizu*, written as 'water', means 'sees not'.

**upon withered bough / a crow has come to its rest ... / autumnal
twilight**
kareeda ni / karasu no tomarikeri / aki no kure
> Bashō. In *Arano* (1689). (An earlier version, in *Azuma nikki* (Eastern
> Diary, 1681), uses a ten-syllabet second phrase (*karasu no tomaritaru
> ya*), to which Sodō replied with: 'a shouldered hoe recedes / into dis-
> tant village mists' (*kuwa katage yuku / kiri no tōzato*).) An acclaimed
> verse, customarily regarded as inaugurating Bashō's mature style – if
> not the so-called 'haiku form' itself – in spite of exceeding seventeen
> syllabets. It presents a bare-bones vignette of a solitary crow alighting
> upon a leafless branch at nightfall in late autumn, poignantly sym-
> bolizing the ultimate existential aloneness in the universe of all living
> beings.
> At least three instances of poetic wordplay reinforce this reading,
> beginning with *karasu*, the thick-billed jungle 'crow' common to Ja-
> pan (*Corvus macrorhynchos*), known for its tenacious scavenging, social
> roosting and loud querulousness. Yet this crow is about to roost alone
> silently, without any full-throated caw-cawing (*kaa kaa* being the Jap-
> anese onomatopoeic form). While one homonym of *karasu* means 'to

make wither', semantically linking 'crow' and 'bare branch', another, written with a graph consisting of the elements 'mouth' and 'summer', means 'to make hoarse'. The striking cacophony of five sporadic *k* consonants, four *k* and *r* combinations and two short *ka* sounds suggests the clipped and therefore distant cawing of *other* crows, as remote as summer from late autumn, or at least the echoes of the lone crow's cry of desperation moments before the action of the verse.

Granted, there has been a long-standing debate about how many crows here are alighting. Technically, since Japanese nouns can be singular or plural, more than one is possible. Bashō himself did not preclude as much, for one of the two extant *haiku* pictures (*haiga*) bearing this verse in his hand (entitled *Kareeda ni kasayadori gasan*) depicts a murder of crows. This runs against the grain of the hallowed theme, in Chinese and Japanese art, of the lone crow. More to the point, it cannot compare to a solitary crow in symbolizing solitude, as seen in Bashō's better-known other composition (reproduced on p. 151).

The second instance of wordplay is *tomarikeri*. The root verb *tomaru*, when used specifically of birds, means 'to alight'. The special auxiliary verb *keri* is conspicuous both for adding two extra syllabets to the verse and for how its meaning, here indicating a realization of the timelessly true nature of something, is not immediately clear. Clarification comes only with the third and final wordplay, *aki no kure*, referring to a particular nightfall in autumn and to the last gasp of autumn itself, thereby revealing the surprise of the until now latent though primary meaning of *tomaru* as 'to cease', either temporarily or permanently.

The extra syllabets could have been avoided by merely truncating *tomarikeri* to *tomari* with no real loss of meaning. Yet Bashō was well aware that hypermetre (*jiamari*) can be used to dramatic effect, as attested by his disciple Hattori Dohō in *Sanzōshi* (1702) (in *NKBZ* 51). In this verse, the above-mentioned *keri* not only conveys a sense of inevitability, confirming the transcendent symbolic reading, and contributes to the soundscape, but as the cut (*kire*) of the verse it freezes the moment spectacularly, not unlike the slow-motion photography of a later age. Two centuries later, Shiki might well have praised the verse for anticipating photorealism, though instead he pooh-poohed it as little more than 'a direct translation of the Chinese phrase "a chilly-looking crow on a bare tree"' (quoted in Ueda (ed. and trans.), *Bashō and His Interpreters*, p. 59). Wallace Stevens, on the other hand, reputedly drew inspiration from it when penning 'Thirteen Ways of Looking at a Blackbird' (1917). Given the emphasis on sound in the original verse, though, an alternative translation might be: 'on a leafless branch / a crow has come to a halt ... / autumnal nightfall'.

snowmelt! / through mountain vapours, / crow-cawing
yukidoke ya / miyama gumori o / naku karasu
   Gyōdai. An eloquent retort, no doubt, to Bashō's well-known verse above, with one or more crows returning to their usual vociferous selves with the coming of spring.

nest feathering! / even the much-despised crow, / a parent's heart
suzukuru ya / nikuki karasu mo / oyagokoro
   Shirao.

fresh green leaves: / cats and crows / squabbling!
wakaba shite / neko to karasu to / kenka kana
   Issa.

at a roadside shrine / glowing before the stone buddha ... / fireflies!
tsujidō no / hotoke ni tomosu / hotaru kana
   Buson. Typically, it is incense sticks burned for the dead that one sees glowing before stone buddha statues. The physical proximity here of buddha (*hotoke*) and firefly (*hotaru*) is echoed in their acoustic similarity.

perched asleep / on the massive temple bell: / a butterfly!
tsurigane ni / tomarite nemuru / kochō kana
   Buson. Apart from the incongruity of the gigantic, suspended, cast-iron bell, meant to be struck with a hanging log at a Buddhist temple, and the minuscule, free-floating, fragile symbol of Zhuangzi's Taoist conundrum about reality and dreams, there is the drama of when the *bell* will be roused from its slumbers, thereby rousing the butterfly – whose slumbers seem echoed in the very rhythms of the verse – from its reveries.

at daybreak / hailstones pitter-pattering / upon camellia
akatsuki no / arare uchiyuku / tsubaki kana
   Buson. Although *uchi-* is an emphatic prefix, it also has a wide range of meanings as a verb in its own right that subtly augment this verse, including 'strike', 'beat (rhythmically)', 'till (soil)' and 'sprinkle'.

evening breeze – / water lapping the shins / of a blue heron
yūkaze ya / mizu aosagi no / hagi o utsu
   Buson. Literally 'blue heron', the *aosagi* (*Ardea cinerea*) is actually grey – though in English 'blue' hints at the latent eroticism of the scene.

steady spring rains ... / doubtlessly growing dark, / this day lingers on

harusame ya / kurenan toshite / kyō mo ari

Buson. Mists arising from the rain diffuse the light of the sun while obscuring it at the same time, making for a disorienting sense of time-lessness.

against the stormclouds / seemingly plum-blossom stars / despite the daylight

amagumo no / ume no hoshi to mo / hiru nagara

Onitsura.

challenge:

no help whatsoever! / no help whatsoever!

sewa shinai koto / sewa shinai koto

response:

hungover yawn – / eyeing offertory saké / upon the altar!

ōakubi / tana no omiki o / mitsukedashi

Author unnamed. In *Yanagidaru* 10 (1775). The verse would appear later under the names Shōga, in *Yanagidaru* 85 (1825), and Chikuka, in *Yanagidaru* 156 (1838–40?). *Ōakubi*, 'huge yawn', contains within it the 'great sin' (*ōaku*) that this person, waking up with a hangover, is contemplating when the offertory saké comes into focus upon the sacred household altar 'shelf' (*tana*, referring to *kamidana*, 'altar').

butterflies! / fluttering a girl's way, / ahead, behind

chōchō ya / onago no michi no / ato ya saki

The nun Chiyo. The *ato* and *saki* can mean 'after' and 'before' in both spatial and temporal senses. With the intentional confusion between dream and reality invoked by the image of the butterfly, this verse is polyvalent.

a fallen petal / back to its bough, reviewed: / a butterfly!

rakka eda ni / kaeru to mireba / kochō kana

Moritake. This verse, one of the poet's best known, at first seems to be merely a visual pun (*mitate*) in which the speaker, in a moment of passionate confusion, mistakes one image for another. However, it also suggests amazement (underlined by the extra syllabet of the first line) at the apparent *untruth* of the Buddhist proverb that a fallen petal never returns to its bough.

water whirligigs? / or butterflies whirling round? / wavelets of petals!

tobu chō wa / maimaimushi ka / hana no nami

Baisei. The visual comparisons (*mitate*) of scattering cherry petals (*hana*) with the droplets of breaking waves (*nami*), and of butterflies (*chō*) with cherry blossoms, are conceits in Japanese poetry going back at least to the first imperially commissioned anthology (*c.* early tenth century). (See Helen Craig McCullough, *Brocade by Night: 'Kokin Wakashū' and the Court Style in Japanese Classical Poetry* (Stanford, CA: Stanford University Press, 1985), p. 416.) What is novel here is their combination. That, and the introduction of the striking term *maimaimushi*, 'round-and-round dancing bug' (also called *mizusumashi* or *amenbō*) or whirligig beetle (*Gyrinus japonicus*). The idea is that just as these steely-grey aquatic bugs are all but imperceptible unless skimming rapidly in circles on water's surface, so too are flitting butterflies all but indistinguishable from falling cherry blossoms.

but for the call / all but indistinguishable – / white heron and snowball

shirasagi no / nakazuba yuki no / hitomaroge

The woman poet Tayojo. Here, only sound can differentiate between the objects of this visual comparison (*mitate*).

beak and legs alone – / inkwash of a white heron / in the snow

hashi to ashi / bakari sumie no / yuki no sagi

Kingyo. In *Yanagidaru* 90 (1826). All of the words in this verse except for one end in either an *i* or *o* sound, and four of the words observe an *a-i* sound pattern.

a line of geese! / and upon the mountain crest / the moon as impress

ichigyō no / kari ya hayama ni / tsuki o insu

Buson. An imaginative visual double take (*mitate*) of an ostensibly observed natural scene as though it were an inkwash landscape painting with some kind of inscribed *haiku*, perhaps, replete with the artist's round seal (*insu*), emphasized by an extra syllabet. Buson has charmingly taken to its logical extreme the classic poetic trope likening a column of wild geese to a vertical line of calligraphy, as with the following *waka* by Tsumori no Kunimoto (*c.*1023–1102): 'how they resemble / the lines of a letter / written in light greys – / those geese returning homeward / through darkening skies' (*usuzumi ni / kaku tamazusa to / miyuru ka na / kasumeru sora ni / kaeru karigane*; poem 71 in the *Gōshūi wakashū* (composed 1086); see *SNKBT* 8, p. 32).

Dutch scribbling: / wild geese in the sky / flying sideways!
oranda no / moji ga yoko tobu / amatsukari

Ishū (aka Shigeyori). Since Japanese customarily was written vertically, the horizontal orientation of Western writing ('Dutch' standing for all things Euro-American) must have seemed so topsy-turvy, if not terribly awry, that it could not have helped but change the way the Japanese regarded the classical poetic trope – as well as the actual sight – of geese on the wing.

skewers of dumplings / more than sprigs of blossoms: / geese flying home
hana yori mo / dango ya arite / kaeru kari

Teitoku. In *Enokoshū* (1633). This verse has long been written off as merely playing with the slangy proverb 'dumplings more than blossoms', favouring pragmatic over aesthetic concerns, to whimsically suggest why geese returning from their winter migration do not stop to admire cherry blossoms. Yet it is only slightly more whimsical than the classic *waka* upon which it riffs, by Lady Ise (c. 875–938): 'paying no heed / to the rising spring mists / those passing geese / must be used to dwelling / in villages without blossoms' (*harugasumi / tatsu o misutete / yuku kari wa / hananaki sato ni / sumi ya naraeru*; poem number 31 in *SNKBT* 5, p. 27). Moreover, there is a a visual pun here: for columns of geese determined to reach home more closely resemble pointed skewers of rice-dough sweets than tangled branches of blossoms.

the fragrance / resides more in the nose / than the nosegay
hana yori mo / hana ni arikeru / nioi kana

Moritake. In *Moritake senku* (1540). Verses such as this one – making use of a trite pun on *hana* as 'nose' and 'flower' – have long been derided for their wordplay as fatuous. Yet the point here is that natural beauty is best articulated through artistic wit.

blowing her nose / with a nosegay of moonflowers – / the young lady
yūgao no / hana de hana kamu / musume kana

Issa. If puns are the lowest kind of wit, then apparently even masters like Issa were not immune from stooping. Although there may be a visual gag (*mitate*) here of sorts, likening the dew on the flower to nasal mucus, the *yūgao* (literally 'evening faces') typically opened up in the evening, not in the morning. Actually a calabash (*Lagenaria siceraria*) with delicately fluffy white blossoms colloquially known as moonflowers, the *yūgao* gourd called to mind the classical ideal of chubby feminine facial beauty.

drops of dew? / or rays of moon / upon the grass!
tsuyu wa isa / tsuki koso kusa ni / musubikere
   Zenma. Two similar-sounding words, *tsuki* (moon) and *tsuyu* (dew),
   likened visually.

vernal seas ... / all day long swelling, falling / swelling, falling!
haru no umi / hinemosu notari / notari kana
   Buson.

rising sun / and nothing else – / misty sea!
izuruhi no / hokani mono nashi / kiri no umi
   Shirō.

rowing clear / through the hazy dimness – / the vast sea
kogi nukete / kasumi no soto no / umi hiroshi
   Shiki.

**cloud and mist alike / rendered unnoticeable – / bright moon
tonight!**
kumo kiri mo / tsuki ni kakururu / koyoi kana
   Kensai. A comic inversion of the usual complaint against anything
   obscuring the moon, for on this particular evening the harvest moon
   is so dazzling that it effectively hides everything else from plain sight.

bright enough / to lose sight of it – / tonight's moon
miushinau / hodo ni akarushi / kyō no tsuki
   Seika.

**mountain fog – / performing shrine safekeeping, / conchshell-
sounds**
yamagiri ya / miya o shugo nasu / hora no oto
   Taigi. The fog and sound of conchshells blend into each other uncan-
   nily. A pivot on *nasu* yields the readings 'the mountain mist *turns into*
   shrine protection' and 'conchshell-sounds *perform* shrine protection'.

glancing behind, / the person met in passing / shrouded in mist
kaeri mireba / yuki aishi hito / kasumikeri
   Shiki. The first line has an extra syllabet.

even behind / even ahead ... / distant mist!
ushiro nimo / mae nimo tōki / kasumi kana
   Ryōta.

heaven and earth / still not rent asunder – / morning mist
ten to chi to / imada wakarezu / asagasumi
  Genkaibō.

bit by bit / the mountainside changes hue – / moonlit night!
dandanni / yama somete yuku / tsukiyo kana
  Fuhaku.

autumn begins! / the summer rainburst blends into / a crisp night drizzle
hatsuaki ya / yūdachi nagabiku / yoru no ame
  Taigi. Captured here is the moment of transition (*kigasanari*) from summer, known for its sudden but short-lived downpours, to autumn, with its dreary drizzles. The second phrase has an extra syllabet that highlights *nagabiku*, 'protracts'.

after sunset / suffuses its vermilion – / autumn dusk
shu o sosogu / irihi no ato wa / aki no kure
  Kitō.

falling clear through / the bottom of loneliness – / freezing rain!
sabishisa no / soko nukete furu / mizore kana
  Jōsō. In Morikawa Kyoriku and Kōno Riyū (eds), *Hentsuki* (c.1699). There is a slight pun on *nukete*, meaning 'to come loose (from something)' and '(for the sky) to be clear'.

cricket / upon hearth's pothook climbs – / frigid night
kirigirisu / jizai o noboru / yosamu kana
  Buson.

the lamplight / holding steady freezes – / frosty night!
tomoshibi no / suwarite koru / shimoyo kana
  Seira.

'the wind is freezing! / freezing, freezing!' / says the night lamp
kaze samushi / samushi samushi to / katō kana
  Issa. Since the slits in a ceramic night lamp tended to be small, for its flame to flicker ominously the wind must be cold and blustery indeed.

first spring breeze / in the lamplight flickering / within the outhouse
hatsukochi no / kawaya no akari / ugokikeri
  Ōemaru.

examined in the palm / the year's first hailstones / revert to water
hatsuarare / te ni tori mireba / moto no mizu
   The woman poet and Gion geisha Sakijo. The Heisenberg uncertainty principle stated eloquently and well ahead of its time.

within my grasp / sadly vanishing! / a firefly
te no ue ni / kanashiku kiyuru / hotaru kana
   Kyorai. A verse on the death of his younger sister, the poet Mukai Chine (d. 1688). The siblings had travelled together to the Ise Grand Shrines, composing verse along the way and recording the results jointly in *Ise kikō* (A Journey to Ise, 1686).

morning glories – / just try to capture their image / and they droop
asagao ya / e ni utsusu ma ni / shiorekeri
   Haritsu. The Japanese morning glory (*Ipomoea nil*) is notoriously fleet of petal. *Shiore*, 'droop', also means 'crestfallen'.

morning glories – / just try to sketch their portrait / and they droop
asagao ya / e ni kaku uchi ni / shiorekeri
   Shiki.

challenge:
a sight to behold! / a sight to behold!
migoto narikeri / migoto narikeri

response:
the classy ones / even when catching z's / grasp books
utatane mo / jōhinna no wa / hon o mochi
   Author unnamed. In *Yanagidaru* 3 (1768).

naptime book – / page by page the breeze / ravishes
utatane no / shomotsu wa kaze ga / kutteiru
   Author unnamed. In *Yanagidaru* 6 (1771). *Kutteiru* has a range of meanings from 'riffling through' to 'tormenting' and even the vulgar 'fucking', suggesting the content of the book if not the dreams of the nap taker.

concealing the face / of the snoozing sneak thief, / *Vatful of Light Verse*
dorobō no / hirune no kao ni / yanagidaru
   Higan. In *Yanagidaru* 87 (1825). At first blush the identity of the burglar is masked by the book. However, it is telling that it is a copy of *Yanagidaru* (Willow Vat) – a verse collection that includes the above

example. Perhaps it even suggests the reason the burglar has been drinking; for *Yanagidaru*, which puns orthographically on the name of its compiler, Karai Senryū, was a willow-wood vat of saké. Were it not for the fact that it is midday, one might easily suppose that a burglar broke into a house and, unwittingly becoming so engrossed in the *senryū* of this book, fell asleep as though intoxicated by saké – a sight the homeowner returns to discover. A similar verse by Yume-suke, in *Yanagidaru* 167 (1840), replaces *yanagidaru* with *koyomizuri*, a sheet of the best ripostes from a verse-capping (*maekuzuke*) competition: 'concealing the face / of the snoozing sneak thief / *Winning Light Verse*' (*dorobō no / hirune no kao ni / koyomizuri*).

the burglar / on his way home commends / the bountiful moon
dorobō no / kaeri ni marui / tsuki o home
Yasharō. In addition to its beauty, which anyone no matter how low can appreciate, the moon has long been associated with karmic fate as well as night-time shenanigans. Here, however, its fullness on the evening in question also provided the burglar enough light by which to bag ample loot, for which he thanks his lucky stars.

the burglar / left it behind – / moon in the window
nusubito ni / torinokosareshi / mado no tsuki
Ryōkan.

bumping into / a woman pickpocket – / hazy moon
aimishi wa / onna no suri ya / oborozuki
Taigi.

through countless rimes / gently this Plantain serves / as my New Year's pine
iku shimo ni / kokorobase o no / matsu kazari
Bashō. In *Atsumeku* (1687). In a bit of self-reflexive wordplay, just as *matsu kazari* (the pine tree decoration associated with the New Year) suggests Matsuo, so too does *kokorobase o* contain the word *baseo*, one way of writing 'Bashō'. This *bashō* is a kind of plantain or so-called Traveller's Palm (*Musa basjoo*). The poet assumed this pen name in 1680 when, having moved away from the hustle and bustle of downtown Edo to a thatch-roofed retreat in Fukagawa on the outskirts of town, a disciple had gifted him with one or more of these exotic plants. Native to Okinawa and parts of the Asian mainland, the *bashō* made for a sturdy symbol both of something or someone far flung (Bashō originally hailed from Iga Province, not far from Kyoto but

a long way from Edo) and of frailty, for its leaves, while providing ample shade from summer heat, none the less were rather easily shredded in the wind.

plantain-shredding windstorm – / rain upon a washbasin heard / all night long!
bashō nowaki shite / tarai ni ame o / kiku yo kana

Bashō. A highly unusual twenty-syllabet verse, in lines of 8–7–5. Of course, this verse would resolve into the usual seventeen syllabets if only the self-advertising word *bashō* (see note to previous verse) were omitted ...

Bashō's plantain / Senryū's riverwillow / equally palmy!
bashō hodo / ha no hiroku naru / kawayanagi

Keisuke. In *Yanagidaru* 99 (1828). Although the literal meaning – 'the riverwillow is as broad-leafed as the plantain tree!' – is exactly false, wordplay yields what must have seemed true: 'Senryū's verses are just as popular as Bashō's!' For 'plantain', see note to Bashō's *iku shimo ni / kokorobase o no / matsu kazari*; for 'riverwillow', see note to next verse.

tree-withering gust! / later bursting forth in buds, / the riverwillow
kogarashi ya / atode me o fuke / kawayanagi

Senryū. This death verse (*jisei*) plays on the literal meaning of Senryū as 'riverwillow' (*kawayanagi*).

come for a loan / he momentarily appears / trustworthy
kari ni kita / toki wa shōjiki / sōna kao

Author unnamed. The duplicitousness is also apparent in the punning phrase *kari ni*, meaning both 'borrow' and 'temporarily'. An associated proverb runs: 'When borrowing, the face of a saint; when repaying, the face of a devil' (*kariru toki no hotokegao, kaesu toki no enmagao*).

more woeful / even than the death poem: / he who lent money!
jisei yori / aware wa kane o / kashita hito

Tamagawa. In *Yanagidaru* 42 (1808). The same verse by one Rōsen (not to be confused with Taniguchi Rōsen) appears in *Yanagidaru* 135 (1834). At first, based on the train of association set up in the first half of the verse, we expect the word *kane* to be a 'bell' tolling for the dead. Instead, rather unexpectedly, it swerves into the graph for 'money' that was lent.

snail / bit by bit ascend! / Mount Fuji
katatsuburi / sorosoro nobore / fuji no yama
　　Issa. Some commentators have suggested that this is a simulacrum
rather than the real mountain. J. D. Salinger quotes this verse in
Franny and Zooey (1961).

to the very brink / of smouldering Mount Asama / cultivated fields
asama ne no / keburu soba made / hatake kana
　　Issa. The eruption of Mount Asama in 1783 killed more than a thou-
sand people straight off. More catastrophically, it extended the Great
Tenmei Famine (1782–8) for several years. Poisonous ash reached
Edo a hundred miles away (where Issa, in his early twenties, was resid-
ing at the time), rendering farmlands barren and no doubt contribut-
ing to the starvation of countless more souls. Farmers responded by
cultivating every possible scrap of land – even up to the verge of the
selfsame volcano that had wrought such devastation in the first place.

Mount Asama / amidst its fumes and ash / fresh young leaves!
asamayama / keburi no naka no / wakaba kana
　　Buson. For the eruption of Mount Asama, see note to previous verse.

bindweed blooms / opening toward the hiss-hissing / sizzling stones
hirugao ya / poppo to moeru / ishikoro e
　　Issa. *Hirugao*, literally 'noon face', is Japanese bindweed (*Calystegia
japonica*) or 'noonflower', opening in the middle of the day and as-
sociated with midsummer. The sizzling stones indicate some kind of
volcanic activity. Although this verse might suggest an impending
eruption, there are also many such areas in Japan, often associated
with hotspring resorts today, that are in little such danger.

worthless weeds! / the taller you grow / the longer the days
mudagusa ya / nanji mo nobiru / hi mo nobiru
　　Issa.

bush warbler! / only a drab-coloured bird / with a song thrown in
uguisu ya / oto o irete tada / aoi tori
　　Onitsura. The Japanese bush warbler or nightingale (*Horornis di-
phone*), more remarkable for its mellifluous singing than its pale
green-brown colour, is hardly ever seen anyway. The second line itself
has an extra syllabet thrown in.

a bush warbler / with too many syllabets / draws out its song
uguisu no / uta no jiamaru / hikine kana
  Buson. Even bush warblers (*uguisu*), like versifiers, sometimes overstep
  their prescribed allotment of syllabets – though this verse does not.

barely springtime / but lo that bush warbler! / in a voice of yore
haru mo yaya / ana uguisu yo / mukashigoe
  Buson.

bush warbler! / alighting upon plum trees / since aeons ago
uguisu ya / ume ni tomaru wa / mukashi kara
  Onitsura. As with many things in life, something that appears to take
  place only in the present turns out to have occurred repeatedly since
  time immemorial.

the years pass ... / greying hairs have I concealed / from my parents
yuku toshi ya / oya ni shiraga o / kakushikeri
  Etsujin.

over there / appears nice and cool – / pines on the ridge
sokomoto wa / suzushisō nari / mine no matsu
  Shikō.

emerging from / the edge of coolness – / ocean moon
suzushisa no / hate yori detari / umi no tsuki
  Shiki.

how enviable! / falling while still resplendent, / the maple leaf
urayamashi / utsukushū narite / chiru momiji
  Shikō. An alternative version has the functionally equivalent *natte* in-
  stead of *narite*. Either way the second line contains an extra syllabet.

**looking as though / spring would nevermore return: / scattered
  leaves!**
mata haru no / kuru tomo mienu / ochiba kana
  Ryōta.

**inner side revealed / outer side being revealed – / tumbling maple
  leaf**
ura o mise / omote o misete / chiru momiji
  Attributed to Ryōkan as his death verse (*jisei*).

city folk / adorned with red maple leaves / on the train home
kyōbito ya / momiji kazashite / modorigisha
    Meisetsu.

heat-shimmers: / even mosquito breeding grounds / brimming
    with beauty
kagerō ya / ka no waku yabu mo / utsukushiki
    Issa. There is a pun here on *waku*, which can refer to hatching or,
    playing with the heat-shimmers, to boiling over.

sure enough! / mushrooms that will kill you, / also gorgeous
hito o toru / kinoko hatashite / utsukushiki
    Issa.

resplendent, / the kite soaring high above / the shanty town
utsukushiki / tako agarikeri / kojikigoya
    Issa. *Kojikigoya* refers to one or more hovels of indigent people.

however sublime, / even the blossoms cannot compare: / tonight's
    bright moon
ikani ikani / hana mo koyoi no / tsuki ichirin
    Sōin. Playing on twin senses of *ichirin* as a counter word for both
    'flowers' (*hana*) and 'moon' (*tsuki*) in a rare double hypermetric verse
    of 6–7–6 syllabets.

plum blossoms / one by one toward / spring's warmth!
ume ichirin / ichirin hodo no / atatakasa
    Ransetsu. Although the plum and warmth are both associated with
    spring, the former had a more transitional feel, appearing even during
    the lingering snows of late winter. The first line has an extra syllabet.

a barren woman / coddling festival dolls – / how poignant
umazume no / hina kashizuku zo / aware naru
    Ransetsu. Perhaps his best-known verse. Most scholars interpret *hina*
    as invoking the dolls (*hinaningyō*) of the doll festival (*hinamatsuri*)
    on the third day of the third lunisolar month. A minority opinion
    maintains that the term refers to hatchlings (*hinadori*). Regardless,
    the springtime setting of this verse contrasts starkly with the infertile
    woman. Since *umazume* can be written 'stone woman', the minority
    reading invokes the mental comparison of eggs and stones.

doll's face . . . / mine unavoidably / wizened with age
hina no kao / ware zehinaku mo / oi ni keri
> The nun Seifu.

door ajar / though nobody home . . . / peach blossoms
to no akete / aredo rusu nari / momo no hana
> The nun Chiyo. Peach blossoms are associated with late spring.

lull in the rain . . . / drifting into the bedroom / a butterfly!
shizuka naru ya / fushido ni irishi / ame no chō
> The nun Seifu. The lovely first line contains an extra syllabet.

spring rains . . . / every thing transformed / exquisitely
harusame ya / utsukushū naru / mono bakari
> The nun Chiyo.

blossoms falling, / it has become still: / the human heart
hana chirite / shizuka ni narinu / hitogokoro
> The nun Matsumoto Koyū. A riff on a classic *waka* by Ariwara no
> Narihira (825-80): 'if in our world / there were no cherry blossoms /
> whatsoever / how serene would be / our hearts in spring!' (*yo no naka
> ni / taete sakura no / nakariseba / haru no kokoro wa / nodokeramashi*; in
> *NKBZ* 8, p. 203).

the wife / buried in their burrow of snow, / while he hawks coal
nyōbō o / yuki ni uzumete / sumi o uri
> Author unnamed. In *Yanagidaru* 1 (1765).

challenge:
ain't that the truth! / ain't that the truth!
honno koto nari / honno koto nari

response:
horse farts perturb / four or five passengers / aboard the ferry
uma no he ni / shigonin komaru / watashibune
> While the challenge verse typically would be written by the referee of
> a verse-capping contest (see Introduction, p. xlviii), this challenge was
> composed by one Ryūsui of Asanuno, who published it in *Senryūhyō
> mankuawase* (1785). The response, which appeared on its own as a
> *senryū*, was composed by Wakamatsu. In *Yanagidaru* 52 (1811). *Shigo*,
> 'four or five', also suggests 'whisper', suggesting farting noises as well
> as something that one wishes to keep quiet. The *watashi* of *watashi-
> bune*, 'ferryboat', can also mean 'private' or 'individual'.

roused by horse farts / to catch a glimpse of / flitting fireflies
uma no he ni / mezamete mireba / tobu hotaru
  Issa.

challenge:
beyond a doubt! / beyond a doubt!
zehini zehini to / zehini zehini to
response:
loan shark / lying in wait outside / the pawnshop
toba no inu / shichiya no kado ni / matteiru
  Author unnamed. In *Yanagidaru* 9 (1774).

valley stream: / stones too do songs croon / 'neath mountain blooms!
tanimizu ya / ishi mo uta yomu / yamazakura
  Onitsura. *Yamazakura*, literally 'mountain cherry' (*Cerasus jamasakura*),
  is a variety of wild cherry that can grow in places other than in
  mountain regions.

willow, bare / clear stream, dry stones / here and there
yanagi chiri / shimizu kare ishi / tokorodokoro
  Buson. A striking verse for its four groupings of repeated vowels, extra
  syllabet in the last line and almost avant-garde grammar: the deliber-
  ately slippery word *kare* ('bare' or 'dry') in the middle of the second
  phrase unusually acts as a pivot between the first and last lines of
  the verse and as a participle (*dried* stones) initiating a fragment that
  straddles two phrases.

hands pressed down / offering up a song – / the frog!
te o tsuite / uta mōshiagaru / kawazu kana
  Sōkan. The second line contains an extra syllabet.

old pond! / a frog plunges into / watersound
furuike ya / kawazu tobikomu / mizu no oto
  Bashō. (*c.*1681–84). The out-of-the-blue diving of one or more young
  'frogs' (*kawazu*) into an age-old pond long 'overlooked' (a homonym
  of *mizu*, 'water'), just beginning to pullulate with life again after the
  dormancy of winter, embodies the delightful surprises of spring.
  (Although the noun *kawazu* can be plural as well as singular, most
  commentators believe that here there is no more than one frog. As
  Fukumoto explains, both of the extant paintings by Bashō on this
  verse have a lone frog. There may also be a possible reference to an

anecdote of Huineng (Enō in Japanese; 638–713), the sixth patriarch of Tang-dynasty China, about a single voice and the sound of water. See *BFD*, pp. 53–61.) For many commentators, this verse is a Zen meditation on the hidden connection between apparent opposites – eternal and momentary, dormancy and awakening, stillness and action – that supposedly epitomizes the haiku form itself. (In the memorable formulation of William Howard Cohen, this verse links 'together seemingly disparate elements by showing their hidden or unsuspected unity' – *To Walk in Seasons: An Introduction to Haiku* (Rutland, VT: Charles E. Tuttle, 1972), pp. 24–45.) For most readers in Bashō's day, however, the pleasure of the verse probably resided far more in its amusing *haiku* twist of having the frog produce a watery sound instead of a croak. For further commentary on this verse, see Introduction, p. xli. See also the image on p. xlii.

philandering ways – / laying off them deflates / his manliness!
asobu ki o / yameru to sagaru / otokoburi
> Author unnamed. (Genroku era, 1688–1704). The equation of playing and ceasing and sapping is driven home in the original by shared *u* sounds.

nobody ever / glances behind himself / in wintry rain
hito no mi no / ushiro e mukanu / fuyu no ame
> Author unnamed.

for a beauty / forty is from head to toe / hideous
utsukushii / onna no shijū / monosugoi
> Author unnamed. *Shijū*, 'forty', has a homonym meaning 'from first to last'.

from forty / when looking in the mirror / one is galled!
shijū kara / kagami o mireba / hara ga tachi
> Author unnamed.

in my handglass / begrudging the departing spring / all alone
yuku haru o / kagami ni uramu / hitori kana
> Seibi.

with great ardour / the freed bird flies smack into / the great arbour!
ureshisa no / ki ni tsukiataru / hanashidori
> Author unnamed. The word 'feeling' (*ki*) pivots into its homonym 'tree' (*ki*) just as the bird smacks into it.

white heron / manoeuvring legs as though / the paddy were unclean
shirasagi no / ta o kitanagaru / ashizukai
  Author unnamed. In *Mutamagawa* 18 (1775).

hew hew! / howls the wind through the sky – / winter peonies
hyūhyū to / kaze wa sora yuku / kanbotan
  Onitsura.

one by one / praising and withdrawing inside – / winter moon
meimei ni / homete hikkomu / fuyu no tsuki
  Senjō. In *Yanagidaru* 26 (1796).

winter orb: / admired then shut out / with a slam
fuyu no tsuki / hometarikeri de / batari tate
  Author unnamed. In *Yanagidaru* 6 (1771).

luminescent / yet completely shut out – / winter moon
sae nagara / shime dasarekeri / fuyu no tsuki
  Ryūichi.

winter moon! / pebbles felt beneath the sole / of one's shoe
kangetsu ya / koishi no sawaru / kutsu no soko
  Buson.

wintry river … / from the trudging ferrymen, / nary a melody
fuyu no kawa / kogu sendō ni / uta mo nashi
  Goyō. *Kogu*, 'paddle', can also mean to make one's way through snow or ice.

cool breeze / breathing deeply into my mouth / a bush mosquito!
suzukaze ga / kuchi e fukikomu / yabuka kana
  Issa. Literally 'bush mosquito', the *yabuka* is a striped (aedine) mosquito that can carry disease.

smoked out / by the next-door neighbour – / bush mosquitoes!
tonari kara / ibushi dasareshi / yabuka kana
  Issa.

challenge:
beyond one's control! / beyond one's control!
mama naranu koto / mama naranu koto

response:

the widow first off / feels lonesome at the emptiness / of the bed netting

goke wa mazu / kaya no hirosa o / sabishigari

Ōkubo of Kirishima. In *Kinkeihyō mankuawase* (1766).

struggling to rise, / to sleep, in searching ... our bed netting's / desolateness!

okite mitsu / nete mitsu kaya no / hirosa kana

The courtesan Ukihashi. Widely misattributed to the nun Chiyo, this celebrated verse first appeared under Ukihashi's name within *Sonotayori* (1694), a *haiku* collection published nearly a decade before Chiyo was born (in Mayama Seika, *Mayama seika zuihitsu senshū* 1, *Kokugen zappitsu* (Dai nihon yūbenkai kōdansha, 1952); cited in *SS*, p. 51).

The rhythm of this verse is fitful, suggesting the tossing and turning of someone unable to sleep. Yet the language is open-ended: *okite mitsu nete mitsu* can mean 'tried to rise, tried to sleep' as well as 'arose and looked, reclined and looked'; *kaya*, the mosquito canopy suggesting the intimacy of a couple's bed, read as the particles *ka ya*, can turn the preceding phrase into an emphatic question; and *hirosa*, 'extent', can also mean the 'vastness' of the bed or of time and space, intimating that the speaker's lover has passed away, therefore hinting at the emptiness in her heart.

diddle weary / Chiyo concocted that bug verse / by a stroke of luck!

kujiriaki / chiyo kaya no ku o / futo anji

Chikuga. In *Yanagi no hazue* (1835). A far-fetched explanation (*kojitsuke*) of the celebrated verse above misattributed to the nun Chiyo. Drawing out the latent phallic associations of mosquitoes (known for 'pricking') and width (*hirosa*), this verse burlesques Chiyo as a stereotypical hard-up widow who overcomes her loneliness by succumbing to horniness. *Anji*, 'devising (a verse)', has a sexualized homonym, 'stroking'. *Futo*, 'suddenly', can also mean 'grand' as well as 'thick'.

sleeping alone / beneath mosquito netting / the wife fuming

hitori neta / kaya de nyōbō / yaite iru

Useki. In *Yanagidaru* 65 (1814). Her husband sleeping elsewhere, a wife tosses and turns in bed alone, *burning* with jealousy, not unlike a *fuming* incense-coil of mosquito repellent. Then again, is a wife so incensed likely to be penetrated in the first place, by mosquito or not?

challenge:
obsessed with the old in-and-out! / obsessed with the old in-and-out!
toritsuki ni keri / toristuki ni keri

response:
the mosquito speaketh: / 'can't even sneak a peep, / damn paper netting!'
ka no iwaku / nozokare mo senu / kono shichō

Author unnamed. In *Omote wakaba* (1732). Literally 'taking and sticking', *toritsuki* in the challenge can mean either 'obsessing' (as with the phallic mosquito's fervent search for blood) or 'clinging together' (as with two lovers in the throes of passion). Insects, animals and inanimate objects were sometimes personified by deploying the 'so-and-so speaketh' formula (*iwakuzuke*) of this verse.

bed netting up, / even mosquitoes are delightful, / flitting in moonlight
kaya tsureba / ka mo omoshiroshi / tsuki ni tobu

Baishitsu. A mildly wry comment on the virtues of being inside a mosquito net. Yet this verse also loosely burlesques a celebrated episode from the *Kojiki* (*c.*711) involving the sun goddess Amaterasu, the putative progenitor of Japan's imperial line. (For an annotated translation of this episode, see Donald L. Philippi (trans.), *Kojiki* (Tokyo: University of Tokyo, 1968), pp. 81–6.) The sun goddess, pouting, has holed up in a cave, plunging the world into darkness. In a ploy to lure her out, the goddess Uzume performs a striptease, baring her breasts and vulva, to the whooping delight of the other deities. Curious about the hullabaloo, the sun goddess peeks out of the cave, her light rays striking Uzume and turning her 'white-faced' (*omoshiroshi*), a term that persists to this day (as *omoshiroi*) to denote that which is de*light*ful. To ensure that Amaterasu could never again withdraw into the cave, a ceremonial straw-woven rope was strung across its opening – not unlike how beds are canopied with netting to keep mosquitoes at bay.

Given the erotic nature of this episode as well as of the setting of the verse, a remotely possible sexualized alternative reading would draw out not only the phallic nature of the mosquito, but also the double entendres on both *tsuki ni tobu* ('flit in moonlight' and 'rise in order to penetrate') and *kaya tsureba* ('when bed netting is draped' and 'when the netted bed beckons') to yield something like: 'when bed netting beckons, / even little prickers are delightful, / rising to penetrate!'

the net that screws not / the mosquitoes screwing her – / swatting all to hell!

kū ka yori / kuwanu kaya made / buchikoroshi

Rekisen. In *Yanagidaru* 33 (1806) and 65 (1814). Who says that *sen-ryū* are seasonless or the Japanese unflappable? Exasperated on a hot summer night, one swats the hell out of the ineffective net as well as the pesky mosquitoes. In addition to meaning 'to eat', *kū* is a vulgar term for having sexual relations with a woman, especially for the first time. *Buchikoroshi*, 'kill by swatting', can also mean 'pawn off'.

swarm of mosquitoes – / fed full with the blood of / fed-up meditators!

amata ka no / chi ni fukureiru / zazen kana

Taigi. In *Taigi kusen kōhen* (1777). The word *fukureiru*, meaning 'enraged' as well as 'engorged', pivots from 'mosquitoes *engorged* with blood' into 'meditators *enraged*'. Although understandably aggravated by the swarming bloodsuckers, these Zen practitioners of seated meditation are helpless to flee, to say nothing of swatting, given the Buddhist injunction against taking even insect life.

mosquito swatting – / the covers of a war epic, / stained with blood!

ka o utte / gunsho no ue ni / chi o insu

Shiki.

poised to retreat, / driving off a yellowjacket / with a book of verse

nigegoshi ni / natte shishū de / hachi o oi

Amenbō. As good a use of a poetry anthology, perhaps, as any. *Hachi* refers to bees, hornets, yellowjackets and other types of wasps.

riled up / by the shears' bare blades: / hornets!

kibasami no / shiraha ni hachi no / ikari kana

Shirao.

bumblebee, / having chased off some person, / returns to its blooms

hito ōte / hachi modorikeri / hana no ue

Taigi.

the maidservant / slept right past their rendezvous / deeply in her cups

yakusoku o / gejo wa tokkuri / nete shimai

Author unnamed. The bottle of saké (*tokkuri*) that caused the maid to completely (*tokkuri*) oversleep the appointed time may perhaps have fuelled her promise to hook up in the first place.

challenge:
given the cold shoulder, / bored alone in bed
furareta ato no / toko temochi nashi

response:
feigning sleep, / then losing sleep before / falling asleep for real!
uso neiri / neiri sokonai / hon neiri
    Shōsui from Kōshū. In Fukaku (ed.), *Niiki* (1693). A young playboy
    finds himself alone in bed waiting for a courtesan. Desperately deter-
    mined to play it cool, he feigns sleep. As time wears on, it becomes
    increasingly apparent that she has stood him up, so he gets too hot
    under the collar to sleep. But exhausted, he falls asleep in spite of
    himself. No doubt this is when the courtesan appears – though being
    asleep, he would never know.

from snowy slumber / bamboo trees shaken awake: / morning sun
yuki ni neta / take o asahi ga / yuriokoshi
    Nyoshun. In *Yanagidaru* 34 (1806). The same verse would reappear
    under the pen names Kisei, in *Yanagidaru* 45 (1808), and Chikugan –
    twice! – in *Yanagidaru* 139 (1835).

challenge:
how devious! / how devious!
zurui koto kana / zurui koto kana

response:
to awaken / a late-morning riser / just say it's midday!
asane suru / hito o okosu wa / hiru to iu
    Author unnamed. In *Yanagidaru* 7 (1772). A slightly different ver-
    sion appears in *Senryūhyō mankuawase* (1757–89) (in Ōmi Sajin and
    Fujiwara Seiken, *Senryū nyūmon: ryūga to sakkuhō* (Ōsaka: Hoikusha,
    1977), pp. 101–2).

challenge:
looking frightened / out of one's wits!
kimo o tsubushite / itaru kaotsuki

response:
a tall tale – / the remedy to cut short / the hiccoughs!
ii kakuru / uso wa shakuri no / tomegusuri
    Shōjin. In *Waka midori* (1691).

challenge:
wanting both to slash / and not to slash
kiritaku mo ari / kiritaku mo nashi

response 1:
that branch / of blossoms concealing / the dazzling moon!
sayakanaru / tsuki o kakuseru / hana no eda
    Author unnamed. In *Inu tsukubashū* (*c.*1530).

response 2:
that housebreaker / caught and unmasked: / *my own kid!*
nusubito o / toraete mireba / waga ko nari
    Sōkan. In *Inu tsukubashū* (*c.*1530). The phrase *toraete mireba*, 'when
captured and looked at', can also mean 'when trying to perceive'.
Unpacking this oft-cited response, the exchange might be rendered: 'to
slash / or not to slash!' / 'looking to apprehend / how the apprehended
housebreaker when unmasked / could be my own kid!'

the sneak thief / apprehended, his mother / stops shrieking
nusubito o / torae hahaoya / koe o sage
    Kinchō. In *Yanagidaru* 26 (1796). Sanbai would publish essentially
an identical version in *Yanagidaru* 58 (1811). *Torae*, 'catch', can also
mean 'grasp (the identity of)'.

'lock up tightly / before sleeping!' repeated, / leaving to thieve
yoku shimete / nero to ii ii / nusumi ni de
    Author unnamed. In *Yanagidaru shūi* 10 (*c.*1796–7). A related proverb
runs: 'Even burglars lock their doors' (*nusubito mo tojimari*; *EST*, p.
309).

to his wife: / 'lock up tightly before sleeping!' / leaving for a job
yoku shimete / neya to nyōbo e / tsutomete de
    Author unnamed. In *Yanagidaru* 2 (1767).

'lock up tightly / before sleeping … with me!' / the widow's depravity
yoku shimete / neyare to goke no / ajikinasa
    Author unnamed. In *Yanagidaru* 6 (1771). One homonym of *shimeru*
(rendered in the form *shimete* here), 'lock up', is 'get wet'.

challenge:
jumping right out! / jumping right out!
tobiagarikeri / tobiagarikeri

response:
more beguiling / than that stunning face: / her put-ons!
utsukushii / kao yori uso ga / migoto nari
> Author unnamed. In Kojui Taiō (ed.), *Urawakaba* (1732). The term *migoto*, meaning something commendable, specifically implies a magnificent performance or act. Moreover, its *mi~* jibes with another reading of *utsukushii*, 'beautiful'.

challenge:
finally settled down! / finally settled down!
ochitsuki ni keri / ochitsuki ni keri

response:
from this day on / she makes herself up / for one man only
kyō kara wa / hitori no tame ni / suru keshō
> Author unnamed. In Chōgetsu (ed.), *(Haikai) Azuma karage* (1755).

challenge:
how despicable! / how despicable!
nikui koto kana / nikui koto kana

response:
the Dear Jane letter, / upon closer inspection, / in a *woman*'s hand!
sarijō o / yoku yoku mireba / onna no te
> Ryūmon of Honjo Ishiwara-chō. In *Senryūhyō mankuawase* (1763). A restoration of the phrase *onna no te* that had come to refer to one Japanese syllabary (*hiragana*) back to its original literal meaning of 'woman's hand'. Although a man could divorce his wife merely by serving her with written notice (*sarijō*), to have his new woman write that notice would be to rub salt in the wound.

challenge:
a pleasant surprise! / a pleasant surprise!
ureshi ya ureshi / ureshi ya ureshi

response:
had it been a dream / her comb would have no business / being here for real
yume naraba / sashigushi no aru / hazu wa nai
> Author unnamed. In *Omote wakaba* (1732). A parody of the classic poetic trope of a male lover coming to a woman at night as if in a dream. The twist here is that, judging by the *sashigushi* – a woman's comb fashioned out of hawksbill sea turtle (*bekkō*) and used as a hair

ornament – it is a woman who has come to the man. Moreover, her comb is the cold, hard physical evidence that punctures any romantic wistfulness.

challenge:
the prank of poking a hole / in the paper sliding-door
shōji ni ana o / akuru itazura

response:
'once crawling, stand! / and once standing, run!' / parental love
haeba tate / tateba hashire to / oyagokoro
    Chōryū. In Fukaku (ed.) *Chiyomigusa* (1692). This proverbial response suggests that the best way to handle a disrespectful young prankster is a good scolding. After all, the kindest thing parents can do for their children is to instil in them respectfulness as well as a healthy appreciation for never being complacent, particularly when it comes to self-improvement. Similar verses include Chijin's nearly identical one a century later: '"once crawling, stand! / once standing, walk!" such is / parental love!' (*haeba tate / tateba ayume no / oyagokoro*). In *Yanagidaru* 45 (1808).

challenge:
a secret that must be kept! / a secret that must be kept!
kakushi koso sure / kakushi koso sure

response:
'bumper crop!' / lyrics not to leave the mouth / in peasant songs
hōnen to / kuchi kara iwanu / tami no uta
    Suisen. In *Chikusaihyō mankuawase* (1748). Playing off the truism that one must not boast about good fortune lest the gods take it away, here it is the government whom the peasant farmers (*tami*) are worried would take food out of their mouths should the words leave their mouths.

rice-planting chant – / not one single aggrievement / goes unaddressed!
taueuta / donna urami mo / tsukinubeshi
    Issa.

challenge:
an extreme grudge / followed by disgrace!
urami sugitaru / ato fushubi nari

response:
the letter snatched / out of his wife's hands / ... from her mother!
tsuma no te o / mogiri hanaseba / haha no fumi
   Suiha. In Fukaku (ed.), *Herazuguchi* (1694).

challenge:
looking forward to it! / looking forward to it!
tanoshimi ni naru / tanoshimi ni naru

response:
**unblackened teeth / and a blank slate of hair – / delightful Miss
   Carte Blanche!**
somenu ha to / egakanu kami no / omoshiroshi
   Fūso. In *Hanabatake* (1711), a collection of verse capping (*maekuzuke*)
   and crown-linking (*kanmurizuke*) verses by an unknown compiler
   but with named authors and groups. *Somenu ha*, 'unblackened teeth',
   signalled a woman's availability throughout premodern Japanese his-
   tory. Such women might be respectable young ladies, but also geisha,
   courtesans, dancing girls and so on (see *NKBZ* 46, p. 271, n. 207).
   In this connection, *kami*, 'paper', can also mean 'hair', an associative
   word of 'teeth'. Tying all of these meanings together is *omoshiroshi*
   (*omoshiroi* in modern Japanese), literally 'white-faced', an image of
   courtesans in their greasepaint, but meaning 'delightful', suggesting
   'coquettish' behaviour (as per the note to Baishitsu's *kaya tsureba / ka
   mo omoshiroshi / tsuki ni tobu*).

**sooner or later / down and dirty in white makeup – / the widow's
   face!**
oshiroi de / kekkyoku yogoreru / goke no kao
   Tōjin. In *Yanagidaru shūi* 3 (*c*.1796-7). *Yogoreru*, 'sullied', also means
   'unchaste'. The second line contains an extra syllabet.

for all people / the seed of daytime napping: / summer moon!
mina hito no / hirune no tane ya / natsu no tsuki
   Teitoku. His assertion that everyone is moved by beauty is consistent
   with the idea of *haiku* as a popular genre. Although the harvest moon
   is regarded as most beautiful, and in fact another version of this verse
   has 'autumn moon' (*aki no tsuki*), the idea of seeds coming to fruition
   is generally more properly associated with summer.

sold filially / into slavery though redeemed / unfilially
kōkō ni / urare fukō ni / uke-dasare

Author unnamed. Typically, courtesans started out as young girls whose impoverished families sold them into the indentured servitude of the pleasure quarters in return for money. Many girls obliged out of a sense of duty to their parents. After becoming courtesans, the more popular ones might have their contracts bought out by wealthy playboys who, paradoxically, depleting their family fortunes with their debaucheries, were anything but filial.

the lucre / for selling his daughter / gone in a flash!
ko o utte / kane inazuma no / yō ni kie

Author unnamed. In *Yanagidaru shūi* 6 (*c.*1796-7).

the follow-up *ah* / *choo!* for which one is braced / goofy-faced
ato no kusa- / me o matteiru / henna tsura

Rekisen. In *Yanagidaru* 44 (1808). This verse captures the frozen moment before a second sneeze not only by describing, but also by enacting. This it does by slowing the reader down several times. Two words contain pregnant pauses: the 'long' or double (geminate) consonants *t* in *matteiru* (waiting) and *n* in *henna* (oddball). And there is the conspicuous enjambment (*kumatagari*) of the word for sneeze (*kusame*) itself. An alternative if not pirated version by one Kiga, replacing *henna* with *bakana* (hare-brained), would appear in *Yanagidaru* 88 (1825).

challenge:
now that's unavoidable! / now that's unavoidable!
zehi mo nai koto / zehi mo nai koto

response:
exasperation / occasionally makes the face / a work of art
kanshaku wa / oriori kao ni / gei o sase

Author unnamed. In *Yanagidaru* 30 (1804).

some blokes / imbibing their winter coats / bundle up with drink!
wataire wa / nonde sake kiru / otoko ari

Author unnamed. In *Yanagidaru shūi* 10 (*c.*1796-7). Hocking one's cotton-padded jacket (*wataire*) for saké is not the most expedient way of staying warm in winter.

crying out / in the driving rain / as though slain
amadare ni / kirareta yōna / koe o dashi
> Kibun. In *Yanagidaru* 29 (1800). Centuries later Mel Brooks would quip: 'Tragedy is when I cut my finger. Comedy is when you fall into an open sewer and die.'

the rain lets up / yet still just as expected / the same heat!
ame yande / yappari moto no / atsusa kana
> Keira.

what rumbling! / rat-grey thunderclouds rouse / summer from slumber
todoroku ya / nezumi kaminari / natsu nezame
> Ichū.

rumbling thunder / heard off in the distance / of the night heat
ikazuchi o / tōku kiku yo no / atsusa kana
> Ganshitsu.

without a moon / to cool down the day – / the night heat!
hi o samasu / tsuki naki yoi no / atsusa kana
> Rōsen.

***irregular shape* / clothiers' secret jargon / for a rare beauty**
gofukumise / fuchō de homeru / ii onna
> Sakakidori. In *Yanagidaru* 33 (1806). The *fuchō*, 'secret jargon', of the couturier can also mean 'poor condition', referring to either an irregularly shaped garment or a business slump.

'monthly visitor' / the pillow word a woman / can rest her head on
okyaku to wa / onna no makura / kotoba nari
> Kinsai. In *Yanagidaru* 29 (1800). The literary device of the 'pillow word' (*makura kotoba*) here is taken literally. According to Watanabe, by invoking the common codeword for a menstrual period, monthly 'visitor' (*kyaku*), thereby abstaining from sex, a woman can actually get some rest (*EBKI*, p. 132; see also *EB*, p. 80).

snagging his clog / with that seeing eye of a stick, / the blindman triumphs
me o geta e / tōshite agaru / zatō no bō
> Teika. In *Yanagidaru* 48 (1809). *Agaru*, 'rise up', also means 'advance' and even 'win' at some kind of game. Hence, this blindman, having

prevailed in the challenge of using his stick to locate and pick up his misplaced or lost wooden clog by its thong, can now progress on his way. The last line contains an extra syllabet.

his seeing eyes . . . / yet still he itches to whip / his dog with his stick!
inu wa me ga / aru noni tsue de / buchitagari
Sesshū. In *Yanagidaru* 17 (1782).

harvest moon . . . / a blindman running smack into me / bursts out laughing!
tsuki koyoi / mekura tsuki atari / waraikeri
Buson. Had the speaker not been gazing up at the brilliant moon he might have seen the visually impaired man coming (conspicuously with the extra syllabet in the second line). Aside from this comic reversal, though, and the two meanings of *tsuki*, 'moon' and 'thrust', Buson playfully alludes to an infamous farce from the now-traditional popular comic theatre (*kyōgen*), entitled *The Moon-Viewing Blindman* (*Tsukimi zatō*). (For more on this play, see Jacqueline Golay, 'Pathos and Farce: *Zatō* Plays of the *Kyōgen* Repertoire', *MN* 28:2 (Summer 1973), pp. 139–49.) In it a gentle blindman (*zatō*), having gone out one night to vicariously enjoy other people viewing the harvest moon, is maliciously knocked down by a man who previously had been kind to him. Buson seems to be giving that blindman a bit of well-deserved comic revenge.

arrived at the blossoms! / seems like people are laughing / upon springtime hill
hana ni kinu / hito waraurashi / haru no yama
Mōichi. This visually impaired poet was also the leader of the *haikai* establishment in Ise.

'they've bloomed!' / relishing plums with his nose, / a blind bloke
saita na to / zatō wa hana de / ume o home
Author unnamed.

rent asunder / by the sound of footsteps: / their silhouette
ashioto de / futatsu ni wareru / kagebōshi
Kakō. In *Yanagidaru* 54 (1811). The verse appears earlier by an unnamed author in *Yanagidaru* 30 (1804) with the challenge verse: 'merged together and yet . . . / merged together and yet . .' (*soroi koso sure / soroi koso sure*), though *soroi*, 'to become complete', can also mean 'careless'.

the wind blows, / twining and untwining / willowstrands
fukimusubi / fukitoku kaze no / yanagi kana
  Gessonsai Sōseki.

tree-withering gust / reaching its ultimate end: / sound of the ocean
kogarashi no / hate wa arikeri / umi no oto
  Gonsui. The sound of the ocean can be heard in the absence of the
  field-withering gales of late autumn.

tree-withering gust / reaching its ultimate end: / firewood for a hut!
kogarashi no / hate wa arikeri / io no maki
  Shūba. In *Yanagidaru* 87 (1825). This parody of Gonsui's verse above
  points out that after the violent late-autumn winds have merged with
  the ocean, there is still the matter of leftover debris, which in this case
  ends up as windfall for a recluse.

tumultuous seas! / stretched out to Sado Isle, / the River of Heaven
araumi ya / sado ni yokotau / amanogawa
  Bashō. This acclaimed meditation on emotional turmoil, displace-
  ment, isolation and the hope of reunion, however fleeting, invokes
  the legend of those long-suffering lovers, the celestial stars Weaver
  Maid (*orihime* or Vega) and Oxherd Boy (*hikoboshi* or Altair), who are
  rejoined only one night each year, on the seventh day of the seventh
  lunisolar month.
  Yet it also invokes the mystique of Sado Island (*Sadogashima*),
  notorious as a remote place of exile (located off the coast in the far
  north-eastern reaches of Japan's mainland). Some involuntary guests
  there have included: Emperor Juntoku (1197–1242), whose bid
  to oust the Kamakura shogunate ended less than swimmingly; the
  Buddhist monk Nichiren (1222–82), who founded the sect named
  after him; and the great dramatist Zeami Motokiyo (*c*.1363–1443),
  credited with having elevated noh to a high art form. Within *Oku
  no hosomichi* (1702), Bashō's alter ego gazes out at Sado during the
  nadir of his wanderings. Nearly three centuries later, Japan's first No-
  bel laureate in literature, Yasunari Kawabata (1899–1972), concluded
  his great novel *Yukiguni* (Snow Country, 1947), involving an annual
  rendezvous between an urbane married man and a rural geisha, with
  a sustained allusion to this verse.
  The rhythm and sound of the vowels in the first line, *ah-ah-oo-eh-
  ah*, conjure up the choppiness and expansiveness of the Sea of Japan,
  infamous for its violent storms. Playing with the term *amanogawa*,
  literally 'Heaven's River', Bashō has the Milky Way span these waters
  to Sado – except that instead of the grammatical 'exist sideways', he

strikingly deploys the transitive verb *yokotau*, 'be existed sideways', implying that some force of creation has moved the very heavens.

how sublime! / through holes in the paper door / the River of Heaven
utsukushi ya / shōji no ana no / amanogawa
> Issa. Although the proverbial frog in a well from the Taoist parable might never know the ocean, a destitute person can see, as well as dream about, the Milky Way.

cold the wind … / through tattered paper doors, / a godless moon
kaze samushi / yabureshōji no / kannazuki
> Sōkan. It was widely believed that during the so-called 'godless month' (*kannazuki* or *kaminazuki*), corresponding to the tenth month of the old lunisolar calendar, the myriad Shinto deities congregated at the Grand Shrine of Izumo (Izumo Taisha), leaving the rest of the country temporarily without guardian deities.

stars on the pond … / again the pitter-pattering / freezing drizzle
ike no hoshi / mata harabara to / shigure kana
> Hokushi. The stars that had appeared reflected upon the surface of a pond, after winter rain clouds had passed, just as suddenly disappear with the coming of yet more rain clouds.

some starlight / spared from being scooped up – / four-handed net
hoshikage wa / sukui nokosu ya / yotsude ami
> Kinsha.

in morning haze / a breeze yearned for and yet … / boat upon the moon!
asagiri ni / kaze hoshi zo omou / tsuki no fune
> Baisei. The boat seems to be stuck on the moon that is somehow reflected on the water in spite of the early morning mist. Although the weary boatman yearns for a wind to help him along (note the extra syllabet in the second line), it would dissipate the beautiful scene.

spring rain – / the belly of a frog / not yet wet
harusame ya / kawazu no hara wa / mada nurezu
> Buson.

sunlight on snow … / the price of oil for desk lamps / falls in Cathay!
yuki no hi wa / kara de abura no / ne ga sagari
> Muchō. In *Yanagidaru* 130 (1834). The humorous logic here is that

the price of oil in Japan naturally rises in winter because of greater demand, whereas in old China it falls; for the Chinese must be such good Confucians as to follow the example of the fourth-century scholar Sun Kang, who, being too poor in his youth to afford a lamp, studied in winter by the sunlight reflected off the snow.

the ninth shogun – / with his demise dog poison / spiked in price
kudaime no / sue ni machin no / ne ga agari

Author unnamed. In *Yanagidaru shūi* 5 (*c.*1796–7). Hōjō Takatoki (1303–33), the ninth and last real Kamakura shogun – whose mental health has long been in question – protected dogs so that he could, paradoxically, have a supply of healthy specimens for mass dogfights at court. Even before his death (by his own hand during the siege of Kamakura), people disobeyed his laws and began hunting down stray dogs.

short-sighted, / a centipede chatting up / a real louse
kingan no / mukade gejigeji o / kudoiteru

Author unnamed. *Gejigeji* means both 'house centipede' (*Scutigeromorpha*) and 'real jerk'. The second line contains an extra syllabet.

as though his own, / the cashier makes change / grudgingly
waga kane no / yōni kaikei / dashioshimi

Bunshō. (Meiji period).

uttered drunk, / true feelings the morning after / turn into lies
yōte iu / honne o asu wa / uso ni suru

Sennosuke.

those boozers / with the most perverse quirks / compose verse!
itchi ii / kuse no namayoi / shi o tsukuri

Author unnamed. In *Yanagidaru* 24 (1791). Alternative versions of this verse replace *ii* with the *yoi* (both meaning 'good') echoed in *namayoi*, 'drunkard'.

within *Who's Who* / nowhere is it written / 'dances when sloshed!'
shinshiroku / yoeba odoru to / kaite nashi

Saika. The earliest *Who's Who* directories (*shinshiroku*) date to the early Meiji period, though throughout the Edo period there were woodblock-printed rankings of sumo wrestlers, courtesans, kabuki actors and so on.

completely different: / one's expression when playing / or paying
kane harau / kao wa asonda / kao de nashi
> Shigetsune.

at a pawnshop / falling in love sight unseen – / summer clothes airing
minu kao ni / horeru shichiya no / doyōboshi
> Ryūge. In *Yanagidaru* 59 (1812) and *Yanagidaru shūi* 2 (*c.*1796–7). Also appears by one Rakushō in *Yanagidaru* 77 (1823). Someone, perhaps with a romantic imagination, catches sight of fine clothes being aired at a pawnshop and fantasizes about their former owner.

on a lone pole / white belly-cutting attire! / midsummer airing
hitosao wa / shinishōzoku ya / doyōboshi
> Kyoriku. *Shinishōzoku*, literally 'attire for death', refers to the white garb used in ritual suicide (*seppuku*). There may be a slight pun here, since *shōzoku* can also mean 'interior decorating'.

challenge:
everything in moderation! / everything in moderation!
hodohodo ga aru / hodohodo ga aru

response:
he who hangs himself / over spiteful remarks: / a real numbskull!
kubikukuri / tsuraate ni to wa / tawakemono
> Author unnamed. In *Yanagidaru* 4 (1769). A similar version of the verse appears in *Senryūhyō mankuawase* (1757–89).

facing Yoshiwara, / a working stiff from Ueno / hanging by the neck
yoshiwara e / muite ueno de / kubi o tsuri
> Author unnamed. Ueno was part of the working-class area (*shitamachi*) of Edo, suggesting that the suicide lacked the resources to continue a relationship with someone in the infamously expensive pleasure district.

'wonder if / I talked in my sleep?' / says Rosei
negoto nado / ii wa senu ka to / rosei ii
> Author unnamed. In *Yanagidaru shūi* 4 (*c.*1796–7). In a famous Chinese story adapted to Japan, the hero Rosei (Lusheng in Chinese) spent a lifetime in the lap of luxury only to wake up and realize it had all been a dream.

mortified / Urashima Tarō / chomped his gums
urashima wa / haguki o kande / kuyashigari

Wari. In *Yanagidaru* 37 (1807). In one of Japan's most enduring folk tales, dating to the earliest extant writings, the young fisherman Urashima Tarō saves a sea turtle, who then transports him to the undersea Palace of the Dragon King. Urashima marries the king's daughter, Otohime, and, though happy together, he eventually wants to go back to visit his home. Otohime agrees on the condition that he bring along a box never to be opened under any circumstance. Having spent only a short time under the sea, Urashima is bewildered to discover that hundreds of years have passed on land. He opens the forbidden box only to find himself suddenly aged by hundreds of years too.

Urashima – / his buttocks riddled / with hexagons!
urashima no / shiri rokkakuna / kata darake

Tsukuda. In *Yanagidaru* 162 (1838-40?). The sea turtle that Urashima rode to the underwater palace (see note to previous verse) must have had a hexagonal pattern on its shell.

Urashima's cock / must've shrivelled up / on the spot!
urashima ga / henoko sokkoku / chijirekomi

Kinsui. In *Yanagidaru* 28 (1799). This particular detail does not seem to be present in any of the myriad versions of the folk tale (see note to Wari's *urashima wa / haguki o kande / kuyashigari*).

Urashima's wife / upon his homecoming: / 'and you would be ...?'
urashima no / kichō nyōbo wa / donata sama

Muho. In *Yanagidaru* 159 (1838-40). This verse answers the hypothetical question 'What if Urashima survived his dramatic ageing and returned to Otohime?' (see note to Wari's *urashima wa / haguki o kande / kuyashigari*). She would have not recognized him or else, knowing he had disobeyed her, pretended not to recognize him.

my hometown: / however misted over, / still grotesque
waga sato wa / dō kasundemo / ibitsu nari

Issa. In the context of Japanese poetry and song prior to the twentieth century, the sentiment of this verse is sui generis. Having lost both his mother and her surrogate, his grandmother, when he was young, Issa became increasingly estranged from his family after his father remarried and shipped him off to Edo, eventually becoming embroiled in an epic legal battle with his stepmother over his father's inheritance.

(He would go on to marry later in life, though losing three children, one after the other, and his wife. As if that were not enough, his house burned down.)

hitting rock bottom / everyone helps each other – / that's humanity
donzoku de / tasukeatteru / ningenmi
    Nokōrō.

giving up his seat / only when disembarking – / whatta guy!
oriru toki / seki o yuzutta / jinkakusha
    Ryūsei.

ticket window / our kid suddenly grows one year / younger
kaisatsu de / waga ko no toshi ga / hitotsu heri
    Author unnamed.

childless / contemplating a seascape / the aged couple
ko mo nakute / umi no e o mite / furu fūfu
    Deirei. The childless old couple are merely glancing at a picture of the sea instead of the sea itself, as though a meditation on the infinity that might have been. The word *furu*, 'aged', has a range of homonyms, including 'abandoned' and 'substitute'.

sleeping together / their copious dream was for / their child's prosperity
tappuri to / soine no yume wa / ko no eiga
    The woman poet Tessen. In *Yanagidaru* 70 (1818).

the bureaucrat's tot / learns about grabby-grabby / an awful lot!
yakunin no / ko wa niginigi o / yoku oboe
    Author unnamed. In *Yanagidaru* 1 (1765). Lightness of tone and punning wordplay accentuate the biting sarcasm in this renowned *senryū*. *Yoku*, 'frequently' or 'well', has homonyms in 'greed' and 'succeeding (generation)'. *Niginigi*, 'clench hold of' in children's parlance, calls to mind an infant reflexively grasping an object – perhaps the finger of a parent, seemingly out of affection. In the case of a government official, by contrast, selfish 'bribe *taking*' or even 'power *grabbing*' may be insinuated. This satire is sometimes read as being aimed at Tanuma Okitsugu (1719–88), reputedly the most corrupt public figure of the period, though Tanuma began serving as senior counsellor (*rōjū*) to the shogun only in 1767, two years *after* publication of this verse. In a society organized according to a hereditary class system, the greater social issue no doubt was generational nepotism.

one's shadow / reaching the ceiling of rank / breaks bad!
tenjō e / tsukaete magaru / kagebōshi
> Gosei. In *Yanagidaru* 22 (1788). Puns on *tenjō*, 'ceiling', as 'palace court', and on *tsukaete*, 'reaching', as 'working', elevate this verse from mere description to satire.

rustic samurai! / muckin' around now more in paddies / than with poetry
inaka bushi / ima wa shi yori mo / ta o tsukuri
> Author unnamed. In *Marumaru chinbun* (1878). As members of the samurai class became ever more financially insolvent during the twilight of the Edo and the dawn of the Meiji period, many had no recourse but to turn to other occupations, even returning to the provinces to take up farming. The fiercely proud and learned samurai are derided – or ironically self-mocked? – by the double meanings of *inaka* as 'uncultured' and 'provincial', and of *tsukuri* as 'composing' poetry as well as 'tilling' the fields.

even walls have *mouths*! / prospering imperial reign / of the telephone
kabe ni kuchi / ari denwaki no / hayaru miyo
> Author unnamed. In *Marumaru chinbun* (1891). A twist on the Japanese proverb 'The walls have ears, the doors have mouths' (*kabe ni mimi ari shōji ni me ari*). Although the telephone was first introduced into Japan in the late 1870s, it would take over a decade before the heavy wall-mounted contraption was made available in post offices for public use. It would not be until the 1920s that telephones began to be installed in private homes.

telegraph pole / toppled down by / the tempest
denshin no / hashira o taosu / nowaki kana
> Shiki. A signal updating of the ravages of late-autumn windstorms, which previously had shredded plantain leaves or thrashed buckets along or toppled scarecrows and the like.

photographers eat / by capturing and roasting / their clientele!
shashin'ya wa / hito o ba totte / yaite kui
> The woman poet Fukui Junko. In Kyōto Nichinichi Shinbunsha (ed.), *Garakuta chinpō* (1880). This verse puns on *totte*, as 'capturing (someone)' and 'taking (a photograph)', *yaite*, as 'roasting' and 'developing (a photograph)', and *kui*, as 'eat' and 'earn a living'.

summer grass! / in the wake of dreams / of legion warriors
natsugusa ya / tsuwamonodomo ga / yume no ato
   Bashō. In *Oku no hosomichi* (1702). One of the poet's most celebrated verses. Looking out upon a field at Hiraizumi in northern Japan, the speaker recalls a historical tragedy that took place on that spot half a millennium earlier, when the renowned hero Minamoto no Yoshitsune (1159–89) was hunted down and forced to kill himself. The word *ato* can mean 'ruins' as well as 'after', in which case the last phrase suggests waking up from a dream. Even in Bashō's day *tsuwamonodomo* was an unusual and old-fashioned term for 'untold valiant warriors'. In the prose passage immediately preceding this verse, Bashō invokes the opening lines from the poem 'Gazing at Spring' ('Chun wang', 757) by the great Chinese poet Du Fu (712–70): 'The state is smashed; rivers and hills remain. / The city turns to spring; grass and trees grow thick' (trans. Paul Rouzer, 'A Dream of Ruined Walls', *Simply Haiku* 4:2 (Summer 2006)).

Nakazu today! / in the wake of dreams / of legion partiers
nakazu ima / bakamonodomo ga / yume no ato
   Chikushi. In *Yanagidaru* 75 (1822). In parodying Bashō's celebrated verse above, Chikushi intimates that unlike the great poets of the past, who invoked Chinese poetry in lamenting tragedies from Japanese history, contemporary Edoites recall nostalgically the mercurial rise and fall of an unlicensed pleasure district. Built in 1772 on reclaimed land on the west bank of the Sumida River, the Nakazu was celebrated for its teahouses, lantern-lit restaurants, firework displays, boat parties, sideshows and even its bed-wetting female hustlers (as per Rekisen's verse *shōben o / shite nigeru no wa / mekake to semi*). Less than two decades later, in 1789, it was dismantled by order of the government, disappointing many dissolute sons of Edo.

in such snow! / the footprints remain / of legion drivellers
kono yuki ni / bakamonodomo no / ashi no ato
   Tagyo. In *Yanagidaru* 79 (1824). See also Bashō's *natsugusa ya / tsuwamonodomo ga / yume no ato*.

the Milky Way … / the sieging camp far below / comes into view!
amanogawa / tekijin shita ni / miyuru kana
   Shiki.

the rose mallow / gracing the side of the road – / devoured by my
   horse!
michinobe no / mukuge wa uma ni / kuwarekeri
   Bashō.

challenge:
now that's crowded! / now that's crowded!
komiai ni keri / komiai ni keri

response:
a tie post / facing the cheap-eats joint – / devoured by my horse!
niuriya no / hashira wa uma ni / kuwarekeri
   Author unnamed. In *Yanagidaru* 1 (1765). A similar version of this
   verse appears in *Senryūhyō mankuawase* (1757–89). In this spoof of
   Bashō's verse above the challenge, a packhorse driver is enjoying a
   little something at a tavern (*niuriya*) selling simple foods such as veg-
   etables, fish and beans as well as saké. The place is so popular, the
   horses are squeezed in together and have limited options for grazing.

unwell on the road / dreams running rampant / o'er withered moors!
tabi ni yande / yume wa kareno o / kakemeguru
   Bashō. His last verse, though not a death verse (*jisei*) per se. Another
   rendering, not anticipating the parody immediately below, would be:
   'ailing on the road / over withered fields my dreams / run rampant'.

unwell in the head / running rampant in dreams / o'er red-light
   whores!
zashikirō / yume ni kuruwa o / kakemeguri
   Richō. In *Yanagidaru* 53 (1811). During the Edo period, *zashikirō*,
   'parlour jails', were used to confine people labelled as lunatics and/or
   criminals. Additionally, *kuruwa*, 'red-light district', suggests *kuruu* or
   kuruwasu, 'drive mad'.

challenge:
a real laugh, *but* ... / a real laugh, *but* ...
warai koso sure / warai koso sure

response:
head over heels / from behind and yet head-on / dead in one's tracks!
ushiro kara / horete mae kara / yame ni nari
   Author unnamed. In *Ame no ochiba* (1733).

challenge:
giggling and yet ... / giggling and yet ...
warai koso sure / warai koso sure

response:
**the house burglar / overhearing sweet nothings / sticks out his
   tongue**
mutsugoto o / kiite nusubito / shita o dashi
   Author unnamed. In *Ame no ochiba* (1733). Suzuki explains that a
   burglar has broken into a house where the couple are so engrossed
   in lovemaking that they fail to notice him (*NKBZ* 46, p. 300). The
   tongue he sticks out at them in contempt is surely suggestive.

'never hang out / with that pecker!' say the fathers / of both peckers
are to deru / na to ryōhō no / oya ga ii
   Author unnamed. In *Yanagidaru* 19 (1784), though originally com-
   posed in 1780. The double entendre on the word *are*, 'that thing',
   used to refer to a person of equal or inferior rank, but serving as a
   euphemism for genitalia – or even sex itself – suggests the nature of
   each father's complaint against the other man's son. What is being
   exposed here, of course, is less youthful shenanigans (presumably in
   the pleasure quarters) than hypocritical parental pride. Then again, to
   the extent that *are* also implies temporal (as well as spatial or social)
   distance, one can speculate that the origins of the gripe between the
   fathers, who seem to be using their sons in a proxy competition, may
   possibly even go back to a jealous rivalry between the two men *them-
   selves* when they were young friends.

challenge:
called out to play ... / called out to play ...
yobidashi ni keri / yobidashi ni keri

response:
their friendship / does not at all please / their fathers
naka no yoi / tomo wa oyaji no / ki ni irazu
   Author unnamed (see *NKBZ* 46, p. 310). The term *yobidashi* of the
   challenge means 'summoning', but also refers to a kind of high-
   ranking courtesan who could only be seen 'by appointment'. *Oyaji*
   means 'father', but it could equally be the 'boss' of the courtesan. In
   answering the challenge, the response also seems to allude to the verse
   are to deru / na to ryōhō no / oya ga ii before it.

Vixen Isle spunk: / dildos fashioned out of fans / from the Shady Shop

nyogo no hari- / kata kosaeteru / mieidō

Ryūsha. In *Yanagi no hazue* (1835). It is fitting that the mythical Isle of Vixens (Nyōgogashima, aka Nyogonoshima) would import its sex toys from the Mieidō, a famous shop in Kyoto specializing in folding fans. Fans not only simulate the manual back-and-forth motion of dildos, they also produce a breeze that calls to mind the seminal southern wind believed to impregnate these vixens. The straddling (*kumatagari*) of *harikata* (dildo) across two lines calls to mind the special 'aplomb' (*hari*) of Yoshiwara courtesans.

Vixen Isle – / so much as sneeze and *wham bam* / the midwife's summoned

nyogonoshima / kushami o suru to / baba o yobi

Author unnamed. In *Yanagidaru shūi* 5 (*c.*1796–7). An oblique 'think-for-yourself' (*kangaeochi*) pun on *kaze* as both the 'common cold' behind the sneeze and the seminal 'breeze' believed to impregnate inhabitants of this mythical island. It may also be possible that the sneeze itself here creates such a breeze, especially given the phallic symbolism of noses. *Suru*, 'to do', also connotes having sex.

challenge:
suddenly it's clear! / suddenly it's clear!
hatsumeina koto / hatsumeina koto

response:
the doctor / takes Kiyomori's pulse / buck naked
kiyomori no / isha wa hadaka de / myaku o tori

Author unnamed. In *Yanagidaru* 1 (1765). An allusion to a famous episode in *Heike monogatari* (*c.* thirteenth century) in which the tyrannical leader of the Taira, Taira no Kiyomori (1118–81), is consumed by an almost supernatural fever.

New Year's greetings / exchanged in a bathhouse / butt naked
yu de atte / gyokei o mōsu / suppadaka
Author unnamed.

New Year's day / even next-door neighbours / stand on ceremony
shōgatsu wa / tonari kara demo / shachikobari
Yamaki. In *Yanagidaru* 53 (1811).

in want of laughs / a New Year's comic duo / gets one laughing!
waraitai / toki manzai wa / warawaseru
  Kijaku of the Ōmi group. In *Yanagidaru* 19 (1784). Comedic duos
(*manzai*) would go door to door at the New Year, presumably to help
people laugh away the travails of the previous year.

laughing loudly / that the loneliness / might be forgotten
takawarai / shite sabishisa o / wasureru ki
  Chigusa.

**as peonies bloom / Christian icons get trampled / at Pure Land
temples**
botan saku / jōdo no tera no / ebumi kana
  Shiki. Throughout most of the Edo period, the authorities period-
ically forced people to step on crosses or other religious icons in an
effort to root out underground Christians. Those who refused were
subjected to harsh punishment, including crucifixion. Shiki seems to
be observing that the so-called 'Pure Land' of Buddhism may not have
been so pure after all.

crowned by both / setting moon and rising sun – / the peony!
zangetsu mo / hi mo itadakeru / botan kana
  Ōemaru.

yellow mustardblooms! / moon to the east / sun to the west
nanohana ya / tsuki wa higashi ni / hi wa nishi ni
  Buson. The *nanohana* (*Brassica napus*) is also referred to variously in
English as rapeseed, oilseed rape and canola.

**yellow mustardblooms! / not even whales in the offing / of a sea
gone dark**
nanohana ya / kujira mo yorazu / umi kurenu
  Buson. Mustardblooms (*nanohana*) are known to blossom in bright
yellow profusion in vast fields in spring. Although whales (*kujira*) are
associated with winter, it is said that when they 'draw close' (*yoru* – of
which *yorazu* is the negative form) to shore in early spring, it bodes
well for the coming fishing season (see *BK*, p. 372). The ocean (*umi*)
'has darkened' (*kurenu*) at dusk, yet somehow the atmosphere feels
more portentous.

upon a world / of yellow mustardblooms, / the setting sun!
nanohana no / sekai ni kyō mo / irihi kana

Tantan. The visual pairing of setting sun and bright yellow blossoms is paralleled in the rhyme of *hana* and *kana*.

even the kerchief / worn during a migraine – / woebegone!
hachimaki mo / zutsū no toki wa / aware nari

Author unnamed. In *Yanagidaru* 1 (1765). The classical aesthetic of 'the pathos of things' (*mono no aware*) is transformed here into something mundane.

second night of the year – / a new flurry of nightmares / the dream beast devours
futsuka no yo / baku shinmai no / yume o kū

Kinga. In *Yanagidaru* 37 (1807). The *baku* is a mythical nightmare-devouring creature with the nose of an elephant, the eyes of a rhinoceros, the tail of an ox, the legs of a tiger and the body of a bear. Since popular belief held that the dream on the second day of the new year would largely determine one's fortune for the coming year, it was customary to place an image of a *baku* under one's pillow to ward off ill-boding dreams (often seen on the first night after celebratory drinking).

for dream beasts / the second night of the year / is New Year's Eve!
akete mazu / futsuka wa baku no / ōtsugomori

Izutsu. In *Yanagidaru* 139 (1835). Also appears in *Yanagidaru* 166 (1838–40?), though written slightly differently. Here the dream beast's frenetic devouring of nightmares on the first dream night (see note to previous verse) is likened to the townsmen's frantic settling of accounts on the last day of the year (*ōtsugomori*), emphasized by an extra syllabet.

'better not turn into a butterfly!' / says the dream beast / about to chow down
chōchō ni / naranu to baku ga / kū tokoro

Kizui. In *Yanagidaru* 57 (1811). The careful dream beast is wary of Zhuangzi's dream of a butterfly lest he find himself in a dream within a dream. (See notes to Kinga's *futsuka no yo / baku shinmai no / yume o kū* and Chiyo's *tanpopo ya / oriori samasu / chō no yume*.)

when there appear / phoenixes and unicorns, / dream beasts get thin
hōō ya / kirin ga deru to / baku wa yase
Banjin. In *Yanagidaru* 56 (1811). Also by Shūrō in *Yanagidaru* 137 (c.1834). Dream beasts, respectful of Taoist immortals, refrain from devouring their dreams (see note to Kinga's *futsuka no yo / baku shinmai no / yume o kū*) and suffer the consequences.

dreams of Mount Fuji / get divvied up evenly / among dream beasts
fuji no yume / susowake o suru / baku nakama
Author unnamed. A group of dream beasts compete for the most auspicious first dreams of the year, which, according to folk belief, are, in descending order: Mount Fuji, hawks, aubergines. (See note to Kinga's *futsuka no yo / baku shinmai no / yume o kū*.)

embroidered ballads / set women's idle grumblings / to sweet music
meriyasu wa / onna no guchi ni / fushi o tsuke
Author unnamed. In *Yanagidaru shūi* 8 (c.1796-7). A *meriyasu*, 'embroidered ballad', was a type of lyrical chanting, usually solo, that accompanied tender scenes on the kabuki stage, frequently depicting the emotional state of a female character.

shrine gate / run aground on the riverbank / or so it seems
dote e tori- / i ga merikonda / yō ni mie
Monryū. In *Yanagidaru* 36 (1807). A visual pun (*mitate*) comparing the uppermost rung of a famous shrine gate (*torii*) at a well-known scenic spot in Edo (the Mimeguri Inari Jinja, located at Mukōjima in present-day Sumida-ku), just southeast of the Yoshiwara pleasure quarter, to a skiff that has struck the embankment on the Sumida River. Although the term *torii*, here rendered by the graphs for 'bird' and 'occupy (a seat)', straddles two phrases, it may be less awkward to parse this verse into 6-6-5 syllabets.

challenge:
how singular! / how singular!
mezurashii koto / mezurashii koto

response:
King of Hell / calls in Sniffing Nose / to buy mackerel
kaguhana o / yonde enma wa / saba o kai
Author unnamed. In *Yanagidaru shūi* 3 (c.1796-7). It stands to comic reason that if Sniffing Nose assists Enma, the King of Hell (or, more precisely, purgatory), sniff out the sins of the dead, she must also be useful in sniffing out rotten fish when he goes grocery shopping.

challenge:
although it came off well . . . / although it came off well . . .
shubi no yoi koto / shubi no yoi koto

response:
getting loose in bed / nothing's so interminable / as a sash!
nete tokeba / obi hodo nagai / mono wa nashi

    Author unnamed. In *Yanagidaru* 3 (1768). *Tokeba*, 'loosen up', can refer to inhibitions as well as belts (see Hamada Giichirō, 'Senryū no okashimi to fūshi', in *Edo bungeikō: Kyōka, senryū, gesaku* (Iwanami shoten, 1988), pp. 111–24, at p. 118).

upon the golden screen / whose negligee could this be?! / – autumn breeze
kinbyō no / usumono wa taga / aki no kaze

    Buson. A category of erotic trompe l'œil called *tagasode* (literally 'whose sleeves?') presented an image of clothing draped over luxurious screens to stimulate the imagination as to which courtesan might be *en déshabillé*.

the young master / smutty prints his handbook / practising strokes!
makurae o / tehon ni musuko / kaku hajime

    Author unnamed. In *Kyōku umeyanagi* 6 (*c.* Tenpō era, 1830–44). Since *kaku*, 'write', can also mean 'stroke', this young man is less starting his writing practice using erotic prints as his handbook (*tehon*) than he is stroking with his hand to his erotic prints.

Sukeroku / hidden beneath her skirts / diddles away
sukeroku wa / kakureta toki ni / kujitteru

    Bunchi. In *Yanagi no hazue* (1835). Alluding to a well-known scene from a kabuki play in which the hero hides beneath the skirts of the courtesan Agemaki before popping out to confront his rival Ikyū, this verse intimates what Sukeroku was really doing down under. The play is *Sukeroku yukari no Edozakura* (Sukeroku, Flower of Edo; first performed in 1713 in Edo).

Willow Vat's Exposé of
'The Treasury of Loyal Retainers'

For more on what is known of the real-life event, see Bitō Masahide, 'The Akō Incident, 1701–1703', *MN* 58:2 (Summer 2003), pp. 149–69. For a translation of the puppet play, see Donald Keene (trans.), *Chūshingura: The Treasury of Loyal Retainers* (New York: Columbia University Press, 1971).

dead drunk / on the outside though deep within / cold sober!
zuburoku to / misete kokoro wa / yoi mo sezu

> Originally by an unnamed author in *Yanagidaru* 50 (1811), this verse alludes to how Yuranosuke, biding his time, has forged the cover story that he is a fall-down drunk who frequents the pleasure quarters. Just prior to this scene, in fact, he was pretending to be inebriated in front of his deceased lord's second-in-command, Kudayū.

playing drunk – / the very mirror of this age / of decadence!
zuburoku no / shiuchi massei / kagami nari

> Originally by Sokō in *Yanagidaru* 50 (1811). Not merely drunkenness but pretending to be drunk is taken to be a symbol of the end of the world. In Buddhism, *massei* refers to the end of the Dharma.

strike the enemy / just like striking a gong – / that's the plan!
dora utsu mo / kataki o utsu no / hakarigoto

> Originally by Kokusui in *Yanagidaru* 50 (1811). This is the gist of the secret letter.

her hairpin / smack-dab between loyalty / and betrayal
kanzashi ga / chū to fuchū no / naka e ochi

> Originally by Shukō in *Yanagidaru* 50 (1811). Okaru's dropped hairpin delineates her loyalty and Kudayū's disloyalty.

Heiemon / makes a terrible demand / of his sister
heiemon / imoto ni hidoi / mushin nari

> Originally by Ryōju in *Yanagidaru* 50 (1811). Having discovered Yuranosuke's intent to kill Okaru, Heiemon persuades her to let him kill her instead.

Kudayū, / hopeful there's silver in it, / gets his hands dirty!

gin naraba / yoi to kudayū / te o nobashi

Originally by Hantō in *Yanagidaru* 50 (1811). The silver here no doubt refers to Okaru's dropped hairpin, which Kudayū reaches to grab, just as much as to the money Kudayū accepts to betray his comrades.

Kudayū / treading with his palms / on cat shit!

kudayū wa / tenoura de fumu / neko no fun

Originally by Tōjin in *Yanagidaru* 50 (1811). Needless to say, there is no mention of cat faeces in the puppet play.

samurai dog / fated to fall underneath / the veranda!

samurai no / inu mo yappari / en no shita

Originally by Shidō in *Yanagidaru* 50 (1811). There is a pun on *en no shita*, 'beneath the veranda' and 'fated'. This of course refers to the ignoble death of the double-crossing Kudayū on all fours beneath the veranda.

[End of *Willow Vat's Exposé of 'The Treasury of Loyal Retainers'*]

pinch her booty / and a maid will brandish / rice-bran hands

gejo no shiri / tsumereba nuka no / te de odoshi

Author unnamed. In *Suetsumuhana* 1 (1776). *Nuka* (or *nukamiso*), a briny paste made by boiling rice bran in saltwater, was a slang term for sexual juices (see Nakamura Yukihiko, Okami Masao and Sakakura Atsuyoshi (eds), *Kadokawa kogo daijiten* 4, 3rd edn (Kadokawa, 2000), p. 927). Associated phrases include 'rice-bran-paste soup for whoring' (*jorōkai no nukamisojiru*) and *nukamisojiru*, a kind of cheap dish that one makes do with in order to afford extravagance elsewhere – particularly the pleasure quarters.

salted rice-bran broth: / with just one gulp losing weight / in the wallet

shinjō wa / nukamisojiru de / gutto yase

Rakuho. In *Yanagidaru* 55 (1811). There is a slight pun on *shinshō*, 'fortune, property', and *shinjō*, 'body'. Economizing on food at home has led not only to bodily weight loss, but also, paradoxically, not to *increased* fortune (as one might expect), but, because one is spending the savings in the pleasure quarter (*nukamiso* implies sexual juices), to increased *poverty*!

'first cicada!' / no sooner thus proclaimed than / it takes a leak
hatsusemi to / ieba shōben / shitarikeri
> Issa. Cicadas pass excess tree sap through their systems and so are said to urinate – often in groups.

those who piss and run: / kept women, / cicadas
shōben o / shite nigeru no wa / mekake to semi
> Rekisen. In *Yanagidaru* 54 (1811). A reference to a well-known swindle (reputedly prevalent in the Nakazu unlicensed quarter – see note to Chikushi's *nakazu ima / bakamonodomo ga / yume no ato*) of a kept woman urinating in order to avoid consummating sex with her sugar daddy. The last line contains an extra syllabet.

thunder letting up, / sunset shining on one tree / where cry cicadas
rai harete / ichiju no yūhi / semi no koe
> Shiki.

woodpecker / upon its one little speck / the sun sets
kitsutsuki ya / hitotsu tokoro ni / hi no kururu
> Issa. The repetition of sounds, in *kitsutsu ... hitotsu* and in *tokoro ... kururu*, suggests the woodpecker's incessant pecking right up until the end of the day.

brocade weaving ... / only a single dragon / and the day darkens
nishikiori / ryū ippiki ni / hi ga kureru
> Author unnamed.

challenge:
her raiment of mist / moistened at the hems
kasumi no koromo / suso wa nurekeri

response:
Princess Sao / springing up and spreading wide / makes peepee!
saohime no / haru tachi nagara / shito o shite
> This well-known verse exchange appears in the first major collection of *haikai*, *Inu tsukubashū* (c.1530). In contrast to the clichéd classical poetic diction of the challenge, this shocking response – by Sōkan, one of the compilers – with its childish if vulgar way of referring to urination (*shito*), is a tour de force of lively wordplay: *haru*, meaning 'spring' and specifically the New Year, also connotes puberty, the prime of one's life and sexuality, though homonyms further suggest 'spread (open)' and 'form (frost on the ground)'; *tachi*, 'rising', refers to mist as well as spring arriving, but also suggests, through several

more homonyms, being caught in a compromising position, being erect (as with nipples or a penis – *sao*, a homonym of the Sao in Sao-hime, being one of many slang terms for the latter), cutting or rending cloth, being clear (an antonym of *kasumino*, 'misty') and the 'dragon' sign of the Chinese zodiac that here symbolizes both morning, when mist rises, and also the third lunisolar month that is early spring.

Princess Sao / swaying, softly, pissing down / the spring rains!
saohime no / shitoshito furu ya / haru no ame
   Teitoku. See note to previous verse.

divinely appearing / upon Luxuriant Reed Plain / His thang dang-a-lang!
furimara de / toyoashihara e / goshutsugen
   Shuchin. In *Yanagi no hazue* (1835). According to the *Kojiki* (*c.*711), the sun goddess Amaterasu-Ohomikami dispatched her son, Masakatsu-Akatsu-Kachihayahi-Ame-no-Oshihomimi, to rule over Japan, then referred to as Toyoashihara (an abbreviation of Toyo-Ashihara-no-Chiaki-Nagaihoaki-no-Midzuho-no-Kuni, though often called Toyo-Ashihara-no-Midzuho-no-Kuni for short). Finding the place too noisy, he beat a hasty retreat.

high priest / in withered fields piously / taking a crap
daitoko no / kuso hiriowasu / kareno kana
   Buson. In spite of the comic incongruity between the polite and the vernacular words, the priest is doing his part to help make this winter field fertile come spring.

even monks / cannot help but ogle / lady flowers
mite oranu / osō wa araji / ominaeshi
   Shigeyori. The lady flower (*Patrinia scabiosifolia*) is a perennial plant with yellow flowers – yellow being the colour of eroticism. This verse seems to allude to a well-known *waka* by the monk Sōjō Henjō (816–90), commended in the *Kokinshū* (*c.* 920) as one of six exemplary poets. Playing on the double sense of *oreru* as 'to snap off (a sprig)' and, being broken, 'to submit', Henjō's *waka* runs: 'drawn to your name / broken, I, off a mere sprig, / lady flower, / that I have fallen for you, / reveal not to others!' (*na ni medete / oreru bakari zo / ominaeshi / ware ochiniki to / hito ni kataru na*; in *SNKBT* 5, p. 80).

stunning nun – / several souls get turned on / to religion
utsukushii / ama nisan hito / shaka mairi

>Author unnamed. In *Yanagidaru* 25 (1794). *Mairi*, 'pilgrimage', can also mean 'infatuation'.

with fingertips / searching for scenic spots – / wide bush pilgrimage
yubisaki de / meisho o sagasu / kai angya

>Yashū. In *Yanagi no hazue* (1835). Wordplay on *yubisaki* (fingertips) as *yukisaki* (destination), on *bobo* (pussy) as *bōbō* (bushy expanse) and on *kai angya* (vulva pilgrimage) – the graph for *kai* alternatively being read as *bobo* (pussy) – as *kaian gyā* (revised itinerary, yikes!) yields two overlapping meanings: 'with fingertips searching for scenic spots on vulva pilgrimage' and 'searching for scenic spots at one's destination across a bushy expanse – yikes, a revised itinerary!'

as a rule / nothing tastes quite like / poontang
bobo no aji / oyoso tatōru / mono wa nashi

>Sekishi. In *Yanagi no hazue* (1835). Sekishi was one of the members of the Edogawa Group that held a 'Great Dirty Sexy Verse Gathering' (*ōbarekai*) during the Tenpō era (1830–44) (see *EBKI*, p. 122). The Spanish term *conchita*, 'little conch', comes closer to capturing the standard pun on the graph that can be read either *bobo*, 'vulva', or *kai*, 'shellfish'.

for the master, / it's a boy, for his wife, / a girl!
teishu wa o- / toko nyōbō wa / onna nari

>Tōgan. In *Yanagidaru* 65 (1814). Although probably about the wished-for-gender of a baby, this verse might possibly defy the general rule that Edo literature acknowledges homoerotic desire between men but not women. Either way, parsing this verse as 7–5–5 or 4–8–5 syllabets might be less odd than straddling the word *otoko* across the first and second lines.

challenge:
ah, how sweet – and yet . . . / ah, how sweet – and yet . . .
amai koto kana / amai koto kana

response:
stretching out / as far as Two Hole street blocks – / the widow's pride
nichō hodo / tsuzuita ga goke / jiman nari

>Author unnamed. In *Yanagidaru* 6 (1771). At first blush, the widow appears gratified that her husband's funeral procession runs two

whole blocks (*nichō*). However, this particular length calls to mind Nichōmachi, the area of the Yoshiwara pleasure quarter devoted to male prostitution. Perhaps the husband met his demise there in some kind of love triangle or sexual act? Perhaps the widow will head there to hire a toyboy herself?

first husband dead / so all the way to Dandytown / for a dandy time
ichi danna / shinde yoshichō / made mo shire

Author unnamed. In *Yanagidaru* 2 (1767). A pun on *shiru*, 'know' and 'have sex', and a pivot on *yoshi*, 'good' and 'Yoshichō', yield the following reading: 'It's fine if your first husband is dead, since you can simply know all the men even as far as Yoshichō!' Yoshichō was a district within Edo's Nihonbashi where male prostitutes (*kagema*) provided services primarily to men, but also to women. According to *Nanshoku saiken* (Detailed Guide to Male–Male Love, 1768), there were thirteen establishments offering the services of some sixty-seven male prostitutes (see *SNKBZ* 79, p. 162, nn. 5 and 6).

women, men – / everybody serviced just dandy / in Dandytown
onna demo / otoko demo yoshi- / chō to ii

Author unnamed (see *EEBT*, p. 184). The verse straddling (*kumatagari*) here occasions the pivot 'dandy' (*yoshi*) within Dandytown (*yoshichō*). (See note to previous verse.)

when craving cock / a widow will head off / to Dandytown
mara ga shita- / kuba yoshichō e / gozare goke

Mokubō. In *Yanagi no hazue* (1835). Another instance of verse straddling (*kumatagari*). (See also note to *ichi danna / shinde yoshichō / made mo shire*.)

just like a clit / bareback riding a dick – / Kindaka's sensation!
mara no se ni / sane kinkō no / kokoromochi

꩜ (Hanasanjin). In *Yanagi no hazue* (1835). An example of a dirty sexy *haiku* (*bareku*) by a famous author of popular literature burlesquing Chinese legend. In a visual pun (*mitate*), the iconic representation of the legendary Chinese immortal Kinkō (aka Kindaka; Qin Gao in Chinese) straddling a giant carp is graphically likened to the act of genital intercourse. In some versions of the story, incidentally, the carp magically transmogrifies into an even larger dragon, transporting Kindaka to heaven.

a maidservant / would have him do *her* / all ninety-nine nights
gejo naraba / kujūku ban wa / saseru toko

Kinshi. In *Yanagi no hazue* (1835). Whereas the storied *waka* poet and beauty Ono no Komachi (*c.* 825–900) had the courtier Fukakusa no Shosho *wait* for her at her gate for one hundred nights in a row before she would consummate the relationship – though he collapsed and died on the ninety-ninth night – contemporary maidservants were reputedly somewhat less modest. There is a slight pun here on *toko*, 'verge' and 'bed'.

outta one hole / but thanks to another hole / into one more hole!
ana o dete / ana e iri mata / ana no sewa

Author unnamed. In *Yanagidaru* 30 (1804). Although many men supposedly spend the first nine months of their lives trying to get out of the womb and the rest of their lives trying to get back into it (or at least other tempting orifices), this verse suggests that the stress of the latter sends them to their graves. *Mata*, 'again', can also mean 'crotch'.

outta one hole / all the way into another hole / thanks to another hole!
ana o dete / ana ni iru made / ana no sewa

Author unnamed. In *Senryūhyō mankuawase* (1757–89) (in *EB*, p. 99).

born of a hole / fooling around with a hole / buried in a hole!
ana o dete / ana ni asonde / ana ni iri

Aryū. In *Yanagidaru* 128 (1833).

how amusing! / the word 'hole' rubbed raw / with red ink
okashisa wa / ana to iu ji o / akaku kaki

The woman poet Konojo. In *(Haifū kanno) Tagusa sakayudaru* 1 (1808). The interpretation of this verse is wide open. The word 'hole' (*ana*) written in red ink conjures up a bodily orifice, making this verse, according to Taira, 'decidedly erotic' (*kiwamete erochiku*) (*RJS*, p. 13). Along these lines, 'written in red' can also mean 'rubbed red', in which case the orifice is probably a vulva; for there is the related phrase *o-ana-sama*, referring to the Ana Kannon – Kannon (goddess of mercy) being a slang term for 'clitoris'. Watanabe, on the other hand, suggests that Konojo is merely pointing out the humorous incongruity between the erotically charged red 'hole' (*ana*) and its prominence in a religious context, in the placards marking the innumerable Inari shrines throughout Edo, which had names such as Ana-Inari (Shinobugaoka Inari Shrine in Ueno) and Ana-Hachiman

(Takada Hachiman in Ushigome) (*EBKI*, p. 115). It may also be possible that the speaker notices the irony of the word 'hole' written in red (ink or even blood) within a blood oath, since not only is red the colour of blood, but the oath has been written because of a sexual relationship.

cherries pink / folks moving in and out – / mound's opening
sakura kara / dehairu hito ya / saka no kuchi
  Ginkō. (1780). Riffing on the slang meaning of *sakura*, 'cherry', as a courtesan, this verse includes visual puns (*mitate*) likening hillside clusters of cherry blossoms above a gateway to a mons pubis and a phalanx of people to a phallus.

on the threshold / of the cherry-red home / a thick bush
akaki ie no / genkansaki e / haeru kusa
  The woman poet Kisenjo. In *Ryūfū kyōku kaisei jinmeiroku* (1899). The first line contains an extra syllabet.

at her barred gate / the roaming monk tried his hand / every which way
todate no to / ni komusō wa / te o tsukushi
  The woman poet Oei. In *Yanagidaru* 104 (1828). Although *todate* generally refers to any kind of blockage, it specifically evokes an obstruction of the vagina (gynatresia). *Komusō*, itinerant monks, were shadowy figures who, when wandering around playing their flutes (*shakuhachi*) in search of alms, donned oversized sedge hats that hid their faces completely. This aura of mystery also helped romanticize them in the popular imagination, not the least because the *shakuhachi* was a phallic symbol (see *RJS*, pp. 14–15).

floating world – / newspapers unearth its loopholes / with the pen!
shinbun wa / fude de ukiyo no / ana o hori
  Author unnamed. In *Marumaru chinbun* (1877). Appearing in the inaugural year of this socio-political satirical magazine, this verse self-reflexively comments on how modern newspapers and magazines have updated the earlier trope of the exposé. Although modern Western-style moveable-type newspapers and magazines began appearing in Japan during the second half of the nineteenth century, there had already been a century-long history of woodblock-printed scandal sheets (*kawaraban*), gossip rags (*yomiuri*) and comic literature (*gesaku*) that exalted the exposé (*ana o hori*, 'loophole unearthing', or *ana o ugachi*, 'loophole uncovering').

newspapers / serve as karmic mirrors / of the world
shinbun wa / yo no jōhari no / kagami nari
> Author unnamed. In *Marumaru chinbun* (1877). *Kagami no jōhari* is
> a crystal mirror used by Enma, King of Hell, to detect the past sins of
> a departed soul.

shining the light / on social enlightenment – / electric lamps!
bunmei no / hikari wa denki- / tō de shire
> Author unnamed. In *Marumaru chinbun* (1889). Japanese people of
> the Meiji period read about modern Western-style 'civilization' (*bun-
> mei*, 'lettered brightness') literally by the very 'electric lighting' (*den-
> kitō*, an oldfangled word for *dentō*) that was part of that civilization.

civilized skies / stretching out into writing / gone sideways
bunmei no / sora yokomoji ni / wataru nari
> Author unnamed. In *Marumaru chinbun* (1889).

even love letters / by civilized young ladies / in block style!
bunmei no / musume wa fumi mo / kaisho nari
> Author unnamed. In *Marumaru chinbun* (1879). *Kaisho*, the block
> style of handwriting associated with the West, can also mean 're-
> sourcefulness'.

beefsteak / as well as Western languages – / just a *soupçon*!
bifuteki to / yōgo mo sukoshi / kuikajiri
> Author unnamed. In *Marumaru chinbun* (1891). *Kuikajiri* means both
> a 'nibble' of food and a 'smattering' of knowledge. The Japanese term
> *bifuteki*, 'beefsteak', entered the language as a loan word from the
> French *bifteck*.

when all else fails, / the interpreter resorts / to hand gestures
magotsuite / kuru to tsūyaku / te o tsukai
> Busui.

socialism: / nothing up and running / except taverns!
shakaishugi / izakaya bakari / aruite i
> Sakai Kuraki. In his *Senryū kurakiten* (1904). And even then, the con-
> versations no doubt consist primarily of griping about socialism.

insufferable / even for politicians – / women's suffrage!
seijika mo / komaru nyōbo no / jiyūshugi
> Author unnamed. In *Chōchōshi koji tsuizen* (1889). Although the women's rights movement began in Japan after the Meiji Restoration, women would not be granted the right to vote until after the Second World War.

misconstruing / libertarianism ... / the widow's looseness!
jiyū no ken / kikimachigaete / goke furachi
> Author unnamed. In *Marumaru chinbun* (1878). According to Robert Bellah: 'Lacking a tradition of philosophical liberalism, Japanese intellectuals in the Meiji period found the Western ideas of freedom and individualism attractive, frightening, and difficult to understand. The commonest misinterpretation was to see them as invitations to license and self-indulgence, and as such dangerous to the nation' (Robert N. Bellah, *Imagining Japan: The Japanese Tradition and Its Modern Interpretation* (Berkeley, CA: University of California Press, 2003), p. 43).

Buddha Colossus / batting not an eye / under hailstones!
daibutsu no / majiroki mo senu / arare kana
> Shiki.

no telling / its head from its ass – / the sea slug
okashira no / kokoromotonaki / namako kana
> Kyorai. In *Sarumino* (1691). The sea slug (*namako*) is actually a kind of sea cucumber (Holothuroidea). (For an entire book of 'haiku' on sea slugs, see robin d. gill, *Rise, Ye Sea Slugs! 1,000 holothurian haiku compiled and translated by robin d. gill* (Key Biscayne, FL: Paraverse Press, 2003).)

heaven and earth: / neither exists apart from / snow fluttering down
ten mo chi mo / nashi tada yuki no / furishikiri
> Hashin.

sky cleared up, / they share a single hue: / moon and snow
sora harete / hitotsu iro nari / tsuki to yuki
> The nun Matsumoto Koyū. *Iro*, literally 'colour', denotes 'love' or even 'sex'.

winter moon! / above a gateless temple, / heaven's vastness
kangetsu ya / mon naki tera no / ten takashi
> Buson.

autumn wind – / for me there are no gods, / no buddhas
aki kaze ya / ware ni kami nashi / hotoke nashi
> Shiki.

from first / to final cleansing tub: / all gobbledygook!
tarai kara / tarai ni utsuru / chinpunkan
> Author unnamed. A well-known death verse (*jisei*), frequently misattributed to Issa. (Makoto Ueda, in his book on Issa, writes: 'A deathbed poem sometimes attributed to Issa ... is merely part of the Issa legend, with no documentary evidence to prove his authorship.' In Ueda, *Dew on the Grass: The Life and Poetry of Kobayashi Issa* (Leiden: E. J. Brill, 2004), p. 165, n. 3.) Building on earlier verses (such as the one immediately below, written in 1757 – half a dozen years before Issa's birth), this one deploys the striking colloquialism *chinpunkan*, meaning something defying comprehension. The verb *utsuru*, 'to move', has a wide range of meanings, from 'fades' to 'elapses'.

from first / to final cleansing tub – / all a dream!
tarai kara / tarai ni kawaru / yume no uchi
> Author unnamed. From *Senryūhyō mankuawase* (1757).

from first / to final cleansing tub – / a mere fifty years!
tarai kara / tarai no aida ga / gojūnen
> Zeraku. In *Yanagidaru* 62 (1812). Fifty years was the proverbial length of a person's lifespan. The second line contains an extra syllabet.

from first / to final cleansing tub – / one long dream!
tarai kara / tarai no aida / nagai yume
> Sajisuke. In *Yanagidaru* 71 (1819).

in all eternity / there's less pain and suffering / than just this one life
goshō yori / tada isshō no / muzukashisa
> Senkyō. In *Yanagidaru* 61 (1812). A nearly identical version written by Kazan would appear in *Yanagidaru* 128 (1833).

even the pine / I planted has grown ancient – / autumnal twilight
ware ueshi / matsu mo oikeri / aki no kure
> Issa. The word *matsu*, 'pine tree', also meaning 'to pine', adds a poignant note. Planting is just as much about burying as it is about sowing.

**this very autumn / how could I have grown so old? / a bird unto
clouds**

kono aki wa / nan de toshiyoru / kumo ni tori

Bashō. Written shortly before the poet's death in 1694, though not a
death verse (*jisei*) per se, this transcendent poem is a fitting swan song:
for the image of a bird diminishing in size as it disappears into the
vast unknown beyond the clouds embodies the ultimate aloneness of
all living beings. Bashō scholar Katō Shūson has observed: 'The force
of the last phrase is beyond words. The deep solitude that has been
given form here is not one that derives from a particular cause. It is a
more basic, existential solitude, the kind of solitude so profound that
nothing can alleviate it' (quoted in Ueda (ed. and trans.), *Bashō and
His Interpreters*, p. 407).

Sources of the Japanese Verses

Verses contained within historical works (see left-hand column below) quoted in the notes to the translations in the Commentary have been drawn from the following modern editions. Modern editions of verses by a named or unnamed poet for whom no historical work is cited in the note to a translation are listed separately below. Where more than one reference is provided for a historical work/poet, modern editions are listed according to those most frequently used. For abbreviated references to works in Japanese, see List of Abbreviations for full details.

Historical Works

Aka eboshi	*NKBZ* 46
'Akuoke no no maki' (The Washbasin Sequence)	See *Sarumino*
Ame no ochiba	*NKBZ* 46
Arano	*NKBZ* 41
Atsumeku	*NKBZ* 41
Beni no hana	*SSS*
Chikusaihyō mankuawase	*NKBZ* 46
Chiyomigusa	*NKBZ* 46
Chōchōshi koji tsuizen	*SMS*
Enokoshū	Matsue Shigeyori (ed.), *Koten bunko* 239, *Enokoshū* (Koten bunko, 1967) *SNKBT* 69
Garakuta chinpō	*SMS*

388   SOURCES OF THE JAPANESE VERSES

(Haifū kanno) Tagusa
sakayudaru   *RJS*
                             EBKI

(Haikai) Azuma karage   NKBZ 46
                             Kokusho Kankōkai (ed.), *Zappai* (Kokusho
                             Kankōkai, 1914)

Haikai kei   *EST*

Haikai shichibushū   SNKBT 70

Hanabatake   NKBZ 46

Hentsuki   Katsumine Shinpū (ed.), *Shōmon haiwa*
                             bunshū, in Nihon Haisho Taikei
                             Kankōkai (ed.), *Nihon haisho taikei* 4
                             (Nihon haisho taikei kankōkai, 1926)

Herazuguchi   NKBZ 46

Inu tsukubashū   NKBZ 46
                             Suzuki Tōzō (ed.), *Inu tsukubashū* (Kadoka-
                             wa shoten, 1965)

Jinensai hokkushū   *SH*

Kawazoi yanagi   NMZ 26

Kinkeihyō mankuawase   NKBZ 46

Kinkōhyō mankuawase   NKBZ 46

Kōmyōshū   Noma Kōshin (ed.), *Teihon saikaku zenshū*
                             11:1 (Chūō kōronsha, 1972)

Kotodama yanagi   *SS*

Kuchiyosegusa   NKBZ 46

Kyōku umeyanagi   *SS*

Mankuawase   Ōmi Sajin and Fujiwara Seiken, *Senryū*
                             nyūmon (Ōsaka: Hoikusha, 1977)

Marumaru chinbun   *SMS*

Minase sangin hyakuin   NKBT 39

Miyage   *SS*

Moritake senku Sawai Taizō (ed.), *Moritake senku kōshō*, in *Aichi Daigaku bungakukkai sōsho* 3 (Kyūko shoin, 1998)

Mutamagawa NMZ 26
Kei Kiitsu and Yamazawa Hideo, *Haikai mutamagawa*, 4 vols (Iwanami shoten, 1984–5)
R. H. Blyth, *Edo Satirical Verse Anthologies* (Tokyo: Hokuseido Press, 1961)

Nanihito hyakuin Esperanza Ramirez-Christensen, *Heart's Flower: The Life and Poetry of Shinkei* (Stanford: Stanford University Press, 1994)

Nanohana ya Ueda, Makoto, *The Path of Flowering Thorn: The Life and Poetry of Yosa Buson* (Stanford, CA: Stanford University Press, 1998)

Niiki NKBZ 46

Omoigo Blyth, R. H., *A History of Haiku* 2, *From Issa up to the Present* (Tokyo: Hokuseido Press, 1964)

Oku no hosomichi NKBZ 41

Omote wakaba NKBZ 46

Oriku taizen SS

Ryūfū kyōku kaisei jinmeiroku RJS

Sarumino NKBZ 32

Senryū kurakiten SMS

Senryūhyō mankuawase SS
Nakanishi Kenji (ed.), *Senryūhyō mankuawase kachikuzuri*, 13 vols (Shizuoka-ken: Senryū zappai kenkyūkai, 1995)
NKBZ 46

Shin hanatsumi NKBT 58

Shūishū	*SNKBT* 7
Shundei kushū	Tsukamoto Tetsuzō (ed.), *Shundei hokku-shū*, in *Yūhōdō bunko* 87 (Yūhōdō, 1914)
Shussemaru	*NKBZ* 46
Suetsumuhana	*SS* *EB* Kasuya Hiroki, *(Shinpen) Senryū daijiten* (Tōkyōdō shuppan, 1995) Okada Hajime (ed.), *Teihon haifū suetsumu-hana* (Yūkō shobō, 1966)
Taigi kusen kōhen	*NMZ* 27 Tsukamoto Tetsuzō and Miura Osamu (eds), *Meika haikaishū*, in *Yūhōdō bunko* 87 (Yūhōdō, 1914)
Urawakaba	*NKBZ* 46
Waka midori	*NKBZ* 46
Yamanaka sangin	*NKBZ* 41 (where it is referred to as *Yamanaka shū*)
Yanagi no hazue	*EBYHT* *YHZ*
Yanagidaru	Okada Hajime (ed.), *(Haifū) Yanagidaru zenshū*, 13 vols, rev. edn (Sanseidō, 1999): *Yanagidaru* 1–13 (covering years 1765–78) are in vol. 1; 14–27 (1779–98) in vol. 2; 28–41 (1799–1808) in vol. 3; 42–55 (1808–11) in vol. 4; 56–71 (1811–19) in vol. 5; 72–85 (1820–25) in vol. 6; 86–99 (1825–28) in vol. 7; 100–112 (1828–31) in vol. 8; 113–24 (1831–3) in vol. 9; 122–34 (1833–4) in vol. 10 (overlapping with vol. 9); 135–150 (1834–40?) in vol. 11; and 151–67 (1838–40) in vol. 12
Yanagidaru shūi	Yamazawa Hideo (ed.), *(Haifū) Yanagidaru shūi* (1796–7), 2 vols, in *Senryū shūsei* 7–8, in *Iwanami bunko* 620 (*ki*-271-7 and *ki*-271-8) (Iwanami bunko, 1995)
Yuki no hana	*SSS*

Individual Poets

Where a poet is unnamed and no further details are provided in the note to the translation, the verse will have been drawn from one of the following works: R. H. Blyth, *A History of Haiku* 1, *From the Beginnings up to Issa* (Tokyo: Hokuseido Press, 1963), *A History of Haiku* 2, *From Issa up to the Present* (Tokyo: Hokuseido Press, 1964), *Japanese Life and Character in Senryu* (Tokyo: Hokuseido Press, 1960), (ed. and trans.) *Senryu: Japanese Satirical Verses* (Tokyo: Hokuseido Press, 1949); Miyamori Asatarō (ed. and trans.), *An Anthology of Haiku, Ancient and Modern* (Tokyo: Taiseido Press, 1932), reprinted as *Haikai and Haiku* (Tokyo: Nippon Gakujutsu Shinkōkai, 1958; reprinted Westport, CT: Greenwood, 1971); Makoto Ueda (ed. and trans.), *Far Beyond the Field: Haiku by Japanese Women* (New York: Columbia University Press, 2003); and *SE*.

Amenbō	Blyth, *Japanese Life and Character in Senryu*
Atsujin	Blyth, *History of Haiku* 2
Baisei	Blyth, *History of Haiku* 1
Baishitsu	Miyamori, *Anthology of Haiku* Donald Keene, *Dawn to the West* 2, *Poetry, Drama, Criticism* (New York: Holt Rinehart & Winston, 1984)
Banan	Ueda, *Path of Flowering Thorn*
Bashō	*NKBZ* 41 Kira Sueo and Sato Katsuaki (eds), *Bashō zenkushū: gendai goyakutsuki* (Kadokawa sofia bunko, 2010)
Bentenshi	Blyth, *Japanese Life and Character in Senryu*
Bishi	Blyth, *Japanese Life and Character in Senryu*
Bokusui	Tōno Kōji (ed.), *Bokusui kushū* (Ōsaka: Rakuyōjusha, 1920)
Bonchō	*NKBZ* 32
Bunshō	Miyamori, *Anthology of Haiku*
Bunson	Miyamori, *Anthology of Haiku*

Buson	*BK* Ogata Tsutomu and Morita Ran (eds), *Buson zenshū* 1 (Kōdansha, 1992)
Busui	Blyth, *Japanese Life and Character in Senryu*
Chigetsu	Ueda, *Far Beyond the Field* *SNKBT* 70
Chigusa	Blyth, *Japanese Life and Character in Senryu*
Chiyo	Blyth, *History of Haiku* 2 Ueda, *Far Beyond the Field* Faubion Bowers (ed.), *The Classic Tradition* *of Haiku: An Anthology* (Mineola, NY: Dover Publications, 1996)
Chora	Miyamori, *Anthology of Haiku* Ueda, *Path of Flowering Thorn*
Deirei	Blyth, *Japanese Life and Character in Senryu*
Etsujin	Harold G. Henderson (ed. and trans.), *An Introduction to Haiku: An Anthology* *of Poems and Poets, from Bashō to Shiki* (Garden City, NY: Doubleday Anchor Books, 1958)
Fugyoku	Miyamori, *Anthology of Haiku*
Fuhaku	Miyamori, *Anthology of Haiku* Blyth, *History of Haiku* 2
Fukoku	Blyth, *History of Haiku* 2
Fusō	Blyth, *Japanese Life and Character in Senryu*
Ganshitsu	Blyth, *History of Haiku* 2
Garyūbō	Blyth, *Japanese Life and Character in Senryu*
Genkaibō	Blyth, *Japanese Life and Character in Senryu*
Ginkō	robin d. gill (ed. and trans.), *Cherry Blos-* *som Epiphany: The Poetry and Philosophy* *of a Flowering Tree* (Key Biscayne, FL: Paraverse Press, 2007)
Goken	Blyth, *Japanese Life and Character in Senryu*

Gomei	Blyth, *History of Haiku* 1 and 2
Gonsui	Blyth, *History of Haiku* 1
Goshun	Daniel C. Buchanan (ed. and trans.), *One Hundred Famous Haiku* (Tokyo and San Francisco: Japan Publications, 1973)
Goyō	Blyth, *Japanese Life and Character in Senryu*
Gyōdai	Blyth, *History of Haiku* 1 Miyamori, *Anthology of Haiku*
Gyokutorō	Blyth, *Japanese Life and Character in Senryu* Stephen Addiss, with Fumiko and Akira Yamamoto, *Haiku Humor: Wit and Folly in Japanese Poems and Prints* (Boston, MA: Weatherhill, 2007)
Hajin	Miyamori, *Anthology of Haiku*
Hanmonsen	Blyth, *Senryu: Japanese Satirical Verses*
Haritsu	Miyamori, *Anthology of Haiku* Bowers, *Classic Tradition of Haiku* Blyth, *History of Haiku* 2
Hashin	Henderson: *Introduction to Haiku*
Hokushi	Bowers, *Classic Tradition of Haiku* Yoel Hoffmann (ed.), *Japanese Death Poems: Written by Zen Monks and Haiku Poets on the Verge of Death* (Rutland and Tokyo: Charles E. Tuttle, 1986) Takahashi Mutsuo, Inoue Hakudo and Takaoka Kazuya, *Haiku: The Poetic Key to Japan*, trans. Miyashita Emiko (Tokyo: PIE Books, 2003)
Hōrō	Blyth, *Japanese Life and Character in Senryu*
Ichū	Blyth, *History of Haiku* 1
Ishū/Shigeyori	Blyth, *History of Haiku* 1
Issa	Shinano Kyōikukai (ed.), *Issa zenshū*, 9 vols (Nagano: Shinano mainichi shinbun-sha, 1976–80) *NKBT* 58

Jisshi	Blyth, *Japanese Life and Character in Senryu*
Jōzen	Blyth, *Japanese Life and Character in Senryu*
Jūkō	robin d. gill (ed. and trans.), *The Fifth Season: Poems for the Re-creation of the World* (Key Biscayne, FL: Paraverse Press, 2007)
Kakujirō	Kadokawa Shoten (ed.), *(Gappon) Haiku saijiki* (Kadokawa shoten, 1997) Takahashi et al., *Haiku: Poetic Key to Japan*
Kanehiko	Blyth, *Japanese Life and Character in Senryu*
Keira	Blyth, *History of Haiku 2*
Kenkabō	Blyth, *Japanese Life and Character in Senryu* Blyth, *Senryu: Japanese Satirical Verses*
Kensai	Steven D. Carter (ed. and trans.), *Haiku Before Haiku: From the Renga Masters to Bashō* (New York: Columbia University Press, 2011)
Kichibō	Blyth, *Japanese Life and Character in Senryu*
Kigin	Blyth, *History of Haiku 1*
Kikaku	Blyth, *Japanese Life and Character in Senryu* Miyamori Asatarō (ed. and trans.), *Classic Haiku: An Anthology of Poems by Bashō and His Followers* (Mineola, NY: Dover, 2002)
Kikusha	Miyamori, *Anthology of Haiku*
Kinbō	Addiss, *Haiku Humor*
Kinsha	Miyamori, *Anthology of Haiku*
Kitō	Blyth, *History of Haiku 1* Miyamori, *Anthology of Haiku* Ueda, *Path of Flowering Thorn*
Kogetsu	Miyamori, *Anthology of Haiku*
Koyū	Miyamori, *Anthology of Haiku*
Kyōdai	Miyamori, *Anthology of Haiku*

Kyokusui	Miyamori, *Anthology of Haiku*
Kyōma	gill, *Cherry Blossom Epiphany*
Kyorai	Miyamori, *Anthology of Haiku*
Kyoriku	Miyamori, *Anthology of Haiku* David Cobb (ed.), *Haiku: The Poetry of Nature* (New York: Universe, 2002)
Mantarō	Takahashi et al., *Haiku: Poetic Key to Japan*
Masahide	Miyamori, *Anthology of Haiku*
Meimei	Blyth, *History of Haiku* 1
Meisetsu	Blyth, *History of Haiku* 1 Miyamori, *Anthology of Haiku*
Meitei	Blyth, *Japanese Life and Character in Senryu*
Mōichi	Blyth, *History of Haiku* 1
Moritake	Blyth, *History of Haiku* 1
Muchō	Blyth, *History of Haiku* 2 Miyamori, *Anthology of Haiku*
Nanboku	Blyth, *Japanese Life and Character in Senryu*
Nangai	Miyamori, *Anthology of Haiku*
Naojo	Miyamori, *Anthology of Haiku*
Nanboku	Blyth, *Japanese Life and Character in Senryu*
Nokōrō	Blyth, *Japanese Life and Character in Senryu*
Ōemaru	Miyamori, *Anthology of Haiku*
Onitsura	Okada Rihei (ed.), *Onitsura zenshū* (Kadokawa shoten, 1968)
Otsuyū	Miyamori, *Anthology of Haiku*
Raizan	Blyth, *History of Haiku* 1 Blyth, *Japanese Life and Character in Senryu* Buchanan, *One Hundred Famous Haiku*
Rankō	Miyamori, *Anthology of Haiku*.
Ransetsu	Miyamori, *Anthology of Haiku*

	Bowers, *Classic Tradition of Haiku*
	Ueda, *Far Beyond the Field*
Ritō	Miyamori, *Anthology of Haiku*
Rohan	Takahashi et al, *Haiku: Poetic Key to Japan*
Roten	Blyth, *History of Haiku* 1
Ryōkan	Cobb, *Haiku: Poetry of Nature*
Ryōta	Miyamori, *Anthology of Haiku*
	Blyth, *History of Haiku* 1
Ryūho	Blyth, *History of Haiku* 1
Ryūichi	Miyamori, *Anthology of Haiku*
Ryūsei	Blyth, *Japanese Life and Character in Senryu*
Saigin	Blyth, *History of Haiku* 1
Saika	Blyth, *Japanese Life and Character in Senryu*
Saikaku	Blyth, *History of Haiku* 1
Saimaro	Blyth, *History of Haiku* 1
Saimu	Blyth, *History of Haiku* 1
Sakijo	Miyamori, *Anthology of Haiku*
Santarō	Blyth, *Japanese Life and Character in Senryu*
Seibi	gill, *Cherry Blossom Epiphany*
	Blyth, *History of Haiku* 2
Seifu	Ueda, *Far Beyond the Field*
	Miyamori, *Anthology of Haiku*
	Ueno Sachiko, *Josei haiku no sekai* (Iwanami shoten, 1998)
Seika	Miyamori, *Anthology of Haiku*
Seimu	Blyth, *Japanese Life and Character in Senryū*
Seira	Blyth, *History of Haiku* 1
Sennosuke	Blyth, *Japanese Life and Character in Senryu*
Shigetsune	Blyth, *Japanese Life and Character in Senryu*

Shigeyori	See Ishū above
Shiki	SZ
	Shibata Nami, *Masaoka Shiki to haiku bunrui* (Kyōto: Shibunkaku shuppan, 2001)
	Janine Beichman, *Masaoka Shiki: His Life and Works* (Boston, MA: Twayne Publishers, 1982)
Shikō	Buchanan, *One Hundred Famous Haiku*
Shinpei	Miyamori, *Anthology of Haiku*
Shirao	Miyamori, *Anthology of Haiku*
	Blyth, *History of Haiku* 1
Shirō	Miyamori, *Anthology of Haiku*
	Blyth, *History of Haiku* 2
Shishōshi	Blyth, *Japanese Life and Character in Senryu*
Shōhaku	Blyth, *History of Haiku* 2
Shōi	Blyth, *History of Haiku* 1
Shōjuen	Blyth, *Japanese Life and Character in Senryu*
Shokyū	Miyamori, *Anthology of Haiku*
Shōkyū	Carter, *Haiku Before Haiku*
Shūda	Miyamori, *Anthology of Haiku*
Shunkō	Blyth, *History of Haiku* 2
Shun'u	Blyth, *Japanese Life and Character in Senryu*
Sodō	Henderson, *Introduction to Haiku*
Sōgi	SS
	gill, *Cherry Blossom Epiphany*
	Ueda, *Path of Flowering Thorn*
Sōin	gill, *Cherry Blossom Epiphany*
	Bowers, *Classic Tradition of Haiku*
Sōjō	Cobb, *Haiku: Poetry of Nature*
Sōkan	Blyth, *Japanese Life and Character in Senryu*
	Blyth, *History of Haiku* 1

Sonojo	gill, *Cherry Blossom Epiphany*
Sōseki	Natsume Sōseki, *Sōseki zenshū* 17 (Iwanami shoten, 1996) Blyth, *History of Haiku* 2
Sōzei	gill, *Cherry Blossom Epiphany*
Suiujo	Miyamori, *Anthology of Haiku*
Sutejo	Miyamori, *Anthology of Haiku*
Taigi	Miyamori, *Anthology of Haiku* Steven D. Carter (ed. and trans.), *Traditional Japanese Poetry: An Anthology* (Stanford, CA: Stanford University Press, 1991)
Takuchi	Miyamori, *Anthology of Haiku*
Tantan	Miyamori, *Anthology of Haiku*
Tatsuko	Takahashi et al., *Haiku: Poetic Key to Japan*
Tayojo	Miyamori, *Anthology of Haiku*
Teishitsu	Cobb, *Haiku: Poetry of Nature*
Teitoku	Blyth, *History of Haiku* 1
Tokugen	Blyth, *History of Haiku* 1
Tonbo	Blyth, *Japanese Life and Character in Senryu*
Toshiko	Blyth, *Japanese Life and Character in Senryu*
Ushichi	Kawamoto Kōji, *Poetics of Japanese Verse: Imagery, Structure, Meter* (Tokyo: University of Tokyo Press, 2000)
Usui	Blyth, *Japanese Life and Character in Senryu*
Yaba	Miyamori, *Anthology of Haiku*
Yachō	Blyth, *Japanese Life and Character in Senryu*
Yasharō	Blyth, *Japanese Life and Character in Senryu*
Zenma	Carter, *Haiku Before Haiku*

Glossary of Terms

Within the glossary entries below, names and terms highlighted in bold constitute a cross-reference either to this glossary or to the Glossary of Poets. See Index of Japanese Verses for verses quoted here that are included in the Commentary.

ageku Concluding stanza of a linked-verse sequence (in *haikai* or *renga*).

ana Literally 'hole'; some kind of loophole in or exposé of common sense. A mainstay of *senryū* (and of comic prose genres collectively known as *gesaku*). Often used as shorthand for the phrase 'loophole uncovering' (*ana o ugachi*). See *ugachi*. See note to *shinbun wa / fude de ukiyo no / ana o hori*.

Analects (*Lunyu* in Chinese, *Rongo* in Japanese; *c.*140 BCE). Collection of sayings attributed to the Chinese socio-political thinker Confucius (Kongzi in Chinese, Kōshi in Japanese; 551–479 BCE).

aware Poignancy. The related term *mono no aware*, referring to the pathos inherent in someone or something felt by empathetic souls (be they readers or poets), is a key aspect of Japanese poetics, according to Motoori Norinaga (1730–1801).

bareku Dirty sexy *haiku*. Literally 'breaking-propriety verse' or 'laying-bare verse' or even 'voluptuous verse' (depending on its **graph**s). Although generally referring to any risqué and/or scatological verse, in the context of witty linked verse (*haikai no renga*), it refers specifically to the vastly popular seventeen-**syllable** comic variety. Its emphasis on humour has meant that it has often been characterized as a subgenre of *senryū*, even though the existence of *bareku*-only collections such as *Yanagi no hazue* suggests it was recognized as a mode in its own right. Like *senryū* (or even modern **haiku**), *bareku* is a retrospective term, having been coined by Okada Hajime in *Yanagi no hazue zenshaku* (1956). Prior to that, other terms included: *aiku* ('love verse', favoured by Karai **Senryū**); *renku* ('coupled verse', burlesquing its more established homonym 'linked verse'); *iroku* (erotic verse); and *waraiku* (giggle verse), appearing in the preface to *Yanagi no hazue*, which playfully but astutely suggested the near union of laughter and sex; *taibi* (referring to the outer limits of acceptability); and *sueban*, the 'lowest-ranked numbers' (as opposed to the 'highest-ranked numbers', *takaban*), meaning the poetic dregs one finds at the proverbial 'bottom of the barrel' of *Yanagidaru*, also implying bodily 'extremities' and excretions.

Bashō Revival *Shōfū kaiki*, literally 'Revival of the Bashō Style'. See **Buson**.

Beni no hana (Blossoms of Pink) and *Yuki no hana* (Snow Blossoms), sister volumes of dirty sexy *haiku* (*bareku*), largely based on *Yanagi no hazue*, with accompanying sexually explicit illustrations (*shunga*) by Koikawa Shōzan (1821–1907), published together in the album *Yanagidaru suetsumuhana yokyō* (The Willow Vat and Safflower Princess Burlesque Show, *c.* 1848–54).

challenge verse Aka 'challenge'. See *maeku*.

daisan Third stanza in a linked-verse sequence, be it *renga* or *haikai*. Moving away from the formal niceties of the *hokku* (initiating stanza) and *wakiku* (second stanza), this seventeen-syllabet stanza was supposed to open the sequence up to exciting new possibilities.

Danrin Literally 'Chatty Woods', aka the Danrin School. Major school of *haiku* founded *c.* 1673 by **Sōin**, whom **Bashō** credited with having elevated *haiku* above the supposed 'drivel' of **Teimon** verse – even though **Onitsura** left the school on account of what he felt to be its over-the-top wordplay. Others involved with Danrin at one time or another include: **Ichū**, Bashō (under the pen name Tōsei) and particularly **Saikaku**.

disciples of Bashō See *Shōmon jittetsu*.

dokugin Linked-verse sequence composed by a single person. *Haiku* examples include *Dokugin senku* (A Thousand Verses Solo, 1540) by **Moritake** and *Saikaku jichū dokugin hyakuin* (Saikaku's Hundred Linked Verses, Annotated by Himself, 1691) by **Saikaku**.

Edo Tokyo. See Chronology.

Edoza The **Edo** Coterie. Branch of the Urban **Shōmon** closely associated with the 'flashy style' (*sharefū*) of the poet **Kikaku** that would come to be condemned as heretical (*jadō*) and is not infrequently written out of standard *haiku* genealogies. Spiritual forebear of *senryū* and perhaps even *bareku*.

enjambment See *kumatagari*.

Enokoshū (Puppydog Collection, 1633). Compiled by **Shigeyori** and **Ryūho**. Major repository of **Teimon** poetry, containing many verses by **Teitoku**. Also contains one of the earliest known *haiku* by a woman, a poet known as 'Mitsutada's wife'.

floating world See *ukiyo*.

Futaba no matsu (Twin-Needled Pine, 1690). Foundational collection of *haiku* verse capping (*maekuzuke*) gleaned from monthly gatherings held in **Edo** and edited by **Fukaku**.

Genji monogatari (The Tale of Genji, *c.* 1000). See Chronology.

gesaku Literally 'frivolous composition', catch-all term for any kind of comic literature primarily in prose. Epitomized by genres such as the yellow-covered adult comicbook (*kibyōshi*) placing an emphasis on the exposé (*ugachi*), verbal wit (*share*) and so on; not unlike *senryū* or even *haikai* more broadly. For more on comicbooks, see notes to Sōseki's *fuyugomori / kibyōshi aruwa / akabyōshi* and Kitō's *ezōshi ni / shizu oku mise ya / haru no kaze*.

graph See *kanji*.

haibun Prose works not only studded with verses from witty linked-verse (*haikai*) sequences, particularly though not exclusively *hokku* (initiating stanzas), but also typically displaying the aesthetics and linking logic of *haikai*. **Bashō** was one of the early great practitioners.

haifū *Haikai*-style.

haiga A *haiku* picture. Probably an abbreviation of *haikai no sōga* (witty linked-verse running-style pictures). Prototypically a deceptively simple-looking inkwash painting in which an image interacts to a sophisticated degree with the calligraphic rendering and content of a *hokku*. However, the term may be applied conceptually to *any* mode of witty linked verse (*haiku*) – including *senryū*, *bareku* and so on – when combined with an image, even if appearing within woodblock prints or media other than inkwashes.

haigō A *haiku* pen name. Typically, poets composed under more than one pen name.

haigon Literally 'witty (linked-verse) words'. Diction allowed in witty linked verse (*haikai*) that was long forbidden to classical poetry (especially *tanka* and *renga*). Includes such things as fleeting colloquial expressions, neologisms, vulgarities and even foreign words (principally Chinese but also Dutch, English, French and German). The playful tension between classical and contemporary diction – not unlike the division between natural or ordinary and elite poetic language – afforded much of the pleasure of *haiku*. Consequently, *haigon* seems to have inspired contemporary *tanka* poets to experiment with freer diction.

haijin One who either composes *haiku* or is possessed of such a sensibility.

haikai Aka *haikai no renga* and *haiku*. Witty linked verse. Relative to serious linked poetry (*renga*), *haikai* was 'witty' because it playfully relaxed if not flouted *renga*'s complex rules of composition (*shikimoku*), strictures of classical poetic diction, elitist aesthetics and privileged status of participants. Customarily derided as lowbrow until **Onitsura**, **Bashō** and others in the latter part of the seventeenth century helped imbue it with highbrow aesthetics and tried to distance it from *maekuzuke* (verse capping), *tentori* (point scoring), *senryū* (comic verse), *bareku* (dirty sexy verse) and other comparatively lowbrow forms. For more on *haikai* and its development as a poetic form, see Chronology and Introduction. See also 'The Washbasin Sequence', pp. 2–7, for an example of verse linking in practice.

haikai no renga See *haikai* and also *renga*.

haiku Pronounced *hah-ee-coo* in English (*ha-i-ku* in Japanese). Shorthand form of *haikai no (renga no) ku*, referring to one or more stanzas (*ku*) of a witty (*haikai*) linked-verse (*renga*) sequence or any of those stanzas taken out of its original linked context. A decidedly premodern, collaborative literary word game in which players devised witty impromptu verses, in a wide range of seventeen- and fourteen-**syllabet** modes, linking with surrounding verses to form a sequence. The term *haiku* was used only rarely until **Shiki** retooled it as the modern **haiku**. For more on *haiku* and its development as a poetic form, see Chronology and Introduction. See also 'The Washbasin Sequence', pp. 2–7, for an example of verse linking in practice.

haiku Pronounced *high-coo*. A decidedly modern form of world poetry, originally devised in the late nineteenth and early twentieth centuries in Japan as a response to modern Western poetry. Prototypically a standalone poem composed by an individual poet in seventeen **syllabets** in Japanese (or seventeen syllables or fewer in other languages). Too often misapplied, following the rhetoric of Masaoka **Shiki**, to pre-twentieth-century *hokku* (the first verse of a linked-verse sequence). For more on haiku and how it evolved out of *haiku*, see Chronology and Introduction.

haiku kakushin Haiku Reform. See **Shiki**.

haramiku Composing a stanza in advance of a verse-composing session. Widely frowned upon not only for its similarity to verse capping (*maekuzuke*) but also because *haiku* valued spontaneity.

Heike monogatari (Tales of the Heike; *c.* thirteenth century). See Chronology (entry for 1180–85).

hiraku Ordinary stanza. That is, any stanza in a linked-verse sequence, be it *haikai* or *renga*, that is *not* a special stanza, such as *hokku*, *wakiku*, *daisan* or *ageku*. It can be either fourteen or seventeen **syllabets**. Although most contain a *kigo* (season word) and a *kire* (cut) or *kireji* (cutting word) – in which case if taken out of their linked context, they can be easily confused for *hokku* – those that do not are typically referred to as *zatsu no ku* (miscellaneous verse) or, in *haiku*, *zappai* (miscellaneous witty verse).

hokku Initiating stanza, prototypically in seventeen **syllabets**, of any linked-verse sequence, be it *haikai* or *renga*. Because this stanza – which convention dictated should include both a *kire* (cut) or *kireji* (cutting word) and a *kigo* (season word) as a kind of benediction of the verse-composing session – set the tone for the other stanzas to come in the sequence, it was often composed by a master poet and/or special guest of honour. Although the modern **haiku** enshrines these formal characteristics (see Introduction, pp. xxxvii–xli) historically there were many modes of witty linked verse other than the *hokku* that dispensed with these.

hosomi Slenderness. The use of understated, objective, egoless, even detached language allowing one to impersonally slip into the quintessence (*hon'i*) of an inanimate object, often resulting in a seemingly paradoxical animation or personification. (See also Introduction, p. xxiv.) Associated primarily with **Bashō** and his school. In what has come to be perhaps his best-known maxim, Bashō is recorded by **Dohō** in *Sanzōshi* (1702) as saying: 'Learn of the pine from the pine; learn of the bamboo from the bamboo' (see *NKBZ* 51, p. 547). Interestingly, Western poets have come around to something similar. One thinks of William Carlos Williams's Imagist catchphrase 'No ideas but in things'.

hyakuin Linked-verse sequence of one hundred stanzas.

iemoto Hereditary atelier system.

ikkudate Standalone verse.

Inu tsukubashū (Mongrel Linked-Verse Collection, *c.* 1530). First major *haikai* collection. Compiled and edited by **Moritake** and **Sōkan**.

Ise monogatari (Tales of Ise, *c.* 880–950). See Chronology.

jiamari Hypermetre, i.e. running over the prescribed **syllabet** count. Far more prevalent in seventeen-syllabet verses than in fourteen-syllabet ones (see *kakurenbō to / yūdan shita haha*). Among its uses, hypermetre frequently can improve rhythm, avoid the awkwardness of verse straddling (*kumatagari*), provide emphasis and impart an air of spontaneity (especially used with popular set expressions). Examples include **Teishitsu**'s 6–7–5-syllabet verse *kore wa kore wa / to bakari hana no / yoshinoyama* and **Bashō**'s 5–9–5-syllabet verse *kareeda ni / karasu no tomarikeri / aki no kure*. Contrast with *jitarazu* (hypometre).

jisei Death verse. Versifiers customarily composed one or more such verses during their final moments, typically on the theme of leaving this world. These were either written by the versifier or taken down by someone at hand.

jitarazu Hypometre, i.e. falling short of the prescribed **syllabet** count. Because of the brevity of individual stanzas in linked-verse sequences (*haikai* or *renga*), hypometre was regarded as a faux pas even if used deliberately and so was exceedingly rare. Even then, it tended to be confined to an individual line lacking a syllabet that was often made up elsewhere in the verse, especially to avoid the awkwardness of verse straddling (*kumatagari*). Contrast with *jiamari* (hypermetre).

jōgo Repeating challenge. Typically a fourteen-**syllabet** challenge verse (*maeku*) in **haiku** verse capping (*maekuzuke*) whose first, seven-syllabet line is repeated using a kind of space-saving ditto mark. Popularized in Tachiba **Fukaku**'s influential *Waka midori*, this became the dominant form of challenge verse from 1692 onwards. Its inherent redundancy eroded the function of the challenge and eventually led to a focus on the comic response (*tsukeku*) that retrospectively would come to be called *senryū*. It may even have planted the seed of the eventual omission of the *tanku*, or fourteen-syllabet *haiku*, as a form of modern **haiku**.

kakekotoba Pivot word. Type of sophisticated wordplay in which the meaning of one phrase 'pivots' into that of another, as with 'Romeo loved Julienned potatoes' or 'I have a townhouse and my sister has a flat behind'.

kana See *kanji*.

kanji Chinese characters or **graph**s (*hanzi* in Chinese). The Japanese writing system combines twin phonetically based syllabary sets (*kana*), known as *hiragana* and *katakana*, with adopted Chinese graphs ranging from pictographs (visually resembling the word they represent) to highly abstract ideographs (with little or no visual basis). Although Chinese graphs are of course read in China according to Chinese pronunciations, in Japan they can have Sinified readings (*on'yomi* – Japanese approximations of Chinese pronunciations) as well as Japanese readings (*kun'yomi*). Sometimes, a graph might playfully be glossed with a non-standard reading. For instance, in several **bareku** in this volume, the graphs for 'shell' (*kai*) and 'opening' (*kai*) are glossed *bobo*, a slang term for vulva, as in Wakō's *goke no bobo / namida no kawaku / hima wa nashi* and **Shuchin**'s *genjina mo / kai wa ōkata / nioumiya*.

kanmurizuke See *maekuzuke*.

karumi 'Lightness' of diction, wit and subject matter. Championed by **Shikō** and others in the manner of **Bashō**, who had been developing it towards the end of his life.

kasen Witty linked-verse sequence of thirty-six stanzas. Most common **haikai** form from the late seventeenth century onwards.

kibyōshi See *gesaku*.

kidai Seasonal topic. See *kigo*.

kigasanari Literally 'season overlap', a verse involving either the moment of transition from one season to another, or two discrete seasons. See, for instance, **Bashō**'s *ume ga ka ni / notto hi no deru / yamaji kana*.

kigo Season word. First and most indispensable of the two major formal requirements of the modern **haiku**, designed to help overcome its radical brevity. In premodern witty linked verse (*haikai*), however, a seasonal reference of some kind was prescribed in the initiating stanza (*hokku*) less to overcome brevity than to set both the tone for the entire sequence and the specific season for the immediate few stanzas to come – stanzas that while not *hokku* none the less tended to include seasons. This difference in function is often obscured by the fact that the very term 'season word' was only rarely if ever used prior to the early twentieth century; for it was in 1908 that Ōsuga Otsuji (1881–1920) coined the term to refer to the seasonal allusion in *both* the premodern *haiku* as well as the modern haiku as if to suggest that these were the same animal. See Introduction, pp. xxxix–xli, for more on this.

kire Cut. See *kireji*.

kireji Cutting word. Technically, a grammatical particle that accomplishes a 'cut' (*kire*), the second of the two major formal requirements that the modern **haiku** has at its disposal for overcoming its extreme brevity. This it does by 'cutting' a verse rhythmically and semantically into two parts whose relationship to each other can only be resolved less by the grammar of the poetry than by some kind of logical or intuitive leap of faith. See Introduction, pp. xxxviii–xxxix, for more on this.

Kojiki (Record of Ancient Matters, *c.*711). See Chronology.

Kokinshū Aka *Kokin wakashū* (Collection of Japanese Verse Old and New, *c.*920). See Chronology.

kumatagari Literally 'verse straddling', a technique of enjambment often associated with experimental modern **haiku**, though also found not infrequently in premodern *haiku*. Typically, *haiku* straddling takes one of three major forms: (1) a word split between two lines to some deliberate effect (as with **Rekisen**'s *ato no kusa- / me o matteiru / henna tsura*, in which the splitting of *kusame* dramatically mimics a pause in sneezing); (2) a cut (*kire*) falling in the middle of a line instead of at its end (as with *ya* in **Issa**'s *kiru ki to wa / shirade ya tori no / su o tsukuru*); or, similarly, (3) two parallel sentence fragments meeting in the middle of a line, usually the second (as with *kōkō ni / urare fukō ni / uke-dasare*). See also *jiamari* and *jitarazu*. In some cases, rather than force a word to straddle two lines, as with *otoko* in Tōgan's verse *teishu*

406   GLOSSARY OF TERMS

wa o- / *toko nyōbō wa* / *onna nari*, it may be less awkward to parse the
verse into a non-standard **syllabet** arrangement, such as 7–5–5, *teishu
wa otoko* / *nyōbō wa* / *onna nari*.

kutsuzuke See ***maekuzuke***.

Kuzu no matsubara (Arrowroot Pine Grove, 1692), by **Shikō** with
Fugyoku, account of the events of the composition of **Bashō**'s 'old
pond' verse (*furuike ya* / *kawazu tobikomu* / *mizu no oto*).

kyōku Madcap verse of typically seventeen **syllabets**. This was one way
of referring to what is now termed ***senryū***. Not to be confused with
kyōka, a madcap ***tanka*** (short poem), typically in thirty-one syllabets.

lunisolar calendar An annual calendar based primarily on the phases
of the moon, adjusted slightly to align with the solar cycle. Most years
consisted of twelve long (thirty-day) and short (twenty-nine-day)
months, with a thirteenth 'intercalary' month inserted occasionally
to correct any gap with the solar year. As such, the lunisolar and solar
calendars do not exactly correspond to each other. Historically, luni-
solar months varied from modern solar months by three to seven
weeks, depending on the year. Imported to Japan from China in the
early seventh century, the lunisolar calendar remained in effect until
1 January 1873, when it was officially replaced by the Western Gre-
gorian solar calendar. For more on this, see Introduction, p. xl.

maeku Literally 'challenge' verse, aka 'challenge'. Typically a fourteen-
syllabet stanza (*tanku*) calling for a seventeen-syllabet response
(*tsukeku*), though other modes also exist (including those prompted
by a single word). See ***maekuzuke***.

maekuzuke Verse capping. The playful practice of adding a witty re-
ply verse (*tsukeku*) to a challenge verse (*maeku*). Heian-period *waka*
poets played a kind of verse capping at court, though during the **Edo**
period *haiku* verse capping became a vital popular phenomenon. Of-
ten derided as a form of poetic training wheels, and even at times
outlawed as a form of gambling, verse-capping contests sometimes
involved tens of thousands of people sending in their verses in the
hope of receiving valuable prizes (see Introduction, p. xlviii, for more
on this). Collections of winning verses – especially **Fukaku**'s ***Futa-
ba no matsu*** and ***Waka midori*** – helped popularize *haiku* itself to
a vast, even national, audience. In *haiku* verse capping, the challenge
was typically a fourteen-**syllabet** set-up verse, issued by a professional
point-scoring judge (*tenja*), calling for a seventeen-syllabet response,
which, when published on its own in collections of winning verses,
would come to be termed ***senryū***.

Roughly speaking, *haiku* verse capping can be divided into two
major forms: 31-syllabet games, where the challenge (*maeku*) was

either a fourteen-syllabet *tanku* (in either complex or 'repeating' form – see *jōgo*) or else a seventeen-syllabet verse, though the former was far more prevalent; and seventeen-syllabet games, such as: (1) 'crown linking' (*kanmurizuke* or *kamurizuke*) or 'sedge-hat linking' (*kasazuke*) in which the challenge takes the form of a five-syllabet verse (called 'crown' or 'sedge hat'), to which one must provide a twelve-syllabet riposte. Subcategories include splice-linking (*kiriku*) varieties, such as *eboshizuke*, *gomojizuke* (or *gojizuke*), *kashirazuke* and so on; (2) 'sash linking' (*obizuke*), in which the challenge is the middle phrase or 'sash' of seven syllabets, to which the player responds with the first and last five-syllabet phrases; (3) 'footgear linking' (*kutsuzuke*), in which the challenge is the last phrase of five syllabets, to which the player responds with the first two phrases of twelve syllabets; (4) various kinds of acrostic verse (*oriku*), in which the first syllabet of each of the three phrases in the response spells the challenge word (not a verse per se); (5) various games of 'step-by-step' linking (*dandanzuke*), in which players offer seventeen-syllabet verses that repeat the last five syllabets of the previous verse (leading some scholars to speculate that this was an offshoot of sash linking; see Satō Yoshifumi, *Senryū bungakushi* (Ōsaka: Shin'yōkan shuppan, 2004), p. 61); (6) twist linking (*mojirizuke*), in which the middle seven syllabets of a seventeen-syllabet verse must perform a pivoting double duty in recasting the first and final phrase (Satō, *Senryū bungakushi*, pp. 61–2); and (7) triple rain-capping (*mikasazuke*), in which three players collaborated to supply each of the three lines of a seventeen-syllabet verse.

makoto Authenticity. **Onitsura** helped elevate *haiku* to a serious art form by devising his influential dictum that 'there can be no witty linked verse without authenticity' (*makoto no hokani haikai nashi*). In the context of the late seventeenth century, this meant that *haiku* should be composed less through the filter of poetic convention than on the basis of experiential truthfulness. See Onitsura's *teizen ni / shiroku saitaru / tsubaki kana*.

makura kotoba Literally 'pillow word', a set poetic epithet, used especially in classical Japanese poetry, as in the phrase *ashibiki yama*, '*foot-dragging* mountain'.

mankuawase Literally 'ten-thousand verses contest'. Printed announcements of winning stanzas (*kachikuzuri*) selected from *maekuzuke* (verse-capping) contests. For instance, *Senryūhyō mankuawase* consisted of winning entries in verse-capping contests from 1757 to 1789 as judged by Karai **Senryū**.

Man'yōshū (Myriad Leaves Collection; late eighth century). See Chronology.

Marumaru chinbun A Meiji-era magazine, published from 1877 to 1907, most infamous for its satirical political cartoons. (The titular *marumaru* playfully referred to the circular blotting out of text by government censors. *Chinbun*, punning on *shinbun*, 'newspaper', literally means 'curious writings'.) Yet it also published socio-politically satirical *haiku* that helped pave the way for the regular publication of 'salaryman *senryū*' in contemporary newspapers in Japan to this day.

mitate Visual pun. A juxtaposition of two images seen with one's actual or mind's eye.

mono no aware See *aware*.

Mutamagawa (Six Crystalline Rivers). Aka *Haikai mutamagawa*. Important eighteen-volume collection of free-standing *haiku*, in both seventeen and fourteen **syllabets**, the former of which would come to be thought of as *senryū*. Although earlier than *Yanagidaru*, this collection did not have the same reach in its day. Its first fifteen volumes were published more or less annually from 1750 to 1761 by Kei Kiitsu (1694–1761), though after his death another three volumes were published sporadically from 1771 to 1775.

(Naniwa miyage) Chūshingura anasagashi yanagidaru (Willow Vat's Exposé of 'The Treasury of Loyal Retainers': Souvenirs from Naniwa; *c.* 1830–44). See pp. 206–9.

nun In Japan, a woman who lost her husband was expected to become a celibate secular 'house nun' (*gokeni*, often abbreviated to *goke*, 'widow'), as opposed to a more devout Buddhist 'nun' (*ama*), though either way her status was typically marked by the addition of the suffix *ni*, 'nun', to her name.

Oku no hosomichi (Narrow Road to the Interior, 1702). Partially fictionalized *haibun* travel account, widely regarded as the masterpiece of its genre, written and edited by **Bashō**, describing his trek of 1689 from **Edo** to Kyoto. Accompanied much of the way by his friend and disciple **Sora**, Bashō proceeded along just about the most circuitous route possible, through the deepest reaches (*oku*) of the northern mainland. In so doing, he retraced the footsteps of the great *waka* poet **Saigyō**. As though to recast himself as a latter-day Saigyō – and to elevate *haiku* itself from lowbrow entertainment to highbrow art – Bashō composed verse on the same celebrated poetic places (*utamakura*) Saigyō had visited and written about five hundred years earlier. The work contains many of Bashō's most highly acclaimed verses and prose as well as verses by many of his disciples and supporters. Bashō was still revising the work at the time of his death in 1694.

onji Syllabet. Technically speaking, an *onji* is more a set mora than a variable syllable. In English, syllables vary from light to heavy, whereas in Japanese *onji* weigh in more uniformly on the lighter side, a fact suggested by the term 'syllabet'. For more on this, see Note on the Translation, pp. lxxvii–lxxix.

onsūritsu Syllabet count. For a guide on counting Japanese syllabets, see Note on the Translation, pp. lxxvii–lxxix.

oriku Acrostic verse. In *haiku* verse capping (*maekuzuke*), this often took the form of a seventeen- or fourteen-**syllabet** response (*tsukeku*) in which the first syllabet of each line together constitute the first part of a challenge verse (*maeku*) or spell out the challenge word. For instance, one seventeen-syllabet acrostic response to the challenge word *ha-na-mi* (flower viewing) was *h̲ahaoya mo / n̲aburarete deru / m̲iai no hi*. And one fourteen-syllabet acrostic response to the challenge word *a-na* (butthole) was *a̲tama mo shiri mo / n̲arabu saotome*.

pivot See *kakekotoba*.

Pure Land *Jōdo*. The celestial or 'pure' realm of a buddha. Pure Land Buddhism, aka Amidism, maintaining that enlightenment can be attained by anyone merely by invoking the name of Amitābha Buddha (*Amida butsu* in Japanese), was introduced into Japan in 1175. For 'Pure Land Gate', see note to **Saimu**'s *yo no akete / hana ni hibiku ya / jōdomon*.

renga Linked verse. A form of sophisticated entertainment, customarily considered 'serious' (*ushin*) compared to both the earlier 'fatuous' (*mushin*) linked verse and the later witty linked verse (*haikai no renga*) owing to its intricate compositional rules (*shikimoku*), reliance on the diction of classical Japanese poetry (*waka*), highbrow aesthetics and elite status of practitioners. Although a form of short linked verse (*tan renga*) can be found in the earliest Japanese poetry collection, the **Man'yōshū**, the extended form flourished from the thirteenth century onwards – until *haikai no renga* increasingly stole its thunder, beginning in the sixteenth century with the publication of *Inu tsukubashū*.

response verse Aka 'response'. See *tsukeku*.

sabi Austere beauty of the forlorn. The almost objective, emotionless, understated, empathetic resignation to the radical solitude of everything in nature.

Sarumino (Monkey's Straw Raincape, 1691). Central text of the **Shōmon**, compiled and edited by **Bonchō** and **Kyorai**, with input from **Bashō**. Also contains verses by the woman poet **Chigetsu**. For an excerpt from *Sarumino*, 'Akuoke no no maki' (The Washbasin Sequence), see pp. 2–7.

senryū Overtly comic verse typically in seventeen **syllabet**s. Arguably the most popular mode of *haiku* historically.

Named for the comic verses associated with Karai **Senryū**, a point-scoring judge (*tenja*) of *haiku* verse-capping (*maekuzuke*) contests, the winning selections of which appeared in **Yanagidaru**. This was a ground-breaking collection of seventeen-**syllabet** witty responses (*tsukeku*) without their fourteen-syllabet challenges (*maeku*), that not only helped catapult *haiku* into the national spotlight but also was probably the first major collection of seventeen-syllabet *haiku* to be published as independent standalone verses.

Like the term **haiku** itself, *senryū* is a retrospective coinage of the late Meiji period (1868–1912). Previously, it had gone by a variety of names, particularly: (1) *tsukeku*, the response in verse capping; (2) *zareku*, 'frivolous verse', suggesting a direct connection to 'frivolous prose' (*gesaku*) (since the **graph** for *zare* can also be read as the *ge* in *gesaku*); and especially (3) *kyōku*, 'madcap verse', suggesting a direct connection to arts imbued with a Buddhist sense of the Absurd (*kyō*). Today, it is customary to differentiate between modern *senryū* and pre-twentieth-century 'old' (*kosenryū*) or '**Edo**-period' (*Edo senryū*) or even 'point-scoring' (*senryūten* or *senryūden*) *senryū*. For more on the development of *senryū*, see Introduction, pp. xlix–liii.

Senryūhyō mankuawase Aka **Mankuawase**. Meaning something like '10,000 Winning Verses Selected by Senryū', this was a huge foundational collection of fourteen-**syllabet** challenge verses (*maeku*) plus winning seventeen-syllabet response verses (*tsukeku*) selected by Karai **Senryū** from a series of his massive *haiku* verse-capping (*maekuzuke*) competitions, held and printed from 1757 to 1789, that would serve as the main source of the **senryū** collections **Yanagidaru** and **Suetsumuhana**. Although 10,000 (*man*) is usually a gross exaggeration, Senryū is believed to have judged millions of response verses in order to publish close to 100,000 in this collection.

Setsumon Literally '[Ran]setsu's Gate', this was the *haikai* school of **Ransetsu** in **Edo**, emphasizing both 'gentle and refined' (*onga*) style and 'subtle charm' (*jūmi*).

shasei Literally 'sketching from life'. Aesthetic of pictorial realism based on direct observation. Although often associated with **Bashō** and his followers, according to **Shiki** the best practitioner was **Buson**. Shiki emphasized this aesthetic as the key to composing modern **haiku**, no doubt because it jibed with the objective photorealism crucial to modernization and Westernization.

Shinto In Japanese, *Shintō*. Collective term referring to diverse pantheistic beliefs and practices indigenous to Japan. The first extant text in Japan, the **Kojiki**, laid out a Shinto world view, notably including stories about the sun goddess Amaterasu, the putative progenitor of

Japan's imperial line. For more on this episode, see note to **Baishi-tsu**'s *kaya tsureba / ka mo omoshiroshi / tsuki ni tobu*.

shōfū Literally '[Ba]shō Style', this was the mature style of **Bashō** and his followers, emphasizing *sabi*, *wabi* (connoting the beauty of imperfection), *tabi* (travel), *karumi*, *hosomi* and so on. For more on this, see **Shōmon**.

Shōmon Literally '[Ba]shō's Gate', aka the Shōmon School. The school of *haiku* most closely associated with the first of the Four Grandmasters of Haiku, Matsuo **Bashō**, that today has come to be virtually if misleadingly synonymous with modern **haiku** itself. An oft-used homonym, no doubt *not* coincidentally, means 'Correct School'. Major collection is widely considered to be *Sarumino*, compiled and edited by **Bonchō** and **Kyorai** under the guidance of Bashō himself. Many of Bashō's most highly acclaimed verses and prose also appear in his *haibun* travel account *Oku no hosomichi*, which he was still revising at the time of his death in 1694.

Succession disputes among his Ten Disciples (*Shōmon jittetsu*) led to factionalization into two major camps: (1) the Urban Shōmon, under **Ransetsu** and **Kikaku** (with his **Edoza**), flourishing in the major metropolises of **Edo**, Kyoto and Osaka and emphasizing a taste for novelty, intellectual cleverness and sophisticated wit that critics found obscure if not cryptic; and (2) the Rural Shōmon, rooted particularly in Ise and Mino provinces respectively under **Otsuyū** and **Shikō**, that by simplifying compositional rules and aesthetics spread throughout the countryside. In spite of this popular appeal, since the **Danrin** and even *maekuzuke* (verse-capping competitions) proved more popular, the clout if not stylistic influence of the Shōmon as a whole waned, at least until **Buson**, **Chora** and others in 1766 helped launch the so-called **Bashō Revival** (*Shōfū kaiki*). **Shiki** suggested that, although the revival extended beyond Buson's death in 1783, had it not been for Buson, *haiku* might never have become firmly equated with Bashō by the end of the eighteenth century as it did.

Shōmon jittetsu Bashō's so-called 'Ten Disciples': Takarai **Kikaku** (aka Enomoto Kikaku, 1661–1707), the principal disciple; Hattori **Ransetsu** (1654–1707); Mukai **Kyorai** (1651–1704); Morikawa **Kyoriku** (1656–1715); Kagami **Shikō** (1665–1731); Naitō **Jōsō** (1662–1704); Ochi **Etsujin** (1656–1739); Shida **Yaba** (1662–1740); Sugiyama **Sanpū** (1647–1732); and Kawai **Sora** (1649–1710). Others sometimes mentioned include Sugiyama Sanputsu (1647–1732), Tachibana **Hokushi** (1665–1718), Hattori Tohō (1657–1730) and Amano Tōrin (1639–1719). Conspicuously does not include several important women, such as Ogawa **Shūshiki** (1669–1725), Shiba

Sonome (1664–1726), Kawai **Chigetsu** (1633–1718) and Kaga no **Chiyo** (1703–75).

shunga Literally 'spring pictures', a modern euphemism applied retro-spectively to pornography, erotica and any other 'libidinous representation' (as Timon Screech has memorably called it, thereby allowing for consideration of genres like the *tagasode* – literally 'whose sleeves?' – meant to excite sexual fantasies by depicting garments rather than flesh; see Screech, *Sex and the Floating World: Erotic Images in Japan 1700–1820* (London: Reaktion Books, 1999)). Contemporary terms included *makurae* (pillow pictures) and *waraie* (giggle pictures). Albums of these images (*shunpon*, 'spring books', in modern Japanese), aside from *makurabon* (pillow books) and *waraibon* (or *shōhon*, 'giggle books'), include *ehon* ('voluptuous books', though written with a different **graph** for *e* than 'picture' in the more common term *ehon*, 'picture book'). **Bareku** were sometimes collected in or composed for such books, as with **Beni no hana** and **Yuki no hana**. Significantly, many if not most of the major artists of **ukiyoe** during the **Edo** period (1600–1868) produced woodblock-printed *shunga* and *shunpon*.

Suetsumuhana *(Haifū) Suetsumuhana* (Safflower Princess, Witty Linked-Verse Style). Collection of *senryū* in four volumes, published in 1776, 1783, 1791 and 1801, containing almost 2,500 dirty sexy *haiku* (*bareku*). (Shimoyama reckons that approximately 2,431 *bareku* appear in the four volumes. See Shimoyama Hiroshi, *Senryū no erotishizumu* (Shinchōsha, 1995), p. 50.)

syllabet See Note on the Translation, pp. lxxvii–lxxix.

tanka 'Short poem' of thirty-one **syllabets** (not to be confused with the fourteen-syllabet *tanku*). Often referred to as *waka* for the way it epitomized Japanese poetry for a millennium, dominating poetic activity during the classic and medieval periods (*c.* 550–1600) if not the **Edo** period (1600–1868), and continuing to be written to this day. Frequently said to consist of a *haiku*-like upper hemistich of seventeen syllabets (in 5-7-5) followed by a lower hemistich of fourteen syllabets (in 7-7).

tanku 'Short verse' of fourteen **syllabets** (not to be confused with the 31-syllabet *tanka*). Appeared primarily in linked verse (*haikai* or *renga*), where it alternated with seventeen-syllabet verses, or in *haiku* verse capping (*maekuzuke*) as a challenge verse (*maeku*). *Mutamagawa* contains a significant number of *senryū* in *tanku* form. Perhaps it is because of its reputation as merely a challenge verse setting up a response that the *tanku* as a form of *haiku* is almost completely obscured by its seventeen-syllabet brethren, which may well be the shortest major verseform in the world today even though in pre-twentieth-century Japan the *tanku* was shorter and hardly scarce. For examples, see the translations, especially 'The Washbasin Sequence' from *Saru-mino* on pp. 2–7.

tanzaku Narrow strip of stiffened, often elegantly patterned, paper upon which verse is written. *Tanzaku* are visible in various stages of completion in several images included in this volume: **Sonome** (p. lv), **Chiyo** (p. 110) and **Kigin** (p. 148).

Tao Literally 'the way' (*dao* in Chinese, *dō* in Japanese), known in English as the Tao or Taoism (aka the Dao or Daoism). Originally a Chinese system of moral thought stressing simple living in harmony with universal nature, based mainly on the collected writings of Laozi (*fl.* sixth century BCE) – especially the *Dao de jing* (aka *Tao te ching*, *c.* late fourth century BCE) – and Zhuangzi (aka Chuang Tzu, *fl. c.* fourth century BCE), that became widely known in Japan during the **Edo** period (1600–1868). Its influence is evident in the poetics and poetry of **Danrin** as well as **Shōmon** poets in particular. (For more on this, see Peipei Qiu, *Bashō and the Dao: The Zhuangzi and the Transformation of Haikai* (Honolulu: University of Hawai'i Press, 2005).) Allusions to Taoist parables, as with the ones about Zhuangzi's dream of the butterfly (see **Chiyo**'s *tanpopo ya / oriori samasu / chō no yume*) or the frog in a well (see **Issa**'s *utsukushi ya / shōji no ana no/ amanogawa*), abound in popular literature such as *haiku*.

Teimon Literally 'Tei[toku]'s Gate'. Earliest major school of *haiku*, most closely associated with **Teitoku** and his followers. Often derided as formalistic and overly bookish, depending on detailed knowledge of the compositional rules of *renga* (linked verse) and mixing obscure references to Chinese and Japanese classics with an understated brand of wit (which **Bashō** characterized as drivel). Also to be credited with loosening the iron grip of classic diction by increasingly admitting colloquialisms and wordplay. Those involved with this school at one time or another include **Shigeyori**, **Saimu**, **Teishitsu**, **Kigin**, **Sute-jo** and **Fukaku**. Although *Enokoshū*, containing many of Teitoku's works, is often hailed as the major repository of Teimon *haiku*, the school would publish more than two hundred collections over the next two centuries.

tenja Referee. Usually an acclaimed poet who agreed to provide commentary on student work for a fee. See also *maekuzuke*.

tsukeai Linking. The artful connection between one stanza and another. Essential to *renga*, *haikai*, *maekuzuke* and so on – though not to modern **haiku**.

tsukeku Response verse. The second verse in any pair of linked verses.

tsukinami Monthly gathering. Commonly associated with ***haiku*** verse capping (***maekuzuke***).

ugachi Exposé. Literally 'digging', as in the phrase *ana o ugachi* (loophole uncovering). See ***ana***.

ukiyo Floating world. The evanescent and therefore scintillating spaces of urban popular culture, particularly kabuki and puppet theatres, pleasure quarters and street spectacles. Punning on the earlier 'fleeting world', conveying Buddhist impermanence, 'floating world' implies that precisely because life is short one should buoyantly pursue transient pleasures. For more on the floating world, especially that of **Edo**, see Introduction, p. xliv.

ukiyoe Literally 'images of the floating world', typically, though not always, woodblock-printed.

ukiyozōshi Novella depicting the floating world. Closely associated with **Saikaku**.

waka Literally 'Japanese poetry', referring to various forms of Japanese (rather than Chinese) poems, but specifically denoting ***tanka***. For more on *waka*, see Chronology.

Waka midori (Young Greens, 1691), edited by **Fukaku**. First work to regularly use a 'repeating challenge' or ***jōgo***.

wakiku Literally 'flanking stanza', the second stanza in a linked verse sequence, be it ***renga*** or ***haikai***. Typically fourteen **syllabet**s and offered by the host of the verse-composing session in response to the ***hokku*** (the initiating stanza presented by the guest of honour) and continuing its season.

Yanagidaru (Willow Vat, 1765–1840). First major collection of what later would come to be called ***senryū***. Published by Hanaya Kyūjirō of Seiundō Publishing in **Edo** in 167 volumes (*satsu*), beginning in 1765, continuing annually from 1767 to 1805, then sporadically until the final volume in 1840. Although **Senryū** judged the verses included in the first twenty-four volumes (1765–91), he neither wrote nor directly collected them. Rather, the main editor was one Goryōken Arubeshi (a pen name meaning something like 'Apologies for the Vetting!'), though others also contributed. See also the Introduction, p. l.

The full title, (*Haifū*) *Yanagidaru* (Willow Vat, Witty Linked-Verse Style), contains nuanced wordplay: the **graph** 'willow', though read *yanagi* in Japanese, by virtue of its Sinified reading *sen*, connotes Karai *Sen*ryū; *daru* refers to a vat or cask (*taru*) of saké, particularly for celebratory occasions, and suggests a homonym of Karai (literally 'base of a well'), meaning 'dry' or 'pungent' in humour as well as flavour. Fully unpacked, the title suggests something like: 'A riverwillow-wood vat of dry saké, full of pungent verses, witty linked-verse style, judged by Karai Senryū'.

Yanagidaru shūi (Further Gleanings from the Willow Vat, 1796–7). An anonymously published twenty-volume collection of what would come to be called *senryū* gleaned from the verse contests held by Karai **Senryū**.

Yanagi no hazue (Willowtip Leaves, 1835). Collection of dirty sexy *haiku* (*bareku*) written at several verse-composing parties (*kuawase*), then selected by Senryū IV (aka Hitomi Shūsuke, 1778–1844). Contains approximately 600–700 verses (though a precise number is hard to determine since the multiple editors did not realize that about seventy-five duplicate verses were included). The title, a portmanteau playing on *yanagi* (willow) and *sue* (extremity), calls to mind both **Yanagidaru** (Willow Vat) and **Suetsumuhana** (Safflower Princess). As Shūsuke explains in his preface, whereas the leaves (an age-old metaphor for poems) at the tip of most trees are admirably lofty, in the case of a willow they trail disgracefully in the muck.

yūgen Profound, mysterious, spiritual beauty.

Yuki no hana See **Beni no hana**.

za Coterie or clique. In linked verse, this was the physical location (*za* literally means 'seat') of a poetic circle as well as that circle itself.

zappai Miscellaneous seasonless verse (*zatsu no ku*), specifically in *haikai*. One work consisting entirely of *zappai* is **Senryū**'s five-volume compilation *Kawazoi yanagi* (Riverbank Willow, 1780). For one of the verses from this work, see *tsuki ochi / karasu naite nyōbo / hara o tate*.

zatsu no ku Miscellaneous verse. Typically one or more seasonless verses within a linked-verse sequence, be it *renga* or *haikai* (where it is typically called *zappai*), that functions as a **pivot** between the previous stretch of verses with a specified season to the following stretch with another specified season. See also *kigo*.

Zen Chan in Chinese. Influential Mahayana Buddhist sect originating in China (where it was influenced by Taoism – see **Tao**) and emphasizing the attainment of spiritual enlightenment through direct experience cultivated by such things as seated meditation (*zazen*) and the contemplation of philosophical conundrums (*kōan*) designed to reveal the inadequacy of language in the face of actual experience.

Glossary of Poets

Japanese poets are listed by their pen name, usually their personal name, which in the Japanese order follows the family name. In the annotations to the translations, the dates of poets whose names are not included below are unknown. Within the glossary entries below, names and terms highlighted in bold constitute a cross-reference either to this glossary or to the Glossary of Terms. See Index of Japanese Verses for verses quoted here that are included in the Commentary.

Aryū The playwright Namiki Ryōsuke (*fl.* mid to late eighteenth century).

Atsujin Endō Atsujin (1758–1836), aka Watsujin.

Baisei Takase Baisei (1611–99). **Teimon** poet.

Baishitsu Sakurai Baishitsu (1769–1852). One of the *haiku* masters of the Tenpō era (1830–44) whom **Shiki** derided as pedestrian 'monthly meeting' (*tsukinami*) poets.

Banan Yoshiwake Tairo (d. 1778).

Bashō Matsuo Bashō (1644–94), aka Matsuo Kinsaku, Matsuo Chūemon Munefusa, Tōsei, etc., among others. (See image on p. xlii.) Assumed the pen name Bashō (also written, in the historical orthography, Baseo or even Haseo), a kind of leafy plantain or so-called 'Traveller's Palm' (*Musa basjoo*), in 1680 after a house-warming present for his new thatch-roofed retreat in Fukagawa on the outskirts of **Edo** (see *iku shimo ni / kokorobase o no / matsu kazari*). Widely acclaimed first and arguably the greatest of the Four Grandmasters of Haiku, having composed the verse supposedly epitomizing the form (see *furuike ya / kawazu tobikomu / mizu no oto*). However, Bashō always considered himself a practioner of *haikai no renga* (witty linked verse), abbreviated as *haiku*. Also head of the school bearing his name. Customarily credited with having elevated *haiku* from mere entertainment to high art. See also **Bashō Revival** and **Shōmon**. For more on his place in the history of *haiku*, see Introduction.

Bishi Active in the Meiji period (1868–1912).

Bokusui Umezawa Bokusui (1875–1914).

Bonchō Nozawa Bonchō (*c.*1640–1714). Important poet in the **Bashō** School (**Shōmon**) of *haikai*. Hailed from Kanazawa but moved to Kyoto where he worked as a physician. Along with **Kyorai** compiled *Sarumino*, a central text of the school. Contributed more verses to this collection than any other poet and, though unusually close to Bashō, his headstrong attitude eventually led to a falling out between the two men. Even supposedly jailed briefly at one point in connection to a criminal investigation.

Bunson Matsui Bunson (d. *c.*1712).

Buson Yosa (no) Buson (1716–84), aka Yoza (no) Buson, Taniguchi Buson and Yahantei Buson. One of the Four Grandmasters of Haiku. Enthusiastic leader of the **Bashō Revival** (*Shōfū kaiki*) if reluctant successor of the Yahantei School of *haiku* a quarter of a century after the death of its founder and his master, **Kikaku** student **Hajin**. Leader of the Sankasha *haikai* coterie that included **Taigi** and others. Professional literati painter and, after resettling in Kyoto, *haikai* master. His present reputation as one of the greatest *haiga* artists deeply influences his reception as a painterly poet – though he also excelled at what might be considered *haiku* sound poetry.

Chigetsu The woman poet Kawai Chigetsu (1633–1718), aka Chigetsu-ni (the **nun** Chigetsu). (See image on p. 111.) **Shōmon** poet, direct disciple of, and reputedly close to, **Bashō** himself. *Sarumino* includes several of her verses.

Chiun (d. 1448), aka Ninagawa Shin'emon Chikamasa.

Chiyo The woman poet Kaga no Chiyo (1703–75), aka Fukuda Chiyo-ni, Kagakuni Mattō no Chiyo, Chiyoni (the **nun** Chiyo) and Chiyo-jo (the woman Chiyo). (See image on p. 110.) Widely renowned as the greatest female master of *haiku*. Heavily influenced by **Bashō**'s renegade disciple and central figure of the Mino faction of the Rural **Shōmon**, **Shikō**. **Kyoshi** recounted in his widely influential essay on the nature of modern **haiku** ('Haiku to wa donna mono ka') how the earliest verse he learned was one by Chiyoni.

Chora Miura Chora (1729–80). *Haikai* poet. Involved in the **Bashō Revival**.

Dohō Hattori Dohō (1657–1730), aka Hattori Tohō. Wrote *Sanzōshi* (1702), which along with Kyorai's *Kyoraishō* (Kyorai's Gleanings, 1704), is one of two major works articulating Bashō's ideas on poetics. (For both works, see *NKBZ* 51.)

Etsujin Ochi Etsujin (1656–1739). One of **Bashō**'s Ten Disciples (*Shōmon jittetsu*).

Fugyoku Itō Fugyoku (1648–97). Along with **Shikō**, he produced *Kuzu no matsubara*.

Fuhaku Kawakami Fuhaku (1714–1807). Tea master in the Omotesenke lineage (and founder of the Edosenke School) who also composed *haiku*.

Fukaku Tachiba Fukaku (1662–1753). (See image on p. xlix.) Influential **Edo**-based *haikai* poet and **Teimon** judge (*tenja*) whose compilations helped popularize *haiku* verse capping (*maekuzuke*) – and thus *haiku* itself – throughout the major urban centres and beyond. Apart from the influential *Futaba no matsu* and *Waka midori*, his other compilations include *Chiyomigusa* (1692), *Ichiiki* (1693), *Niiki* (1693), *Herazuguchi* (1694), *Hirutsubute* (1695), *Futagoyama zenshū* (1697) and *Watatsumi* (1703).

Gansui Active *c.*1791.

Gomei Kikkawa Gomei (1731–1803).

Gonsui Ikenishi Gonsui (1650–1722).

Goshun (1752–1811), aka Gekkei.

Gyōdai Katō Gyōdai (1732–92). High-ranking samurai from Nagoya who became an important **Shōmon** poet.

Gyokutorō Takashima Gyokutorō (1887–1953).

Hajin Hayano Hajin (1676–1742), aka Yahantei Sōa. Disciple of **Kikaku** and master of **Buson**.

Hanasanjin Hosokawa Yōjirō (1790–1858), aka Tōrisanjin and Bisanjin. Renowned author of comic literature (*gesaku*). His pen name literally meaning 'Nosy Wanderer', Hanasanjin often signed his verse with a 'peony nose' mark ◌.

Hanmonsen Probably the poet Kimura Hanmonsen (1889–1953).

Haritsu Ogawa Haritsu (1663–1747), né Naoyuki. Lacquerware artist and painter.

Hashin Kajiwara Hashin (b. 1864).

Hokusai Katsushika Hokusai (1760–1849), celebrated *ukiyoe* artist, *haiku* poet under the pen name Manji and father of the woman poet **Oei**.

Hokushi Tachibana Hokushi (1665–1718). Often included as one of **Bashō**'s Ten Disciples (*Shōmon jittetsu*).

Ichū Okanishi Ichū (1639–1711), aka Ichijiken. A leading poet of the **Danrin** and disciple of **Sōin**.

Issa Kobayashi Issa (1763–1827). Third of the Four Grandmasters of Haiku. Widely acclaimed as one of Japan's most beloved poets. The majority of his verses appear within his prose diaries, as with *Oraga*

haru (Spring of My Life, 1819). For an example, see *tsuyu no yo wa /*
tsuyu no yo nagara / sari nagara. For more on Issa, see Introduction,
p. liii.

Jōsō Naitō Jōsō (1662–1704). One of **Bashō's** Ten Disciples (*Shōmon*
jittetsu). Former samurai who turned to *haiku* and **Zen**.

Jūkō Dates unknown, but verse included here dates from 1786.

Kenkabō Inoue Kenkabō (1870–1934).

Kensai Inawashiro Kensai (1452–1510).

Kigin Kitamura Kigin (1624–1705). (See image on p. 148.) Leading
poet of the **Teimon**. His conviction that classical literature should be
made accessible to everyone no doubt influenced his most famous
disciple, **Bashō**.

Kikaku Takarai Kikaku (1661–1707), aka Enomoto Kikaku. (See im-
age on p. 101.) One of **Bashō's** Ten Disciples (*Shōmon jittetsu*) and
author of *An Account of the Last Days of Our Master Bashō*. (For a trans-
lation, see Nobuyuki Yuasa, *Springtime in Edo: A Kasen to Commem-*
orate the 300th Anniversary of Kikaku's Death (Hiroshima: Keisuisha,
2006).) After Bashō's death, Kikaku developed his own 'flashy style'
(*sharefū*), drawing inspiration particularly from **Shikō** and **Yaba** (see
SNKBT 72, p. 476). This would become the mainstay of **Edoza** *hai-*
ku that, in its more exuberant iterations, was damned as heretical
(*jadō*) and resulted in its exclusion from many *haiku* dictionaries and
genealogies. Kikaku and Edoza *haiku* may be regarded as spiritual
forebears of *senryū* and perhaps even *bareku*. See also *dokugin*.

Kikusha The **nun** Tagami Kikusha (1752–1826).

Kinbō Yano Kinbō (1894–1936).

Kisenjo The woman poet Ōuchi Yoshitakejo (*fl. c.* Meiji period, 1868–
1912). Not to be confused with Ōuchi Jukō (1537–1551), daughter
of the warlord Ōuchi Yoshitaka (1507–51).

Kitō Takai Kitō (1741–89). Major disciple of **Buson** and articulator of
Buson's school of poetics.

Kōbai Asakusa Kōbai (known to be active 1775–86).

Koyū The **nun** Matsumoto Koyū (*fl. c.* eighteenth century).

Kyōdai Kumura Kyōdai (1732–93).

Kyokusui Suganuma Kyokusui (1660–1717).

Kyōma Verse included here dates from 1773.

Kyorai Mukai Kyorai (1651–1704). One of **Bashō's** Ten Disciples
(*Shōmon jittetsu*). Along with **Bonchō** co-edited *Sarumino*, a cen-
tral text of the **Shōmon**. Along with Hattori **Dohō's** *Sanzōshi* (1702),
his *Kyoraishō* (Kyorai's Gleanings, 1704) is one of two major texts
articulating Bashō's ideas on poetics, including such things as cutting
words (*kireji*) and seasonal associations (*kidai*). (For both works, see

NKBZ 51.) Along with his sister Chine co-wrote the poetic travel account *Ise kikō* (A Journey to Ise, 1686).

Kyoriku Morikawa Kyoriku (1656–1715), aka Gorōsei Kyoriku. One of Bashō's Ten Disciples (*Shōmon jittetsu*). His inkwash of a lone crow on a branch, with calligraphy by Bashō himself, is a well-known *haiga* illustrating the verse *kareeda ni / karasu no tomarikeri / aki no kure* (see pp. 150–51 and 330–31). Bashō praised Kyoriku's verses. **Buson** marvelled that some were beyond his own comprehension.

Kyoshi Takahama Kyoshi (1874–1959). Influential modern poet and major articulator of the 'Grand Narrative of Haiku'. Favoured disciple of Masaoka **Shiki** who declined to succeed his master until years after Shiki's death. For more on Kyoshi, see Introduction, pp. xxx–xxxi.

Mantarō Kubota Mantarō (1889–1963).

Masahide Mizuta Masahide (1657–1723), aka Seishū.

Meimei (d. 1824).

Meitei Tsukakoshi Meitei (1894–1965).

Meisetsu Naitō Meisetsu (1847–1926).

Mōichi Sugiki Mōichi (1586–1643), aka Moichi. Visually impaired poet from a family of Shinto priests tending to the Grand Shrines at Ise, where he was one of the leaders of the *haikai* establishment. Emulated the *haiku* style of **Moritake**.

Moritake Arakida Moritake (1472–1549). (See image on p. 155.) One of the pioneers of *haikai no renga*. Along with **Sōkan** jointly compiled and edited *Inu tsukubashū*.

Muchō Ueda Akinari (1734–1809). One of the key literary figures of the period, best known for his adaptations of Chinese supernatural tales as well as nativist scholarship, including an important study of cutting words or *kireji* (*Ya kana shō*, 1774).

Nangai Tanaka Nangai (*fl. c.* mid nineteenth century).

Narihira See *Ise monogatari* (*c.* 880–950) in the Chronology.

Oei The woman poet Katsushika Oei (1793–1859), aka Wei and Ōi. Best known as the third daughter of woodblock artist **Hokusai** and (thanks to the animated movie *Miss Hokusai*, 2015) as an artist in her own right. Yet Oei also composed verse. After her marriage failed, she moved back home at the age of thirty. Hokusai, who himself wrote *senryū* under the pen name Manji, brought her along with him to poetry gatherings (see Taira Sōsei (ed.), *Ryōran josei senryū: Meiji irai hyakunen o utai tsugu 48-nin no chisei to jōnen no sekai* (Midori shobō, 1997), pp. 14–15). Verses by father and daughter alike appear in *Yanagidaru*, especially volume 85 (1825), though several dirty sexy *haiku* (*bareku*) of hers alone appear in volume 104 (1828).

Ōemaru Ōtomo Ōemaru (1722–1805). Disciple of **Ryōta**.

Onitsura Uejima Onitsura (1660–1738), aka Kamijima Onitsura and Itami Onitsura (since he was born to a family of saké merchants in Itami, present-day Hyōgo Prefecture). (See image on p. 58.) Arguably the greatest *haiku* grandmaster of whom most people have never heard. Studying in the **Danrin** early on, Onitsura came to condemn its humour, in his treatise *Hitorigoto* (Soliloquy, 1718), as formulaic and 'frivolous'. Helped elevate *haiku* to the status of a true art form, through both his influential concept of *makoto* (poetic authenticity) and his poetry – though **Bashō** customarily gets the credit. For more on Onitsura, see Introduction, pp. xlv–xlvi.

Otsuyū Nakagawa Otsuyū (1675–1739).

Raizan Konishi Raizan (1654–1716). (See image on p. 146.) Studied under **Sōin** and was active in Osaka as a point-scoring judge (*tenja*) of miscellaneous verse (*zappai*).

Rankō Takakuwa Rankō (1726–*c*.1798).

Ransetsu Hattori Ransetsu (1654–1707). One of **Bashō**'s Ten Disciples (*Shōmon jittetsu*) and head of the **Setsumon** (literally '[Ran]setsu's Gate') in **Edo**, emphasizing both 'gentle and refined' (*onga*) style and 'subtle charm' (*jiimi*). Notably, Bashō admired Ransetsu his poetic austerity. **Buson** once advised that to master *haikai* one must 'Seek **Kikaku**, visit Ransetsu, recite **Sodō** and escort **Onitsura**'. However, Ransetsu may have been too austere – **Kyoriku** denounced him as someone who having invited guests for a banquet would serve only menus. After his first wife, a bathhouse prostitute, died in childbirth, Ransetsu married a geisha or courtesan before eventually turning to **Zen**.

Rekisen (b. 1748). Poet of *senryū* and one of the few known judges of *oriku* (acrostic) verse.

Ritō Sakurai Ritō (1680–1754).

Rohan Kōda Rohan (1867–1947).

Rōsen Taniguchi Rōsen (1699–1783).

Roten Naitō Roten (1655–1733).

Ryōkan Ryōkan Taigu (i.e. 'Ryōkan the Great Fool', 1758–1831). Sōtō **Zen** Buddhist monk who wrote *haiku*.

Ryōta Ōshima Ryōta (1718–87). **Ransetsu** disciple and influential **Shōmon** poet whose writings included an early study (1743) of Bashō's *Oku no hosomichi*.

Ryūho Nonoguchi Ryūho (1595–1669), aka Hina'ya Ryūho. Along with **Shigeyori** compiled the first major *haikai* work, *Enokoshū*. Supposedly a student of the great painter Kanō Tan'yū (1602–74), Ryūho is also renowned as an early *haiga* master.

Saigin Mizuta Saigin (d. 1709), aka Rakugetsuan. **Danrin** poet who studied under **Sōin** and **Saikaku**.

Saigyō Satō Norikiyo (1118–90). Priest and major *tanka* poet whose poetic travels and emphasis on the aesthetics of such things as *sabi* and *mono no aware* inspired **Bashō** five hundred years later.

Saikaku Ihara Saikaku (1642–93), aka Naniwa Saikaku. (See image on p. 65.) One of Japan's greatest humorists, both as a leader of the **Danrin** and also as a vastly popular author of floating-world novellas (*ukiyozōshi*). According to Howard Hibbett: 'His witty portrayal of his sharply observed world has earned him an uncontested place in history as Japan's first and greatest comic novelist' (see Hibbett, *The Chrysanthemum and the Fish: Japanese Humor Since the Age of the Shoguns* (Tokyo, London and New York: Kodansha International, 2002), p. 47). Nicknamed 'Dutch' (Oranda) Saikaku, to humorously emphasize the outlandishness of his brand of *haiku* after **Teimon** partisan Nakajima Zuiryū had condemned the **Danrin** as 'Red-Haired' Christians. In the twentieth century, when there was a resurgence of interest in Saikaku, his poetry sometimes drew comparisons with the puzzling non sequiturs of Dadaism.

Saimaro Shiimoto Saimaro (1656–1738).

Saimu Yamamoto Saimu (1606–78). Edited one of the major **Teimon** collections.

Sakijo The woman poet Sakijo (*c.* late eighteenth century or early nineteenth century). Reputedly a geisha of Gion in Kyoto.

Sanpū Sugiyama Sanpū (1647–1732). One of **Bashō**'s Ten Disciples (*Shōmon jittetsu*), he was supposedly deaf.

Seibi Natsume Seibi (1749–1816).

Seifu The **nun** Enomoto Seifu (1732–1815).

Seira (1740–91).

Senryū Karai Senryū (1718–90), aka Karai Hachiemon. (See image on p. l.) Profoundly influential point-scoring judge (*tenja*) of *haiku* verse-capping (*maekuzuke*) contests, some of them drawing over one hundred thousand participants, and major popularizer of the overtly comic *haiku* that would come to be named after him. Along with **Fukaku**, he helped popularize *haikai* as well as *haiku* verse capping. Verses he selected and published in *Yanagidaru* and other collections eventually gave rise to the modern term *senryū*.

Shigeyori Matsue Shigeyori (1602–80), aka Ishū. Influential *haikai* poet. Originally active in the **Teimon**, compiling the *Enokoshū* with **Ryūho**, but going his own way after the two men had a falling out. Disciples include both **Sōin**, who went on to play the leading role in the **Danrin**, and the great poet **Onitsura**, whose concept of poetic authenticity (*makoto*) no doubt owes much to Shigeyori's motto of 'witty linked verse from the heart' (*kokoro no haikai*).

Shiki Masaoka Shiki (1867–1902), aka Masaoka Noboru. Last of the Four Grandmasters of Haiku. One of Japan's greatest poetic modernizers, launching the Haiku Reform (*haiku kakushin*) and thereby mostly responsible for the invented tradition of **haiku**. In a rhetorical ploy to locate a basis for modern Western-style individualism within the Japanese poetic past, he appropriated the term *haiku* – hitherto an abbreviation of *haikai no (renga no) ku* (witty linked verse) – and retooled it as the haiku in the modern sense of a standalone poem. A fan of baseball and persimmons, Shiki died at the age of thirty-five after a slow painful decline from tuberculosis. For more on Shiki, see Introduction, p. xxv–xxix.

Shikō Kagami Shikō (1665–1731). (See image on p. 166.) Influential *haiku* poet if arguably the most controversial among **Bashō**'s Ten Disciples (*Shōmon jittetsu*). Founded the Mino branch of the Rural **Shōmon** and mentored Kaga no **Chiyo**. Became wildly popular championing the aesthetic of *karumi* (lightness) that Bashō had been developing in his final years. Perhaps jealous of this success, Shikō's detractors accused him of a self-serving departure from his master's 'true' teachings. Along with **Fugyoku** produced *Kuzu no matsubara*.

Shirao Kaya Shirao (1738–91). *Haiku* poet also involved in the **Bashō** Revival (*Shōfū kaiki*).

Shirō Inoue Shirō (1742–1812). Medical doctor and famous *haiku* poet from Nagoya.

Shōha Kuroyanagi Shōha (1727–71), aka Shundei.

Shōi Tashiro Shōi (*fl. c.* late seventeenth century). Leader of the **Danrin** in **Edo**.

Shokyū The woman poet Arii Shokyū (1714–81), aka Shokyūni (the nun Shokyū), Nagamatsu Nami and Namijo. Wrote *Akikaze no ki* (Autumn Wind Collection, 1771) commemorating her walk in **Bashō**'s footsteps.

Shōkyū (d. 1552).

Shuchin Known to be active 1811–35.

Shunkō Kubota Shunkō (1772–1850). Husband of the better-known poet Kubota Seifu and supporter of **Issa**.

Shūshiki The woman poet Ogawa Shūshiki (1669–1725). *Haiku* poet of **Edo** known for urbane witty verses.

Sōchō Saiokuken Sōchō (1448–1532). Disciple of **Sōgi** and important *renga* poet.

Sodō Yamaguchi Sodō (1642–1716). *Haiku* poet from Kai who studied the Chinese classics under prominent scholar Hayashi Shunsai (son of the even more prominent scholar Hayashi Razan). Friends with **Bashō** and instrumental in establishing an offshoot of the **Shōmon** known as the Katsushika Branch.

Sōgi Iio Sōgi (1421–1502). (See image on p. 62.) Widely considered to be one of the greatest poets of *renga*. Helped infuse an aesthetics of *yūgen* (profound beauty) that elevated *renga* above its status as mere entertainment – thereby setting the example for **Onitsura**, **Bashō** and others who would do much the same for *haikai no renga*. Although there had been a recognition as far back perhaps as the twelfth century that the *hokku* (initiating stanza) was a special kind of verse within a sequence, by imbuing the *hokku* with a certain gravitas Sōgi was among the first to recognize its potential as a standalone verse, thereby paving the way for the modern **haiku**.

Sōin Nishiyama Sōin (1605–82), aka Baiō (Old Man Plum). (See image on p. 38.) Having studied *renga* under **Moritake**, went on to found the **Danrin**. **Bashō** famously credited Sōin with having elevated *haiku* above the supposed 'drivel' of **Teimon** verse.

Sōjō Hino Sōjō (1901–56).

Sōkan Yamazaki Sōkan (1465–1553), né Shina Norishige. (See image on p. 118.) One of the key pioneers of *haikai no renga*. Along with **Moritake** jointly compiled and edited *Inu tsukubashū*, the first major collection of *haikai* (though there were earlier collections, such as *Chikuba kyōginshū*, 1499 – see Chronology). The humour of his verses (as with *waga oya no / shinuru toki ni mo / he o kokite*) was immensely influential, not only inspiring the development of **Danrin** *haikai* (that would emerge fully in the early seventeenth century), but also no doubt contributing to the development of the *senryū* as its own mode within *haikai*.

Sonome The woman poet Shiba Sonome (1664–1726), aka Sonojo. (See image on p. lv.) **Shōmon** poet. One of the first women to work professionally as a *haiku* master (*sōshō*).

Sora Kawai Sora (1649–1710). One of **Bashō**'s Ten Disciples (*Shōmon jittetsu*). Wrote *Sora tabi nikki* (Sora's Travel Diary), about the famed journey he and Bashō took mostly together in 1689 that formed the basis for the latter's *haibun* masterpiece *Oku no hosomichi*. The sometimes drastic discrepancies between the two works, which only came to light after *Sora tabi nikki* was rediscovered in 1943, suggest that Bashō took poetic licence, thereby casting doubt on the putative factuality of parts of *Oku no hosomichi* itself.

Sōseki Gessonsai Sōseki (1474–1533). *Renga* master. Disciple of **Sōgi**.

Sōseki Natsume Sōseki (1867–1916). One of the greatest modern Japanese writers and literary reformers, Professor of English Literature at Tokyo Imperial University (now University of Tokyo) and close friend of **Shiki**. Not to be confused with the *renga* poet Gessonsai **Sōseki** (1474–1533) or the **Zen** master Musō Soseki (1275–1351).

Sōzei Takayama Sōzei (d. 1455).

Suiujo The woman poet Miwa Suiujo (1766–1846).

Sutejo The woman poet Den Sutejo (1633–98). (See image on p. 61.) Prominent **Teimon** poet.

Taigi Tan Taigi (1709–71). Point-scoring judge (*tenja*) and vastly popular poet in his own day, perhaps just as much as **Buson**, with whom he was close. Infamously set up shop within a pleasure-quarter establishment and was involved with the Urban **Edo** School (**Edoza**) of *haiku*.

Takuchi Tsuruda Takuchi (1768–1846).

Tantan Matsuki Tantan (1674–1761). Important *haiku* poet. Helped spread **Kikaku**-style point-scoring to western Japan.

Tatsujo A woman poet (*fl. c.* seventeenth century).

Tatsuko Hoshino Tatsuko (1903–84).

Tayojo The woman poet Ichihara Tayojo (1776–1865).

Teishitsu Yasuhara Teishitsu (1610–1713), aka Masaakira. Successor to **Teitoku** in the **Teimon**, whose detractors criticized its frivolity and artfulness.

Teitoku Matsunaga Teitoku (1571–1653). (See image on p. 184.) One of the spiritual granddaddies if not fathers of *haikai*, helping to elevate it from mere pastime to literary art. In spite of classical training in *waka* under the likes of Hosokawa Yūsai (1534–1610), Teitoku dabbled in *haikai* and was heavily represented in the important *Enokoshū*. Although the **Teimon** is named after him, he was not its leader per se.

Tessen A woman poet who composed *bareku* and other *haiku* (*fl. c.* 1818).

Tokugen Sakai Tokugen (1559–1647).

Ukihashi The courtesan Ukihashi (d. *c.* 1716–36).

Ushichi Minoda Ushichi (1663–1727).

Yaba Shida Yaba (1662–1740). One of **Bashō**'s Ten Disciples (*Shōmon jittetsu*). His airy wit contributed to the 'flashy style' (*sharefū*) of **Kikaku** associated with the *haiku* of **Edoza**.

Yachō Known to be active Shōwa period (1926–89).

Yahantei See **Buson**.

Yasui Okada Yasui (1658–1743). **Shōmon** poet.

Acknowledgements

As one of those pernicious corrupters of taste whom poet-translator Kenneth Rexroth once damned for traducing Japanese haiku into a foreign tongue, I wish to thank several partners in crime. At Harvard, teachers and colleagues: Howard Hibbett, for sparking my curiosity about the interplay between witty linked verse and humour; Haruko Iwasaki, for taking me under her wing in reading frivolous prose; the late Nagatomi Masatoshi, for fomenting my interest in Buddhism and the Absurd; Edwin Cranston, for sharing the secrets of his alchemistical transformation of Japanese poetry into the gold standard of English renderings; and Jay Rubin, for mischievously unleashing Penguin on me.

At Penguin: Mariateresa Boffo, for backing this project from the get-go; Isabelle De Cat, for the stylish handling of the cover art; Matt Bacon, Bianca Bexton, Dinah Drazin, Katie Jarvis, Ruth Pietroni and Louise Willder, for their various contributions; and particularly Kate Parker, for the brilliant copyediting, Stephen Ryan, for the meticulous proofreading, Anna Hervé and Richard Duguid, for the editorial managing, and Jess Harrison, for aiding and abetting me at every turn, even when work proceeded waddlingly. In Madison (where seemingly lingers in the ether the shade of Robert Spiess of the Modern Haiku Press), at the University of Wisconsin, friends, colleagues and staff in Asian Languages and Cultures as well as Memorial Library. And others who shall remain unnamed – save Marjeta and Robert Jeraj, Robin Mittenthal, Kayo Tada, Asakawa Seiichirō, Glynne Walley, John Solt, robin d. gill, David McCann, Iwata Hideyuki, Robert Campbell, Richard Gilbert and above all, for his acumen, generosity and camaraderie, Lee Gurga. Any shortcomings or infelicities herein are my own.

Several institutions have touched me with their big-heartedness: the Japan Foundation, for a peripatetic summer of archival exploration across Japan; Tokyo Metropolitan Central Library, for unfettered access to the Special Collections; Kakimori Bunko in Itami, especially Okada Urara and Director Imai Miki; the National Institute of Japanese Literature; Kyūshū University Central Library; the Museum of Haiku Literature in Shinjuku; Harvard's Reischauer Institute of Japanese Studies and UW-Madison's Graduate School, for supplemental travel support and research assistantships; and UW-Madison's Center for East Asian Studies and its director, Gene Phillips, for subsidizing my guest speaker series featuring scholar-translator David Barnhill, poet-blogger Melissa Allen and then-editor of *Frogpond*, Francine Banwarth.

I am likewise grateful to those who, having invited me to speak on this project, were gracious hosts: Ed Cranston, at Harvard's Reischauer Institute; Esperanza Ramirez-Christiansen, at the University of Michigan-Ann Arbor's Center for Japanese Studies; Jill Casid at UW-Madison's Center for Visual Cultures; Sara Geyer at UW-Madison's Center for the Humanities; Peter Nosco, at a faculty development workshop run by the University of Hawai'i's East–West Center; Jeffrey Angles, at Western Michigan University's Soga Japan Center; Gayle Bull, at Foundry Books in Mineral Point; Richard Torrance, at Ohio State University's Institute for Japanese Studies; Jason Abbott, at the University of Louisville's Center for Democracy; Benedetta Lomi, at the University of Virginia; Hsien-Hao Sebastian Liao, at National Taiwan University in Taipei; Wenchi Lin, at National Central University in Chungli; Earl Jackson Jr, at National Chiao Tung University in Hsinchu; Catherine Turley, at the University of Colorado's Asian Studies Graduate Conference; Sumie Jones and Russell Valentino, at Indiana University's Institute for Advanced Study; and Will Fleming, at Yale's Center for East Asian Studies.

Students in my undergraduate courses and graduate seminars at Harvard and Wisconsin have my appreciation for their insights and patience with work in progress, particularly Alicia Foley, Genesie Miller and Michael Toole, as do my undergraduate research scholar Stephen Zellmer, my teaching fellow Ethan Bushelle and my graduate project assistant Giovanni Bottero. My deepest gratitude, however, goes to Hasegawa Makoto and Terumi, Wakana Tomoko, Judy Kern, Ruth Earl and Gene Kern. This book is dedicated to my children, Mika Alana and Elias Zen.

Index of Japanese Verses

nedaru ko no / mikata ni natte / joten'in   283
negoto nado / ii wa senu ka to / rosei ii   362
neko no ashiato / kobore ume   302
neko no ko no / kakurenbo suru / hagi no hana   312
neko no koi / yamu toki neya no / oborozuki   258
neko no me no / mada hiru suginu / haruhi kana   259
neko no me ya / kōri no shita ni / kurū uo   238
neko no rin / botan no atchi / kotchi kana   327
nemuredomo / ōgi wa ugoku / atsusa kana   306
nenrei o / ukete ima no wa / dare datta   227
neta ie o / niramu yō nari / kyō no tsuki   318
nete okite / ōakubi shite / neko no koi   259
nete tokeba / obi hodo nagai / mono wa nashi   373
neteite mo / uchiwa no ugoku / oyagokoro   306
nichō hodo / tsuzuita ga goke / jiman nari   378
niganigashiku mo / okashikarikeri   305
nigaoe de / ateire o suru / nagatsubone   265
nigegoshi ni / natte shishū de / hachi o oi   350
niji o haite / hirakan to suru / botan kana   324
nikui koto kana / nikui koto kana   353
nisanjaku / chōchō neko o / tsuriageru   259
nishikie to / sumie to gyōja / motte kuru   265
nishikiori / ryū ippiki ni / hi ga kureru   376
niuriya no / hashira wa uma ni / kuwarekeri   367
niwakusa ni / hotaru ari to wa / shirazarishi   322
no mo yama mo / yuki ni torareta / nanimo nashi   300
no ni yama ni / ugoku mono nashi / yuki no asa   300
nomi shirami / uma no nyō suru / makuramoto   314
noraneko ga / hotoke no hiza o / makura kana   323
noridashite / kaina ni amaru / haru no koma   223
nusubito ni / deau kitsune ya / uribatake   249
nusubito ni / torinokosareshi / mado no tsuki   339
nusubito o / torae hahaoya / koe o sage   352
nusubito o / toraete mireba / waga ko nari   352
nyōbō ni / shikarareteiru / ii shūto   278
nyōbō no / yaku hodo teishu / mote mo sezu   290
nyōbō o / motte ninsō- / zura ni nari   289
nyōbō o / yuki ni uzumete / sumi o uri   344
nyōbō wa / ofukuro yori mo / jamana mono   279
nyogo no hari- / kata kosaeteru / mieidō   369
nyogonoshima / kushami o suru to / baba o yobi   369

O

THE TALES OF ISE

'Was it you who came to me,
or I who went to you?
I cannot tell.
Was I awake or sleeping?
Was it real, or just a dream?'

The Tales of Ise is one of the most famous and important works of Japanese literature. Consisting of 125 poem tales loosely based on the life of the hero, Narihira, a model lover of the Heian period, they evoke a world in which beauty and refinement were a way of life. Covering such themes as forbidden love, devotion between friends and pleasure in nature, these lyrical episodes combine great elegance with a subversive, experimental wit. This delightful, groundbreaking translation brings out the sophisticated humour and playfulness of the original, which has inspired Japanese art and literature for a millenium.

Translated with a Commentary by Peter Macmillan
Foreword by Donald Keene

ISBN: 978 0 14 139 257 8

THE PENGUIN BOOK OF JAPANESE
VERSE

'The sea dark,
The call of the teal
Dimly white'

The Penguin Book of Japanese Verse contains 700 poems from
the third century to the twentieth, including both *tanka* ('short
poem') and *haiku*, and covering such classic themes as nature,
love, partings and time. Displaying the full wit, sadness and subtlety
of Japanese poetry, this collection also illustrates the continued
popularity of the poetic form in Japan. Introducing the more
complex 'New-Style' verse, the anthology offers a complete picture
of Japan and its culture through the centuries.

Translated with Introductions by Geoffrey Bownas and
Anthony Thwaite

ISBN: 978 0 14 119 094 5

THE NARROW ROAD TO THE DEEP NORTH AND OTHER TRAVEL SKETCHES

Matsuo Basho

'It was with awe
That I beheld
Fresh leaves, green leaves,
Bright in the sun'

In his perfectly crafted haiku poems, Basho described the natural world with great simplicity and delicacy of feeling. When he composed *The Narrow Road to the Deep North*, he was an ardent student of Zen Buddhism, setting off on a series of travels designed to strip away the trappings of the material world and bring spiritual enlightenment. He wrote of the seasons changing, of the smell of the rain, the brightness of the moon and the beauty of the waterfall, through which he sensed the mysteries of the universe. These seventeenth-century travel writings not only chronicle Basho's perilous journeys through Japan, but they also capture his vision of eternity in the transient world around him.

Translated with an Introduction by Nobuyuki Yuasa

ISBN: 978 0 14 044 185 7

THE PILLOW BOOK

Sei Shonagon

'I wonder if it's wrong to feel a fascination with the way those in
high places live'

Written by the Court gentlewoman Sei Shonagon (c. 966–1017)
ostensibly for her own amusement, *The Pillow Book* is one of the
greatest works of Japanese literature. A fascinating exploration
of life amongst the nobility at the height of the idyllic Heian period,
it describes the exquisite pleasures of a confined world in which
poetry, love, fashion and whim dominated, and harsh reality was
kept firmly at a distance. In sections ranging in size from brief
reflections to longer, lyrical tales, Shonagon moves elegantly across
a wide range of themes including nature, society and her own
flirtations and frustrations, to provide a witty, unique and deeply
personal insight into a woman's life at Court in classical Japan.

Translated with an Introduction and Notes
by Meredith McKinney

ISBN: 978 0 14 044 806 1

THE TALE OF GENJI

Murasaki Shikibu

Written in the eleventh century, this exquisite portrait of courtly life in medieval Japan is widely celebrated as the world's first novel – and is certainly one of its finest. Genji, the Shining Prince, is the son of an emperor. He is a passionate characeer whose tempestuous nature, family circumstances, love affairs, alliances, and shifting political fortunes form the core of this magnificent epic.

Edited and translated by Royall Tyler

ISBN: 978 0 14 303 949 5

AS I CROSSED A BRIDGE OF DREAMS

Lady Sarashina

'I lie awake,
Listening to the rustle of the bamboo leaves,
And a strange sadness fills my heart'

As I Crossed a Bridge of Dreams is a unique autobiography in which the anonymous writer known as Lady Sarashina intersperses personal reflections, anecdotes and lyrical poems with accounts of her travels and evocative descriptions of the Japanese country-side. Born in 1008, Lady Sarashina felt an acute sense of melancholy that led her to withdraw into the more congenial realm of the imagination – this deeply introspective work presents her vision of the world. While barely alluding to certain aspects of her life such as marriage, she illuminates her pilgrimages to temples and mystical dreams in exquisite prose, describing a profound emotional journey that can be read as a metaphor for life itself.

Translated with an Introduction by Ivan Morris

ISBN: 978 0 14 044 282 3

THE ART OF WAR

Sun-Tzu

'Ultimate excellence lies not in winning every battle but in
defeating the enemy without ever fighting'

For more than two thousand years, Sun-Tzu's *The Art of War* has
provided military leaders with essential advice on battlefield tactics,
managing troops and terrain, and employing cunning and decep-
tion. An elemental part of Chinese culture, it has also become a
touchstone for the Western struggle for survival and success,
whether in battle, in business, or in relationships.

Edited and translated with an Introduction by John Minford

ISBN: 978 0 14 310 575 6

TAO TE CHING

Lao Tzu

'Have little thought of self and as few desires as possible'

Whether or not Lao Tzu was a historical figure is uncertain, but the wisdom gathered under his name in the fourth century BC is central to the understanding and practice of Taoism. One of the three great religions of China, Taoism is based upon a concept of the Tao, or Way, as the universal power through which all life flows. The *Tao Te Ching* offers a practical model by which both the individual and society can embody this belief, encouraging modesty and self-restraint as the true path to a harmonious and balanced existence.

Translated with an Introduction by D. C. Lau

ISBN: 978 0 14 044 131 4

THE SONGS OF THE SOUTH

An Ancient Chinese Anthology of Poems by Qu Yuan and Other Poets

'From of old things have always been the same:
Why should I complain of the men of today?'

Chu chi (*The Songs of the South*) and its northern counterpart, *Shi jing*, are the two great ancestors of Chinese poetry and contain all we know of its ancient beginnings. *The Songs of the South* is an anthology first complied in the second century AD. Its poems, originating from the state of Chu and rooted in Shamanism, are grouped under seventeen titles. The earliest poems were composed in the fourth century BC and almost half of them are traditionally ascribed to Qu Yuan. Covering subjects ranging from heaven to love, work to growing old, regret to longing, they give a penetrating insight into the world of ancient China, and into the origins of poetry itself.

Translated with an Introduction and Notes by David Hawkes

ISBN: 978 0 14 119 870 5